Progress in IS

Jens Dibbern • Jens Förderer • Thomas Kude •
Franz Rothlauf • Kai Spohrer

Editors

Digitalization Across Organizational Levels

New Frontiers for Information Systems
Research

Editors
Jens Dibbern
Institute of Information Systems
Universität Bern, Bern, Switzerland

Jens Förderer
Technical University of Munich
Heilbronn, Germany

Thomas Kude
Information Systems, Decision Sciences
and Statistics
ESSEC Business School
Cergy, France

Franz Rothlauf
Information Systems and Business
Administration
University of Mainz
Mainz, Germany

Kai Spohrer
Frankfurt School of Finance & Management
Frankfurt am Main, Germany

ISSN 2196-8705   ISSN 2196-8713   (electronic)
Progress in IS
ISBN 978-3-031-06545-3   ISBN 978-3-031-06543-9   (eBook)
https://doi.org/10.1007/978-3-031-06543-9

This Springer imprint is published by the registered company Springer Nature Switzerland AG
The registered company address is: Gewerbestrasse 11, 6330 Cham, Switzerland

Preface

We have edited this book in honor of Prof. Dr. Armin Heinzl to celebrate his 60th birthday. We feel deeply indebted to Armin, who served as our academic advisor and supporter during our own academic careers. Clearly, Armin has had a tremendous impact on our academic careers.

In the tradition of a "Festschrift", we invited all of Armin's former Ph.D. students, who continued in academia afterward, to contribute to this book. Moreover, we invited contributions from three outstanding academics who have been influencing and accompanying Armin's work and life since the early days of his career, namely Wolfgang König (advisor and reviewer of Armin's dissertation and habilitation), Rudy Hirschheim, and Dorothy Leidner. The result is an edited book consisting of 11 chapters. Each chapter sheds light on the topic of digitalization from different perspectives and focuses on different emergent digitalization phenomena. Accordingly, we entitled the book "Digitalization Across Organizational Levels", with the subtitle *New Frontiers for Information Systems Research*. The title of the book resonates with Armin's impressive research output, which he has generated since he entered the academic field as a doctoral student in 1986 at the WHU Koblenz.

Throughout his career, Armin has published numerous groundbreaking articles and books which were often far ahead of their time. As one of the pioneers in the research area, Armin studied IS outsourcing and related IT management questions in his doctoral and habilitation theses (published in 1991 and 1996). Already at that time, Armin went beyond what we would today consider traditional IS research questions to also study forward-looking IT-related challenges, e.g., on the evolution of IS. Besides his interest in organizational phenomena related to IS, he also developed interest in emergent technologies in practically relevant contexts, e.g., applying agent technology for patient scheduling in hospitals or using genetic algorithms for optimizing flight schedules. Building on these earlier contributions, Armin has always worked at the forefront of IS research and pushed the frontiers, e.g., in the context of implications of digital technology for individuals or on digital ecosystems. For Armin, it is always essential that his research creates impact and is relevant for societies, organizations, and individuals. He considers adhering to the highest standards of scientific rigor not as a goal in and of itself, but as a matter of course and a necessary condition for conducting high-quality research. Armin has never engaged in a research project just for the sake of publishing, but only if he saw value. In this light, his list of publications, which is filled with articles in our discipline's top-ranked outlets and highly cited papers, is all the more impressive.

In his teaching, Armin was equally visionary as in his research. The strategic importance of IS—as opposed to representing a mere secondary function within organizations that would support business—has been a key pillar of Armin's courses from the beginning of his career. Armin also recognized the value of new digital technologies, such as mobile computing or predictive analytics, early on and included them in his classes. Thus, Armin's students would learn about digital transformation long before it made the news, and his courses continue to be at the forefront of digital innovation. Armin's pedagogical approach is characterized by innovation and participant focus, both in his courses and in building new programs and institutions, as evidenced by his role in the foundation of the Mannheim Business School and its Digital Academy. Another important element of Armin's pedagogical activities—from which we all benefited tremendously—is doctoral education. He has also served in various roles for the key business administration and IS associations in Germany. For instance, he served as the junior scholars' chairman ("Nachwuchsobmann") of the German-speaking IS community for many years and used this role to establish yearly meetings among the IS postdocs of the German-speaking countries. This portrays his strong interest in supporting junior scholars and in helping the IS discipline flourish throughout his entire career.

Armin has always been highly active in terms of community services and in setting the German IS discipline on a course toward global relevance. He built bridges and took various roles in our primary IS journals and conferences. For instance, Armin has served as the vice editor-in-chief of *Business & Information Systems Engineering*, the flagship journal of the German-speaking IS community. In this role, he opened the journal—still called *WIRTSCHATFSINFORMATIK* at the time—to the international IS community by introducing English as a secondary and eventually as the primary journal language. He co-organized and co-chaired various workshops and conferences, among them the International Conference on the Outsourcing of Information Services (ICOIS in 2001 2007, 2013, and 2019), sponsored by partners from the IT services industry, and the International Conference on Information Systems at Fort Worth, Texas, in 2015. Armin has also been a great contributor to the national and international impact of IS. He initiated and participated in various individual and collaborative research projects funded by industry and agencies at the federal (DFG, BMBF) and state levels, such as in Bavaria (e.g., FORWIN) and Baden-Württemberg (e.g., CollaBaWü, Cloud Mall BW).

We are grateful that we have had and continue to have Armin as our mentor and advisor. We have always appreciated his ambition, leadership, kindness, and humor, and we look forward to working with him on research projects and spending time with him in the years to come.

Bern, Switzerland	Jens Dibbern
Heilbronn, Germany	Jens Förderer
Cergy, France	Thomas Kude
Mainz, Germany	Franz Rothlauf
Frankfurt am Main, Germany	Kai Spohrer

Contents

Part I
Introduction

Studying Digitalization Across Levels: An Overview and Introduction

Thomas Kude and Jens Dibbern

Abstract Advances in digital technologies have significantly increased the speed of digitalization in the new millennium. Such digitalization occurs across various levels, such as the individual, team, organization, and ecosystem levels. This paper seeks to provide an overview of how information systems (IS) research addresses digitalization phenomena across different levels. Thereby, it distinguishes between two interrelated perspectives: one referring to the management of IS and digital transformation; the other relating to the design of digital artifacts and the implications arising from their application and use, i.e., IS impacts. The respective digitalization research streams are illustrated with examples from past and current IS research.

1 Introduction

The past decade has witnessed tremendous changes of the capabilities and roles of information systems (IS) in organizations. Information systems—which are located at the intersection of information technology (IT), people, and tasks (Heinrich et al., 2011; Davis & Olson, 1985)—have long played a crucial role for organizations. Traditionally, the management of IS used to be a secondary function in organizations, whose role was to support the business side in creating value (Porter, 1985). This supportive role can be characterized from a technological perspective, in terms of the systems in place to support business, and from an organizational perspective, in terms of the related organizational challenges (Markus & Robey, 1988).

T. Kude
Information Systems, Decision Sciences & Statistics, ESSEC Business School, Cergy, France
e-mail: kude@essec.edu

J. Dibbern (✉)
Universität Bern, Bern, Switzerland
e-mail: jens.dibbern@iwi.unibe.ch

© The Author(s), under exclusive license to Springer Nature Switzerland AG 2022
J. Dibbern et al. (eds.), *Digitalization Across Organizational Levels*, Progress in IS,
https://doi.org/10.1007/978-3-031-06543-9_1

From a technological perspective, IS management has often been concerned with enterprise systems, such as enterprise resource planning (ERP) systems (Dibbern et al., 2002; Heinzl & Brehm, 2006; Brehm et al., 2001) or knowledge management systems (Alavi & Leidner, 2001). From an organizational perspective, key concerns of IS management have included sourcing decisions and IT governance (Heinzl, 1991, 1996; Weill, 2004). Given the high complexity and cost of IS services, as well as the lack of human resources, the question of whether to outsource IS services or provide them in-house has been a critical one (Heinzl, 1991, 1996). While questions related to outsourcing focus on whether the service is provided in-house or through the market, organizations have implemented IT governance frameworks to specify decision rights and accountabilities and ensure desirable behavior in the use of IT (Weill, 2004) and thereby enable alignment between IT and business (Luftman & Brier, 1999).

While these systems and organizational challenges remain highly relevant and have often become even more critical, the role of IS management has evolved as a result of recent technological developments. Various innovations, e.g., in terms of sensor and communication technology, have contributed to the ubiquity of technological devices such as smart phones. The resulting data, along with advances in computing power and algorithms, have made machine learning a viable technology that is now widely used across industries (Bichler et al., 2017), such as manufacturing or health care (Jussupow et al., 2021b). As another example, Blockchain technology is making its way into organizational applications, for instance, in the context of the digitalization of supply chains or the Internet of Things (Risius & Spohrer, 2017).

Given these technological developments, the role of IS management—once focused mostly on the reliable provision of enterprise systems to support business—has expanded considerably. Digital technology has evolved from tools to support value creation to also become a substantial part of the value itself, as products and services are partly or even entirely digitalized. For example, whereas banking services used to be provided in physical branches or through ATMs, these branches lose importance for most people, as banking services are often consumed through apps and payments are made electronically, e.g., through platforms like Ant Financial. As another example, the media industry shifted from newspapers or DVDs to digital content and video streaming, resulting in struggles for previously flourishing companies such as Blockbuster.

To digitally transform and remain successful despite digital disruptions, incumbent organizations need to adjust their business models and their operating models (Venkatraman, 2017). From a business model perspective, incumbent organizations increasingly need to find their place in digital ecosystems consisting of digital giants such as Apple or Alibaba, numerous technology entrepreneurs, and other incumbent organizations. From an operating model perspective, organizations need to move away from traditional hierarchies to enable agility and digital innovation. In the next section, we discuss how the evolution of IS management in organizations is reflected by changing research foci in the Information Systems (IS)[1] discipline.

2 The Evolution of Information Systems Research Across Organizational Levels

Reflecting on the evolution of IS research has been an important issue in the IS discipline (Alavi & Carlson, 1992; Somogyi & Galliers, 1987; Galliers, 1993; Heinzl, 1996). Here we reflect on research on digitalization and the associated evolution of IS management within organizations focusing on key research themes that have been studied in academic research in the IS discipline. This is illustrated in Fig. 1, which shows exemplary IS research questions pertaining to two broad categories—the management of IS and digital transformation (on the left) and the design and implications of digital artifacts (on the right). The questions are situated on different organizational levels, from teams and individuals, over intra- and inter-organizational levels, to the level of digital ecosystems (see dark grey triangle in the center of Fig. 1).

The evolution of major themes in IS research is depicted in Fig. 1 through the light grey arrows connecting the different levels and themes in a circular way. In line with the role of IS in organizations as a secondary, supportive function, the focus of early research on IS management has often been at the intra- and inter-organizational levels.[2] In light of the changes outlined above—most notably that incumbent organizations are increasingly embedded in digital ecosystems and rely on agile teams to develop digital innovation—IS research on the management of IS and digital transformation has expanded from the intra- and inter-organizational level to digital ecosystems at a higher organizational level and to teams and individuals at a lower organizational level.

In tandem with the study of questions on how to manage IS and digital transformation, IS research has also examined the design and implications of digital artifacts as well as broader questions related to the industry and regulatory context. Importantly, the circular arrows in Fig. 1 are not meant to propose a rigid process that would connect research across organizational levels and themes in a deterministic way. Instead, the arrows illustrate that IS research streams across levels of analysis and genres constantly influence and fertilize each other. For example, technological advancements and the digital transformation of organizations raise

---

[1] We follow an inclusive view of the IS discipline, comprising the business & information systems engineering ("Wirtschaftsinformatik" in German) discipline with its origins at the intersection of management and computer science as well as the more management oriented IS field originating from business schools (Heinrich et al., 2011).

[2] Beyond IS management, a major research stream of traditional IS research was concerned with the use of IS at the individual level (Burton-Jones et al., 2017).

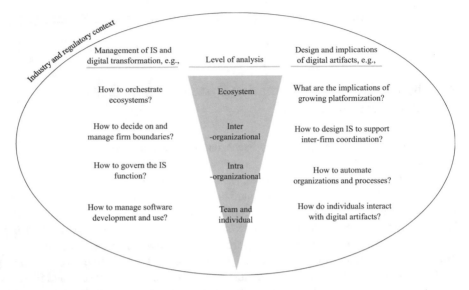

Fig. 1 Overview of levels of analysis and exemplary research questions

important novel questions for the established literature stream on IS outsourcing (Hirschheim et al., 2020). The evolution of these different streams is outlined next, with some illustrative examples of notable research work.[3]

As noted above, mirroring some of the enduring challenges of IS management in practice, IS research has often studied questions at the intra- and inter-organizational levels. At the intra-organizational level, the question of how to govern the IS function has received particular attention by IS researchers. For instance, Kude et al. (2018) studied regulation-oriented and consensus-oriented IT governance capabilities and their impact on IT-based synergies. Based on an exploratory field study that included interviews with CIOs and other IT executives, the authors propose that IT governance capabilities lead to IT-based synergies through IT relatedness and business process relatedness. At the intra-organizational level, the question of how to decide on and manage firm boundaries has often taken center stage (Dibbern & Heinzl, 2009; Dibbern et al., 2008, 2012; Winkler et al., 2009; Heinzl, 1991, 1996). For example, Dibbern et al. (2008) examined variations in client extra costs across offshored IS development and maintenance projects. The authors integrated transaction-cost and knowledge-based arguments to develop a theoretical framework, which was empirically corroborated based no qualitative data from six projects in a large German financial services institution. The findings show that different types of client extra costs arise after contractual agreements

---

[3] In keeping with the goal of this book to honor the research contributions of Armin Heinzl, as well as his comprehensive works covering various parts of the framework in Fig. 1, we specifically draw on his contributions to illustrate research streams across levels of analysis and genres.

have been made, and that these extra costs are particularly high in projects where a large amount of client-specific knowledge is required. Notably, these costs are less caused by the threat of opportunistic behavior—as transaction-cost arguments would predict—but rather by the efforts associated with knowledge transfer, i.e., in line with knowledge-based reasoning.

With technological advances and the increasing ubiquity of technology across industries, IS researchers have also long been interested in the management of IS and digital transformation at the team and individual level. This stream of research did not only include IS use—a long-time mainstream of the IS discipline (Burton-Jones et al., 2017)—but also IS development, in particular following the widespread reliance on agile software development methodologies in practice (Kude et al., 2019; Scheerer et al., 2013, 2015; Gholami & Heinzl, 2013; Bick et al., 2017; Hildenbrand et al., 2008). For instance, Kude et al. (2019) examined how applying the agile practice of pair programming in software development teams contributes to team performance. In particular, the authors hypothesize that pair programming helps teams to establish shared understanding and backup behavior, which is particularly beneficial if task novelty is high. The hypotheses are corroborated through a survey study of software development teams at a large enterprise software firm.

One key element of digital transformations is that organizations are increasingly embedded in digital ecosystems, as opposed to being monolithic entities with clear-cut boundaries. Given the important role of digital platforms in this context, studying the orchestration of platform ecosystems has become an important stream in the IS literature (e.g., Foerderer et al., 2018b, 2019, 2021; Halckenhäußer et al., 2020; Kude et al., 2012; Arndt et al., 2009). One particular focus in this research was the software industry, for instance, in terms of enterprise software platforms (Foerderer et al., 2019) or mobile operating systems (Foerderer et al., 2018b). Much of this work has focused on questions around platform governance (Halckenhäußer et al., 2020; Hurni et al., 2022; Huber et al., 2017), such as the implications of competing with app developers (Foerderer et al., 2018b) or the question of how to enable complementors to develop add-on functionality (Foerderer et al., 2019).

Since its inception, IS research has not only focused on improving our under-standing of phenomena related to the management of IS (see left hand side of Fig. 1) but has also studied the design and implications of digital artifacts (see right hand side of Fig. 1). Often, this work has focused on the individual and team level as well as the intra-organizational level. At the individual and team level, research often followed a design-science approach (Hevner et al., 2004) and developed solutions for teams and individuals to collaborate, for instance, in the context of software development teams (Geisser et al., 2007; Hildenbrand et al., 2009). Another stream of research studied the implications of the ubiquity of digital artifacts on individual users (Jussupow et al., 2018, 2020; Seeger et al., 2021; Fallon et al., 2019; Spohrer et al., 2021; Neben et al., 2015). For example, Seeger et al. (2021) examined the interaction of human actors and human-like conversational agents. Drawing on the psychological theory of anthropomorphism the authors developed and tested—through an online experiment—a theoretical framework on the design of human-like chatbots.

At the intra-organizational level, IS research was often interested in the question of how to automate organizations and processes in various industries. For instance, prior work studied the design and the implications of digital artifacts for organizations in the health care sector (Jussupow et al., 2021a; Paulussen et al., 2013; Denz et al., 2008; Baumgart et al., 2007), the software industry (Stuckenberg et al., 2014), the aviation industry (Grosche et al., 2001, 2007), the construction sector (Deibert et al., 2009), or for financial services organizations (Schoberth et al., 2003, 2006).

At the inter-organizational and ecosystem levels, IS researchers have also been interested in the design and implications of digital artifacts. For instance, in one stream of IS research, studies have looked at the question of how inter-firm coordination in the software industry can be supported through digital artifacts (Hoffmann et al., 2019; Kramer et al., 2017; Klimpke et al., 2014). At the ecosystem level, researchers have started to turn attention to the implications of platformization across industries (Foerderer et al., 2022). These questions go beyond particular platform ecosystems, such as Apple's or Google's mobile operating ecosystems, to include the wider industry level and questions of regulation that policymakers are interested in (Foerderer et al., 2018a, see large circle in Fig. 1).

3   Contributions in This Book

The book is structured into six parts and 11 chapters, starting with this introductory chapter (Part I) that introduces a multi-level perspective of research on digitalization and that provides an overview of the book. The overview includes a summary of the subsequent 10 chapters organized into five parts (Parts II–VI). Each part addresses different perspectives as introduced in the framework depicted in Fig. 1.

Part II, including the chapters on "The Early History of IT Outsourcing: A Personal Reflection" and "How to Ensure Collective Action in Multinational Projects: Insights from the EurHisFirm Project", is dedicated to the inter-organizational perspective. The digitalization and digital transformation of organizations often involve the inclusion of multiple parties (Dibbern & Rudy, 2020). The parties involved may be organized differently. One widely established form refers to contract-based client-vendor IT outsourcing arrangements (Dibbern et al., 2004; Kern & Willcocks, 2002). Another form refers to coalitions of multiple organizations with shared interests, such as in a multi-party project that seeks to achieve a common goal (Malhotra et al., 2001). Yet another form may be characterized as a hybrid organizational arrangement (Borys & Jemison, 1989), such as a multivendor outsourcing arrangement, that relies on formal contracts between the client and its vendors, while also seeking to achieve a common objective (Krancher et al., 2022). In the following two chapters, the authors share their experiences and provide reflections on two of these organizational forms, the first on the history of IT outsourcing and the second on the challenges of achieving collective action in a multi-party transnational IT project.

In the chapter "The Early History of IT Outsourcing: A Personal Reflection", Rudy Hirschheim reflects on the history of IT outsourcing and how it has changed over time. He attributes its beginnings to the early 1990s, when the first multi-billion-dollar IT outsourcing deals created quite a stir in the IS community. It did not take long until IS research recognized the importance of this new phenomenon, which led to a significant stream of IS outsourcing research that continues to evolve and grow. Rudy Hirschheim, together with Mary Lacity, were among the pioneers in researching IS outsourcing in the U.S. (Lacity & Hirschheim, 1993a, b), in the same vein as Leslie Willcocks (U.K.) and Armin Heinzl (Germany) were among the academic trailblazers in Europe (Willcocks et al., 1995; Heinzl & Stoffel, 1991; Heinzl, 1991, 1993). Soon on, IS outsourcing had become a global phenomenon that went through various stages (or waves), which are described and reflected on by Rudy Hirschheim in his introductory chapter. Following the idea of waves, IT outsourcing may also be seen as a forerunner of many related phenomena of the division of labor among organizations in the digitalization process, among them the emergence of IT as a service (via the cloud), crowdsourcing, open-source communities, and (digital) platform ecosystems.

It is also notable that not only organizations, but also countries and their governments increasingly realize the need of spanning together in addressing digitalization challenges that cannot be addressed by individual actors alone. Often, such collective digitalization challenges arise from organizational interdependencies and network effects in exploiting the benefits of digital assets, such as shared IT infrastructures and pooled data.

In the chapter "How to Ensure Collective Action in Multinational Projects: Insights from the EurHisFirm Project", Wolfgang König, Muriel Frank, Jefferson Braswell, Lukas Ranft and Pantelis Karapanagiotis, reflect on such a challenge of ensuring collective (as opposed to individual) action in a transnational multi-party project. As such, they take the exemplary case of EurHISFirm as a basis (https:// eurhisfirm.eu). EurHISFirm is a project funded by the European Union's Horizon 2020 research and innovation program. Its key objective is to provide an open-access platform for company-level data in Europe, as a basis for researchers, policymakers, and other stakeholders for the purpose of data analysis. As such, various IT artifacts (e.g., a common data model) have to be developed collaboratively across the various involved parties. König et al. present their lessons learned from this project as participants and observers of the project, thereby shedding light on the challenges of collective action among organizations and European states.

The third part of this book (*Part III*) zooms into two issues that colloquially are often referred to as "soft factors" when it comes to understanding digitalization processes and capabilities. Both are closely linked to the individual perspective, acknowledging the human factor in IS. The first paper falling into this category addresses the role of culture in the context of knowledge management systems; the second the role of gender, specifically the role of females in taking on IT careers.

In the chapter "A Theory of Organizational Information Culture", Dorothy Leidner develops a theory that recognizes the role of culture as an often-overlooked aspect in the design, implementation, and use of knowledge management systems.

Specifically, she introduces the notion of information culture as complementary to widely established concepts of individual and organizational culture. As such, she distinguishes four information cultures, i.e., information hoarding, selective information sharing, random information sharing, and full information sharing. Her theory elaborates on the implications of these different information cultures for the sharing of tacit knowledge and how individual and organizational cultures influence such different information cultures towards the sharing of tacit knowledge.

In the chapter "IT or Not IT? A Female View on Inhibiting and Promoting Factors in Young Women's Decisions for a Career in IT", Birte Malzahn, Jessica Slamka, and Daniela Scheid problematize and analyze the digital gender gap in higher IT education, specifically the underrepresentation of women in IT-related courses of study, such as computer science. They argue that the digital gender gap has its roots in differences as to how females experience and get in contact with IT education throughout different phases of their life, i.e., the growth and exploration phases, which then influences their initial decision for an occupation qualification (IT- or non-IT-related). In each phase, they analyze the inhibiting and promoting factors and approaches.

The fourth part of the book (*Part IV*) zooms out to the IT platform and ecosystem perspective. Digital platforms and platform ecosystems may be seen as combinations of technical, organizational, and partly social innovations (Gawer & Cusumano, 2014; Tiwana, 2014). On the technical side, the Internet has provided the basis for a more networked economy, in that it enabled easy access to and sharing of digital (and digitalized) resources, such as data, information, content, software, hardware storage, and processing power. Internet-based architectural innovations (e.g., service-oriented architectures, web services, or application programming interfaces) and other innovations, e.g., in scaled data base management, distributed computing, and cryptography (just to name a few), provide the basis for emerging technology platforms, such as cloud computing infrastructures, or, more recently, blockchain infrastructures (Weinhardt et al., 2009; Tapscott & Tapscott, 2017; Felin & Lakhan, 2018). On the organization side, this is mirrored by the emergence of platform ecosystems that have considerably changed the IT (services) industry (Tiwana, 2014; Huber et al., 2017). On the one hand, this change is visible through new players having entered the market. For example, Salesforce, having started as a CRM Software-as-a-Service (SaaS) provider, not only has become one of the biggest and fastest growing software companies in the world, but also has transformed into a key (cloud services) platform provider with an ever-growing ecosystem of complementors. Moreover, new intermediaries, such as Airbnb or Uber, have entered the market, that define themselves as digital platforms or multi-sided markets, the core business model of which lies in connecting supply and demand (i.e., consumption) of digital and non-digital assets in new innovative ways. Another form of connection of supply and demand refers to social networking platforms (e.g., Facebook, Twitter) that may also be seen as social innovations increasingly substituting common practices of communicating and networking. On the other hand, established IT giants, such as SAP or Oracle, had to re-invent their business models from on-premises software (license) sellers to cloud service providers, establishing themselves as platforms and ecosystems. The emergence of such digital platforms and ecosystems has led to a growing stream of research that has begun to study various issues around them, such as their various forms and functions, their governance, their key value propositions, their emergence, growth, and evolution, and their outcomes and implications (Ghazawneh & Henfridsson, 2013; Jacobides et al., 2018; Karhu et al., 2020; Foerderer et al., 2018b).

The next two chapters contribute to the existing body of knowledge by taking two different views; the one takes the perspective of dyadic relationships between a platform owner and its particular complementors to understand the conditions under which value in the form of innovation is created on platforms; the other takes a holistic network perspective of digital platforms seeking to understand their wider consequences and implications—some of them rather unintended and neglected, but becoming increasingly important.

In the chapter "How Access to Resources Affects Complementor Innovation in Platform Ecosystems", Thomas Huber, Thomas Hurni, Oliver Krancher, and Jens Dibbern examine the conditions under which complementors contribute to product and process innovations on software platforms (e.g., SAP, IBM, or Apple). Specifically, they argue that this depends on the extent to which the partnership with a platform owner provides access to valuable resources, such as technical, social, and commercial capital, but that it is also important that the platform owner is willing to share critical information relevant for the particular partnership. Data from platform partnerships in the Swiss software industry provides support for the combined role of access to resources and information sharing for stipulating complementor innovation.

In the chapter "The Economic and Social Consequences of Digital Platforms: A Systematic and Interdisciplinary Literature Review", Michaela Lindenmayr, Tobias Kircher, Alexander Stolte, and Jens Förderer examine the economic and social consequences of digital platforms. Specifically, they focus on three challenges that come along with running and participating in digital platforms, which are privacy, the generation and distribution of harmful content, and implications for innovation and competition. Considered concertedly, these three challenges show mutual dependencies that can enhance or dampen the particular challenges— also depending on the particular context and perspective taken. For example, guaranteeing anonymity on digital platforms may enhance privacy, but also may allow particular users to distribute harmful content under the cloak of anonymity.

As noted above, technological innovations provided the backbone for the emergence of digital platforms and platform ecosystems. While it is important to understand the implications of such new organizational forms and how to manage them, it is also important to note that technologies are constantly evolving, leading to new opportunities with novel transformational potentials.

Part V contributes two chapters that examine two of these emerging technologies. The first refers to blockchain technology, which is essentially a shared, immutable ledger that facilitates the process of recording transactions and tracking assets in a business network (Beck et al., 2017). This emerging technology has led to various digital innovations, the most prominent being Bitcoin, the first and still most widely used cryptocurrency network established by its anonymous founder Satoshi Nakamoto (Kher et al., 2021). Today, various blockchain platforms have been established that allow for various applications of the blockchain technology, thereby enabling follow-up digital service innovations (Felin & Lakhan, 2018; Lacity, 2018). The second refers to process mining, in terms of a class of techniques that support the automatic discovery of business process models from event log data (vom Brocke et al., 2021). As such, it has been established as an outgrowth of process modeling and data mining techniques over the past 20 years but is still further developed and in the process of reaping its full potential.

In the chapter "The Affordances of Blockchain Platforms: Why Service Providers Use Blockchains", Kai Spohrer and Marten Risius examine the affordances of blockchain platforms from the perspective of service providers that draw on the resources provided on such platforms to create their own blockchain applications and serve their customers in new innovative ways. Based on multiple cases of such service providers that make use of a blockchain platform for their own business and using affordance theory as a theoretical basis, they identify five types of affordances. These affordances draw on different material properties of the blockchain technology, and they partially enable and constrain each other. Based on the actualized affordance, the service providers can be categorized into four groups, i.e., authenticity services, efficiency services, consultancy services, and consumer orchestration services. Beyond this typology of affordances and service providers, the authors take a dynamic view of affordance actualizing, finding that as blockchain platforms constantly evolve, service providers may either focus and extend their engagement with a particular platform or decouple and diversify to other specific platforms. This process of change hinges on whether the service provider values stay aligned with enacted community values of the platform or become misaligned over time.

In the chapter "Process Mining for Carbon Accounting: An Analysis of Requirements and Potentials", Lars Brehm, Jessica Slamka, and Andreas Nickmann elaborate the requirements and potentials of process mining for supporting organization-specific sustainability goals. Specifically, they use expert interviews to explore the supporting role of process mining for carbon accounting—an increasingly established practice in organizations to document and analyze their carbon footprint as a basis to take measures to reduce CO_2 emissions. One of the requirements for reaping the potential of process mining for carbon accounting lies in linking carbon-related data to the particular event logs of business processes. To automate such retrieval and integration of carbon data, external data sources could be tapped into via application programming interfaces. This can help realize various potentials for reaching sustainability goals both at the corporate and ecosystem levels.

Finally, the sixth part of this book (Part VI) bridges different perspectives, including organization, network as well as the industry and regulatory environment. It includes two papers that both take a strong market-related perspective in that they examine structural elements of markets (i.e., centrality or concentration measures)—on the one hand, the online book market, exemplified by a large online bookstore; on the other hand, the airline market in Europe.

In the chapter "The Impact of Product Recommendation Networks on Sales: The Moderating Influence of Product Age", Nils Herm-Stapelberg and Franz Rothlauf examine how online stores can make sense of the mass of data that they have about their online sales in order to gain knowledge about future sales. This is exemplified by an online bookstore that seeks to make sense of its data. Specifically, they analyze how the page rank centrality of a book (as an indication of the attractiveness of the book) is associated with its actual sales. They also examine how this relationship is influenced by the age of the book. The results suggest that page rank matters for online sales, but that the age of products (i.e., books) should also be taken into account. This suggests that combinations of product attributes from the past need to be considered for market predictions.

In the chapter "Airline Market Concentration in Europe", Tobias Grosche examines the structural properties of the airline market, which provides an important basis for airline flight scheduling (Grosche et al., 2007). Specifically, he assesses the level of competition in the European Airline market by measuring market concentration for particular routes (city pairs). This allows analyzing market competition on different levels, i.e., the city, the country, or region level. The results also show that Europe has a higher market concertation than the United States. While one may assume that this has to do with the reduction of the number of airlines in Europe, the opposite is the case; the reduction of the number of airlines has come along with an increase in market concertation in Europe. Overall, the results provide important insights into market concentration development and its source, which is informative not only for the design of airline yield management systems, but also for industry regulators.

4 Conclusion

The objective of this chapter was to provide an overall umbrella for studying digitalization in the IS field and to introduce this book, which presents a collection of papers that viewed the phenomenon from different perspectives and with different thematic orientations. As this book is written in honor of Armin Heinzl and his 60th birthday, our introductory chapter was also largely inspired by his impressive collection of research contributions over the last 30 years. In fact, his contributions (up to date) provide a microcosm of digitalization research that by itself has taken an evolution. For example, he has also examined IS phenomena from different perspectives, and while he has studied some research themes enduringly (e.g., IS outsourcing), he has also undergone a transformation both thematically and with respect to the level of analysis taken. In illustrating our framework, we drew on Armin's work, but we also tried to develop the framework as an umbrella for the chapters of this book (and of course were influenced by our own view on the IS world). We therefore belief that the framework is of general interest and applicability, helping to guide future research endeavors on digitalizing. It may be viewed as a navigation instrument that helps researchers to find their home in the digital research landscape and see linkages to related fields of study—either across levels or across thematic orientations (e.g., from management to design and vice versa).

In general, the future of research on digitization appears wide open with many emerging questions. We have tried to articulate some important questions, but there are many more. Hopefully, this book will help motivate individuals to either begin research in the field or continue engaging in digitalization research. Much has been done, but there is still much more to be done. We hope the readers enjoy the papers in this volume. Happy reading!

References

Alavi, M., & Carlson, P. (1992). A review of MIS research and disciplinary development. *Journal of Management Information Systems, 8*(4), 45–62.

Alavi, M., & Leidner, D. E. (2001). Knowledge management and knowledge management systems: Conceptual foundations and research issues. *MIS Quarterly, 25*, 107–136.

Arndt, J. M., Kude, T., Dibbern, J., & Heinzl, A. (2009). The emergence of partnership networks in the enterprise application software industry-an SME perspective. In A. Heinzl, P. Dadam, S. Kirn, & P. Lockemann (Eds.), *PRIMIUM: Process innovation for enterprise software. Lecture Notes in Informatics - Proceedings* (pp. 179–194).

Baumgart, A., Zoeller, A., Denz, C., Bender, H-J., & Heinzl, A., & Badreddin, E. (2007). Using computer simulation in operating room management: Impacts on process engineering and performance. In *Hawaii International Conference on System Sciences* (pp. 131–131). IEEE.

Beck, R., Avital, M., Rossi, M., & Thatcher, J. B. (2017). Blockchain technology in business and information systems research. *Business and Information Systems Engineering, 59*(6), 381–384.

Bichler, M., Heinzl, A., & van der Aalst, W. M. P. (2017). Business analytics and data science: once again? *Business and Information Systems Engineering, 59*(2), 77–79.

Bick, S., Spohrer, K., Hoda, R., Scheerer, A., & Heinzl, A. (2017). Coordination challenges in large-scale software development: a case study of planning misalignment in hybrid settings. *IEEE Transactions on Software Engineering, 44*(10), 932–950.

Borys, B., & Jemison, D. B. (1989). Hybrid arrangements as strategic alliances: theoretical issues in organizational combinations. *Academy of Management Review, 14*(2), 234–249.

Brehm, L., Heinzl, A., & Markus, M. L. (2001). Tailoring ERP systems: A spectrum of choices and their implications. In *Hawaii International Conference on System Sciences*.

Burton-Jones, A., Stein, M.-K., & Mishra, A. (2017) IS use. *MIS Quarterly Research Curation.*

Davis, G. B., & Olson, M. H. (1985). *Management information systems conceptual foundations, structure, and development*. McGraw-Hill Series in Management Information Systems.

Deibert, S., Hemmer, E., & Heinzl, A. (2009). Mobile technology in the construction industry–the impact on business processes in job production. In *Amercias Conference on Information Systems*.

Denz, C., Baumgart, A., Zöller, A., Schleppers, A., Heinzl, A., & Bender, H.-J. (2008). Perspektiven zur Weiterentwicklung des OP-Managements: Von der Prozessanalyse zur simulationsbasierten Planung und Steuerung. *Anaesthesiol Intensivmed, 49*, 85–93.

Dibbern, J., & Heinzl, A. (2009). Outsourcing der Informationsverarbeitung im Mittelstand: Test eines multitheoretischen Kausalmodells. *Wirtschaftsinformatik, 51*(1), 118–129.

Dibbern, J., & Rudy, H. (2020). Introduction: Riding the waves of outsourcing change in the era of digital transformation. In R. Hirschheim, A. Heinzl, & J. Dibbern (Eds.), *Information systems outsourcing: The era of digital transformation* (Vol. 5). Springer.

Dibbern, J., Brehm, L., & Heinzl, A. (2002). Rethinking ERP-outsourcing decisions for leveraging technological and preserving business knowledge. In *Hawaii International Conference on System Sciences*.

Dibbern, J., Goles, T., Hirschheim, R. A., & Jayatilaka, B. (2004). Information systems outsourcing: A survey and analysis of the literature. *ACM Sigmis Database: The DATA BASE for Advances in Information Systems, 35*(4), 6–102.

Dibbern, J., Winkler, J., & Heinzl, A. (2008). Explaining variations in client extra costs between software projects offshored to India. *MIS Quarterly, 32*(2), 333–366.

Dibbern, J., Chin, W. W., & Heinzl, A. (2012). Systemic determinants of the information systems outsourcing decision: A comparative study of German and United States firms. *Journal of the Association for Information Systems, 13*(6), 466–497.

Fallon, M., Spohrer, K., & Heinzl, A. (2019). Wearable devices: a physiological and self-regulatory intervention for increasing attention in the workplace. In *Information systems and neuroscience* (pp. 229–238). Springer.

Felin, T., & Lakhan, K. (2018). What problems will you solve with Blockchain? *MIT Sloan Management Review, 60*(1), 32–38.

Foerderer, J., Bender, M., & Heinzl, A. (2018a). Regulation of digital platform ecosystems: Evidence from Russia's Google vs Yandex ruling. In *International Conference on Information Systems*.

Foerderer, J., Kude, T., Mithas, S., & Heinzl, A. (2018b). Does platform owner's entry crowd out innovation? Evidence from Google photos. *Information Systems Research, 29*(2), 444–460.

Foerderer, J., Kude, T., Schuetz, S. W., & Heinzl, A. (2019). Knowledge boundaries in enterprise software platform development: Antecedents and consequences for platform governance. *Information Systems Journal, 29*(1), 119–144.

Foerderer, J., Lueker, N., & Heinzl, A. (2021). And the winner is...? The desirable and undesirable effects of platform awards. *Information Systems Research, 32*(4), 1155–1172.

Foerderer, J., Heinzl, A., & Kude, T. (2022). Plattformökosysteme. In S. Roth & H. Corsten (Eds.), *Handbuch Digitalisierung* (pp. 137–160). Vahlen.

Galliers, R. D. (1993). Research issues in information systems. *Journal of Information Technology, 8*(2), 92–98.

Gawer, A., & Cusumano, M. A. (2014). Industry platforms and ecosystem innovation. *Journal of Product Innovation Management, 31*(3), 417–433.

Geisser, M., Heinzl, A., Hildenbrand, T., & Rothlauf, F. (2007). Verteiltes, internetbasiertes requirements-engineering. *Wirtschaftsinformatik, 49*(3), 199–207.

Ghazawneh, A., & Henfridsson, O. (2013). Balancing platform control and external contribution in third-party development: the boundary resources model. *Information Systems Journal, 23*(2), 173–192. https://doi.org/10.1111/j.1365-2575.2012.00406.x

Gholami, B., & Heinzl, A. (2013). Leading agile self-organizing teams: A collective learning perspective. In *International Conference on Organizational Learning, Knowledge and Capabilities*.

Grosche, T., Heinzl, A., & Rothlauf, F. (2001). A conceptual approach for simultaneous flight schedule construction with genetic algorithms. In *Workshops on Applications of Evolutionary Computation* (pp. 257–267).

Grosche, T., Rothlauf, F., & Heinzl, A. (2007). Gravity models for airline passenger volume estimation. *Journal of Air Transport Management, 13*(4), 175–183.

Halckenhäußer, A., Foerderer, J., & Heinzl, A. (2020). Platform governance mechanisms: An integrated literature review and research directions. In *European Conference on Information Systems*.

Heinrich, L. J., Heinzl, A., & Riedl, R. (2011). *Wirtschaftsinformatik: Einführung und Grundlegung*. Springer.

Heinzl, A. (1991). *Die Ausgliederung der betrieblichen Datenverarbeitung: Eine empirische Analyse der Motive, Formen und Wirkungen*. Poeschel.

Heinzl, A. (1993). Outsourcing the information systems function within the company: An empirical survey. In *International Conference of Outsourcing of Information Services*, May 20–22, 1993.

Heinzl, A. (1996). *Die Evolution der betrieblichen DV-Abteilung: eine lebenszyklustheoretische Analyse*. Physica-Verlag.

Heinzl, A., & Brehm, L. (2006). Organisatorische Gestaltung und Erfolgsfaktoren der Postimplementierungsphase von ERP-Systemen. *Die Unternehmung, 60*(6), 407–425.

Heinzl, A., & Stoffel, K. (1991). Formen, Motive und Risiken der Auslagerung der betrieblichen Datenverarbeitung. *DV-Management, 4*, 161–173.

Hevner, A. R., March, S. T., Park, J., & Ram, S. (2004). Design science in information systems research. *MIS Quarterly, 28*(1), 75–105.

Hildenbrand, T., Rothlauf, F., Geisser, M., Heinzl, A., & Kude, T. (2008) Approaches to collaborative software development. In *Workshop on Engineering Complex Distributed Systems*.

Hildenbrand, T., Heinzl, A., Geisser, M., Klimpke, L., & Acker, T. (2009). A visual approach to traceability and rationale management in distributed collaborative software development. In A.Heinzl, P. Dadam, S. Kirn, & P. Lockemann (Eds.), *PRIMIUM: Process innovation for enterprise software. Lecture notes in informatics – Proceedings* (pp. 161–178).

Hirschheim, R. A., Heinzl, A., & Dibbern, J. (2020). *Information systems outsourcing: The era of digital transformation*. Springer.

Hoffmann, P., Mateja, D., Spohrer, K., & Heinzl, A. (2019). Bridging the vendor-user gap in enterprise cloud software development through data-driven requirements engineering. In *International Conference on Information Systems*.

Huber, T. L., Kude, T., & Dibbern, J. (2017). Governance practices in platform ecosystems: Navigating tensions between co-created value and governance costs. *Information Systems Research, 28*(3), 563–584.

Hurni, T., Huber, T. L., & Dibbern, J. (2022). Power dynamics in software platform ecosystems. *Information Systems Journal, 32*(2), 310–343.

Jacobides, M. G., Cennamo, C., & Gawer, A. (2018). Towards a theory of ecosystems. *Strategic Management Journal (John Wiley & Sons, Inc), 39*(8), 2255–2276. https://doi.org/10.1002/smj.2904

Jussupow, E., Spohrer, K., & Heinzl, A. (2018). *Link C I am; we are—Conceptualizing professional identity threats from information technology*.

Jussupow, E., Benbasat, I., & Heinzl, A. (2020). Why are we averse towards algorithms? A comprehensive literature review on algorithm aversion. In *European Conference on Information Systems*.

Jussupow, E., Meza Martínez, M. A., Mädche, A., & Heinzl, A. (2021a). Is this system biased?–How users react to gender bias in an explainable AI system. In *42nd International Conference on Information Systems*.

Jussupow, E., Spohrer, K., Heinzl, A., & Gawlitza, J. (2021b). Augmenting medical diagnosis decisions? An investigation into physicians' decision-making process with artificial intelligence. *Information Systems Research, 32*(3), 713–735.

Karhu, K., Gustafsson, R., Eaton, B., Henfridsson, O., & Sørensen, C. (2020). Four tactics for implementing a balanced digital platform strategy. *MIS Quarterly Executive, 19*(2), 105–120. https://doi.org/10.17705/2msqe.00027

Kern, T., & Willcocks, L. (2002). Exploring relationships in information technology outsourcing: The interaction approach. *European Journal of Information Systems, 11*(1), 3–19.

Kher, R., Terjesen, S., & Liu, C. (2021). Blockchain, Bitcoin, and ICOs: A review and research agenda. *Small Business Economics, 56*(4), 1699–1720. https://doi.org/10.1007/s11187-019-00286-y

Klimpke, L., Kude, T., & Heinzl, A. (2014). *Ein integrierter Mikroblogging-Ansatz zur Unterstützung verteilter Softwareentwicklungsprojekte*. Multikonferenz Wirtschaftsinformatik.

Kramer, T., Heinzl, A., & Neben, T. (2017). Cross-organizational software development: Design and evaluation of a decision support system for software component outsourcing. In *Hawaii International Conference on System Sciences*.

Krancher, O., Oshri, I., Kotlarski, J., & Dibbern, J. (2022). Bilateral, collective, or both? Formal governance and performance in multisourcing. *Journal of the Association for Information Systems*.

Kude, T., Dibbern, J., & Heinzl, A. (2012). Why do complementors participate? An analysis of partnership networks in the enterprise software industry. *IEEE Transactions on Engineering Management, 59*(2), 250.

Kude, T., Lazic, M., Heinzl, A., & Neff, A. (2018). Achieving IT-based synergies through regulation-oriented and consensus-oriented IT governance capabilities. *Information Systems Journal, 28*(5), 765–795.

Kude, T., Mithas, S., Schmidt, C. T., & Heinzl, A. (2019). How pair programming influences team performance: The role of backup behavior, shared mental models, and task novelty. *Information Systems Research, 30*(4), 1145–1163.

Lacity, M. C. (2018). Addressing key challenges to making enterprise blockchain applications a reality. *MIS Quarterly Executive, 17*(3), 201–222.

Lacity, M. C., & Hirschheim, R. A. (1993a). The information systems outsourcing bandwagon. *Sloan Management Review, 35*(1), 73–86.

Lacity, M. C., & Hirschheim, R. A. (1993b). *Information systems outsourcing: myths, metaphors, and realities*. Wiley.

Luftman, J., & Brier, T. (1999). Achieving and sustaining business-IT alignment. *California Management Review, 42*(1), 109–122.

Malhotra, A., Majchrzak, A., Carman, R., & Lott, V. (2001). Radical innovation without collocation: A case study at Boeing-Rocketdyne. *MIS Quarterly, 25*(2), 229–249.

Markus, M. L., & Robey, D. (1988). Information technology and organizational change: causal structure in theory and research. *Management Science, 34*(5), 583–598.

Neben, T., Xiao, B. S., Lim, E., Tan, C.-W., & Heinzl, A. (2015). *Measuring appeal in human computer interaction: A cognitive neuroscience-based approach* (pp. 151–159). Information Systems and Neuroscience. Springer.

Paulussen, T., Heinzl, A., & Becker, C. (2013). Multi-agent based information systems for patient coordination in hospitals. In *International Conference on Information Systems*.

Porter, M. E. (1985). *Competitive Advantage: Creating and sustaining superior performance*. The Free Press.

Risius, M., & Spohrer, K. (2017). A blockchain research framework. *Business & Information Systems Engineering, 59*(6), 385–409.

Scheerer, A., Schmidt, C. T., Heinzl, A., Hildenbrand, T., & Voelz, D. (2013). *Agile software engineering techniques: The missing link in large scale lean product development*. Software Engineering.

Scheerer, A., Bick, S., Hildenbrand, T., & Heinzl, A. (2015). The effects of team backlog dependencies on agile multiteam systems: A graph theoretical approach. In *Hawaii International Conference on System Sciences* (pp. 5124–5132).

Schoberth, T., Preece, J., & Heinzl, A. (2003). Online communities: A longitudinal analysis of communication activities. In *Hawaii International Conference on System Sciences* (p. 10). IEEE.

Schoberth, T., Heinzl, A., & Preece, J. (2006). Exploring communication activities in online communities: A longitudinal analysis in the financial services industry. *Journal of Organizational Computing and Electronic Commerce, 16*(3–4), 247–265.

Seeger, A.-M., Pfeiffer, J., & Heinzl, A. (2021). Texting with humanlike conversational agents: Designing for anthropomorphism. *Journal of the Association for Information Systems, 22*(4), 931–967.

Somogyi, E. K., & Galliers, R. D. (1987). Applied Information Technology: From data processing to strategic information systems. *Journal of Information Technology, 2*(1), 30–41.

Spohrer, K., Fallon, M., Hoehle, H., & Heinzl, A. (2021). Designing effective mobile health apps: Does combining behavior change techniques really create synergies? *Journal of Management Information Systems, 38*(2), 517–545.

Stuckenberg, S., Kude, T., & Heinzl, A. (2014). Understanding the role of organizational integration in developing and operating Software-as-a-Service. In *Information systems outsourcing* (pp. 313–345). Springer.

Tapscott, D., & Tapscott, A. (2017). *Realizing the potential of blockchain: A multistakeholder approach to the stewardship of blockchain and cryptocurrencies*. World Economic Forum.

Tiwana, A. (2014). *Platform ecosystems: Aligning architecture, governance, and strategy*. Elsevier LTD.

Venkatraman, V. (2017). *The digital matrix: New rules for business transformation through technology*. LifeTree Media.

vom Brocke, J., Jans, M., Mendling, J., & Reijers, H. A. (2021). A five-level framework for research on process mining. *Business and Information Systems Engineering, 63*(5), 483–490.

Weill, P. (2004). Don't just lead, govern: How top-performing firms govern IT. *MIS Quarterly Executive, 3*(1), 1–17.

Weinhardt, C., Anandasivam, A., Blau, B., Borissov, N., & Meinl, T. (2009). Cloud computing - A classification, business models, and research directions. *Business and Information Systems Engineering, 1*(5), 391–399.

Willcocks, L. P., Fitzgerald, G., & Feeny, D. (1995). Outsourcing IT: The strategic implications. *Long Range Planning, 28*(5), 59–70.

Winkler, J. K., Dibbern, J., & Heinzl, A. (2009). The impact of cultural differences in offshore outsourcing: Case study results from German–Indian application development projects. In *Information systems outsourcing* (pp. 471–495). Springer.

Part II
Outsourcing and Multi-party Projects: Reflections and Experiences

The Early History of IT Outsourcing: A Personal Reflection

Rudy Hirschheim

Abstract In this chapter, I attempt to document the early days of Information Technology Outsourcing, starting with the initial EDS facilities management contracts, which then led to the notion of IT outsourcing and its proliferation. I will present the history of the mega-deals, and some of the ideas, lessons, and rationale, which drove early outsourcing. By understanding the early history of IT outsourcing, it better positions us to appreciate the evolution and challenges facing today's new forms of outsourcing.

1 Introduction

While there have been a number of papers surveying the field of Information Technology (IT) Outsourcing (cf. Dibbern et al., 2004; Hatonen & Eriksson, 2009; Lacity et al., 2009; Liang et al., 2016), the actual *history* of the field has been given scant attention. This seems odd and inconsistent with the Information Systems field's interest in—and recognition of the importance of—history (Hirschheim et al., 2012; Bryant et al., 2013) and the historical method (Mason et al., 1997; Porra et al., 2014). Without a documented history, there is no sense of shared understanding of how IT outsourcing got to where it is, and what challenges it faces now and possibly in the future. However, with a shared understanding of IT outsourcing, each of us who is engaged in the field can achieve a sense of the larger meaning of our individual contributions and the contribution of others. It leads to shared concepts and the ability to communicate with others across boundaries, especially across the academic/practitioner divide. It allows us to appreciate the work that came before and helps establish a cumulative tradition. With this in mind, I will offer my thoughts on the historical antecedents which lie behind the evolution of IT outsourcing.

R. Hirschheim (✉)
Lousiana State University, Baton Rouge, LA, USA
e-mail: rudy@lsu.edu

© The Author(s), under exclusive license to Springer Nature Switzerland AG 2022
J. Dibbern et al. (eds.), *Digitalization Across Organizational Levels*, Progress in IS,
https://doi.org/10.1007/978-3-031-06543-9_2

21

2   Three Waves of IT Outsourcing[1]

The history of IT outsourcing is a rich one. We can see that outsourcing has evolved considerably since the late 1980s when large IT outsourcing vendors such as EDS and IBM, signed multibillion-dollar deals with clients involving the transfer of corporate IT to these vendors. While the types of outsourcing arrangements have evolved to include business processes, offshoring, crowdsourcing and the like, the current trend is now firmly associated with organizations' desire for digital transformation (cf. Willcocks & Lacity, 2012).

Digital transformation has been defined as "the use of new digital technologies, such as mobile, artificial intelligence, cloud, blockchain, and Internet of things (IoT) technologies, to enable major business improvements to augment customer experience, streamline operations, or create new business models" (Warner & Wäger, 2019). Essentially, digital transformation changes the way organizations use technology, people and processes to fundamentally change business performance (Westerman et al., 2014). While the notion is not particularly new (cf. Scott Morton, 1991; Markus & Benjamin, 1997; Andal-Ancion et al., 2003), the role of outsourcing within this transformation has only somewhat recently been considered. The emphasis has shifted from outsourcing legacy and/or traditional services to outsourcing for digital transformation. Organizations are looking for vendors, consultants, and researchers who can assist them in this transformation. This is evident in the academic research which is now exploring sourcing topics such as crowdsourcing (Blohm et al., 2013; Geiger & Schader, 2014), platform ecosystems (Constantinides et al., 2018; Foerderer et al., 2018; Ghazawneh & Henfridsson, 2013; Huber et al., 2017; Schmeiss et al., 2019; Tiwana, 2002), cloud computing (Venters & Whitley 2012; Schneider & Sunyaev, 2016; Yinghui et al., 2018), service innovation (Barrett et al., 2015; Lusch & Nambisan, 2015), service automation (robotic process automation—RPA) (Lacity & Willcocks, 2016; Rutschi & Dibbern, 2020; Willcocks & Lacity, 2016), impact sourcing (Heeks, 2013; Sandeep & Ravishankar, 2018); artificial intelligence/machine learning (Davenport & Ronanki, 2018), process mining/analytics (Fogarty & Bell, 2014), internet of things (Dijkman et al., 2015), and blockchain (cf. Lacity & Willcocks, 2018).

---

[1] The three waves of IT outsourcing are based on a chapter that Jens Dibbern and I collaborated on Dibbern and Hirschheim (2020).

The current growth of digital transformation has led to a changing IT outsourcing landscape which could be thought of as three commingling "waves of change." They are:

2.1 Wave 1: The Evolving Traditional Outsourcing of IT Services

This wave refers to the outsourcing of IT functions and IT tasks, such as software development or data center operations, that are performed by external IT work forces. In such labor-intensive traditional outsourcing of IT services, enduring trends include offshoring and multi-sourcing, which have been around for some time. But also new sourcing arrangements that are characterized by novel value propositions, such as striving for innovation through outsourcing rather than simply cost savings or getting access to scarce resources. The development of "impact sourcing" emerged as a new way of looking at the notion of value. Here, clients and vendors consider how their outsourcing arrangements contribute to creating social and society-wide (rather than purely firm) economic value (Lacity et al., 2014; Babin & Nicholson, 2020; Carmel et al., 2016; Lacity et al., 2016; Kahn et al., 2018).

2.2 Wave 2: The Emergence of Cloud Computing and Platform Ecosystems

This wave involves a new approach to service development and delivery by the IT industry where IT services are developed in large platform ecosystems and provided via platforms. These comprise new pricing models (i.e., renting readily available services) and the provision of services via the internet (i.e., cloud) as Software as a service (SaaS), Infrastructure as a service (IaaS), or Platform as a service (PaaS) (Weinhardt et al., 2009; Ceccagnoli et al., 2012). The move toward platforms also includes the provision of labor as a service and has led to entirely new business models that disrupt traditional industries (Willcocks et al., 2018). This includes crowdsourcing, i.e. engaging the crowd in a new service delivery model, and embracing the use of digital platforms to expose untapped supply and demand of services that are based on the sharing of individually owned resources and assets as exemplified by Airbnb and Uber.

2.3   Wave 3: The Development of Robotic Process Automation and "Outsourcing" to Software Bots

This wave embodies an arrangement where entire tasks or business functions are taken over by some type of automation such as a chatbot. Thus, the goal is not to support humans with cheaper or better IT services that may stem from external providers, but rather to replace humans by IT (Przegalinska et al., 2019; Adam et al., 2021; Rutschi & Dibbern, 2020). AI/machine learning, data analytics, and blockchain are all integral elements of this wave.

It is important to note that although this description is of three distinct waves of change, they are in fact commingled and entangled. They overlap both within and between the waves. For example, a software bot may be developed by an external service provider using a traditional outsourcing arrangement with an external vendor and the bot may take over work from the former in-house personnel of the client and hence the work is outsourced to the bot. The bot may then also be provided as a SaaS via cloud computing. So the waves are really a simplifying vehicle to make sense of the broad evolution of IT outsourcing from the late 1980s through today. However, IT outsourcing has a richer tradition that extends back into the 1960s when Ross Perot, and his company EDS, first started managing IT facilities for a number of companies, which eventually evolved into the first IT outsourcing arrangements (cf. Mack & Quick, 2002). It is to this early history of IT outsourcing that I turn next.

3   The Early, Early Days of Outsourcing

Given this chapter is about IT outsourcing and its early history, it is important to define what is meant by "outsourcing." I define *outsourcing* as the practice of engaging with a third-party entity for the provision of goods or services to either replace, supplement, or provide specific activities or tasks; and it has been around for centuries. According to Jones (2018), one of the earliest occurrences of outsourcing can be traced back to the ancient Roman Empire where *publicans* ('men engaged in public business') were hired to collect taxes and harbor dues, provide military and civilian supplies, build and repair roads, bridges and aqueducts, handle waste disposal, and so on. In the late seventeenth century in America, the production of wagon covers and clipper ships' sails was outsourced to laborers in Scotland, where they used raw material imported from India. As Ghimire (2005) writes: *"England's textile industry became so efficient in the 1830s that eventually Indian manufacturers couldn't compete, and that work was outsourced to England."* Outsourcing remained popular in the manufacturing sector, with part of the assembling in many industries being subcontracted to other organizations and locations where the work could be done more efficiently and cheaply (Momme, 2002; Akbari, 2018). Commenting on this trend, Pastin and Harrison (1987) note that such outsourcing of manufacturing functions was creating a new form of organization which they termed the "hollow corporation" (i.e., an organization that designs and distributes, but does not produce anything). They note that such an organizational form would require considerable changes in the way organizations were managed. But this has not stopped the inexorable growth of outsourcing in virtually every industry. As Hatonen and Eriksson (2009) write: *"What we have been witnessing is an outsourcing revolution, which has changed the way firms compete in as diverse industries as automobiles, aerospace, telecommunications, computers, pharmaceuticals, chemicals, healthcare, financial services, energy systems and software just to name a few."* (p. 142).

It was not long before the idea of outsourcing was applied to the procurement of information technology (IT) services also. Initially, when organizations looked to external sources for the provision of IT services, the vendor provided a single basic function to the customer, exemplified by facilities management arrangements where the vendor assumed operational control over the customer's technology assets, typically a data center. Electronic Data Systems (EDS) contract with Frito-Lay in 1963 was the first major example of such an arrangement. However, EDS's agreement with Blue Cross/Blue Shield of Texas in 1966 was different from previous 'facilities management' contracts in that EDS was responsible for handling Blue Cross/Blue Shield's data processing services. EDS took over the responsibility for Blue Cross's IT people extending the scope of the agreement beyond the use of third parties to supplement a company's IT services. EDS and Blue Shield of California inked a similar deal in 1969. EDS's client base grew to include customers such as HCA Inc., the U.S. Department of Defense, and the U.S. Government's National Flood Insurance Program in the seventies. In 1982, the U.S. Army awarded EDS a 10-year $650 million contract, which at the time was the largest in the history of the information services industry. EDS signed a $350 million contract with the U.S. Navy the following year. In 1984 General Motors bought EDS for $2.5 billion. These deals portended a new type of IT services provision—large-scale IT outsourcing.[2] Such IT outsourcing agreements were entered into with three large companies headquartered in Houston—Continental Airlines, First City Bank and Enron in the late eighties. These EDS arrangements were not simply IT service contracts but typically involved EDS either purchasing stock in the companies they were providing IT services to and/or providing an upfront cash payment for the client company's IT assets. So these were financial arrangements that allowed all three companies to receive a cash infusion to help stave off potential chapter "Airline Market Concentration in Europe" filings. In 1989, other players besides EDS entered the outsourcing arena, the most noteworthy of these being the ISSC division of IBM. In fact, ISSC's deal with Kodak in 1989 heralded the arrival of the IT outsourcing mega-deal and legitimized the role of outsourcing for IT. Following the success of the Kodak deal, well-known companies around

---

[2] In the IT world, the term "outsourcing" has been attributed to Morton Meyerson of EDS who used the term to refer to EDS's business model of providing IT services to its clients, often in the context of facilities management (Yost, 2017).

the world quickly followed suit. In 1991, General Dynamics signed a $3 billion deal with CSC. Equifax signed a $650 million outsourcing contract with ISSC in 1993. EDS signed a $3.2 billion deal with Xerox in 1994. In 1997, IBM, Telstra and Lend Lease of Australia entered into a major IT deal valued at $2 billion. In the same year, EDS inked an IT outsourcing deal with the Commonwealth Bank of Australia for $3.8 billion. In 1997, Swiss Bank signed a $3 billion outsourcing deal with Perot Systems. The same year, saw Dupont/Conoco ink a deal with CSC and Anderson worth $4.2 billion. And in 1996, General Motors sold off EDS and then signed a 10-year IT outsourcing deal with them valued at $38 billion. Other major multi-billion-dollar deals were implemented by McDonnell Douglas, AT&T, JP Morgan/Chase, Bell South, Delta Airlines, and the U.S. Military in the U.S.; Lufthansa in Germany; Rolls Royce, Inland Revenue, Bank of Scotland, and British Aerospace in Britain; KF Group in Sweden; Canada Post in Canada; Government of South Australia in Australia; Bank di' Roma in Italy; and ABN Amro in the Netherlands (Dibbern et al., 2004).

It is interesting to note that a number of the outsourcing deals in the 1990s were very creative and became models for future arrangements. Here are two which are worth considering, both from outside the US. The first example is a 1996 deal, that was struck with EDS and the Government of South Australia in Adelaide. This is an arrangement that allows the South Australian Government to outsource its IT to a third-party provider, in this case EDS. What was interesting about that deal, was that EDS was required to spend approximately 10% of the revenue of the outsourcing deal to spur economic development in the state of South Australia. Thus, the interesting aspect about this deal was, that it was not simply an outsourcing arrangement, where a vendor provided IT services for a set dollar amount. It was the IT vendor providing services but also spurring the economy of this state by creating new jobs, spending money in the state of South Australia to bolster its economy. This was clearly a very creative venture even though it had its difficulties in terms of determining what was the value of EDS' contribution to the State of South Australia's economy. A second example is the co-sourcing arrangement that EDS structured with Rolls Royce in the UK. It was a £2 billion arrangement. EDS' co-sourcing arrangement was that Rolls Royce would provide EDS £500 million to manage and deal with the higher-level IT arrangements for Rolls Royce. The other £1.5 billion would be spent on either EDS providing initial services or EDS subcontracting to third-party providers for the provision of system development, system maintenance and the like. That deal shows the breadth of the kind of arrangement a client can strike with an outsourcing vendor. There are also a number of other arrangements which have led to so-called win-win operations. One is Telstra (Australia) signing a deal with IBM Global Services. In this deal, Telstra outsourced its IT to IBM. Telstra and IBM then formed a company called Advantra whose purpose was to provide telecommunication services to Pacific Rim countries. This is an example of a joint venture between the outsourcing vendor and client with the intention of offering the prospect of a new source of revenue for them. Such new joint ventures would allow the industry skills provided by the client with the technology skills of the vendor coming together to provide a new venture which would offer both expertises in a particular industry segment to sell these skills to others in that same industry. (Although how successful such joint ventures are, or could be, is far from clear.)

Similar joint venture and/or spinoff arrangements were not uncommon in the early days of outsourcing. Important examples of IT spinoffs that competed in the IT outsourcing space include Debis Systemhaus (a spinoff of Daimler-Benz's IT department in 1990); T-Systems (a spinoff of Deutsche Telekom in 2000 which in 2002 acquired Debis Systemhaus); Shell Services Company (the spinoff of Royal Dutch Shell in 1994 to compete in the IT outsourcing market); and General Motors spinning off EDS in 1996 (having purchased it in 1984). Spinoffs and joint ventures have only increased in number, size, and scope since the early days of IT outsourcing (cf. Lacity et al., 2004; McIvor, 2010). A recent example can be found in IBM's announced spinoff of its Managed Infrastructure Services division as a new company called Kyndryl (Enderle, 2021).

Figure 1 offers a timeline of the growth of IT Outsourcing focusing on the early period of this history.

	1966	EDS wins Blue Shield of Texas account
	1969	EDS wins Blue Shield of California account facilities management, contract programming, systems integration, service bureau, time sharing
The early days	1982	US Army signs $650 million contract with EDS
	1984	GM buys EDS
	1988-1991	EDS involved in financial outsourcing deals - Continental Airlines - First City Bank - Enron
FIRST WAVE	1989	IBM announces ISSC Kodak outsources to ISSC which legitimizes outsourcing (The era of the megadeal begins)
Best of Breed "Pinnacle Alliance" - JP Morgan	1993	BP, KF Group (Sweden), Canada Post (Outsourcing becomes international) Alliances, partnerships grow
	1994	Xerox outsources to EDS - $3.2 billion
	1996	Cosourcing – EDS and clients share the risks and rewards of the services EDS provides
Creativity in deal Making, *cf.* South of Australia	Mid 90s	Outsourcing moves beyond simple cost savings…value –based sourcing/equity-based outsourcing Other functions considered for outsourcing; IT is seen as the "leader" Lots of renegotiating of contracts
	Mid/late 90s	Business Process Outsourcing (BPO)
	Late 90s	70+% of companies outsource some piece of IT… selective sourcing is totally accepted as sound business practice
Web and eBusiness helping to drive outsourcing…	1999	The emergence of ASPs and net sourcing
	2001	Offshoring
	2003	BPO (offshoring): HR & payroll, F&A, KPO, R&D, Legal, Engineering services, Customer contact
SECOND WAVE	2005	Rural sourcing
"Virtualization of business process outsourcing assets"	2007-10	OM/G tools; multisourcing; New titles: Chief Sourcing Officer, Head of Resourcing, Head of Transformation
	2011	Microsourcing/Crowdsourcing
THIRD WAVE	2015	Cloud computing / platform ecosystems outsourcing; impact sourcing
	2019	Robotic Process Automation (RPA), chabots, AI

Fig. 1 IT outsourcing timeline

3.1   Why Do Companies Really Outsource?

A question that drove much of the early IT outsourcing research was "why do companies really outsource?" The conventional wisdom suggested that while organizations outsource IT for many reasons, the growth was largely attributed to two primary phenomena: (1) a focus on core competencies and (2) a lack of understanding of IT value (Lacity et al., 1994). First, motivated by the belief that sustainable competitive advantage can only be achieved through a focus on core competencies, the management of organizations chose to concentrate on what an organization does better than anyone else while outsourcing the rest. As a result of this focus strategy, IT came under scrutiny. Did it make sense for companies to devote so much time, money, and effort to keeping up with IT advances, particularly when IT was simply a "support" function? As such, the IT function was viewed as a non-core activity in organizations, so much so that Carr (2003) went so far as to argue that IT was simply a commodity. Further, senior executives believed that IT vendors possessed economies of scale and technical expertise to provide IT services more efficiently than internal IT departments. Second, and perhaps more telling, the growth in outsourcing was also due to a lack of clear understanding of the value delivered by IT (Porra et al., 2005; Lacity & Hirschheim, 1993a). Though senior executives viewed IT as essential to the functioning of the organization,[3] it was viewed as a cost that needed to be minimized. Believing that outsourcing would help meet the IT needs of the organization less expensively, it was hardly surprising that organizations jumped on the outsourcing bandwagon (Lacity and Hirschheim 1993b; Willcocks & Fitzgerald, 1994).

Although early research documented the orthodox thinking on why companies "supposedly" outsourced their IT, i.e., cost savings, focusing on core competencies, and the like, Lacity and Hirschheim (1993a) questioned the validity of this orthodoxy. Deciding that the best way to *really* understand what was happening with outsourcing was to undertake detailed case studies of organizations who had outsourced their IT. The cases involved large companies who had signed high dollar value outsourcing contracts with well-known outsourcing vendors such as EDS and IBM. Using an interpretive research approach, they found a much more nuanced approach to IT outsourcing that involved shifts in organizational power, as well as financial issues that were less to do with overall IT cost savings, and more to do with the desperate need for an immediate cash infusion. Indeed, the early outsourcing deals (for example, EDS's arrangement with Enron, First City Bank, and Continental Airlines), were primarily short-term financial transactions where EDS would inject significant amounts of capital through cash and stock purchases in

---

[3] Davis et al. (2006) make the interesting observation that while IT was indeed not a core competence for most organizations, it was nevertheless "special," i. e., a critical success factor that was necessary but not sufficient for the success of a firm. Initially it was thought that such functions could not be outsourced, but either (a) IT was not "special," or (b) the logic that "special" functions could not be outsourced was fallacious. In either case, the outsourcing of IT continued to grow.

exchange for long-term IT outsourcing contracts. Companies either in, or very close to, chapter "Airline Market Concentration in Europe" filings, desperately needed such cash infusion to survive, so it is hardly surprising they entered into these long-term, mega-outsourcing contracts. Such announcements were promoted to the stock market as an indication that these companies had made a strategic decision to "reign in the runaway costs of IT and focus on their own specific core competencies." The stock market was only too willing to reward these companies with increased stock prices believing that IT outsourcing meant that the company was "putting its house in order." But did it? Were the promulgated benefits of outsourcing real?

The Lacity and Hirschheim research on Insourcing (Lacity & Hirschheim, 1995; Hirschheim & Lacity, 2000) paint a rather perplexing picture of the results of early IT outsourcing. They report that the impact of IT outsourcing was not as simple or as straightforward as the literature—both academic and practitioner—was contending. In fact, they found that IT outsourcing had not yielded the benefits that organizations had hoped for. Indeed, for a number of companies, IT outsourcing increased the overall cost of IT, although the way IT was accounted for and reported, made this calculation difficult to see and comprehend. Moreover, IT outsourcing created new problems that seemed to be overlooked in the zeal to outsource. In particular, two thorny issues were identified.

3.2 Unresolved Issues of Early Outsourcing Research: Loss of Internal Skills and Succession

While much of the literature focused on the short-term reasons and value of outsourcing, the question of what happens in the longer term, seemed to be rarely asked. The focus was squarely on the decision to outsource which was typically motivated by cost savings, irrespective of any collateral damage that might occur in the long term. In particular, what were the long-term consequence of turning over strategic parts of the business to third-party providers; would there be lost opportunities of not having these strategic parts internal to the organization? And who should be involved in making the decision of what to outsourcing and what not to outsource? Then there was the concern of what happens when the company no longer has the individual skills sets possessed by those individuals who have been outsourced. Often those skills were exactly what was needed in the making of important decisions. Lastly, there was the issue of succession. When a company turns over a significant number of functions to third-party providers and the people working in these functions then go to the outsourcing vendor, where does the next generation of senior executives come from? Essentially, those individuals who formerly worked for the company—and formed the base for the next generation of top management—have now gone over to the vendor. Thus, in the long-term outsourcing can lead to the difficult situation of how organizational succession occurs, because the executives or the executives in training have been outsourced to third-party providers. Issues such as loss of internal skills and succession were left for future research to explore.

4 Academic Initiatives on IT Outsourcing

4.1 Academic Conferences

Reports from well-known IT consulting companies such as Gartner, Forrester, McKinsey noted that outsourcing would continue to rapidly grow both domestically and globally and embrace emerging domains such as offshoring, business process outsourcing, crowdsourcing, and the like. Indeed, IT outsourcing was a "proof of concept" that even strategic functions such as IT, could be turned over to third-party providers. It was, as it were, a continuation of converting fixed assets and costs into variable ones. The trend was unmistakable. It, therefore, became apparent to many in the academic community that IT outsourcing was not a passing fad and needed to be studied by academics. Early academic IT outsourcing research was undertaken around the same time in various countries such as the USA, UK, the Netherlands, Germany, and Finland among others. In the early 90s, it became apparent that there was a need for individual researchers around the globe to come together to take stock on what research was being done and what was known about the phenomenon. To this end, Markku Saaksjarvi, Arje Wassenaur, and Rudy Hirschheim got together and decided it was time to have an academic conference on IT outsourcing. The outcome was the first academic conference to explore this global phenomenon was held on May 20–22, 1993 at the University of Twente, in Enschede, the Netherlands. It was called the "Conference on Outsourcing of Information Systems Services (OUT'93)" with the intention that it would be the first of more to come. Indeed, that has been the case. Noting that the growth of academic research had been dramatic (by 2001, over 100 academic papers, along with numerous doctoral dissertations had been published on IS outsourcing), motivated the team of Rudy Hirschheim, Armin Heinzl, and Jens Dibbern to conduct the "Second International Conference on Outsourcing of Information Services (ICOIS'2001)" which was carried out at Castle Thurnau, Bayreuth, Germany, June 22–23, 2001. This was followed by the "Third International Conference on Outsourcing of Information Services (ICOIS'2007)" held at Villa Bosch in Heidelberg, May 29–30, 2007. In 2013, ICOIS continued with the "Fourth International Conference on Outsourcing of Information Services (ICOIS'2007)" held at Mannheim Castle in Mannheim, June 9–11, 2013. And in 2019, the "Fifth International Conference on Outsourcing of Information Services (ICOIS'2019)" was held again at Mannheim Castle, in Mannheim, June 16–18, 2019.

Another academic conference initiative was the Global Sourcing Workshop initiated by Leslie Willcocks, Julia Kotlarsky, and Ilan Oshri as part of the AIS Special Interest Group on Outsourcing—SIGSourcing. The first conference was held in 2007 and has been an annual event ever since. 2019 marked the 15th Global Sourcing Workshop. More recently, Julia Kotlarsky, Ilan Oshri, and Ji-Ye Mao started the Asia-Pacific Global Sourcing Conference with the first event being held on September 23–25, 2016, and the second, September 14–16, 2018.

In addition to these specialized academic outsourcing conferences, mainstream IS academic conferences such as ICIS, AMCIS, ECIS, ACIS, and PACIS had specific tracks on outsourcing. These included not only conference papers but also panel sessions and keynote sessions. So it is clear, that IT outsourcing had a rich history in the IS academic conference scene.

4.2   Journals/Institutions

Following the success of outsourcing in academic conferences, 2008 saw the introduction of a new journal—*Strategic Outsourcing: An International Journal*—that focused exclusively on outsourcing. While mainstream journals such as: *MIS Quarterly, Information Systems Research, Journal of MIS, Journal of the AIS, European Journal of Information Systems, Information Systems Journal, Journal of Information Technology, Journal of Strategic Information Systems, Information & Management, Communications of the ACM, Communications of the AIS, International Journal of Information Management,* and *Information & Organization* as well as many other IS-oriented journals, published individual articles on outsourcing, *Strategic Outsourcing: An International Journal* was the first journal whose mission statement was to publish outsourcing papers. In that sense, it was unique and was an outlet that all outsourcing researchers could count on to provide a knowledgeable and fair treatment of their research.

Interestingly, the so-called "applied" journals, such as *Harvard Business Review, California Management Review, Sloan Management Review,* and *Business Horizons* published many papers on outsourcing. This suggested that practitioners, who made up the lion's share of the audience of these journals, felt that outsourcing was an important topic. In the IS field, *MISQ Executive* also published a number of outsourcing papers which is suggestive of a topic that had wide appeal.

More specifically, the broad area of IT outsourcing can be seen as one of a rather small number of IS academic research domains that practitioners were interested in and led to significant interaction between academics and practitioners: for example, practitioners speaking at academic outsourcing conferences, academics speaking at practitioner outsourcing conferences, academics advising companies on outsourcing decisions, academics working with practitioners on outsourcing research projects, and the like. Another example of this interaction can be seen by The International Association of Outsourcing Professionals (IAOP) inducting both Mary Lacity and Leslie Willcocks into the IAOP Hall of Fame in 2013.

Another indication of the importance of outsourcing to the IS academic IS field can be seen by the commencement of several interest groups on outsourcing. For example, in the early 2000s, the Association for Information Systems (AIS) formed a special interest group—SIG IS Outsourcing (SIGISO) which later became SIGOUT, that offered an opportunity for outsourcing researchers to get together and share experiences and research at various IS conferences. SIGOUT has now been superseded by SIGSourcing which not only holds sessions at the AIS conferences (in particular ICIS) but also has its own annual conference—The Global Sourcing Workshop.

5 Conclusion

My personal reflection on the early days of IT outsourcing contains, of course, my own biases of what I chose to include in my interpretation of the history of outsourcing.[4] My recollection of the early outsourcing history is no doubt incomplete and there might be some mistakes in terms of dates of when certain outsourcing events occurred. It is also likely that additional academic outsourcing research was done by others around the globe that I am unfamiliar with.[5] Additionally, considerable work on outsourcing was undertaken by the many outsourcing consulting firms that formed in and around that time period. Those were heady days in the evolution of outsourcing! Case in point was the excellent work done in the early days of IT outsourcing by Technology Partners International (TPI) (which has now become ISG). Other advisory firms also helped the outsourcing industry to grow and prosper. Lastly, it is important to recognize how IT outsourcing has transformed from the arrangements in the late 1980s and 90s to include Business Process Outsourcing (BPO), Offshore Outsourcing, Crowdsourcing, Impact Sourcing, Cloud Computing/Platform Ecosystems Outsourcing, Robotic Process Automation (RPA), bots, and AI Outsourcing. But I shall leave that subject for another paper!

References

Adam, M., Wessel, M., & Benlian, A. (2021). AI-based chatbots in customer service and their effects on user compliance. *Electronic Markets, 31*(2), 427–445.

Akbari, M. (2018). Logistics outsourcing: A structured literature review. *Benchmarking: An International Journal, 25*(5), 1548–1580.

Andal-Ancion, A., Cartwright, P., & Yip, G. (2003). The digital transformation of traditional businesses. *MIT Sloan Management Review, 44*(4), 34–41.

Babin, R., & Nicholson, B. (2020). Impact sourcing (socially responsible outsourcing). In E. Beulen & P. M. Ribbers (Eds.), *The Routledge companion to managing digital outsourcing*. Routledge.

---

[4] Appendix provides a bibliography of the published papers in the first decade of IT outsourcing.

[5] An excellent survey of the early literature of outsourcing can be found in Dibbern et al. (2004). See also Lacity et al. (2009).

Barrett, M., Davidson, E., Prabhu, J., & Vargo, S. (2015). Service innovation in the digital age: key contributions and future directions. *MIS Quarterly, 39*(1), 135–154.

Blohm, I., Leimeister, J. M., & Krcmar, H. (2013). Crowdsourcing: How to benefit from (too) many great ideas. *MIS Quarterly Executive, 12*(4), 199–211.

Bryant, A., Black, A., Land, F., & Porra, J. (2013). Information systems history: what is history? What is IS history? What IS history? . . . and Why even bother with history. *Journal of Information Technology, 28*, 1–17.

Carmel, E., Lacity, M., & Doty, A. (2016). The impact of impact sourcing: Framing a research agenda. In B. Nicholson, R. Babin, & M. Lacity (Eds.), *Socially responsible outsourcing* (pp. 16–47). Springer.

Carr, N. G. (2003). IT doesn't matter. *Harvard Business Review, 38*, 24–38.

Ceccagnoli, M., Forman, C., Huang, P., & Wu, D. (2012). Cocreation of value in a platform ecosystem. *MIS Quarterly, 36*(1), 263–290.

Constantinides, P., Henfridsson, O., & Parker, G. (2018). Introduction—platforms and infrastructures in the digitalage. *Information Systems Research, 29*(2), 381–400.

Davenport, T., & Ronanki, R. (2018). Artificial intelligence for the real world. *Harvard Business Review, 96*(1), 108–116.

Davis, G., Ein-Dor, P., King, W., & Torkzadeh, R. (2006). IT offshoring: History, prospects and challenges. *Journal of the Association for Information Systems, 7*(11), 770–795.

Dibbern, J., & Hirschheim, R. (2020). Introduction: Riding the waves of outsourcing change in the era of digital transformation. In R. Hirschheim, A. Heinzl, & J. Dibbern (Eds.), *Information systems outsourcing in the era of digital transformation* (5th ed., pp. 1–20). Springer.

Dibbern, J., Goles, T., Hirschheim, R., & Jayatilaka, B. (2004). Information systems outsourcing: A survey and analysis of the literature. *The DATA BASE for Advances in Information Systems, 35*(4), 6–102.

Dijkman, R., Sprenkels, B., Peeters, T., & Janssen, A. (2015). Business models for the internet of things. *International Journal of Information Management, 35*(6), 672–678.

Enderle, R. (2021). The IBM Kyndryl Spin-Off: When separation makes sense. *Datamation,* November 22, 2021. https://www.datamation.com/big-data/ibm-kyndryl-spin-off-separation-makes-sense/

Foerderer, J., Kude, T., Mithas, S., & Heinzl, A. (2018). Does platform owner's entry crowd out innovation? Evidence from Google photos. *Information Systems Research, 29*(2), 444–460.

Fogarty, D., & Bell, P. (2014). Should you outsource analytics? *MIT Sloan Management Review, 55*, 41–45.

Geiger, D., & Schader, M. (2014). Personalized task recommendation in crowdsourcing information systems—Current state of the art. *Decision Support Systems, 65*, 3–16.

Ghazawneh, A., & Henfridsson, O. (2013). Balancing platform control and external contribution in third-party development: The boundary resources model. *Information Systems Journal, 23*(2), 173–192.

Ghimire, B. (2005). IT job outsourcing. *Ubiquity,* Volume 2005, Issue August https://ubiquity.acm.org/article.cfm?id=1088430

Hatonen, J., & Eriksson, T. (2009). 30+ years of research and practice of outsourcing – Exploring the past and anticipating the future. *Journal of International Management, 15*, 142–155.

Heeks, R. (2013). Information technology impact sourcing. *Communications of the ACM, 56*(12), 22–25.

Hirschheim, R., & Lacity, M. (2000). Information technology insourcing: Myths and realities. *Communications of the ACM, 43*(2), 99–107.

Hirschheim, R., Saunders, C., & Straub, D. (2012). Historical interpretations of the IS discipline: An introduction to the special issue. *Journal of the Association for Information Systems, 13*(4), i–viii.

Huber, T. L., Kude, T., & Dibbern, J. (2017). Governance practices in platform ecosystems: Navigating tensions between co-created value and governance costs. *Information Systems Research, 28*(3), 563–584.

Jones, P. (2018). Outsourcing, a long history. *The Spectator*, February 3, 2018.

Kahn, S., Lacity, M., & Willcocks, L. (2018). Entrepreneurial impact sourcing: a conceptual framework of social and commercial institutional logics. *Information Systems Journal, 28*, 538–562.

Lacity, M., & Hirschheim, R. (1993a). *Information systems outsourcing: Myths, metaphors, and realities.* Wiley.

Lacity, M., & Hirschheim, R. (1993b). The information systems outsourcing bandwagon. *Sloan Management Review,* Fall 1993 (pp. 73–86).

Lacity, M., & Hirschheim, R. (1995). *Beyond the information systems outsourcing bandwagon: The insourcing response.* Wiley.

Lacity, M., & Willcocks, L. (2016). A new approach to automating services. *Sloan Management Review, 58,* 40–49.

Lacity, M., & Willcocks, L. (2018). *Robotic process and cognitive automation: the next phase.* Steve Brookes Publishing.

Lacity, M., Hirschheim, R., & Willcocks, L. (1994). Realizing outsourcing expectations: Incredible expectations, credible outcomes", *Information Systems Management,* Vol. 11, No. 4, Fall 1994, pp. 7–18.

Lacity, M., Willcocks, L., & Feeny, D. (2004). Commercialising the back office at Lloyds of London: Outsourcing and strategic partnerships revisited. *European Management Journal, 22*(2), 127–140.

Lacity, M., Khan, S., & Willcocks, L. (2009). A review of the IT outsourcing literature: Insights for practice. *Journal of Strategic Information Systems, 18,* 130–146.

Lacity, M., Rottman, J., & Carmel, E. (2014). Prison sourcing: 'doing good' or 'good for business'? *Journal of Information Technology Teaching Cases, 4,* 99–106.

Lacity, M., Khan, S., & Carmel, E. (2016). Employing U.S. military families to provide business process outsourcing services: A case study of impact sourcing and reshoring. *Communications of the Association for Information Systems, 39*(9), 150–175.

Liang, H., Wang, J.-J., Xue, Y., & Cui, X. (2016). IT outsourcing research from 1992 to 2013: A literature review based on main path analysis. *Information and Management, 53,* 227–251.

Lusch, R., & Nambisan, S. (2015). Service innovation: A service-dominant logic perspective. *MIS Quarterly, 39*(1), 155–175.

Mack, D., & Quick, J. (2002). EDS: An inside view of a corporate life cycle transition. *Organizational Dynamics, 30*(3), 282–293.

Markus, M. L., & Benjamin, R. (1997). The magic bullet theory in IT-enabled transformation. *Sloan Management Review, 38,* 55–68.

Mason, R., McKenney, J., & Copeland, D. (1997). An historical method for MIS research: Steps and assumptions. *MIS Quarterly, 21*(3), 307–320.

McIvor, R. (2010). *Global services outsourcing.* Cambridge University Press.

Momme, J. (2002). Framework for outsourcing manufacturing: Strategic and operational implications. *Computers in Industry, 49*(1), 59–75.

Pastin, M., & Harrison, J. (1987). Social responsibility in the hollow corporation. *Business and Society Review, 87*(63), 54–58.

Porra, J., Hirschheim, R., & Parks, M. (2005). Forty years of corporate information technology at Texaco Inc. – An interpretation using a systems theoretical lens. *MIS Quarterly, 29*(4), 721–746.

Porra, J., Hirschheim, R., & Parks, M. (2014). The historical research method and information systems research. *Journal of the Association for Information Systems, 15*(9), 536–576.

Przegalinska, A., Ciechanowski, L., Stroz, A., Gloor, P., & Mazurek, G. (2019). In bot we trust: a new methodology of chatbot performance measures. *Business Horizons, 62,* 785–797.

Rutschi, R., & Dibbern, J. (2020). Towards a framework of implementing software robots: Transforming human-executed routines into machines. *ACM SIGMIS Database: The DATA BASE for Advances in Information Systems, 51*(1), 104–128.

Sandeep, M., & Ravishankar, M. (2018). Sociocultural transitions and developmental impacts in the digital economy of impact sourcing. *Information Systems Journal, 28*(3), 563–586.

Schmeiss, J., Hoelzle, K., & Tech, R. (2019). Designing governance mechanisms in platform ecosystems: Addressing the paradox of openness through blockchain technology. *California Management Review, 62 1*, 121–143.

Schneider, S., & Sunyaev, A. (2016). Determinant factors of cloud-sourcing decisions: Reflecting on the IT outsourcing literature in the era of cloud computing. *Journal of Information Technology, 31*(1), 1–31.

Scott Morton, M. (1991). How information technologies can transform organizations. In M. S. Morton (Ed.), *The corporation of the 1990's: Information technology and organizational transformation*. Oxford University Press.

Tiwana, A. (2002). *The knowledge management toolkit: orchestrating IT, strategy, and knowledge platforms*. Prentice Hall International.

Venters, W., & Whitley, E. (2012). A critical review of cloud computing: Researching desires and realities. *Journal of Information Technology, 27*(3), 179–197.

Warner, K. S. R., & Wäger, M. (2019). Building dynamic capabilities for digital transformation: An ongoing process of strategic renewal. *Long Range Planning, 52*(3), 326–349.

Weinhardt, C., Anandasivam, A., Blau, B., Borissov, N., & Meinl, T. (2009). Cloud computing - a classification, business models, and research directions. *Business and Information Systems Engineering, 1*(5), 391–399.

Westerman, G., Bonnet, D., & McAfee, A. (2014). The nine elements of digital transformation. *MIT Sloan Management Review, 55*(3), 1–6.

Willcocks, L., & Fitzgerald, G. (1994). *A business guide to IT outsourcing*. Business Intelligence.

Willcocks, L., & Lacity, M. (2012). *The new IT outsourcing landscape – From innovation to cloud services*. Palgrave Macmillan.

Willcocks, L., & Lacity, M. (2016). *Service automation: Robots and the future of work*. Palgrave Macmillan.

Willcocks, L., Oshri, I., & Kotlarsky, J. (2018). *Dynamic innovation in outsourcing – theories, cases and practices*. Palgrave Macmillan.

Yinghui, Z., Deng, R., Liu, X., & Zheng, D. (2018). Blockchain based efficient and robust fair payment for outsourcing services in cloud computing. *Information Sciences, 462*, 262–277.

Yost, J. (2017). *Making IT work: A history of the computer services industry*. The MIT Press.

Appendix: Bibliography of the First Decade of IT Outsourcing Research

Ang, S., & Cummings, L. (1997). Strategic response to institutional influences on information systems outsourcing. *Organization Science, 8*(3), 235–255.

Ang, S., & Slaughter, S. (1998). Organizational psychology and performance in IS employment outsourcing. In *Proceedings of the 31st Annual Hawaii International Conference on System Sciences* (pp. 635–643).

Ang, S., & Straub, D. (1998). Production and transaction economies and IS outsourcing: A study of the U.S. Banking Industry. *MIS Quarterly, 22*(4), 535–551.

Apte, U. M., & Mason, R. (1995). Global disaggregation of information-intensive services. *Management Science, 41*(7), 1250–1262.

Apte, U. M., Sobol, M. G., Hanaoka, S., Shimada, T., Saarinen, T., Salmela, T., & Vepsalainen, A. P. J. (1997). IS outsourcing practices in the USA, Japan, and Finland: A comparative study. *Journal of Information Technology, 12*, 289–304.

Aubert, B., Patry, M., & Rivard, S. (1998) Assessing the risk of IT outsourcing. In *Proceedings of the 31st Annual Hawaii International Conference on System Sciences* (pp. 685–691).

Aubert, B., Dussault, S., Patry, M., & Rivard, S. (1999). Managing the risk of IT outsourcing. In *Proceedings of the 32nd Annual Hawaii International Conference on System Sciences*. doi:https://doi.org/10.1109/HICSS.1999.772972.

Beath, C., & Walker, G. (1998). Outsourcing of application software: A knowledge management perspective. In *Proceedings of the 31st Annual Hawaii International Conference on System Sciences* (pp. 666–674).

Chalos, P., & Sung, J. (1998) Outsourcing decisions and managerial incentives. *Decision Sciences, 29*(4), 9 pp. 01–919.

Chaudhury, A., Nam, K., & Rao, H. R. (1995). Management of information systems outsourcing: A bidding perspective. *Journal of Management Information Systems, 12*(2), 131–159.

Cheon, M., Grover, V., & Teng, J. (1995). Theoretical perspectives on the outsourcing of information systems. *Journal of Information Technology, 10*, 209–219.

Clark, T. D., Zmud, R. W., & McCray, G. E. (1995). The outsourcing of information systems: transforming the nature of business in the information industry. *Journal of Information Technology, 10*, 221–237.

Clemons, E. K., Reddi, S. P., & Row, M. C. (1993). The impact of information technology on the organization of economic activity: The 'move to the middle' hypothesis. *Journal of Management Information Systems, 10*(2), 9–35.

Cross, J. (1995). IT outsourcing: British petroleum's competitive approach. *Harvard Business Review*, May–June, 1995 (pp. 94–102).

Currie, W. L. (1996). Outsourcing in the private and public sectors: an unpredictable IT strategy. *European Journal of Information Systems, 4*, 226–236.

Currie, W. L. (1998). Using multiple suppliers to mitigate the risk of IT outsourcing at ICI and Wessex Water. *Journal of Information Technology, 13*, 169–180.

Currie, W. L., & Willcocks, L. P. (1998). Analysing four types of IT sourcing decisions in the context of scale, client/supplier interdependency and risk mitigation. *Information Systems Journal, 8*(2), 119–143.

DeLooff, L. (1995). Information systems outsourcing decision making: A framework, organizational theories, and case studies. *Journal of Information Technology, 10*, 281–297.

DiRomualdo, A., & Gurbaxani, V. (1998). Strategic intent for IT outsourcing. *Sloan Management Review, 39*(4), 67–80.

Duncan, N. (1998). Beyond opportunism: A resource-based view of outsourcing risk. In *Proceedings of the 31st Annual Hawaii International Conference on System Sciences* (pp. 675–684).

Earl, M. (1996). The risks of outsourcing IT. *Sloan Management Review*, Spring 1996 (pp. 26–32).

Elitzur, R., & Wensley, A. (1997). Game theory as a tool for understanding information services outsourcing. *Journal of Information Technology, 12*, 45–60.

Fitzgerald, G., & Willcocks, L. (1994). Contracts and partnerships in the outsourcing of IT. In *Proceedings of the Fifteenth International Conference on Information Systems* (pp. 91–98).

Fowler, A., & Jeffs, B. (1998). Examining information systems outsourcing: A case study from the United Kingdom. *Journal of Information Technology, 13*, 111–126.

Gable, G. (1996). A multidimensional model of client success when engaging external consultants. *Management Science, 42*(8), 1175–1198.

Gallivan, M. J., & Oh, W. (1999). Analyzing IT outsourcing relationships as alliances among multiple clients and vendors. In *Proceedings of the 32nd Annual Hawaii International Conference on System Sciences*. doi:https://doi.org/10.1109/HICSS.1999.772970.

Goodstein, J., Boeker, W., & Stephan, J. (1996). Professional interests and strategic flexibility: a political perspective on organizational contracting. *Strategic Management Journal, 17*, 577–586.

Grover, V., Cheon, M. J., & Teng, J. T. C. (1994). An evaluation of the impact of corporate strategy and the role of information technology on IS functional outsourcing. *European Journal of Information Systems, 3*(3), 179–190.

Grover, V., Cheon, M. J., & Teng, J. T. C. (1996). The effect of service quality and partnership on the outsourcing of information systems functions. *Journal of Management Information Systems, 12*(4), 89–116.

Hancox, M., & Hackney, R. (1999). Information technology outsourcing: Conceptualizing practice in the public and private sector. In *Proceedings of the 32nd Annual Hawaii International Conference on System Sciences*. doi:https://doi.org/10.1109/HICSS.1999.772971.

Heckman, R., & King, W. (1994). Behavioral indicators of customer satisfaction with vendor-provided information services. In *Proceedings of the Fifteenth International Conference on Information Systems* (pp. 429–444).

Heinzl, A. (1993). Outsourcing the information systems function within the company: An empirical survey. In *OUT'93 Outsourcing of Information Systems Services Conference,* Enschede, May 20–22, 1993 University of Twente.

Heiskanen, A., Newman, M., & Similae, J. (1996). Software contracting: A process model approach. In *Proceedings of the Seventeenth International Conference on Information Systems* (pp. 51–62).

Hirschheim, R., & Lacity, M. (1994). IS outsourcing evaluations: Lessons from the field. In Glasson, B., Hawryszkiewycz, I., Underwood, B., & Weber, R. (Eds.), *Business process re-engineering: Information systems opportunities and challenges* (pp. 363–373). (*Proceedings of the IFIP TC8 Conference on Business Process Re-engineering: Information Systems Opportunities and Challenges*), Gold Coast, May 8–12, 1994.

Hirschheim, R., & Lacity, M., (1998) Reducing information systems costs through insourcing: Experiences from the field. In: H. Watson (ed) *Proceedings of the Thirty-First Annual Hawaii International Conference on System Sciences* (pp. 644–653). IEEE Computer Society Press, Kona, Hawaii, January 6–9, 1998.

Hu, Q., Saunders, C., & Gebelt, M. (1997). Diffusion of information systems outsourcing: A reevaluation of influence sources. *Information Systems Research., 8*(3), 288–301.

Huber, R. (1993) How continental bank outsourced its 'Crown Jewels'. *Harvard Business Review,* Jan–Feb 1993 (pp. 121–129).

I/S Analyzer. (1990). Taking an objective look at outsourcing, 28(8), September 1990.

Jurison, J. (1995). The role of risk and return in information technology outsourcing decisions. *Journal of Information Technology, 10,* 239–247.

Kern, T. (1997). The *Gestalt* of an information technology outsourcing relationship: An exploratory analysis. In *Proceedings of the Eighteenth International Conference on Information Systems* (pp. 37–58).

Klepper, R. (1995). The management of partnering development in I/S outsourcing. *Journal of Information Technology, 10,* 249–258.

Klotz, D., & Chatterjee, K. (1995). Dual sourcing in repeated procurement competitions. *Management Science, 41*(8), 1317–1327.

Lacity, M., & Hirschheim, R., (1993) Implementing information systems outsourcing: Key issues and experiences of an early adopter. *Journal of General Management, 19*(1), Autumn 1993, pp. 17–31.

Lacity, M., & Willcocks, L. (1995). Interpreting information technology sourcing decisions from a transaction cost perspective: Findings and critique. *Accounting, Management and Information Technologies, 5*(3/4), 203–244.

Lacity, M., & Willcocks, L. (1997). Information systems sourcing: examining the privatization option in USA public administration. *Information Systems Journal, 7*(2), 85–108.

Lacity, M., & Willcocks, L. (1998). An empirical investigation of information technology sourcing practices: Lessons from experience. *MIS Quarterly, 22*(3), 363–408.

Lacity, M., Willcocks, L., & Feeny, D. (1995). IT outsourcing: Maximize flexibility and control. *Harvard Business Review,* May–June 1995, pp. 85–93.

Lacity, M., Willcocks, L., & Feeny, D. (1996). The value of selective IT sourcing. *Sloan Management Review,* Spring 1996, pp. 13–25.

Lee, J.-N., & Kim, Y.-G. (1999). Effect of partnership quality on is outsourcing success: Conceptual framework and empirical validation. *Journal of Management Information Systems, 15*(4), 29–61.

Loh, L. (1994). An organizational-economic blueprint for information technology outsourcing: Concepts and evidence. In: *Proceedings of the Fifteenth International Conference on Information Systems* (pp. 73–89).

Loh, L., & Venkatraman, N. (1992a). Diffusion of information technology outsourcing: Influence sources and the kodak effect. *Information Systems Research, 3*(4), 334–358.

Loh, L., & Venkatraman, N. (1992b). Determinants of information technology outsourcing: A cross-sectional analysis. *Journal of Management Information Systems, 9*(1), 7–24.

Loh, L., & Venkatraman, N. (1995). An empirical study of information technology outsourcing: Benefits, risks, and performance implications. In: *Proceedings of the Sixteenth International Conference on Information Systems*, pp. 277–288.

Marcolin, B., & McLellan, K. (1998) Effective IT outsourcing arrangements. In: *Proceedings of the 31st Annual Hawaii International Conference on System Sciences* (pp. 654–665).

McFarlan, F., & Nolan, R. (1995). How to manage an IT outsourcing alliance. *Sloan Management Review*, Winter 1995, pp. 9–23.

McLellan, K., Marcolin, B., & Beamish, P. (1995). Financial and strategic motivations behind IS outsourcing. *Journal of Information Technology, 10*, 299–321.

Michell, V., & Fitzgerald, G. (1997). The IT outsourcing market-place: Vendors and their selection. *Journal of Information Technology, 12*, 223–237.

Nam, K., Rajagopalan, S., Rao, H., & Chaudhury, A. (1996). A two-level investigation of information systems outsourcing. *Communications of the ACM, 39*(7), 36–44.

Nelson, P., Richmond, W., & Seidman, A. (1996). Two dimensions of software acquisition. *Communications of the ACM, 39*(7), 29–35.

Pearce, J. (1993). Toward an organizational behavior of contract laborers: Their psychological involvement and effects on employee co-workers. *Academy of Management Journal, 36*(5), 1082–1096.

Poppo, L., & Zenger, T. (1998). Testing alternative theories of the firm: Transaction cost, knowledge-based, and measurement explanations for make-or-buy decisions in information systems. *Strategic Management Journal, 19*, 853–877.

Quinn, J. B. (1999). Strategic outsourcing: Leveraging knowledge capabilities. *Sloan Management Review*, Summer 1999, pp. 9–21.

Quinn, J. B., & Hilmer, F. (1994). Strategic outsourcing. *Sloan Management Review*, Summer 1994, pp. 43–55.

Reponen, T. (1992). Outsourcing or insourcing? In: *Proceedings of the Thirteenth International Conference on Information Systems* (pp. 103–113).

Sääksjärvi, M. (1993). Outsourcing of information systems. In *OUT'93 Outsourcing of Information Systems Services Conference*, Enschede, May 20–22, 1993. University of Twente.

Sääksjärvi, M., & Saarinen, T. (1993). Empirical evaluation of two opposite IS outsourcing strategies in Finnish Pulp and Paper Industry. In *OUT'93 Outsourcing of Information Systems Services Conference*, Enschede, May 20–22, 1993 University of Twente.

Saarinen, T., & Sääksjärvi, M. (1993). Empirical evaluation of two different outsourcing strategies in the Finnish Wood Working Industry. In *OUT'93 Outsourcing of Information Systems Services Conference*, Enschede, May 20–22, 1993 University of Twente.

Sabherwal, R. (1999). The role of trust in outsourced IS development projects. *Communications of the ACM, 42*(2), 80–85.

Sarkar, S., & Ghosh, D. (1997). Contractor accreditation: A probabilistic model. *Decision Sciences, 28*(2), 235–259.

Saunders, C., Gebelt, M., & Hu, Q. (1997). Achieving success in information systems outsourcing. *California Management Review, 39*(2), 63–79.

Sharma, A. (1997). Professional as agent: Knowledge asymmetry in agency exchange. *Academy of Management Review, 22*(3), 758–798.

Slaughter, S., & Ang, S. (1996). Employment outsourcing in information systems. *Communications of the ACM, 39*(7), 47–54.

Smith, M. A., Mitra, S., & Narasimhan, S. (1998). Information systems outsourcing: A study of pre-event firm characteristics. *Journal of Management Information Systems, 15*(2), 61–93.

Sobol, M., & Apte, U. (1995). Domestic and global outsourcing practices of America's most effective IS users. *Journal of Information Technology, 10*, 269–280.

Sridhar, S., & Balachandran, B. (1997). Incomplete information, task assignment, and managerial control systems. *Management Science, 43*(6), 764–778.

Teng, J. T. C., Cheon, M. J., & Grover, V. (1995). Decisions to outsource information systems functions: Testing a strategy-theoretic discrepancy model. *Decision Sciences, 26*(1), 75–103.

Timbrell, G., Gable, G., Underwood, A., & Hirschheim, R., (1998). Government IT&T insourcing/outsourcing: A model and guidelines. In B. Edmundson and D. Wilson (eds.) *Proceedings of the Ninth Australasian Conference on Information Systems* (pp. 672–684), Sydney, Sept 30–Oct 2, 1998.

Van Mieghem, J. (1999). Coordinating investment, procurement, production, and subcontracting. *Management Science, 45*(7), 954–971.

Venkatraman, N. (1997). Beyond outsourcing: Managing IT resources as a value. *Sloan Management Review, 38*(3), 51–64.

Wang, E. T. C., Barron, T., & Seidmann, A. (1997). Contracting structures for custom software development: The impacts of informational rents and uncertainty on internal development and outsourcing. *Management Science, 43*(12), 1726–1744.

Whang, S. (1992). Contracting for software development. *Management Science, 38*(3), 307–324.

Willcocks, L. P., & Kern, T. (1998). IT outsourcing as strategic partnering: The case of the UK Inland Revenue. *European Journal of Information Systems, 7*, 29–45.

Willcocks, L., Fitzgerald, G., & Lacity, M. (1996). To outsource IT or not? Recent research on economics and evaluation practice. *European Journal of Information Systems, 5*, 143–160.

How to Ensure Collective Action in Multinational Projects: Insights from the EurHisFirm Project

Wolfgang Koenig, Muriel Frank, Jefferson Braswell, Lukas Ranft, and Pantelis Karapanagiotis

Abstract This chapter analyzes a central part of an EU-funded, seven-nations development project for the comprehensive interdisciplinary design of a European system to collect and collate historical financial and firm data (named EurHisFirm)—the responsibility of the authors was the design of a Common Data Model (CDM). Against the background that successful information systems are of the type "sociotechnical systems" between human applicants and information technology—mutually driving each other but likewise also depending on the input of the respective opposite side—we have strong indications that in complex decision situations human cooperation deficiencies substantially outweigh expectable exponential advancements of the information technology. The reason is presumably that amongst diverse and self-confident nations—actually persons—(likewise in important sub-national groups of responsibility, e.g., communal authorities or firms) reaching an agreement on data and other standards is an overly lengthy process that often ends with foul compromises. We understand our contribution to bundle substantial indications toward a possible enhancement of the state-of-the-art—however, fellow researchers should thoroughly investigate the approach.

W. Koenig (✉) · M. Frank · L. Ranft
Chair of Information Systems and Information Management, Goethe University, Frankfurt am Main, Germany
e-mail: wkoenig@wiwi.uni-frankfurt.de; frank@wiwi.uni-frankfurt.de; lranft@wiwi.uni-frankfurt.de

J. Braswell
Tahoe Blue Ltd, San Francisco, CA, USA
e-mail: ljb@tahoeblue.com

P. Karapanagiotis
EBS University, Wiesbaden, Germany
e-mail: karapanagiotis@ebs.edu

1   Introduction

The sociotechnical perspective—focusing sociotechnical systems (Mumford 2006, Bednar and Welch 2020)—is our fundamental research lens for our analysis. On top of that, we investigate standards. Standards are between multiple (independent) actors agreed-upon processes or products that make "things go somehow together," thus reducing production costs and increasing user benefits (Farrell and Saloner 1985). Recurring on the network theory, which looks at "actors" (persons or machines), represented for instance as nodes, and "interactions" (communication) between actors, represented by arcs, standards occur so-to-say "in nodes" (e.g., standardized business experience levels) or "in arcs" (for instance communication standards in the Internet). The second-generation theory of collective action helps understand the "production" of a standard as a common good. Often this cannot be created by singular persons or institutions. Rather, a group of persons (small groups like a set of University institutes or larger groups like a Non-Governmental Organization) has to produce such a good coordinatively using own resources which are on limited supply—in free societies (we restrict our studies to this case) the respective persons will often feel competition between the individual benefit and the benefit of the group, thus having to decide under which circumstances to choose which strategy—and, as theory and experience indicate, often prefer individual goals, in particular when feeling themselves kind of "lost in scrub" which seems in Europe *not* seldomly the case.

With respect to producing common goods in—interrelated—groups of humans, the political body, the institution to discuss and decide in our case upon standards, is a multi-level federated European deliberation and decision hierarchy comprising six or more interconnected decision levels, each following a respective constitution with democratic participation rights. Each deliberation and decision level acts within limits set by its constitution and within its restrictions of the action space set by decisions on the superior level. We have tested a simplified version of such a federated multi-level hierarchy on our project—involving all work packages.

However, in such a federated hierarchy, the imperative of subsidiarity enjoys high importance, which means that a particular decision has to be delegated to the lowest possible level in order to properly involve local knowledge into the decision-making—but of course also to tie in local actors "into the common." This seems to amplify the coordination problem substantially. It is a well-acknowledged nexus that political rights always go hand-in-hand with respective responsibilities toward fellow members or communities—on the same decision level as well as up and down the hierarchy—and thus with, for instance, ready-enough preparedness to knowledgeably evaluate and decide upon urgently needed collective actions in due course.

Amongst a set of results—one being the agreed-upon CDM—our most important experience is: In such a federated multi-level hierarchy, substantial risks reside with the lower-level members of the hierarchy (although lower-level members often complain about decision-makers on higher levels). They seem to be often not sufficiently prepared with respect to content- and time-readiness when faced with complex threats. But without their on-time qualified bottom-up "feeds" of superior units in this hierarchy, the latter starve from the void of air decision space. We conjecture that even the massive information technology advancements cannot properly make up for missing readiness and thus qualified and timely cooperation on the lower end of this hierarchy.

In such a case—in a particular environment—, we need leadership which we call a *performant center* that is prima facie a contradiction to the subsidiarity imperative. Thus, the majority of similarly strong actors residing on the lower levels must also tolerate such a performant center. And unfortunately, also the higher-level actors in such a hierarchy expose deficiencies. Both effects almost "invite" anyhow observant members of this hierarchy to firstly strive for their individual benefits—even when this behavior may unduly damage the interests of the "common." So, all actors of this hierarchy have to improve performance, but in particular the actors on the lower levels have to increase their participation in the consensus finding and feeding their local knowledge into the upper levels of the hierarchy.

This article ends with proposals on how to alleviate the "dichotomy" and against the background that the latter doesn't easily disappear we call our highly diverse continent for the foundation of an independent European Agency (as for instance given in the case of the European Central Bank for financial supervision founded in 1988) to profoundly substantiate the goal of building-up a European repository of historical and contemporary data that makes European culture (including business) digitally evaluable.

2   The EurHisFirm[1] Case

In Economics and Business Administration, for decades, scholars and farsighted practitioners worldwide profoundly raise the community's attention to missing digitized historical data—for instance, on the application of very old financial instruments like stocks. As a consequence, both policymakers and students have no access—or at least no comfortable access—to historical data. Learning from past is substantially hindered. Subsequently, often, "the wheel has to be invented multifold." This deficiency is evident in Europe with its 27[2] highly diverse and simultaneously very self-confident national states. Moreover, Europe has been troubled by an array of massive wars in the nineteenth and the first half of the twentieth century (with lots of territorial changes and substantial losses of data

---

[1] We highly acknowledge the EU support for this project under the H2020 grant # 777489. And we thank our European fellow researchers and staff members in the other work packages for numerous discussions and valuable insights.

[2] For simplification, we concentrate on the 27 member States of the EU, and later on the seven EurHisFirm States.

on paper). The complex task of standardizing and harmonizing historical data is substantially magnified in this very diverse Europe. Under the guidance of the Paris School of Economics (PSE) and referring to an initial relational database at the Antwerpen University (with datasets starting in 1780), European financial historians inaugurated a yearly conference series named Eurhistock (History of European Stock Exchanges) more than a decade ago[3] and over time laid the foundation for the EurHisFirm project.

The United States of America (USA),[4] in contrast, provides (a substantial amount of) such digitized, curated and harmonized historical financial and economic data starting from 1925. These data are offered with a profound price tag[5] to universities and research institutes worldwide, and firms (there the saying "data is the new oil of economies" is realized). The USA started its respective data gathering more than 50 years ago—of course, based on its advantage of dealing with only one language, one currency, and one national jurisdiction for 200 years. Since then, the USA has complemented its collection—actually: a set of collections—year after year. Moreover, the USA is considered the highly successful founder of modern Information and Communication Technology (ICT) as well as of modern Marketing (also with respect to monetarizing innovations). In fact, Europe trails the USA in a rather substantial set of overarching ICT developments (like operating systems, but also like end-user data collections).

The respective European situation is bleak: In the aftermath of World War II—facing immense destructions—first steps towards integration have been undertaken with the foundation of the European Coal and Steel Community in 1951 (comprising six states). Subsequently, these six states founded in 1957 the European Economic Community, which then—after the fall of the iron curtain in 1990—was further developed into the European Union (EU) in 1992, an Association of now 27 Member States.

For 30 years, Europe has tried to find and exercise a substantial modern common understanding in *all* important fields. Geared toward our case topic, Europe has very limited national digitized data—only a few university institutes—(like at

---

[3] https://eurhistock.hypotheses.org/date/2010/

[4] For simplification, we abstract from Canadian and Mexican data.

[5] The underlying business model is considerable. An example: 20 years ago, the German National Science Council (Wissenschaftsrat) formulated a recommendation that in universities advanced Economics and Business Administration students in their final thesis should not only describe concepts for innovatively solving a problem (for instance novel ways to reorganize the social security system) but have to prove-run the respective concepts against real-world data. Immediately, both the students and professors (in Germany, likewise in Europe and in the world) started to look for existing and easily accessible data. As in Europe they very often did not find appropriate data sources, they accessed the readily available data sources in the USA. So, Europe not only co-funds the data collection in the USA (the Faculty of Economics and Business Administration of Goethe University alone pays Euro 60,000 each year for just one of these databases) but European students are in the end more inclined to contribute to solve US problems in their academic training—and their results often are not applicable to European challenges—, because there they can easily access its available historical (and in wake contemporary) data.

Antwerpen and Paris) have collections—and these are not publicly available via self-service Internet access. Against this background, the EU financed within Horizon 2020 and there within its pan-European research infrastructures support program INFRADEV[6] our project named European Historical Financial and Firm Data (EurHisFirm)[7] (aimed at data from 1815 to 1970[8]). This project covered the first of aspired four consecutive phases: *Comprehensive Design* (the next phases should have been[9]: fine specification of the desired overarching system, procurement/development and kick-off, and continuous operation (for—presumably—30+ years). So, with respect to EurHisFirm, the EU regarded research *data*—a "data backbone"—as a similar infrastructure as, for instance, the support of polar research by co-financing an ice-exploration ship in development and operation.

The overall goal is to design a comprehensive system to acquire, collect, ingest and harmonize European historical financial and firm data.[10] In this way, data has to be consolidated (as data collection occurs in various places and under different circumstances), cleansed, de-duplicated, and reconciled. Two main work packages (WPs) dealt with the foundations of a semi-automated AI-based extraction of historical financial and firm data by applying OCR to paper sources (WP 7), and the discussion of business model options for the endeavor (WP 10), which were based on results from other WPs, for instance on data availability (digitized), integration and interoperability with respect to other repositories—and legal options and restrictions.

A third important research subject that also used this input was the development of a Common Data Model[11] (CDM) for EurHisFirm (WP 5), which was concentrated in Frankfurt and which makes up the background of this chapter. The genesis of the CDM in some sense resembles on the technical level the overall development path, which we may name the counter-current method (or mixed top-down and bottom-up planning): After an initial proposal of a for the whole community "good-willing" expert (in the private sector, this is for instance the Board of an incorporation; or in the language of the old ages: a patriarch[12]) the comprehensive

---

[6] https://ec.europa.eu/research/participants/data/ref/h2020/wp/2018-2020/main/h2020-wp1820-infrastructures_en.pdf

[7] EurHisFirm (eurhisfirm.eu) comprised 11 research institutes in seven European states and was composed of ten work packages plus an overarcing management work package.

[8] Since 1970 professional data offerings are available.

[9] Meanwhile, the EU has discontinued the H2020 support program. The specification of the succeeding support program is as of Jan. 2022 not yet finished.

[10] One would also expect as an objective that already available digitized data—probably after having undergone a brush-up process—have to be published (at least in a reasonable percentage). This goal was *not* part of the project.

[11] https://docs.microsoft.com/en-us/common-data-model/

[12] We use "patriarch" as the designation of a—for a whole citizenship—well-meaning leader without appreciable own interests who acts knowledgeable, experienced and determined. Of course, we do not want to discriminate females—so we could also see this highly respected person as a 'matriarch'.

design of such a complex multi-disciplinary endeavor occurs in repetitive circles of involving new data to be taken care of, new actors and new solution approaches followed by standardization, reconciliation and integration steps and vice-versa—repetitively going down and up in the federative deliberation and decision hierarchy. Of course, such a process is lengthy and consumes a lot of resources, but—like in politics—we do not yet know a better design approach. In particular with respect to future wants for data needs, no one can today top-down prescribe which technical developments will prevail in—for example—15+ years[13], and likewise no one fully foresees which specific application needs will be important then.

In addition, legal options and restrictions had to be considered (WP 3). It was lodged at the University of Frankfurt as well. The EurHisFirm project—phase 1 in INFRADEV—started in April 2018 and ended in June 2021. End of 2021, the EU signed off our phase 1 results after an evaluation session.[14]

The following chapter depicts the most important design decisions with respect to the data structure specifics of the CDM (including interoperability)—subject to a step-wise development process of a series of future versions of a comprehensive CDM—starting from an initial specification and catering for detailing a previous CDM data structure, altering previous design decisions, expanding existing lists of attributes of objects and expanding existing objects by, for example, newly discovered historical data. Also, the re-integration of stepwise altered data structures has to be taken care of.

3   Important Research Lenses

3.1   Sociotechnical Perspective

The sociotechnical perspective is one of the fundamental viewpoints for the Information Systems discipline (Sarker et al., 2019). Its origins can be traced back to several studies in the 1950s that looked at technical innovation in British coal mines and were the first to bridge the gap between socially and technically oriented approaches (Trist & Bamforth, 1951). Two decades later, scholars built on these ideas and emphasized the importance of sociotechnical systems theory (STS) for understanding problems and failures of information systems (Bostrom & Heinen, 1977). Broadly speaking, sociotechnical systems comprises of two interacting and mutually influencing components (see Fig. 1): first, the technical component, which

---

[13] Please consider the tremendeous developments of modern data management options in the last 15 years, and assume over the thumb that an exponentially increasing amount of substantial advancements will in the future be realized already in much less time. The advancement of the technical benefit of basic ICT will downright explode over the years.

[14] Final report of EurHisFirm: EURHISFIRM consortium. (2021). EURHISFIRM D1.14: Final report. Zenodo. https://doi.org/10.5281/zenodo.4980412

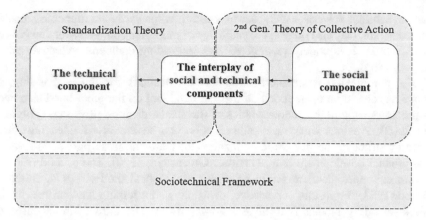

Fig. 1 Relationship between theories and the sociotechnical framework [Adapted from Sarker et al. (2019)]

consists of hardware, software, and techniques used to achieve organizational goals or solve organizational issues, and second, the social component, which includes individuals or collectives and their relationships within specified structures (Bostrom et al., 2009; Lee et al., 2015). The theory does not favor one component over the other but assumes that both are essential to achieve instrumental as well as humanistic goals (Bostrom et al., 2009; Sarker et al., 2019).

Figure 1 illustrates how standardization theory and the second generation of collective action theory influence the sociotechnical framework. Standardization theory pertaining to the technical component specifies the technical artifacts that meet the requirements of the collective (Fomin et al., 2003). The second generation of collective action theory, on the other hand, is related to the social component, as it can be used to explain why actors voluntarily contribute to a collective good (Ostrom, 2000), here the design of a European database for historical financial and firm data. Only the interaction of both, social and technical, components contributes to understanding the success or failure of such information systems projects.

3.2 Standardization Theory

Standards in hardware, software, or data are widely seen as a necessity to developing global and comprehensive information systems (Deans et al., 1991). A standard is conceived to be a set of technical specifications to which a set of actors have agreed to adhere (David & Greenstein, 1990). Basically, standardization involves creating a set of artifacts that meets the requirements related to the standard as well as the mobilization of a set of independent players who do not necessarily have the same interests but are willing to follow such deviations (Fomin et al., 2003). Moreover, an agreement is required on what compliance with the codified specifications actually means (Schmidt & Werle, 1998). Because common standards simultaneously enable and constrain, they also present the challenge of mobilizing collective action (Garud et al., 2002). It is widely recognized that free-riding dampens collective action (Olson, 1965).

The complexity of standardization has implications for theory building, as concepts need to be open-ended on the one hand, but on the other hand also need to precisely capture the characteristics of the standardization processes (Fomin et al., 2003). Previous work on standardization can be broadly divided into three research strands: The first strand considers standardization as part of innovation and product development (e.g., David & Greenstein, 1990). The second research stream examines standardization as a game-theoretical model[15] (e.g., Besen & Farrell, 1994). From this perspective, decisions about joining standardization are based on utility models (Farrell & Saloner, 1985). The third strand focuses on standardization as a sociotechnical continuum and therefore examines the social and technical components that influence standardization outcomes (e.g., Williams & Edge, 1996).

3.3   The Second-Generation Theory of Collective Action

The theory of collective action goes back to Mancur Olson (1965), who was concerned with how people make decisions in social dilemma situations, here: the collective good problem. Olson demonstrated that rational and self-interested actors would not engage in collective action to obtain a public good, even if all members of the group would be better off if the action was taken. Instead, individuals will prefer to free-ride. According to him, sustaining collective action is even more difficult in larger groups than in smaller groups because the share of benefit getting to the individual is less in larger groups. However, his conception has been challenged mainly for two reasons. First, contrary to the zero contribution thesis, cooperative behavior is prevalent in all walks of life (Oliver & Marwell, 1988). Second, his theory ignores contextual influences (Volacu & Goloptenţa, 2013), though they help understand behaviors (Ostrom, 2000).

Consequently, theorists invested considerable effort into providing a revised theory of collective actions accounting for context (Ostrom, 2000). The second generation of collective action models assumes that individuals' decisions to contribute are influenced by social norms and rules that impose certain moral constraints and facilitate the development of cooperators (Ostrom, 2000; Ostrom & Basurto, 2011). Individuals are no longer seen as self-interested rationalists but conditional cooperators (Ostrom, 1998) because they are willing to contribute to collective action if and as long as they feel that others will reciprocate (Ostrom, 2000). While norms—actions that are forbidden or permitted—are contingent on

---

[15] It is noteworthy that game theory also helps to explain collective action problems.

social and cultural settings, rules in the form of procedures or policies implicitly or explicitly determine the mechanisms, responsibilities, and interdictions within a particular situation (Ostrom, 1986). Empirical findings support this notion. Ledyard (Ledyard, 1995), for instance, shows that voluntary contribution is strongly affected by marginal payoffs and communication and weakly affected by economic (e.g., homogeneity), systemic (e.g., group identity), and institutional factors (e.g., sequencing).

4   The EurHisFirm Common Data Model Design Decisions

To better comprehend the EurHisFirm CDM standards, we start with a quick overview of the common action process, which is then detailed in chapter "The Human and Organizational Realm of EurHisFirm: Multi-level Federated Standardization".

Soon after the EurHisFirm project had started, the Work Group on Identification and Standardization (WGIS) was inaugurated as joint discussion and decision board overarching the various WPs. All WPs had been invited to participate in this group to ensure the best analysis and solutions. After in-depth deliberation, binding decisions were taken based on the one-WP[16] one vote rule on two different experience and argumentation levels: the operative (often very technical) level regarding the specifics (comprising staff members) and the overarching strategic level (comprising all WP leaders). After a set-up phase in the first 9 months, we convened WGIS first monthly, in the latter 2 years each 14 days.

With the WGIS approval,[17] four fundamental development lines guided our first steps into the CDM design progress:

(a) After profound discussions of handling structured data (comprising data values that follow controlled formats like in a relational database) vs. unstructured data (text interpretation like in Wikibase), we decided to apply the triplestore data concept[18] (graph database[19] concept) (see Sect. 4.5) as a kind of com-

---

[16] On the EU level, this resembles the one-state-one-vote rule.

[17] *All* CDM design decisions have been approved unanimously. However, we must concede that WPs with less proximity to technical questions in general and to standards in particular were sometimes absent. This is one reason that we bet on more and more thorough education with respect to "federalism at work," also in technical challenges.

[18] A triplestore is a purpose-built database for the storage and retrieval of triples through semantic queries. "Subject-predicate-object" triples are stored as atomic data entities in the Resource Description Framework (RDF) data model. The "Simple Knowledge Organization System" (SKOS) is a World Wide Web (W3C) recommendation designed for the representation of thesauri, classification schemes, taxonomies, subject-heading systems and other type of controlled vocabulary – as part of the Semantic Web family of standards. It builds upon RDF and is geared toward an easy publication of such vocabularies as linked data. (www.w3.org/TR/PR-rdf-syntax/Overview.html) (1999).

[19] A graph database is a generalization of triplestore.

mon denominator of both worlds—however, putting more design emphasis on the structured data part, because statistical evaluations of mass data for the next decade or more request structured—and thus pre-harmonized—data. Yes, unstructured data may also be statistically evaluated using interpretative (rather than compilation-based) techniques—but because of the expected sheer explosion of data sizes over time, only the previous one will render sufficient efficiency[20] for an unaware end user—at least for the next decade.

In a nutshell, graph databases capture networks comprised of:

(i) Nodes (for instance: the object "firms").
(ii) Arcs as relationships between nodes (for instance: supply chain relations).
(iii) Properties (attribute values of nodes or edges following a property format).

(b) Compared to classic applications in firms, the CDM evolves with substantial alterations. Our historical data treasure can only be appropriately managed in an archeological approach, like when scientists find in Patagonia first splitters of a bone of a yet unknown dinosaur and expect to dig several decades for necessary additional discoveries—but the early data shall be made publicly accessible right-away and not only in—say—30 years. One straightforward data management derivative is to store—in our case—also the source of historical papers.

(c) Given substantial IT developments over time (which we expect to continue for a further decade and more), in this first phase of the INFRADEV funding we concentrated on logical—conceptual—data design solutions rather than investing too much time in the transformation options from logical to physical data structures. We have moved the latter decisions to be addressed into the second phase of INFRADEV (which meanwhile was abandoned).

(d) In our environment of highly diverse and at the same time self-assured member States of the EU, we—in a first approach, that later may be altered by the states—assume that each state wants to keep its treasure of historical data sustained "on the own soil." Our design caters to a comprehensive central copy—but the data "owners" will be the respective states. The local data will be stored in a cloud-type (networked) data infrastructure.

Based on these foundational design decisions, the subsequent chapters are organized as follows: CDM-content-wise, we start with an overarching design model that provides a rough overview of required functionalities and the respective

---

[20] It is intelligent to store compiled standardised statistical analyses procedures rather than to "invent" from scratch new analysis routines, for instance each time a new user request comes in.

standardization and identification necessities. We sketch a selection of important logical implementations. Chapter "The Human and Organizational Realm of EurHisFirm", we layout the continuous process of adding new input data and refining or altering existing data structures.

4.1 Design Model of Bridging EurHisFirm User Requests and Solution Options Based on Standards and a Thorough Identification

The following design model was generated at the beginning of our WGIS process to help project participants who are not deeply into such data design and respective process questions to better understand the "right" challenges and the solution options.[21] This design model was not meant to be implemented 1:1—rather, the derived—logical—data structures and processes differ from the design model.

Figure 2 shows the semantic distance that EurHisFirm has to bridge with respect to data accessibility. We enumerate its layers from top to bottom. The top layer (layer 1—"Data Consumers") comprises—in our case—four user types of EurHisFirm data, for instance:

- Scientists who want to evaluate new concepts (e.g., for a better social security system) against historical data.
- Practitioners in firms who want to improve the firm's business strategy.
- Practitioners in public regulatory bodies who want to test aspired changes in their regulation before introducing these in business practice.
- Practitioners of the EurHisFirm organizational unit that will offer the Common Data Access Service to customers—for instance, for training purposes.

Their different data requests have to be mapped into the CDM data structure of the "Common Data Access Service" (CDAS) on layer 2 "Common Data Access Standards." There, EurHisFirm-wide ("European") data governance and metadata management functions are assisted by support systems (e.g., a technical or human data dictionary service helping a (type of) data administrator, and a metadata management expert system supporting other data administrators). These functions also help map the different user requests onto the different data provisions depicted on layer 4 "Data Source Standards," and map the data results back from the sources to the end user via the CDAS.

---

[21] This design model is another indicator that "only bottom-up" planning is not successful in such complex environments. This model was brought in by a professional expert who had – in other environments—already three times solved this kind of problems and worked with such structures over decades. And this approach molted to the "pivotal" starting point to get diverse collaborators think in the same direction. A bottom-up routine of developing such a concept by a systematic sequence of "trial and error" binary selections ("better vs. worse alternative") of combinatorial solution options amongst the diverse participants would have lasted almost endless.

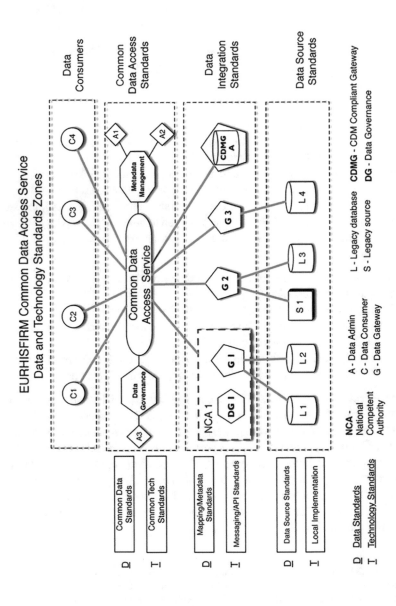

Fig. 2 Design model of the Common Data Model—centered around the Common Data Access Service (CDAS), also depicting data and technology standards zones

Layers 2–4 are all technical layers subject to the availability of standards. We distinguish on each level two-sided integrated data standards (semantic standards of respective data management tasks, for instance data governance on level 2) and technology standards (e.g., standards of the local storage system—layer 4 "Data Source Standards").

The lowest layer—the opposite side to the data consumers (layer 4 in Fig. 2)-comprises the data sources accessible via the CDAS to the users. Here we distinguish legacy databases—these are already existing databases like SCOB in Antwerpen and DFIH in Paris.

Between layer 2 and layer 4, layer 3 "Data Integration Standards" performs the bulk of the mapping work. A gateway transforms in an ideally completely programmed way top-down a user request to possible queries against—for instance—databases on layer 4, and helps to integrate different bottom-up answers from different data sources on their way back via the CDAS to the respective user.

In addition, Fig. 2 denotes three complementing specifics: If a source database is already implementing the CDM—as depicted in the CDM Compliant Gateway on layer 3—then we can use this database without further provisioning as accessible from the CDAS (logically, the CDMG is a combination of database and gateway).

The second specific in Fig. 2 deals with organizational issues prima-facie related to the gateway function: The primary function of each gateway is the translation/transformation of regional or local data conventions into the common definitions and standards of the CDM that enables consistent access to data by end-users in a federated network of information sources and individual repositories. As such, the implementation of the appropriate transformation and translation functions necessary to perform this mapping will typically be required—by human developers or users—to integrate each gateway into the network federation that comprises the CDAS. In any case, the gateway function is assisted by a data governance unit on layer 3, and we call such a respective organizational unit now a "National Competent Authority." This denomination was chosen because we expect the nations within which the source data is provided will emphasize keeping the ownership of their data in their national hands. Moreover, financial historians easily understand that data often can only be seriously interpreted against the respective national background (because of specifics of their legal system, language, inherent cultural understandings, customs etc.). On the other side, it was and is also possible to create multi-national authorities, like (human rights or trade) courts and central banks. Present day examples are Central Commission for Navigation on the Rhine and the Principat d'Andorra, a sovereign state, jointly governed by the bishop of Urgell in Spain and the President of France (in succession of the Compte de Foix). Nevertheless, these kinds of deviations do not harm the overall logical four-layer concept, as depicted in Fig. 2.

A third specific is not depicted in Fig. 2: All the National Competent Authorities in regard of EurHisFirm are members of a respective network with the desire to exchange national experiences, but moreover with the task to profoundly handle supra-national problem cases, like financial instruments of firms that are registered in one country but have their stocks also listed in a different jurisdiction.

4.2 Implementation of the Gateway Function by Data Staging

A highly important EurHisFirm CDM design decision is that a data staging concept implements the "logical gateway function" shown in Fig. 2—by realizing a sequence of data melioration actions to stepwise improve data quality from "raw data" (for instance, newly acquired data from applying OCR on a novel paper source), which are not yet compliant to EurHisFirm standards (stage 1), to another stage which provides that data in full CDM-compliance to the users. Such standardization and harmonization processes consume, however, a substantial amount of resources, not the least time, and are in procedure and result uncertain. Therefore, the data backbone of the EurHisFirm data architecture must be flexible enough to adapt to yet unknown demand and challenges.

The number of melioration stages may "breathe," depending on (national or other) circumstances, as the individual entry point of a dataset into that staging sequence may vary (depending, for instance, on how much compliance to the CDM is already taken care of in a "feeder database" of digitized data). Specifics have to be decided upon by the Network Integration Centers (NICs). Figure 3 provides an overview of the data staging concept.

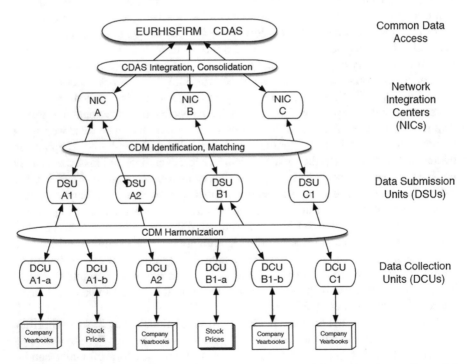

Fig. 3 EurHisFirm Data Staging concept—stepwise (bottom-up) improving data quality to full CDM-compliance

We explain the staging concept from bottom to top, introducing additional organizational units to perform the respective tasks. As data inputs we distinguish raw data obtained via OCR from (paper-based) sources (yearbooks, stock prices from newspapers etc.) in the form of (digital) files. These are fed into local Data Collection Units (DCUs) that, for instance, provide a local identifier for each data record in order to, e.g., provide basic identification of data for local corrections. Thus, one of the most important steps further up is to standardize the identifier, which means: to select, if at all possible, just one overarching identifier, e.g., for firms, financial instruments, data sources, documents, etc. Ideally, only one (or very few) identification schemes are necessary for, e.g., deduplication purposes (e.g., a stock is traded in two states). "Overarching" means *at least* a Europe-wide[22] perimeter of the identification scheme. In the next chapter, we specify our identification approach.

Going up in Fig. 3 sketches a workflow that provides a framework for collecting, tagging, harmonizing, and integrating these data on different levels—ultimately reaching the CDAS—which means full CDM-compliance—on the top level ("Common Data Access"). "Data Collection Units (DCUs)" provide interfaces to handle different data input modes and enable data tagging. Moreover, DCUs perform "first-level" integration between two or more different local data sources. Subsequently, the "Data Submission Units (DSUs)" execute a data harmonization step (for instance, adjusting different data formats for the same properties) of objects (like firms, financial instruments) and relations between objects which are in stage 1 collected from databases and files in different European places, according to local collection and collation conditions. Further on, the Network Integration Centers (NICs) provide the common identifier and offer matching services of local identifiers to the CDM-compliant identifier. Also, NICs perform a "next step" of integration between the inputs of different DSUs. Finally, the top layer named "Common Data Access"—under European control—is responsible for offering Europe-wide integration and consolidation of the EurHisFirm data, according to the CDM, and offering these data to end-users—ideally in a self-service access mode.

4.3 The EurHisFirm Identification Scheme

Object identification (ID) in information systems occurs with different approaches. One basic approach is that each data owner uses or even individually invents a unique identification scheme, like customer numbers of retail merchants, banks,

---

[22] If we would choose "only" a Europe-wide common identifier—probably following the argument that, for competitive reasons, other large economic powers would also strive for their "own" respective identification systems—, we automatically introduced "endless" mapping necessities with likewise identifiers in other important parts of the world-wide economy, like in the USA or in China. A better choice is to choose a world-wide *common* identifier under an international (global) control (with substantial European control participation).

or airlines. Here, each application perimeter is confined to the respective firm and customers have to manage multifold customer IDs in parallel. The identification problem has been solved to a great deal by using cookies, fingerprinting, iris scans etc., all known for decades and grossly underestimated in their impact on personality rights by the legal system. The opposite extreme is a worldwide appreciated standard identification scheme for specific objects that provides an exact "one object to one dataset with that one identifier value" property (we call this "triple unity").

A prominent example for an overt identification system is the Legal Entity Identifier (LEI[23]) in the financial world provided by the Global LEI Foundation (www.gleif.org). It has started in 2014 and comprises by the end of 2021 roughly 2 Mio. LEIs in operation—one for each organization unit of a firm, which may cause systemic risks. Although the LEI was originally targeted toward financial problem fields, the "legal entity identification" was conceptualized along the entire financial supply chain, extending from pure financial institutions to e.g., large enterprises who issue, e.g., financial instruments. Thus, the LEI was meant to act as a worldwide acknowledged broad identifier for firms in different industries.[24]

Between those extreme points, manifold inter-solutions and implementations exist where in some cases we encounter fractures of the triple unity concept. In general, each identification scheme that is not CDM-compliant needs to be supported by a matching algorithm from one identification scheme to the other one. Frequently, these matchings need human assistance for interpretations of local (as opposed to global) identifications.

Looking at the historical dimension of EurHisFirm, almost all of the above mentioned approaches concentrate their efforts on contemporary objects and their identification. So, EurHisFirm has further developed the LEI to also cater to historical objects and their identification. One four-digit value out of the 20 GLEIF characters has been denoted to indicate historical objects—for instance, firms— and in addition the "start date" and the "end date" of the life of a historical firm is recorded—indicating the validity period of properties and its values. Moreover, we have further developed the LEI also to support the identification of public-sector economic units (like state railroads, various types of public law banks, state broadcasting units, churches as entities of public law etc.). The respective identification scheme is now called EurHisFirm LEI (ELEI). This approach also provides systematic matching options between historical data (bases) like Compustat (or repositories, like the British Archive) and contemporary data (bases) (or

---

[23] The ISO-standardized LEI comprises 20 alphanumeric digits. The LEI was introduced in the aftermath of the 2008 financial crises to strive for a comprehensive overview on network risks (for instance, failure risks of mutually issued financial instruments (debt obligations, bonds etc.) between two or more financial institutions). The Global LEI Foundation (GLEIF) provides also a set of highly developed routines to ensure that firms are operational, for instance, and not only shell companies.

[24] It is interesting to note, that GLEIF has not dealt with the question of identifying natural persons, although individuals are important members of the financial risk network—and they are also of course important actors.

repositories, like EUROFIDAI). Moreover, EurHisFirm can also use an array of high-powered and well-established GLEIF procedures, for instance for deduplication efforts.

4.4   The EurHisFirm Standardized Core Class Model

At the present stage, it appears impossible to unilaterally prescribe the EurHisFirm standards. Instead, (almost) all project members have to develop and agree on commonalities and formulate consensus between them—we strive to solve dissents over time.[25] Details will be discussed in chapter "The Human and Organizational Realm of EurHisFirm". Due to the absence of the power to impose rules on the participating units, our fundamental design approach had to be less than complete. A detailed, consistent and clean comprehensive CDM design could not be provided. Rather we resort to as much flexibility as possible on the data structure side—and take precautions to be capable of altering or re-adjusting or even re-formulating previous design decisions in the future.

As a consequence, the extensibility of the data structure is an integral design approach. For instance, relational database systems allow adding new object occurrences or new properties of objects and relations without running into the necessity to change existing structures. Moreover, we can use property descriptions formulated in the lingua franca XML to be semi-automatically imported/exported between different database architectures. A complementary approach is to use adjacent standards like the Entity Legal Form (ELF) ISO standard[26] to declaratively introduce new legal forms of firms into the database. These are techniques toward the extensibility of a data structure (without substantial reprogramming necessities) that we use in EurHisFirm.

Our specific approach is that we formulate a EurHisFirm core class model as the common denominator of all future developments (see Fig. 4). The core class model comprises "EurHisFirm Legal Entities" (identified by the ELEI), EurHisFirm Financial Instruments (identified by the EFII), (Financial) Markets (for instance exchanges, identified by the ELEI and EFII) and Currencies (identified by the ELEI, EFII, and markets). This core class model may be specified, completed or expanded in the future—as circumstances permit and request. The CDM's "development in life" has to be debated and decided in a sustained systematic cooperation and its realization has to be controlled by the respective European or local oversight organizations (see chapter "The Human and Organizational Realm of EurHisFirm").

The core class model of EurHisFirm is centered around two pivotal elements: The first one, which is to be found left to the vertical center axis in Fig. 4, starts

---

[25] External pressure on Europe (like fierce crises) may help shorten the time to agree on important steps forward. But we are not eager for such external pressure.

[26] https://www.gleif.org/en/about-lei/code-lists/iso-20275-entity-legal-forms-code-list

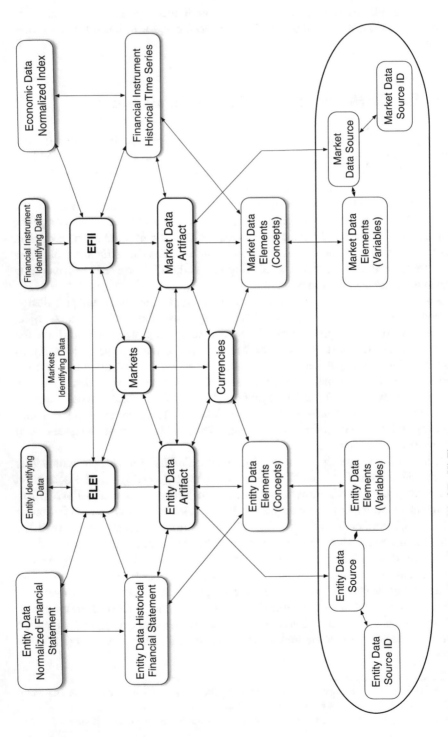

Fig. 4 Extensible standardized core class model of EurHisFirm

from north to south with the "Entity Identifying Data" of legal entities, for instance banks and non-bank firms, that are in the unit underneath equipped with the ELEI. Subsequently, we provide a declarative artifact of the respective object (entity)—a bank being for instance differently modeled than a non-bank firm. Afterward, the artifact is conceptualized ("which properties describe which object?"), and in the lower end (southern end), the respective variables are introduced. Finally, a likewise data structure is to be seen right of the center axis of Fig. 4—here for "financial instrument" that results in "financial market data."

Two extensions are added in Fig. 4: The left and the right "ears" of the core class model make up for common complementary and—in a somehow logical sense—external data: In the upper-left corner, we see for each "firm"—on the left side of "ELEI"—how historical financial statements can be captured—and the northern end of that far-left data structure is specified in a normalized way, putting, for instance, yearly ROI values in relation to the average value over the last 5 or 10 years. Likewise, we capture national aggregated economic figures on the right-hand side, for instance time series on national inflation or (un-) employment.

The second extension is located bottom transverse on Fig. 4—depicted by an oval circle. This is the interface to capture the data sources from where we obtain objects occurrences and properties values. The sources for legal entity data and market data are—again—identified in a standardized way.

For the three center columns in Fig. 4, we have spelled out in specification handbooks the (almost) ready to compile data structures of the identification of legal entities, financial instruments and markets, also the declarative artifact specification of legal entities and markets.

This core class model can be extended and specified in many ways. We expect it to be sufficiently flexible in itself by already available data management routines. It is also extensible to be, for instance, complemented by results of opinion surveys or sociological research. Transformed into the political—federative—deliberation and decision hierarchy (see chapter "The Human and Organizational Realm of EurHisFirm"), this core class model becomes part of the constitutions of all decision bodies in the European federated deliberation and decision hierarchy.

4.5   Overarching Semantic Equivalence

Parallel to rapid progress of information technology the user requirements on EurHisFirm data will develop too. Even if a serious prognosis of the respective progress is almost impossible, we know that in the past user demands regularly have outgrown systems supply. The resulting "optimization necessities" lead to problem descriptions that require lots of technical performance. Optimizations may be calculated faster and more precisely. We must consider that along with that time span different information technologies may be more appropriate at certain points in time—or specific circumstances—than others. After acquiring data via OCR at different places and in different local environments, the subsequent collection of facts and their respective sources may benefit from the flexibility of a data store or repository that facilitates "just these" issues—without immediately requiring to marshaling data into structures or standards that are part of the CDM which is geared-up for end-user access.

These are important reasons to strive for a semantic equivalence among machine-readable data persistence implementations. Figure 5 gives an overview of involved technology architectures and physical models to be set into a hierarchical relation. Although Fig. 5 also comprises physical models, our momentary perspective is mere logically.

The reasoning for the overarching semantic equivalence starts with (see: top left side in Fig. 5) the "Business Architecture" layer, materialized in a "Business and Process Modeling and Analysis" (see: northern end of the center vertical axis in Fig. 5). In the EurHisFirm design development process, we early on performed this first step following the software development methodology The Open Groups Architecture Framework (TOGAF). (https://www.opengroup.org/togaf).

Figure 5—underneath in the center column—depicts subsequently three layers of logical models for the "data architecture" and the "application architecture" which we abbreviate with (**a**), (**b**), and (**c**). (**a**) shows the desired overarching "semantic modeling and analysis" which provides automatic problem description transformations between the three predominant data persistence implementations (types) of the "application architecture": *Relational databases* express entities, relationships and respective attributes. *Object-oriented databases* reflect properties and attributes. *Data types databases* show data elements and structures. Subsequently, the logical layer c) then "explodes" each of the three persistence types of layer (b). Then—further down—the "technology architecture" and finally the "physical model" layers follow—expanding into a substantial set of traditional, contemporary, and advanced technologies.

This semantic equivalence is an easy-to-comprehend approach to systematically link structured data (bases) (for instance, the relational databases SCOB and DFIH) and unstructured Wikibase type of textual data. A graph database[27]—see in Fig. 5 the layer c)—is a reasonable candidate for a respective persistence platform. However, the concept bears two occurrences—Labeled Property Graph (LPG) and Resource Description Framework (RDF)—that show mutually exclusive processing advantages when being used at a very early stage of (in our case: distributed) data collection and common data usage after intermediate melioration steps. Wikibase, however, is a bit of a hybrid that has aspects of both LPG and RDF triple stores[28] and can provide the kind of "schema-less" flexibility that makes it a good "landing zone"for data collected in the previous stage.

---

[27] A graph database mainly comes in two distinct flavours: A Labeled Property Graph (LPG) or a graph based on the Resource Description Framework (RDF) which is a World Wide Web Consortium (W3C) standard that is the basis for the creation of factual assertions in 'triple stores' that can reference each other via the Internet ("semantic web") and may be queried with a standard query language (SPARQL).

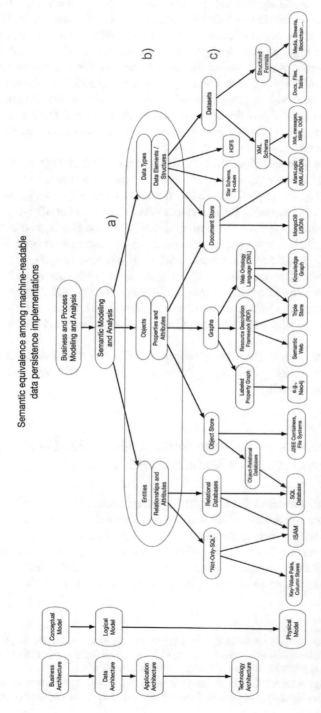

Fig. 5 Semantic equivalence among machine-readable data persistence implementations

The relative flexibility and schema-less aspects of Wikibase also mean that additional steps are needed to harmonize, consolidate, cleanse, de-duplicate and reconcile data that has been collected and captured by different teams independently and without the requirements to align with a common schema or set of semantic standards. However, storage and access will be needed for significant subsets of data (e.g., years of daily historical market prices of securities) in structured forms of data organization. Also, "transformations"of historical time series for normalizing data in order to, e.g., adjust for inflation and stock splits will require a "classic" form—or a today not yet known form—of data storage and access. The same holds true when we want to develop indices from primary data.

Summing up the technical part of the logical CDM design decisions, we conjecture that, in the end, solving the data structure challenges will not at all be easy. Probably the request for novel, not yet known data storage and access forms will nevertheless *not* be the decisive bottleneck of the overall highly complex endeavor. Rather, we foresee the real problem to lay on the human side of the sociotechnical EurHisFirm system. A substantial amount of European states and citizens with highly diverse backgrounds and wants will have to agree on substantial common next steps forward which will bring the aspired advancements for all, but will presumably also touch (almost) every collaborator in a potentially negative way, because even the rapid information technology developments cannot make up for substantial dissens with regard to weighing benefits and burdens of the potential solutions.

Therefore, in a next step the appropriate deliberation and decision process in Europe with all its peculiarities, inconsistencies, and idiosyncrasies will be examined more in-depth.

5   The Human and Organizational Realm of EurHisFirm: Multi-level Federated Standardization

Ideally, standards are defined as an agreed-upon existence of equalities[29] between at least two cooperating actors (which may be humans or machines). The more actors participate in such a network, the more common benefits may be exploited, but the more difficult the agreement is. A technical example is the worldwide telephone network, where each new participant (a new "phone number") can easily access all other existing telephone numbers. With a relatively limited own investment the

---

[28] The links between two data items in Wikibase technically fit the definition of a "triple" (subject, predicate, object), but individual items can be tagged with an arbitrary number of properties that are similar to the key-value pair attributes of the items that are used in LPGs.

[29] A variant of the standards definition "only" requests "compatibility" (instead of equality)— technical provisions often allow to solve real-world problems in the first-mentioned (less expensive or more flexible) way.

access perimeter of the new member is huge. Also, the existing network members profit from the new member although the individual benefit may be very small.

To systematize standardization objects, we use the network paradigm, which comprises sets of nodes and of arcs between the nodes representing the actors. Standardization objects for EurHisFirm thus are:

- Communication standards ("arcs"), e.g., agreements which protocols are used for the exchange of contents between actors.
- Content standards ("nodes"), e.g., often minimal standards that regulate the content of an object—e.g. the "triple unity" identification request (see Sect. 4.3).

In the absence of standard setting by (technical) evolution or market forces it has to be organized by the interested collective, regularly a societal or governmental entitiy. A particularly challenging environment is Europe with its peculiarities and idiosyncrasies, as has already been pointed out. The multi-level European deliberation and decision hierarchy is sketched in Fig. 6. On the national level we often experience the goal "consensus (for common advantage)" outplayed by the goal "individual benefits"(of course this problem also occurs in the subsequent levels). Thus, we must unite both worlds, not only in abstract words but with concrete actions toward more commonalities. In such an environment, each state (and each political deliberation and decision unit below that level) has to be actively involved in consensus-finding and -conclusion. An easy-to-be-agreed-upon request is the "one state one vote" rule (often expanded by the request of unanimity, but this makes consensus-finding a very costly process). Variants of such a consensus approach may be "one firm one vote" or "one research institute one vote."

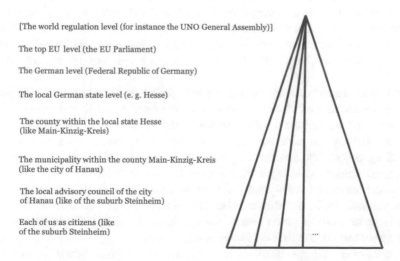

[The world regulation level (for instance the UNO General Assembly)]

The top EU level (the EU Parliament)

The German level (Federal Republic of Germany)

The local German state level (e. g. Hesse)

The county within the local state Hesse
(like Main-Kinzig-Kreis)

The municipality within the county Main-Kinzig-Kreis
(like the city of Hanau)

The local advisory council of the city
of Hanau (like of the suburb Steinheim)

Each of us as citizens (like
of the suburb Steinheim)

Fig. 6 European multi-level federated deliberation and decision hierarchy

The common denominator in overarching European consensus-finding is a multi-level federated deliberation and decision hierarchy which we explain in the following paragraph. Afterward, we discuss the WGIS process sequence that was performed in a simplified version as a kind of self-testing of the validity of such an approach.

5.1 European Multi-level Federated Deliberation and Decision Hierarchy

The political federated deliberation and decision hierarchy might comprise seven deliberation and decision levels. We take as an example the German situation. For our European purposes, we can abstract from the UN level:

In this simplified—but for our purposes sufficiently correct—model, each citizen (here: of the suburb Steinheim) has to obey laws (ordinances) of the village and—going further up—the parliaments of the overarching city, the county, of the sub-central (local German) state ('Land'), of the German Federation ('Bund') and of the EU. Like in all decentralized systems rules on conflicts of law have to exist which govern which norm prevails in case of conflict. In modern systems usually the norms of the higher level prevail in effect with variations in detail.

On each, level basically two types of deliberation and decision actors can be distinguished: One is of type "parliament" (with representatives elected by popular votes, usually by the citizens of the constituency), and the second unit is a type of executive organ. According to the limits set by the superior body, each political unit can design and amend its own constitution and enjoys some autonomy with many variations in details. In addition, usually courts ensure that the laws and regulations on the different levels of this hierarchy are obeyed. Such an organizational set-up is quite time- and resource-consuming. Moreover, it seems to be not optimal as regards standard setting in a technical environment. More details are discussed below, in Sect. 5.2.

Deliberations and decisions in a multi-level *federated* hierarchy mean, that, as an imperative, all possible decisions have to be executed at the lowest possible level in that multi-level hierarchy—this concept is named subsidiarity (Kistenkas, 2000). The idea behind this imperative is that a central deliberation and decision unit—according to multifold practical experiences—cannot quickly collect and properly evaluate all relevant data regarding a decision on the level of, for instance, a city or a suburb. Moreover, future-proof solutions on complex decision objects have to be in some sense "based on" the contribution—at least the "felt contribution"—of the persons concerned with such a decision—we have to somehow tie in such persons on the lower levels into the decision-making process.

The number and specification of levels vary between different (in our case: European) states. For instance, Poland is not organized as a federal state, i.e. composed of (sub-central) states (with each its own constitution and parliament) but does have "voivodeships" ("provinces") where the national government installs the administration. They might be considered as decentralized units of the (one) state administration.

In EurHisFirm, we decided to strive for a multi-level federated deliberation and decision hierarchy as the most important instrument for evaluating and selecting communication ("arcs") and content ("nodes") standards. We regard members of this hierarchy—across the various levels—as a network striving for—in our case—decisions on standards and also overseeing that these decisions are transferred into reality.

Moreover, the participants in EurHisFirm could decide which of the different roles (like DCU, DSU, NIC) they wanted to concentrate on which organizational unit(s) and which political body shall exert the oversight on these units. Of course, these assignments may also vary over time.

5.2   The Circular-Incremental Deliberation and Decision Process: The WGIS Example

We tested a simplified process model on ourselves in EurHisFirm. Soon after the project started, we inaugurated the "work group on identification and standardization" (WGIS). Our overarching goal was to have *all* work packages—and respectively all seven participating states—be actively involved in the discussions and joint selections of identification schemes and communication and content standards. Aside from a formal project management WP, this was the only "political body" that was driven by all WPs. Its purpose was to collect challenges, technical solution options and circumstantial solution conditions, and commonly discuss techno-political options (including sociological influences). These debates were performed on two levels: Preparatory tasks have been exerted on the operative level where staff members of each WP were included, and 14 days later, the WP leaders were presented a solution proposal of the operative level to deliberate and, if necessary, alter the approach—or finally approve it.

With respect to the software development process, Information Systems literature distinguishes between three fundamental process models:

- Top-down development (e.g., linearly detailing a comprehensive solution description over several specification levels).
- Bottom-up development (linearly composing solutions elements from the bottom over several generalization levels up to something comprehensive).
- Circular development[30] (often used in modern agile development systems) (starts out with a subset of solution elements that seem to fit the sought-for comprehensive solution and strive to quickly integrate these into a first draft of

---

[30] www.circulardesignguide.com/methods

a comprehensive solution—and then respecify a vital part of the comprehensive solution to be better capable to integrate existing solution elements—or identify missing solution elements to better fit into the overarching goal—and thus, repetitively step-by-step—approach a solution concept <in our deliberation and decision hierarchy> that fits the respective demands of "the top" and "the bottom").

Each of these three alternatives has its clear disadvantages—in particular in complex application environments. Top-down planning may result in not realizable solution components. The bottom-up approach bears the danger of solving another comprehensive solution—not the one we actually strive for. Moreover, all three concepts are plagued with ample time and resource demands—in particular, experienced and willing collaborators are needed with respect to the application subject matter as well as to the ICT world—that bring different educational and job backgrounds to the table. However, for modern software design, in complex cases, circular development is *the* way to go forward for most practitioners and researchers—but clearly, it is not free of problems.

Thus, we also adopted the circular-incremental approach in WGIS. The deliberation and decision process for this concept was very challenging for the members of WGIS, in particular for the non-IT experts. To raise the chances of project success, it was necessary to have at least one expert who has already experienced and co-solved similar problems in the past and thus could give the novices in the team confidence to properly turn a design challenge into a kind of a one-experience-in-life solution—we had such an infrastructure software development expert in the field of financial and firm data. However, such an expert must be "neutral" with respect to other influencing factors that other members of the team pursue (like, for instance, statisticians). And: This expert must be as such acknowledged in the team.

Our experience is: Get this process of deliberation and decision as quickly as possibly started because you cannot, for non-experts, "simulate" the unwanted outcomes of previous (or higher-level) decisions. This, of course, makes the start of such a process sequence very demanding with respect to both the time and the content dimension.

To gear-up productive WGIS works at the start of the project, we performed tutoring sessions[31] with The Open Group Architecture Framework (TOGAF) and designed preliminary flow diagrams of how the process sequence in detail should be executed (for instance: how to change a—from the past—given data design and how to alter or amend a "constitution"). Actually, due to capacity reasons and time constraints, we have not formally laid down written constitutions as such, but we have produced extensive documentation of the session's contents.

With respect to subsidiarity and leadership necessities in general, we conjecture that the distribution of central vs. decentralized decisions on standards may also be a

---

[31] In general, one should always care for precautions to involve external experts into such processes – on both the operative as well as on the leader's level.

function of the extent of experience in the different locations or states when working in such structures.

6 "The Fish Does Not Only Rot from the Head Down." Now What?

We have discussed the substantial challenges and the solution options to design a European CDM in a highly diverse action space and we have laid out procedures that facilitate consensus-building and presented important first results of—with relative ease- expandable data structures signed-off by the participants. Are we now—so-to-say—*done*?

A substantial hint signals: pay attention. After 5 years of work (including the preparatory time to create our EU application), we do not see one more collected and collated data being openly accessible on the Internet.[32] Although this was _not_ part of our application and thus not part of the agreed-upon deliverables,[33] and although some more data was collected for training purposes (for instance, of the AI component for the interpreter of the OCR results), this outcome calls for more analyses. This re-evaluation helps benefit our data aspirations, but moreover—beyond this subject matter—it sheds light on other important European challenges and ultimately on the politically desired European integration (see chapter "The Human and Organizational Realm of EurHisFirm").

Having strived for the CDM, our main challenge boils down to the contradiction that on the one hand we are obliged to perform subsidiarity in the European multi-level federated deliberation and decision hierarchy—"delegate each decision to the lowest possible level!" and on the other hand the necessity to have a performant *center* of our network, a "strong kernel" that in this capacity is acknowledged by the other members. Both (!) "movements" are apparently prerequisites for the network's success. More specific: In this hierarchy with expectable substantial contradicting local interests—also among the colleagues on the same level—and global desires, both sides must be powerful and self-assured, and both sides nevertheless must—in "broadband," not in "narrowband"—knowledgeably and trustfully cooperate productively without unduly harming the respective other. And ideally no one should free-ride at the expense of a colleague or another institution in the network.

These aspects constitute very high demands on systematic cooperation in Europe. Performant leaders as well as powerful actors on lower levels are requested to cooperate in the repetitive steps to specify solution parts—and all actors must refrain from enriching themselves at the expense of colleagues and rather concentrate on the big picture, which is in the micro-sphere very detailed. We have indications that

---

[32] We researchers had and still have the opportunity to access the desired available data, but this was and is not yet openly possible in a kind of—for instance: web-based—self-service.

[33] In contrary, EU regulations kind of forbid to use INFRADEV funds for collecting more data.

we encounter not just one underperforming part of the whole process sequence—for instance: "the fish rots from the head down!"—but we conjecture that the actors on the lower end of this European hierarchy are much more challenged (just look at the increasing masses of people which have to be somehow addressed when going down this hierarchy). And the lower-level actors often seem not sufficiently experienced and staffed (financed). We have to examine these types of factors with the desire to better the situation and thus the real test of this solution procedure is still outstanding.

So, aside of a pile of written and somehow signed papers the "test in reality" is another step to offer additional data and also additional services to the users. This is a severe necessity because, in the end, following the crowd intelligence approach, the users—better: the subject matter experts within the user crowd—will be capable of evaluating whether the data values and the data structure in the database(s) are correct. Looking at the hindrance factors to publish data, the main argument that was easily discussed in the research context was: "It took us such a long time and such an effort to collect and collate these data sets, that we first want to exploit these data in own publications—for our own qualification—before opening-up our data wealth to the public." However, even the answer "o.k., then let us agree to make our data openly accessible 5 years after these came into the system" has not affected a move toward opening existing data.

We analyze possible reasons that humans do not easily live up to desired actions and derive possible strategies to improve the human behavior—with the conjecture that we see deficits on all levels of the hierarchy, but the more severe ones on the lower levels.

6.1 Analysis of the "Dichotomy" Between Subsidiarity and a Performant Center

Aside from the already mentioned arguments, we see three important causes:

6.1.1 Not Every European State Is Set-Up as Federated as Others: Lack of Experience

Several states in Europe are not composed of independent local states which enjoy their own constitution and, for instance, their own treasury. It is almost incomprehensible for citizens of such states to understand and, when necessary, realize federalism. So, an important step forward could stem from increasing efforts to educate project members on federalism. This approach would also help citizens of European states organized as federations (like Germany) to earlier and better understand—after the 60 years of European integration—deficiency potentials and solution options of these processes.

6.1.2 Proper Federative Work Requires on Lower Levels Precautionary Knowledge and the Willingness to Answer Demands from Higher Levels Quickly Enough

EurHisFirm staff comprised ~25 experts in various fields, organized in 11 work packages geographically dispersed in seven states. One main division runs between the historical financial experts and the data system specialists with only very few colleagues having been educated and experienced "in both worlds". Against the background of the growing importance of ICT developments in modern digitized socio-economic systems, we experienced in general a pronounced willingness to learn the most important design options and restrictions of the respective other side. However, the tightly knitted project plan posted substantial time restrictions on each staff member and in the second half of the EurHisfirm project, also the pandemic hindered quicker results. And in such multidisciplinary and multinational projects, too tight environmental corsets give chances to resort on one's original field of expertise. And some chances have been used. It is known in literature that business subject matter experts often are not too eager to struggle with ICT requests to make use of their subject matter options enabled by ICT (Torre and Sarti 2020). This was also experienced in the WGIS context, in particular as the necessity to understand technical challenges (see Chapt. 4) was substantial.

The WGIS work sequence requested a substantial amount of attention in the last 18 months - we convened each 4 weeks all staff members as well as the WP leaders to introduce (new) standardization topics, discuss it and decide upon it. That resulted in some absences in such sessions, which gives us reason to conjecture that in the multi-level federated deliberation and decision hierarchy the (greater number of the) lower level staff members experience capacity bottlenecks which then may result in lack of precautionary knowledge that would enable a staff member to easily and quickly answer complex questions "from above" and further we conjecture that the respective persons know about their deficiencies and try to circumvent such decision necessities.

But higher levels in the federative deliberation and decision hierarchy (who, by the way, probably enjoy more often assistants capacities) need quick and educated or experienced feed-back bottom-up for making better decisions. In other words: The delegation of decisions in the multi-level federative hierarchy to the lowest possible level requires appropriate staffing of those lower levels-otherwise the decentralized unit(s) cannot live up to the responsibility requests that the local constitution imposes on them.

6.1.3 The Role of the "Mass" of the Citizens

The member States of the EU are organized as democracies: majorities rule.

We need the mass of citizens[34] for evaluating the data of our databases and for backing up the actors in the federated hierarchy caring for digitized historical data that we want to use in research and for training purposes. But the mass of citizens—at least a reasonable number of individuals—should also agree to and tolerate their leaders. Again, education seems a necessity, complemented by field exercises.

All in all, the European multi-level system has deficits in performing efficiently and smoothly. In complex situations, it can be observed that in particular (but not restricted to) the actors of the lower levels just kind of step-back and "highly-performant wait" for the colleagues on the upper levels now to do something—leading to a form of deadlock—whereas the higher levels mutually accuse the opposite side of "sinning" but often do not appreciate own deficits in this coordination game.

Before we discuss a selection of possible ways out of this dilemma, we shortly examine also deficiencies on the top levels of the European decision hierarchy.

6.2   Insertion: Deficiencies of the "European Head"

A presumably[35] substantial negative effect on the functionality of the European multi-level federated hierarchy was that the INFRADEV support program of the EU was discontinued and is not yet succeeded by a follow-up program—and this is not to be expected until 2024. Knowledgeable young persons do not have a career prospect in such a setting and choose other occupations.[36] Both big contesters of Europe concerning ICT and data availability seem to do a better job in creating an environment where the lower-level members of the "network" see enough chances to improve their stand.

6.3   Possible Ways Out of the Dilemma

Our overall experience says that, when facing complex design challenges, the subsidiarity imperative (accentuating the bottom-up intelligence of the federative multi-level European deliberation and decision hierarchy) and the necessity to have a performant center for making a network successful (emphasizing the respective top-down intelligence) do not quickly go hand in hand. When striving for improved

---

[34] Clearly, the mass of citizens will be in the case of fighting the pandemic larger compared to the number of citizens to be convinced to profoundly strive for harmonized European historical (and contemporary) data.

[35] We could not test in our case how the European hierarchy would have functioned if the follow-up funding problem would have been dissolved approximately 18 months after project start.

[36] This is not a big problem, because EU programs also strive to disseminate European cooperation in the field which was of course successfully exercised in EurHisFirm. However, INFRADEV looked toward decades of operation of EurHisFirm which should not end after a 3 year—logical—design phase.

ways to deal with the semantic difference between EurHisFirm users and data availabilities in storage systems, we cannot make up for human deficiencies by only relegating to the expectedly exponential improvements of the price-performance ratio of modern ICT. As we do not yet have these digitized historical data available to train, for instance, machine learning algorithms, we must take care of the cognition gap by ourselves. The ICT improvements will presumably help in the forward development of our sociotechnical man-machine systems—in particular with respect to more classic administration tasks (like overseeing system tune-ups and similar functions). But the necessary intellectual input to overcome shortages—often referred to as "subject-matter (business) concept" (in our case: document concept for historical firms)—must be provided by human experts.

We regard the deficiencies on the human (organizational) side of the sociotechnical system as more severe than the deficiencies on the technology side. As a result, we concentrate on the human side and propose six ways out of the dilemma that should be thoroughly researched in the future.

6.3.1 Education and Exercising Federalism

For European societies profound knowledge of federalism and its practice seem to be a fundamental requirement for the further development. All citizens and states have to step up their efforts to close that knowledge and experience gap. This should begin in school, and should be deepened in academic course programs. Likewise, continuing education in firms and organizations must thematize federalism.

People who do not yet have seriously dealt with a data infrastructure should have their opinion, but should not pretend that—if outvoted—an unbearable harm would be inflicted on them.

We assume that classic presentation-only education will not fill the cognition gap. Instead, we have—on the different educational levels—to exercise federated cooperation, for instance, on small-scale overarching projects in communities, firms, or schools.

6.3.2 Step-Up Research on Federalism

There are ample research results on federalism, but given the high importance of this concept in European developments and given the "skewed (two-sided)"—more on the lower levels, but also on the upper levels—deficiencies in fulfilling the requirements of the European federated multi-level deliberation and decision hierarchy, we should invest substantially more into researching this field. To explicate just one example: Europe's competitive stand is already kind of sandwiched between the USA and China with respect to fundamental ICT developments—a challenge we cannot overcome by just relying on regulation (as quite an amount of managers and citizens do). Regulation has a fundamental character of "you independent citizen are no longer allowed to do something you enjoy," and this desire is formulated after unwanted important societal developments occurred that urgently need to be corrected. All this has a smell of negativeness. Rather, we must step-up contributions beforehand to have Europe not being regarded as an "avenging angel" when things have fallen into the fountain. The collaboration must be stepped-up in this hierarchy—both from the bottom-up as well as the top-down perspectives ("broadband team work"). Substantial challenges in this highly demanding cooperation have to be "checked" by complementing research results.

6.3.3 Role Models

In modern societies, role models (Merton, 2010) are important to convince the broad (democratic) public to join forces toward—for instance—standards. However, specifying the desired characteristics of a role model is a double-edged sword: The European Parliamant (EP), for instance is for some citizens a "damaged" European institution because these people, e.g., do not fully endorse further European integration. But we have learned to know the EP as an institution that pursues common European interests much more than others. Also, other European institutions move strongly forward in this way, for instance, the European Space Agency (ESA). Also, the European Central Bank (ECB) seems to be an example which is constituted in the legal form of an European state with a "tightly-knitted" task (European price stability) and the respective constitution (the own statehood guarantees the formal independence from other European states).

6.3.4 Brush-Up Constitutions in Europe to Strengthen Federalism

We conjecture that in European states which do not know or do not value federalism in their internal organization, citizens have less opportunity and incentive to learn and exercise federalism. Given the overall European necessity of a federated architecture, this challenge should be overcome.

6.3.5 Allow More Flexibility on the Lower Levels of the European Multi-level Federated Deliberation and Decision Hierarchy

We have to take the megatrend toward more individualism—in particular with respect to the lower levels of our hierarchy—seriously. We expect to face an increase in the number and the severity of decision problems on lower levels of the European deliberation and decision hierarchy (and supposedly increase the funding of the lower level actors).

Again, we concentrate our proposals to better the cooperation routines in the European multi-level federated deliberation and decision hierarchy on the human side, specifically with respect to collaboration. We call for reasonable advancements on this subject matter. Otherwise we cannot sincerely exploit the expected massive progress of the ICT technology in the years to come—despite furthering the ICT-supported classic administrative functions of a modern Europe (but this is not the most important bottleneck).

6.3.6　Overarching Grand Challenge for Europe

A grand challenge is an—ideally—from important forces in a community commonly accepted complex problem that has to be solved with priority to the substantial common benefit. It is very difficult to accomplish, and ought to be solved by this community and/or the society (Ferraro et al., 2015). The first landing on the moon was such a grand challenge (for the US and some allies). Fighting cancer is another example (worldwide). We formulate a grand challenge candidate for Europe:

Europe ought to develop a European culture representation by data not only contemporarily but also by using the rich treasure of European diversity in its past. Or, in other words: How could we imagine that Europe really is capable of furthering its specific culture, when we as continent cannot provide our own digitized historical data in a minimally harmonized fashion? The answer seems to be: We cannot! The grand challenge is then to fill this severe gap with a profound effort to build up such a data repository—referring to all paper sources of our past, which of course is not confined only to financial and firm data but should include *all* disciplines of the Humanities and related Technology. And, this repository then should also bridge the gap between historical and contemporary data sets. We regard our CDM as a—of course to be stepwise expanded—"kernel" of such a common data infrastructure of Europe. Then, for instance, European students (see chapter "The EurHisFirm Case"; Footnote 5) can—at their will—use European data for their research theses—and this is only the least necessity. We—Europe—must also be better positioned to escape the strategic sandwich between the USA and China. Reflecting the substantial problems in performing the appropriate top-down and bottom-up communications in the European multi-level federated deliberation and decision hierarchy, we conjecture that without a substantial alteration of this institutional set-up an "emergent" solution will take "forever" or, in other words: This problem seems to be unsolvable. Thus, we propose the following institutional intervention: We take the European Central Bank (ECB) as role model for introducing an independent European Data Agency with the duty to preserve and make available European culture contemporarily as well as historically in form of digitized data. We conjecture that without such a data representation of European culture as an European data infrastructure we as Europe will be overly hampered to identify our competitive wealth of diversity against the other world powers-probably we even will not be capable to sustain our (often postulated) cultural advantage. Such an European Data Agency could be an—independent from other European states-"own state" in Europe (also independent from specific interests of important societal groups like companies or administrations), devoted to substantially further the availability of European data and the better understanding of the wealth of data in Europe.

7 Summary

This chapter analyzed a central part of an EU-funded, seven-nations development project for the comprehensive interdisciplinary design of a European system to collect and collate historical financial and firm data (named EurHisFirm)—the responsibility of the authors was the design of a Common Data Model (CDM). We have strong indications that in complex decision situations—and developing a CDM in Europe belongs to that class of problems—human cooperation deficiencies substantially outweigh expectably exponential advancements in information technology. The reason is presumably that a federative approach asks for involving the concerned in a European deliberation and decision hierarchy, which among diverse and self-confident nations—actually persons—(likewise in important sub-national groups of responsibility, e.g., communal authorities or firms) makes reaching an agreement on data and other standards an overly lengthy endeavor. Such a process is often accompanied by undue recurred allegations that not heeding the one or the other individual conviction will result in a catastrophe at least for the concerned. Such a "mine field" often ends with foul compromises. We understand our contribution to bundle substantial indications toward a possible furthering of the state-of-the-art, and we beg fellow researchers to thoroughly investigate this approach.

European projects request an organization and decision structure based on a federative approach that gives each European state an equal vote. We conjecture a multi-level European deliberation and decision hierarchy with the EU level (e.g., the European Parliament) placed on top and a research institute placed on the pre-bottom level, where the decision-making is performed by parliaments on each level which democratically represents the concerned citizens. Moreover, work on each level is regulated by the level-specific constitution and the action space is restricted by decisions of the superior level.

A federated deliberation and decision hierarchy also requests subsidiarity—placing a decision on the lowest possible level in the hierarchy. Our experience indicates a substantial "dichotomy": On one hand, the local knowledge has to actively be channeled into the upper levels of the hierarchy, but we suspect that the lower level actors are not well-prepared to content- and time-wise live-up to such a request in complex problem cases. Our experience also says that—in order to reduce design errors and time necessities for a multitude of deliberation and decision processes in parallel—we need a performant center—ideally an expert who has no own interests and has already solved such a complex problem in the past. However, such an expert must also be acknowledged by the majority of the actors on the lower levels, which we wish us as "powerful" to be capable of profoundly playing the required interaction.

We conjecture the following chain of argumentation in such a hierarchy: Actors on the lower level are not sufficiently prepared to fill the void of air in upper decision levels with local arguments. But we also see deficiencies on the upper level, which may help decision-makers on the lower levels to be "observant." Both sides then kind of wait for the respective other side before getting into concrete action. In such an environment it can be expected that more or less all actors look first for the individual advantage rather than on the benefit of the common.

The second important set of results of our analysis comprises the concrete design decisions of the European CDM. All decisions in our simplified test deliberation and decision hierarchy have been taken unanimously. Important cornerstones of the CDM are:

- Expandable data structure with ideally no reprogramming necessities in case of future changes.
- Melioration staging (say: a sequence of five[37] melioration steps) between raw data and fully CDM-compliant data.
- Selection of a worldwide identification scheme that allows "triple unity" of objects: worldwide just one identifier for just one data object and vice versa—and this is also the identifier of the one respective real-world object.
- Standardized Core Data Model.
- Semantic equivalence among machine-readable data persistence implementations.

In addition, we have furthered the biunique LEI identification scheme to cater to historical firms and financial instruments (we call the respective worldwide identifiers ELEI and EFII). And we have spelled out in handbooks the (almost) ready-to-compile data structures for these identifiers,[38] also for the declarative inclusion of the Entity Legal Form (ELF) standard.

Our conjecture is that the expected dramatic price/performance advancements of Information Technology will not be capable of making up for the above-mentioned severe deficiencies on the human side. So, the technical side of the CDM is not at all an easy self-runner. But we regard the deficiencies on the human (organizational) side as more severe and important. So, all actors of this hierarchy have to improve performance, in particular, the actors on the lower levels have to increase their participation in the consensus finding and feeding their local knowledge timely into the upper levels of the hierarchy.

The chapter ends with proposals on how to alleviate or even to overcome the "dichotomy". Our far-reaching proposal is the foundation of an (independent) European Data Agency tasked with systematically collecting and collating cultural data contemporarily and historically to make European diversity digitally available

---

[37] Again, this number is "breathing."

[38] We also provide, as an example, an installation guide for the ELEI and EFII. (EURHIS-FIRM consortium. (2021). EURHISFIRM D1.14: Final report. Zenodo. https://doi.org/10.5281/zenodo.4980412), see page 46).

in (partly) harmonized data. We conjecture that, if we don't embark on this proposal, combating severe crises in Europe is substantially hampered, and in the end, the comprehensive European political harmonization process may suffer severely. It is mainly on *us*—on the lower levels of the European federated multi-level deliberation and decision hierarchy—to change for the better! Our main proposal is to step-up education on federalism "at work" and to provide occasions to exercise this concept in real-world challenges.

Acknowledgement The authors thank Helmut Siekmann, Uwe Walz, Dennis Gram, Marius Liebald, Lut de Moor and Marion Wiebel for their valuable contributions and support.

References

Bednar, P. M., & Welch, C. (2020, April). Socio-technical perspectives on smart working: Creating meaningful and sustainable systems. *Information Systems Frontiers, 22*(2), 281298. doi:https://doi.org/10.1007/s10796-019-09921-1

Besen, S. M., & Farrell, J. (1994). Choosing how to compete: Strategies and tactics in standardization. *Journal of Economic Perspectives, 8*(2), 117–131. https://doi.org/10.1257/jep.8.2.117

Bostrom, R. P., & Heinen, J. S. (1977). MIS problems and failures: A socio-technical perspective. Part I: The causes. *MIS Quarterly, 1*(3), 17–32. https://doi.org/10.2307/248710

Bostrom, R. P., Gupta, S., & Thomas, D. (2009). A meta-theory for understanding information systems within sociotechnical systems. *Journal of Management Information Systems, 26*(1), 17–48. https://doi.org/10.2753/MIS0742-1222260102

David, P. A., & Greenstein, S. (1990). The economics of compatibility standards: An introduction to recent research. *Economics of Innovation and New Technology, 1*, 3–41. https://doi.org/10.1080/10438599000000002

Deans, P. C., Karwan, K. R., Goslar, M. D., Ricks, D. A., & Toyne, B. (1991). Identification of key international information systems issues in U.S.-based multinational corporations. *Journal of Management Information Systems, 7*(4), 27–50. https://doi.org/10.1080/07421222.1991.11517902

Farrell, J., & Saloner, G. (1985). Standardization, compatibility, and innovation. *The Rand Journal of Economics, 16*(1), 70–83.

Ferraro, F., Etzion, D., & Gehman, J. (2015). Tackling grand challenges pragmatically: robust action revisited. *Organization Studies, 36*(3), 363–390. https://doi.org/10.1177/0170840614563742

Fomin, V., Keil, T., & Lyytinen, K. (2003). Theorizing about standardization: Integrating fragments of process theory in light of telecommunication standardization wars. *Sprouts: Working Papers on Information Environments, Systems and Organizations, 3*(1), 29–60.

Garud, R. J., Jain, S., & Kumaraswamy, A. (2002). Institutional entrepreneurship in the sponsorship of common technological standards: The case of Sun Microsystems and Java. *Academy of Management Journal, 45*(1), 196–214. https://doi.org/10.5465/3069292

Kistenkas, F. (2000). European and domestic subsidiarity. *Tilburg Law Review, 8*(3), 247–254. https://doi.org/10.1163/221125900x00044

Ledyard, J. O. (1995). Public goods: A survey of experimental research. In J. Kagel & A. Roth (Eds.), *The handbook of experimental economics* (pp. 111–194). Princeton University Press. https://doi.org/10.1021/ed024p574

Lee, A. S., Thomas, M., & Baskerville, R. L. (2015). Going back to basics in design science: From the information technology artifact to the information systems artifact. *Information Systems Journal, 25*, 5–21. https://doi.org/10.1111/isj.12054

Merton, R. K. (2010). *Sociology of Science and Sociology as Science*. Columbia University Press.
Mumford, E. (2006, October). The story of socio-technical design: reflections on its successes, failures and potential. *Information Systems Journal, 16*(4), 317342. doi:https://doi.org/10.1111/j.1365-2575.2006.00221.x. S2CID 6943658
Oliver, P., & Marwell, G. (1988). The paradox of group size in collective action. *American Sociological Review, 53*(1), 1–8.
Olson, M. (1965). *The logic of collective action: Public goods and the theory of groups*. Harvard University Press.
Ostrom, E. (1986). An agenda for the study of institutions. *Public Choice, 48*(1), 3–25. https://doi.org/10.1007/BF00239556
Ostrom, E. (1998). A behavioral approach to the rational choice theory of collective action: Presidential address. *American Political Science Review, 92*(1), 1–22.
Ostrom, E. (2000). Collective action and the evolution of social norms. *Journal of Economic Perspectives, 14*(3), 137–158. https://doi.org/10.1080/19390459.2014.935173
Ostrom, E., & Basurto, X. (2011). Crafting analytical tools to study institutional change. *Journal of Institutional Economics, 7*(3), 317–343. https://doi.org/10.1017/S1744137410000305
Sarker, S., Chatterjee, S., Xiao, X., & Elbanna, A. (2019). The sociotechnical axis of cohesion for the IS discipline: Its historical legacy and its continued relevance. *MIS Quarterly, 43*(3), 695–719. https://doi.org/10.25300/MISQ/2019/13747
Schmidt, S. K., & Werle, R. (1998). *Coordinating technology. Studies in the international standardization of telecommunications*. The MIT Press.
Torre T. & Sarti, D. (2020). The "way" Toward E-leadership: Some Evidence From the Field. *Frontiers in Psychology, 11*, https://doi.org/10.3389/fpsyg.2020.554253.
Trist, E. L., & Bamforth, K. W. (1951). Some social and psychological consequences of the longwall method of coal getting. *Human Relations, 4*(3), 3–38. https://doi.org/10.1177/001872675100400101
Volacu, A., & Goloptenţa, I.-P. (2013). First and second generation theories of collective action. *Modern Dilemmas. Understanding Collective Action in the 21st Century* (pp. 27–56).
Williams, R., & Edge, D. (1996). The social shaping of technology. *Research Policy, 25*, 865–899. https://doi.org/10.1016/0048-7333(96)00885-2

Part III
Culture and Gender: Recognition of Promotion

A Theory of Organizational Information Culture

Dorothy E. Leidner

Abstract This chapter presents an integrated theory of information, knowledge management systems, and culture in organizations. The knowledge-based theory of the firm suggests that knowledge is the organizational asset that enables sustainable competitive advantage in hypercompetitive markets. Since 2000, systems to manage knowledge in organizations, regardless of the system label—intranets, organizational social media, knowledge management systems and more—have become important aspects to most organizations' information systems strategy. Systems designed to facilitate knowledge management are intended to facilitate the quality, creation, storage, distribution and use of knowledge in organizations. However, such systems are often seen to clash with corporate culture and, as a result, have limited positive benefits. This chapter bridges the literature on information, culture, and knowledge sharing to develop a theoretical framework for assessing those aspects of organizational culture that are likely to be the source of implementation challenges for systems intended to facilitate knowledge processes. In so doing, the chapter associates various organizational subunit cultures with different information cultures, and presents a series of propositions concerning the relationships among individual, organizational, and information cultures.

1 Preface

Theorizing is among the most challenging undertakings facing scholars. In the past several decades, many editorials and papers have been written with a view toward explaining what theory is (Feldman, 2004; Lee, 2014), what it is not (Sutton & Staw, 1995; DiMaggio, 1995), what types of theories there are (Gregor, 2006; Burton-Jones et al., 2015), and what the attributes of "good" theory are (Bacharach, 1989). Others have provided suggestions for assessing theoretical contribution (Corley &

D. E. Leidner (✉)
Baylor University, Waco, TX, USA
e-mail: Dorothy_Leidner@baylor.edu

© The Author(s), under exclusive license to Springer Nature Switzerland AG 2022
J. Dibbern et al. (eds.), *Digitalization Across Organizational Levels*, Progress in IS,
https://doi.org/10.1007/978-3-031-06543-9_4

Gioia, 2011; Whetten, 1989; Bergh, 2003; Leidner, 2020) and understanding what makes a theory interesting (Davis, 1971; Barley, 2006; Bartunek et al., 2006). Yet others attempt to help the fledging theorist with advice for theorizing (LePine & King, 2010; Shepherd & Sutcliffe, 2011; Poole & van de Ven, 1989; Weick, 1989), often highly abstract advice itself based on theory. Recently, a series of editorials has provided a first-hand account from several theorists of the theorizing they employed in developing their recently published theory (Leidner & Tona, 2021a, b; Young et al., 2021; Gregory & Henfridsson, 2021).

An implicit assumption of much of these papers is that theorizing is something that is consciously learned—it is not enough to read widely cited theories and emulate in a vicarious manner of learning; rather, one must reflect on the meanings of theory in order to learn to theorize. Yet at the same time, theorizing cannot be learned simply by reading everything that has been written about theory and theorizing. At some point, one must begin to theorize; indeed, there is no substitute for experience. Theorizing requires reflecting with profound depth on a variety of literature, experience, and perspectives and then composing something new and interesting. Over two decades ago, I drafted a theory by myself. I had an interest in theorizing and had worked on at least one conceptual paper that had many characteristics of theorizing (Leidner & Jarvenpaa, 1995) but was wanting to learn more. I never submitted the draft and never asked anyone to read it and provide feedback. I lacked confidence, thinking the paper was too simple. I was later to learn as a scholar that theory often feels simple as it is being developed and this is no reason to abandon the theory. Part of the theorization process is a constant urge to push the theory to greater depth of explanation and more insightful implications. The theorizing is only beginning once the initial theory has been put to words.

The theory presented in this chapter was an attempt to combine two areas of my research interest at the time—knowledge management and culture. The chapter was uploaded to the university website where I was working at the time and where it still resides as of this writing (Leidner, 1998a, b). In honor of Prof. Armin Heinzl, and in recognition of our shared past interests in issues related to information, knowledge, and culture (Heinzl & Leidner, 2012; Hemmer et al., 2014), I here present this theory in its original form. In terms of the phenomenon of study, it provides a glimpse into the not-so-distant past, but a past that feels drastically different than the present. In terms of theorizing, it provides a glimpse into the thinking of an aspiring theorist. Even while I abandoned the theory without so much as soliciting any feedback from peers or from a conference or journal, the effort was highly rewarding, laying a foundation for future papers on related topics (Alavi et al., 2005; Ravishankar et al., 2011) and future theorizing efforts (Leidner & Kayworth, 2006; Chipidza & Leidner, 2019; George & Leidner, 2019; Leidner & Tona, 2021a, b). I hope the publication of the chapter in this book will inspire young aspiring theorists to write a theory, free from the worries of whether the theory is published or not but simply for the sake of their own personal learning and growth as a scholar.

2 Introduction

When asked about why the organization was building a worldwide Intranet and knowledge management system, the Chief Knowledge Office of a large multi-national consulting firm replied "we have 80,000 people scattered around the world that need the information to do their jobs effectively. The information they needed was too difficult to find and, even if they did find it, often inaccurate. Our Intranet is meant to solve this problem" (Leidner, 1998a, b). Roughly a decade ago, case studies of organizations implementing executive information systems (EIS) suggested that a major reason behind these systems was a need for timely, accurate, and consistent information and to help managers cope with the problem of information overload (Rockart & DeLong, 1988; Houdeshel & Watson, 1987). And although a goal of management information systems (MIS) was to provide relevant information for managerial control and planning, MIS was unable to provide timely, complete, accurate, and readable data of the type executives needed for strategic decision-making. Even earlier, in 1967, Ackoff notes that "I do not deny that most managers lack a good deal of information that they should have, but I do deny that this is the most important information deficiency from which they suffer. It seems to me that they suffer from an overabundance of irrelevant information." Interestingly, in 1997, Courtney et al. state that "omitting the unimportant information (from corporate intranets) may be as important as concentrating on the important. The mere availability of 'information' may have a distracting effect . . . ". Is information systems' history repeating itself over and over again in a continuous cycle of providing more information in greater detail in a more timely manner in a more graphical format, yet forever doomed to be providing "too much irrelevant" information while leaving the important information "too hard to find"? Or, is it that each time progress is made on one front, new forms of barriers to the impact of IS are encountered? Alternatively, has the real culprit in IS's seeming failure to impact organizational effectiveness not yet been discovered?

Recommended approaches to helping ensure that information systems result in organizational improvements have included structuring information systems requirements analysis (Yourdan & Constantine, 1978), involving users in analysis (King & Rodriguez, 1981; Ives & Olson, 1984), attempting to link IT to the business strategy (Pyburn, 1983), and improving change agentry skills (Markus & Benjamin, 1996). All of the approaches merit consideration, as do contingency theories which would suggest that the success of information systems (IS) in an organization depends upon the proper fit of IT to the organization's structure and design. Yet despite the prescriptive advice, information-based systems still seem to fail to live up to expectations and often fail to provide the dramatic improvements in organizational effectiveness for which they are designed (Lyytinen & Hirschheim, 1987; Mowshowitz, 1976). Moreover, there appears to be almost a crisis in the image of IS in organizations, with such problems as high CIO turnover, executives not recognizing the strategic importance of IS, and declining top management commitment to large IS investments.

This article offers a new exegesis to the reasons why information-based systems appear to be encountering the same problems repeatedly despite significant advances in planning and implementation methodologies and theories, as well as in the technology itself: an incongruity with corporate culture. It posits that information systems implementation efforts must take into account corporate culture when designing the plan for change; if not, such systems might produce results, some anticipated others not, but the systems will fall way short of providing the major improvements expected in most large systems implementation efforts.

This article will first trace briefly information-based systems advancements and the dominant organizational paradigms used to investigate the organizational effects of IS, and will then examine current developments in information-based systems, namely knowledge management systems. It will show how these systems in particular call for a new paradigm of interpretation, that of organizational culture theory. The article will introduce the notion of information culture in the context of knowledge management systems and will present a brief overview of the relevant work on organizational culture. The article offers the existence of information culture as a framework for assessing those aspects of organizational culture that are likely to be the source of implementation challenges. Propositions will be offered concerning the relationship between organizational subunit culture and information culture and these will be tied to managerial prescriptions on managing the implementation of knowledge management systems.

3   Advances in Information Systems

Information systems can be classified in several ways, including: according to their broad function, to the organizational function they serve, to the underlying technologies, or the organizational level at which they are used (Laudon & Laudon, 1997). This article will consider information systems by broad function since much of the IT literature focuses on particular systems classified in this manner, such as decision support systems, expert systems, and electronic mail. In particular, we are interested in systems designed to provide information to managers and professionals at any organizational level. Hence, we will focus primarily on MIS and EIS (as both systems aim to supply managerial information) and knowledge management systems (a new line of systems oriented to providing professionals and managers unstructured information).

3.1   MIS and the Structuring of Organizations

As noted in Somogyi and Galliers (1987), as firms began to computerize in the 1950s, the first applications were in the area of transaction processing. Transaction processing systems are computerized systems that perform and record the daily routine transactions necessary to the conduct of business such as payroll, sales order entry, shipping, order tracking, accounts payable, material movement control (Laudon & Laudon, 1997). These systems were designed to facilitate data collection and to improve the efficiencies of organizational transactions. Soon thereafter, with advances in programming languages, databases, and storage, systems oriented toward providing performance information to managers emerged (Somogyi & Galliers, 1987). Management information systems (MIS) are computer-based information systems that provide managers with reports, and in some cases, with on-line access to the organization's current performance and historical records. MIS primarily serve the functions of planning, controlling, and decision-making at the management level. Generally, they condense information obtained from transaction processing systems and present it to management in the form of routine summary and exception reports.

Simon (1977) predicted that computers, namely MIS, would recentralize decision-making, shrink line organizational structures, decrease the number of levels, and result in an increase in the number and size of staff departments. It was believed that information technology would enable greater centralization of authority, clearer accountability of subordinates, a sharper distinction between top management and staff, and the rest of the organization, and a transformation of the planning and innovating functions. The organizational theory used to evaluate the effect of MIS on organizations was contingency theory of organizational structure, technology, and the environment. Research prior to 1970 indicated that IT provided a means of collecting and processing large amounts of data and information, thus enabling a small number of persons effectively to control authority and decision-making; hence, IT was said to facilitate centralization (Klatzky, 1970; Whisler, 1970; Stewart, 1971). Research after 1970 seemed to find that IT, by enabling organizations to gather and process information rapidly, facilitated decentralizing decision-making (Carter, 1984; Foster & Flynn, 1984; Dawson & McLaughlin, 1986). For example, Carter (1984) felt that as the extent of computer utilization increased in subunit applications, the locus of decision-making authority would become more decentralized in the organization, and the division of labor as reflected by functional diversification, functional specialization and functional differentiation would increase. Carter found in her study of newspaper organizations that as computers become the predominate technology, upper management was released from the day-to-day encumbrances of centralized decision-making, fostering a decentralized organizational structure. In other cases, IT appeared to have had no effect when changes were expected (Franz et al., 1986). Considering the weak relationships found when using technology as an independent variable, other researchers employed technology as a moderator variable between the environment and structure or as a dependent variable. Robey (1977) found that IT supported an existing decentralized structure in organizations with uncertain environments but that in more stable environments, IT strengthened a centralized authority structure.

In summary, early research on the impact of IT, namely MIS, on organizations focused on the effect of IT on organizational structures. The results were highly mixed, leading to an emergent imperative that argued that the particular effects of IT were dependent on a given organization's context and hence, were not predictable or systematic across organizations. An alternative perspective was that certain inherent limitations of MIS prevented predictable improvements to organizational effectiveness. Among the limitations of MIS are that they have highly limited analytical capabilities, they are oriented almost exclusively to internal, not environmental or external, events, and that the information content is fixed and not tailored to individual users (Laudon & Laudon, 1997).

3.2 DSS, EIS, and Organizational Decision-Making

Decision support systems (DSS) and executive information systems (EIS) aimed to provide what MIS were unable to: specific online information relevant to decision-makers in a flexible format. DSS are interactive model-oriented systems, and are used by managers and knowledge workers, analysts, and professionals whose primary job is handling information and making decisions (Keen & Morton, 1982; Sprague & Carlson, 1982). DSS assist management decision-making by combining data, sophisticated analytical models, and user-friendly software into a single powerful system that can support semi-structured or unstructured decision-making (Keen & Morton, 1982; Sprague & Carlson, 1982). DSS tend to be isolated from major organizational information systems and tend to be stand-alone systems developed by end-user divisions or groups, not under central IS control (Hogue, 1987). EIS are computer-based information systems designed to provide managers access to information relevant to their management activities. Originally designed for senior managers, the systems quickly became popular for managers at all levels. Unlike DSS which are tied to specific decisions and which have a heavy emphasis on models, EIS focus on the retrieval of specific information, particularly daily operational information that is used for monitoring organizational performance. Features distinguishing EIS from such systems as management information systems and decision support systems include a non-keyboard interface, status access to the organizational database, drill-down analysis capabilities (the incremental examination of data at different levels of detail), trend analysis capabilities (the examination of data across desired time intervals), exception reporting, extensive graphics, the providing of data from multiple sources, and the highlighting of the information an executive feels is critical (Kador, 1988; Mitchell, 1988). Whereas the traditional focus of MIS was on the storage and processing of large amounts of information, the focus of EIS is on the retrieval of specific information about the daily operational status of an organization's activities as well as specific information about competitors and the marketplace (Friend, 1986).

Huber (1990) advanced a theory of the effects of advanced decision and information-providing technologies, such as DSS and EIS, on organizational decision-making. While he also made propositions concerning the effect of such systems on organizational design and structure, the dominant paradigm for examining the organizational effects of information technology was turning toward decision-making. Huber and McDaniel (1986) argued that decision-making was the most critical management activity and that the effectiveness of IS rested more in facilitating organizational decision-making than enabling structural responses to environmental uncertainty. A wide body of research emerged examining organizational decision-making and the decision-making consequences of IS. However, most of the IS literature focused on the individual level of analysis, which was reasonable given that DSS were designed in most cases for individual decision-makers, and most of the EIS research also supported individual rather than organizational improvements.

While some of Huber's propositions have been substantiated (Leidner & Elam, 1995; Molloy & Schwenk, 1995), the organizational level effects have received little substantiation and have been overshadowed by the individual-level effects (Elliott, 1992). Moreover, research on DSS showed that decision-makers used the tools in such a manner as to reduce time, but not necessarily to increase quality (Todd & Benbasat, 1991) but in the cases where the systems did appear to increase quality, the decision-makers seemed not to subjectively perceive this improvement (Le Blanc & Kozar, 1990). Empirical evidence has shown that EIS enable faster decision-making, more rapid identification of problems, more analysis before decision-making, and greater understanding of the business (Leidner & Elam, 1995; Elliott, 1992). Evidence also suggests that EIS allow single and double-loop learning (Vandenbosch & Higgins, 1996). Other promises for EIS, which have not been empirically substantiated, involved helping companies cope with reduced staff levels (Applegate, 1987; Applegate & Osborn, 1988), substantial monetary savings (Holub, 1988), power shifts and a change in business focus (Applegate & Osborn, 1988), and improving service (Holub, 1988; Mitchell, 1988; Kador, 1988). Interestingly, these promises sound reminiscent of the promises that were made for MIS and that are now being made for Intranets, as will be discussed later.

Among the most serious challenges to EIS implementation involved overcoming information problems, namely organizational subunits feeling ownership of information that was suddenly being accessed by senior managers who previously had relied on these subunits to summarize and analyze their own performance in periodic reports. Such ownership problems led to system failure in some cases, when subunits consciously and covertly altered data to be more favorable to the unit and thereby rendered the EIS inaccurate (Leidner, 1992). Other weaknesses of EIS are the difficulty of pulling information from multiple sources into a graphical PC-based interface, justifying the costs of the systems given the unclear payoff, and ensuring that the information remains relevant as the needs of managers changes (Leidner, 1992). In summary, DSS and EIS research adopted an organizational decision-making paradigm as a reference theory for determining the organizational impacts of these systems. While the systems have well-documented individual-level benefits, the organizational-level benefits have been less lucid.

3.3   Knowledge Management Systems and Organizational Culture

A new line of systems based on web technology has emerged which compensates for some of the limitations of EIS, namely the difficulty of integrating information across platforms. These systems return control for information content to organizational subunits, hence bypassing some of the informational problems encountered with EIS, yet also require active participation of users not only in the design process but also in the process of information provision. Corporate Intranets are private web-based networks, usually within a corporation's firewalls, that connect employees to vital corporate information. They let companies speed information and software to employees and business partners (Thyfault, 1996; Vidal et al., 1998). The primary incentive is their ability to provide "what computer and software makers have frequently promised but never actually delivered: the ability to pull all the computers, software, and databases that dot the corporate landscape into a single system that enables employees to find information wherever it resides" (Cortese, 1996). While there is a business case for the value of Intranets, there is little proof of the economic value of such systems (Rooney, 1997).

Among the most lauded potential applications of intranets is the provision of tools for knowledge management. Knowledge includes the insights, understandings, and practical know-how that employees possess. Knowledge management is a method of systematically and actively managing ideas, information, and knowledge of employees. Knowledge management systems refer to the use of modern information technologies (e.g., the Internet, intranets, extranets, browsers, data warehouses, software filters and agents) to systematize, enhance, and expedite intra- and inter-firm knowledge management (Alavi & Leidner, 1999). Knowledge management systems (KMS) are intended to help organize, interpret, and make widely accessible the expertise of an organization's human capital to help the organization cope with turnover, rapid change, and downsizing. KMS are being built in part from increased pressure to maintain a well-informed, productive workforce.

The concept of systematically coding and transmitting knowledge in organizations is not new—training and employee development programs have served this function for years. The integration of such explicit knowledge involves few problems because of its inherent communicability (Grant, 1996). Explicit knowledge is that knowledge that is transmitted in formal systematic language (Nonaka, 1994). It is externally documented tacit knowledge (Brown & Duguid, 1991). It is declarative and procedural knowledge which can be divorced from the context in which it is originally created and transferred to various other contexts with little if any modification. Advances in information technology have greatly facilitated the integration of explicit knowledge through increasing the ease with which explicit knowledge can be codified, communicated, assimilated, stored, and retrieved (Huber, 1991). However, what has in the past proved elusive—that context-dependent knowledge obtained by professional workers (referred to as "tacit

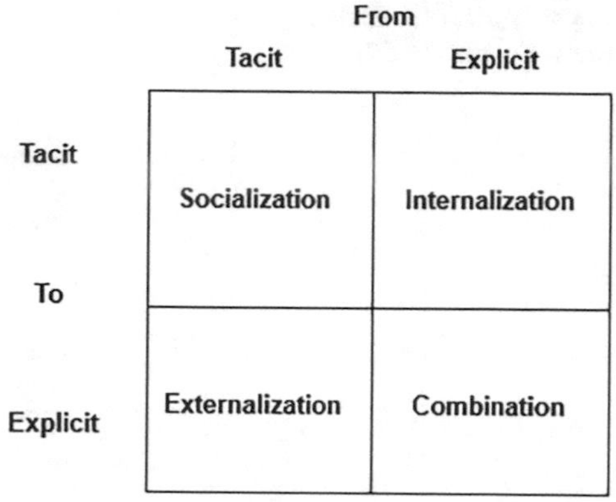

Fig. 1 The knowledge creation process [from Nonaka (1994)]

	From Tacit	From Explicit
To Tacit	Socialization	Internalization
To Explicit	Externalization	Combination

knowledge" (Nonaka, 1994)—is a focus of KMS. Figure 1 classifies knowledge creation into tacit and explicit, based on Nonaka (1994).

Nonaka focused on knowledge creation, although the knowledge management process must give equal attention to knowledge storage, knowledge distribution, and knowledge integration in order to achieve significant organizational improvements (Alavi & Leidner, 1999). Indeed, the major challenge of tacit knowledge is less its creation than its integration (Grant, 1996; Davenport, 1997a); such knowledge is of limited organizational value if it is not shared. With KMS, it is not sufficient that users use the system, they must actively contribute their knowledge. This is a large departure from previous information systems where user involvement was needed primarily at the analysis and design phase, not the content provision phase. Moreover, such systems make information readily available at a low cost across functions and business units, hence implying the capacity for an integration of information even if the functions and units themselves remain unintegrated.

While there is not yet empirical evidence of the organizational impacts of KMS, preliminary descriptive research suggests that KMS may require a change in organizational culture and that the values and culture of an organization have a significant impact on the learning process and how effectively a company can adapt and change (Sata, 1989). Respondents in the Alavi and Leidner (1999) study suggested that the information and technology components of knowledge management constituted only 20% of the challenge whereas overcoming organizational cultural barriers accounted for the major part of effective knowledge management initiatives. Similarly over half the respondents in Skyrme and Amidon (1997) recognize that corporate culture represents the biggest obstacle to knowledge transfer and a similar proportion believe that changing peoples' behaviors represents the biggest challenge to its continuing management.

Junnarkar and Brown (1997) suggest that knowledge managers interested in the role of IT as an enabler of knowledge management should not simply focus on how to connect people with information but how to develop an organizational environment conducive to tacit knowledge sharing. Similarly, Newman (1997) sees

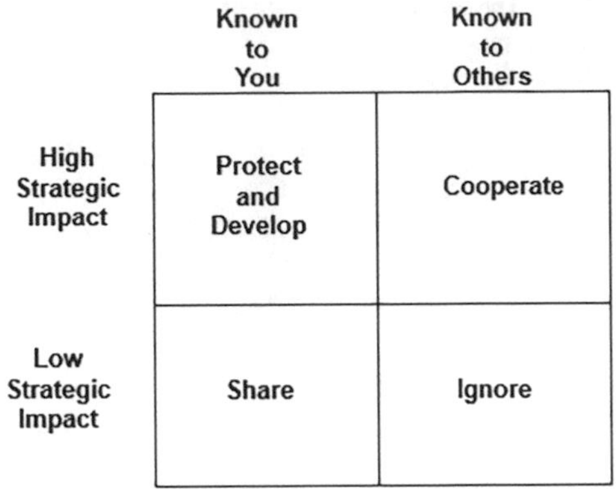

Fig. 2 The Johari window
[from Newman (1997)]

	Known to You	Known to Others
High Strategic Impact	Protect and Develop	Cooperate
Low Strategic Impact	Share	Ignore

information hoarding behavior resulting from perceptions of the strategic value of information. His modified Johari Window (see Fig. 2) provides a view of when individuals are likely to cooperate and when they are unlikely to do so.

Poor communication between people can be a major barrier to learning. In many organizations, information and knowledge are not considered organizational resources to be shared, but individual competitive weapons to be kept private (Davenport, 1997b). Organizational members may share personal knowledge with a certain trepidation—the perceived threat that they are of less value if their knowledge is part of the organizational public domain. Research in organizational learning and knowledge management suggest that some facilitating conditions include trust, interest, and shared language (Hanssen-Bauer & Snow, 1996), fostering access to knowledgeable members (Brown & Duguid, 1991), and a culture marked by autonomy, redundancy, requisite variety, intention, and fluctuation (Nonaka, 1994).

Hence, in understanding the potential impact of KMS on organizations, it is first necessary to understand the cultural implications of such systems. We would argue that the division of knowledge creation into tacit versus explicit, while interesting, does little to advance our understanding of the users' view of the knowledge or information included in KMS. The Johari Window of knowledge sharing likewise does not explicitly deal with the users' view of their own knowledge (except to classify apparent knowledge as "high or low in strategic value" although it is unclear if this is value to the individual, organization, or both). If we consider the user as a contributor of information to the KMS, we can think of information as having a certain value to the user as an individual asset and a certain degree of value as a corporate asset. This is depicted in a simple matrix in Fig. 3.

According to Fig. 3, we would expect certain individuals to share knowledge willingly, others to hoard knowledge, others to be indifferent (labeled random sharing), and others to engage in selective sharing. Moreover, it should be noted that certain types of knowledge will be viewed differently than other types of knowledge. For example, explicit knowledge such as a company training manual is unlikely to be perceived as valuable as an individual asset. However, the very type of knowledge that KMS are designed to amalgamate—tacit knowledge such as lessons learned

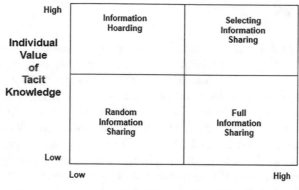

Fig. 3 Information culture matrix

on a project—is likely to be the type of knowledge with the greatest potential for being viewed as an individual asset. One could try to classify various categories of knowledge into the four quadrants; for our propositions, we will consider the primary challenge of knowledge management to be that of fostering the sharing of tacit knowledge.

Based on the above discussion and Fig. 3, we would venture the following propositions:

Proposition 1 Individuals perceiving their tacit knowledge to be high in individual value and high in corporate value will engage in selective sharing, sharing that knowledge that might bring recognition and reward to them but concealing that knowledge that might be successfully used by others with no reward for them.

Proposition 2 Individuals perceiving their tacit knowledge to be high in individual value and low in corporate value will engage in information hoarding, choosing to avoid sharing their knowledge but attempting to learn as much as possible from others.

Proposition 3 Individuals perceiving their tacit knowledge to be low in individual value and high in corporate value will engage in information sharing, sharing freely with others for the benefit of the organization.

Proposition 4 Individuals perceiving their tacit knowledge to be low in individual value and low in corporate value will engage in random sharing, sharing freely when their knowledge is requested but not consciously sharing otherwise.

In determining the factors that might influence information culture (i.e., the perceptions on the value of tacit knowledge to the individual and to the organization), an understanding of corporate culture is in order. This will be discussed in Sect. 4.

3.4 Summary

New classes of information systems for managers and professionals are continuing to emerge, yet the perennial problem of obtaining systematic benefits from
such systems remains. IS researchers have attempted to explain the impact of
IS on organizations by considering the effect of IS on organizational structure
and decision-making. The former line of research led to mixed findings and the
latter, findings more at the individual than organizational level. With the changes
in systems, summarized in Table 1, the role of the user has progressed from
involvement in system design (MIS), to in many cases system designer (DSS), to
interactive system user (EIS), to information content provider (KMS). This shift
in the role of the user requires a concomitant shift in our conceptualization of
information systems with less emphasis on the "systems" aspect and more on the
"information" aspect, namely the users' view of information as an individual or
corporate asset. Information has been classified according to its accuracy, timeliness,
reliability, completeness, precision, conciseness, currency, format, accessibility, and
perceived usefulness (Delone & McLean, 1992). Previous systems' design focused
on these aspects as the foundation of information quality. What is missing is an
understanding of the information culture issue. As we have seen, the latest class of
systems requires far greater activity of users in not just information requirements
processes, but in supplying information for the system.

Moreover, we seem to have moved from a "one for all" to a "one for one"
to an "anyone anytime anywhere" information provision strategy as we have
advanced from MIS to DSS and EIS, to KMS. The latter strategy requires
greater horizontal and vertical integration of information in an organization. It
is arguable that the potential impact of systems is greater when a larger part of
the organization is affected, such as with systems integrated organization-wide,
or even across organizations. Yet the greater the required integration, the greater
the potential implementation difficulties. As the degree of horizontal integration
increases, we would expect structural constraints. For example, enterprise-wide
systems are transaction-based systems that most effectively operate in environments
with horizontal coordination. In organizations where little horizontal coordination
existed, i.e., where units were highly decentralized, we would expect greater
implementation challenges than in already centralized organizations. Likewise,
vertical integration is expected to pose control challenges. In loosely formalized
organizations, for example, email systems would not be expected to pose threats
to power distributions (in that employees can easily communicate upward without
hesitation) but in rigidly formalized organizations, the possibility of lower-level
employees by-passing individuals in the hierarchy via electronic communication
might create difficulties. Systems requiring both vertical and horizontal integration
will create the greatest cultural challenges for organizations (see Fig. 4). We will
next examine organizational culture and its implication for KMS implementation.

Table 1 Summary of information-based systems

	MIS	DSS	EIS	KMS
Purpose:	Provide summarized performance reports to management	Provide tools, models, and data for aid in decision analysis	Provide online access to real-time financial and operational information	Provide online access to understand information and knowledge throughout the organization
Users:	Managers at various levels	Analyst and middle managers	Senior and middle managers	Professionals and managers throughout an organization
Role of users:	Participation in design	Participation as designer, active user	Participation in design, active user	Participation in design, active user, content provider
Information strategy:	All-for-all	One-for-one	One-for-one	Anyone, anytime, anywhere
Interpretive framework:	Organizational structure	Organizational decision-making	Organizational decision-making	Organizational culture

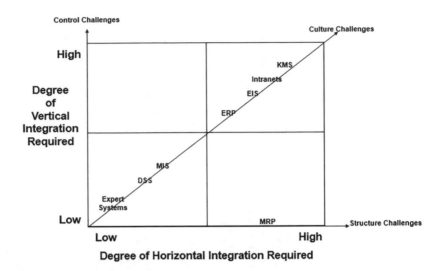

Fig. 4 Systems and organizational integration

4   Organizational Culture and Its Implication for KMS

Schein (1996) defines organizational culture as "the set of shared, taken-for-granted implicit assumptions that a group holds and that determine how it perceives, thinks about, and reacts to its various environments." Burack (1991) defines culture as the "organization's customary way of doing things and the philosophies and assumptions underlying these," and Johnson (1992), as "the core set of beliefs and assumptions which fashion an organization's view of itself." These are similar to Hofstede's (1980, 1991) definition of national culture as the "collective program-ming of the mind that distinguishes one group of people from another." Culture is hence viewed as a shared mental model which influences how individuals interpret behaviors and behave themselves, often without their being aware of the underlying assumptions. Schein (1996) states that the members of a culture are generally unaware of their own culture until they encounter a different one.

Culture is manifested in rituals and routines, stories and myths, symbols, power structures, organizational structures, and control systems (Johnson, 1992). Whereas a wealth of inconclusive contingency research examines the appropriate structure and technology in various environments to maximize organizational effectiveness, we are only now beginning to see research aimed at determining the contribution of organizational culture to organizational effectiveness. Part of the reason for this has been the difficulty of categorizing and measuring organizational cultures. Furthermore, there may have been an unstated view that cultures evolve and are beyond the control of organizational decision-makers; hence, research focused on more malleable constructs such as structure, technology, and decision-making processes.

In the organizational culture literature, culture is examined either as a set of assumptions or as a set of behaviors. Behaviors, or norms, are a fairly visible manifestation of the mental assumptions, although some argue that the behaviors should be considered "organizational climate" and the norms, as comprising organizational culture. We will present a brief discussion of both the values and behavioral perspectives of culture.

4.1   The Value View

Denison and Mishra (1995) studied the impact of organizational culture on organizational effectiveness and looked for a broad set of cultural traits that were linked to effectiveness in various environments. Denison and Mishra suggested that, from a values perspective, culture could be thought of as including degrees of external versus internal integration and tradeoffs of change and flexibility with stability and direction. They classified cultures as being adaptability oriented, involvement oriented, mission oriented, or consistency oriented. Their classification is drawn from Quinn and Rohrbaugh's (1983) value set which argued that organizations focus to various degrees internally or externally, and, in terms of structure preferences, have tradeoffs in stability and control versus flexibility and change.

Denison and Mishra found that in two of four organizations studied, organizational effectiveness appeared to be tied to consistency and mission, yet the cases also seemed to support the idea that involvement oriented cultures led to organizational effectiveness. In a survey, Denison and Mishra found that mission and consistency, traits of stability, predicted profitability whereas involvement and adaptability, traits of flexibility, predicted sales growth.

Chatman and Jehn (1994) argue that organizational cultures within a given industry tend to deviate very little; in other words, they argue that the environment dictates to a certain extent cultures in organizations (at least for organizations that survive in the industry). A problem with Denison and Mishra's study is its inability to consider the effect of the environment on cultures given that there was not sufficient industrial variation in the sample. Thus, we are unable to deduce if the environment might have influenced their findings.

Hofstede et al. (1990) examined culture both in terms of values and behaviors. In terms of value, they found that organizational culture was tied to the national culture dimensions identified by Hofstede (1980) and reflected preferences for centralized versus decentralized decision-making (power distance), preferences for the degree of formalization of routines (uncertainty avoidance), degree of concern over money and career versus family and cooperation (masculinity/femininity dimension), and degree of identification with the company and preference for individual versus group reward systems (collectivistic/individualistic dimension). When the authors eliminated the effects due to nationality, the value differences between organizations were primarily dependent upon subunit characteristics rather than overall membership in the organization. Hence, the authors concluded that organizational subunits were the more appropriate level of analysis for organizational culture study. Moreover, they found that behaviors were a better means of distinguishing subunit cultures than were value systems.

4.2   The Behavioral Perspective

Although popular literature insists that shared values represent the core of organizational culture, the empirical data from Hofstede et al. (1990) showed shared perceptions of daily practices formed the core of organizational subunit culture. The behavioral dimensions isolated by the authors were:

1. process versus results oriented: this dimension refers to a focus on improving the means by which organizational goals are achieved (process) as opposed to a focus on the attainment of goals.
2. employee vs. job oriented: employee orientation suggests a concern for people whereas a job orientation refers to a concern over performing tasks effectively.
3. parochial vs. professional: a parochial orientation suggests that individuals are loyal to their organization whereas a professional orientation suggests that individuals are loyal to their profession.
4. open vs. closed system: this dimension describes the communication climate in the subunit.
5. loose vs. tight control: the control dimension reflects the degree of internal structuring, with loose organizations having few written or unwritten codes of behavior and tight organizations having strict unwritten and written policies.
6. normative vs. pragmatic: pragmatic units are market driven and customer oriented whereas normative units are product oriented. Interestingly, some units were found to be pragmatic but not results oriented (i.e., a goal of improving customer service might not imply a goal of improving the bottom line).

The process/results, parochial/professional, loose/tight, and normative/pragmatic were found to relate partly to the industry, confirming Chatman and Jehn's (1994) conclusion that industry or environmental factors more generally affects organizational cultures, whereas the employee/job orientation and open/closed system were more determined by the philosophy of the founders and senior managers. These latter dimensions might therefore be more malleable.

In considering the possible influence of the behavioral dimensions of subunit culture on information culture, one dimension in particular appears more relevant to predicting the quality of the knowledge contributed to a system rather than to predicting the value placed on the knowledge. Specifically, loose versus tight control might influence whether individuals follow organizational rules and procedures about sharing knowledge but would not necessarily influence their beliefs about whether the knowledge was properly theirs or the organization's and hence, might influence the quality of the knowledge they elected to contribute to a system but would not likely influence their attitude about the value of that knowledge to them or

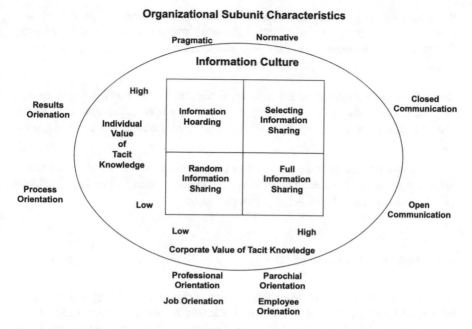

Fig. 5 Subunit and information culture relationship

the organization. We, therefore, do not include this dimension in predictions about the influence of subunit culture on information culture. If we map the remaining dimensions into Fig. 3 to form Fig. 5, we might expect that certain of these subunit cultural behaviors would tend to foster the view of tacit knowledge as an individual asset whereas others would encourage viewing tacit knowledge as a corporate asset.

Proposition 5 Individuals in subunits characterized by a results orientation will view tacit knowledge largely as an individual asset whereas individuals in subunits characterized by a process orientation will view tacit information less as an individual asset.

Proposition 6 Individuals in subunits characterized by a professional orientation will view tacit knowledge less as a corporate asset whereas individuals in subunits characterized by a parochial orientation will view tacit knowledge more as a corporate asset.

Proposition 7 Individuals in subunits characterized by an open communication culture will view tacit knowledge less as an individual asset whereas individuals in subunits characterized by a closed communication climate will view tacit knowledge more as an individual asset.

Proposition 8 Individuals in subunits characterized by a pragmatic culture will view tacit knowledge less as a corporate asset whereas individuals in subunits characterized by a normative culture will view tacit knowledge more as a corporate asset.

Proposition 9 Individuals in subunits characterized by an employee culture will view tacit knowledge more as a corporate asset whereas individuals in subunits characterized by a job orientation will view tacit knowledge less as a corporate asset.

The above propositions are intended to predict the possible influence of subunit cultural factors on information culture. A final consideration will be the dimension of culture at the individual level, as discussed next.

4.3   *Individual Cultures*

Although Hofstede et al. (1990) discount the utility of considering culture at the individual level, others propose that individual-level cultures interact either synchronously or disharmoniously with organizational culture (Patterson et al., 1996; Chatman & Barsade, 1995). Chatman and Barsade (1995) examined individual-level culture in organizations using the individualistic/collectivistic dimension of culture which has been the topic of extensive communication research at the individual level of analysis (Gudykunst et al., 1996).

Individualism versus collectivism was first identified by Hofstede (1980) as a dimension distinguishing national cultures. Individualism is the preference for a loosely knit social framework in society in which individuals are supposed to take care of themselves and their immediate family as opposed to collectivism in which there is a larger in-group to which is given unquestioning loyalty (Hofstede, 1980). Individualism is related to a low-context communication style wherein individuals prefer information to be stated directly and exhibit a preference for quantifiable detail whereas collectivism is related to a high-context communication style in which individuals prefer to draw inferences from non-explicit or implicit information (Hall, 1976; Gudykunst, 1997). In individualistic cultures, the needs, values, and goals of the individual take precedence over the needs, values, and goals of the ingroup. In collectivistic cultures, the needs, values, and goals of the ingroup take precedence over the needs, values, and goals of the individual (Gudykunst, 1997; Hofstede, 1980). Research suggests that those who are associated with individualistic values tend to be less concerned with self-categorizing, are less influenced by group memberships, and have greater skills in entering and leaving new groups than individuals from collectivist cultures (Hofstede, 1980; Hall, 1976). Individualistic values are associated with preferences for individual rewards (or a norm of justice, meaning that an individual is rewarded according to his/her input rather than a norm of equality in which all individuals who work as a group are rewarded equally) (Gudykunst & Ting-Toomey, 1988).

Earley (1994) argued that organizations could also be thought of as being dominantly individualistic or collectivist. Organizations encouraging individuals to pursue and maximize individuals' goals and rewarding performance based on individual achievement would be considered as having an individualistic culture whereas organizations placing priority on collective goals and joint contributions and rewards for organizational accomplishments would be considered collectivist (Chatman & Barsade, 1995).

On an individual level, Chatman and Barsade (1995) propose that workplace cooperation—the willful contribution of employee effort to the successful completion of interdependent tasks—is as much dependent on individual culture as organizational culture. They suggest that individuals with cooperative dispositions place priority on working together with others toward a common purpose while persons with a low cooperative disposition place priority on maximizing their own welfare irrespective of others. Cooperative persons are more motivated to understand and uphold group norms and expect others to cooperate whereas individualistic people are more concerned with personal goals and expect others to behave in like manner. Chatman and Barsade (1995) proposed that people who have a high disposition to cooperate and who work in a collectivistic organizational culture will be the most cooperative while people who have a low disposition to cooperate and who work in an individualistic culture will be the least cooperative. This may suggest that individualistic cultures are results oriented and tend to be closed whereas cooperative cultures are process oriented and tend to be open. It might be that cooperative people in a cooperative culture could be more willing to share tacit knowledge than individualistic individuals in a cooperative culture or cooperative individuals in an individualistic culture. When mapped into Fig. 3, we would expect the following influence of individual culture on information culture (see Fig. 6):

If we consider the relationship between individual-level culture, subunit culture, and information culture, we propose the following:

Proposition 10 Individualistic individuals in collectivistic organizational subunits will engage in selective sharing of tacit knowledge.

Proposition 11 Cooperative individuals in collectivistic organizational subunits will engage in full sharing of tacit knowledge.

Proposition 12 Individualistic individuals in individualistic organizational subunits will engage in hoarding of tacit knowledge.

Proposition 13 Cooperative individuals in individualistic organizational subunits will engage in random sharing of tacit knowledge.

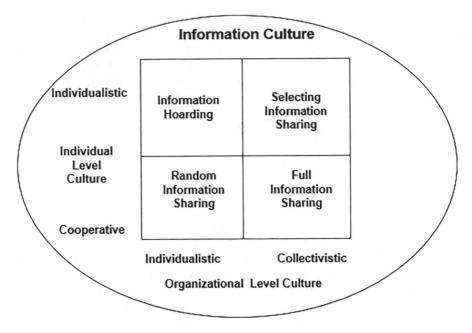

Fig. 6 Individual culture's relationship to information culture

4.4 *Summary*

This section has presented a brief summary of organizational subunit cultures and has made propositions concerning the relationship of subunit culture and individual culture with the information culture discussed in Sect. 3. The propositions, in abbreviated form, are summarized in Table 2.

The above propositions reflect an organizational imperative—that organizational factors, in this case organizational subunit and individual culture, influence the successful implementation and use of knowledge management systems. It is also conceivable that KMS will affect organizational cultures (a technology imperative). There is evidence that as systems integrate information vertically and horizontally, organizational cultures are altered. For example, in the case of EIS, it has been found that by virtue of the fact that top managers are viewing detailed daily information previously viewed in monthly or weekly reports in a summarized fashion, all levels in the organization take notice of the information being tracked by the senior managers and alter their behavior in such a manner as to focus on the measures being examined by the top managers. In some cases, this was part of a planned attempt to help focus the attention of employees on the factors considered most critical by the top managers (Carlsson et al., 1996). Over time, the underlying values might shift to become consistent with the new behavior. KMS are being implemented in a time of increasing global competition and the need to be "flexible"; as such, part of the implementation goal may be directed toward enabling a more flexible,

Table 2 Summary of propositions

Nature of proposition	Proposition number	Proposition (abbreviated)
Information culture	1	Individuals perceiving their tacit knowledge as high in individual and corporate value will engage in selective sharing of tacit knowledge.
	2	Individuals perceiving their tacit knowledge as high in individual and low in corporate value will engage in information hoarding.
	3	Individuals perceiving their tacit knowledge as low in individual and high in corporate value will engage in full sharing.
	4	Individuals perceiving their tacit knowledge as low in individual and corporate value will engage in random sharing.
Organization subunit culture influence on information culture	5	Results, as opposed to process, oriented subunits will foster a view of tacit knowledge as an individual asset.
	6	Parochial, as opposed to professional, oriented cultures will foster a view of tacit knowledge as a corporate asset.
	7	Closed, as opposed to open, subunit communication climates will foster a view of tacit knowledge as an individual asset.
	8	Normative, as opposed to pragmatic, oriented cultures will foster a view of tacit knowledge as a corporate asset.
	9	Employee, as opposed to job, oriented cultures will foster a view of tacit knowledge as a corporate asset.
Individual and organizational culture influence on information culture	10	Individualistic individuals in collectivistic cultures will engage in selective sharing of tacit knowledge.
	11	Cooperative individuals in collectivistic cultures will engage in full sharing of tacit knowledge.
	12	Individualistic individuals in individualistic cultures will engage in hoarding of tacit knowledge.
	13	Cooperative individuals in individualistic cultures will engage in random sharing of tacit knowledge.

adaptable culture. In this case, by implementing the system and inculcating desired sharing behaviors, over time the organizational culture may itself become more open, flexible, and employee oriented. However, the current article purports to evaluate the constraints posed by organizational culture on the implementation of KMS rather than the potential long-term consequences of KMS on organizational culture. The latter interesting question is left for future research.

5 · Implications and Conclusion

It can be argued that the first step in developing an implementation plan is understanding where barriers might be encountered and why. The above analysis is intended to help evaluate where and why such barriers might exist when implementing KMS. Several strategies for KMS implementation have been suggested: one strategy is to include information of high value such as corporate directories which make users comfortable with, and dependent upon, the corporate intranet. Another is education on the need and potential of such a system to improve individual productivity and customer service. Another commonly used strategy is providing rewards and incentives, such as bonuses, based on the amount and quality of knowledge one contributes. The strategy used to implement KMS should be tied to the organizational subunit culture. For example, individuals in reward-oriented subunits might respond well to incentive systems whereas individuals in process-oriented subunits might require greater education and training on the benefits of such a system. Furthermore, changes in reward systems will do little to change the information culture; in which case, at most, we would expect that subunit cultures which foster a view of knowledge as a high individual asset (results-oriented, professional-oriented subunits) will be able to encourage selective information sharing but not the full sharing of the most valuable of tacit knowledge. To obtain full sharing in subunits that are results oriented, closed, professional oriented, and job oriented, the change management plan might need to first focus on changing the culture and only secondly, on implementing the system. It would be misleading to think that the system would encourage full sharing in organizations where the information culture ran contrary to such sharing, just as it has been found that electronic mail systems do not encourage greater communication among subunits with infrequent, irregular communication (Vandenbosch & Ginzberg, 1997). However, in organizations with cultures that foster the attitude of tacit knowledge as primarily a corporate asset, it would be expected that KMS could be implemented with little resistance.

This article has taken the view that organizational effectiveness in the highly competitive global environment will depend largely on an organization's capacity to manage individual employee knowledge. We have argued that knowledge management systems will be important computer-based information system components to such effectiveness but that the success of these systems will depend on an appropriate match with organizational subunit and individual culture. The article has offered propositions in an attempt to provide a framework for understanding where potential incongruity between these new IS and organizational culture might exist.

One way to consider the advances of information-based systems in organizations is to consider the dominant organizational theory underlying the assumptions of the need for information. The era of MIS can be thought to correspond to the organizational theory termed the "information processing view of the organization" This view posited that organizations process information to reduce uncertainty—the absence of information and to reduce equivocality—the existence of multiple and conflicting interpretations about an organizational situation (Daft & Lengel, 1986). According to this view, information systems are needed to help organizations understand the environment and make appropriate plans in response. As DSS and EIS came into vogue, so was the information-processing view of the firm replaced with the decision-making view of the firm espoused by Huber and McDaniel (1986) wherein decision-making was seen as the most critical managerial activity. This view placed the primary purpose of IS as supporting organizational decision-makers by providing tools, timely information, and ready access to important operational and financial information. More recently, it is being argued that the most critical organizational activity is creating, sharing, and utilizing the knowledge that resides in employees (Nonaka, 1994). To understand the potential organizational effect of systems designed to harness knowledge, it is argued that the traditional paradigms of structure and decision-making are insufficient, but a perspective incorporating organizational culture is needed.

The major intent of the article has been to encourage thinking about the important topic of current IS and its relationship to organizational culture rather than to offer a complete set of guidelines on implementing KMS or evaluating the effectiveness of KMS in given organizational cultures. It is hoped that the reader leaves with a framework for assessing the potential conflicts resulting from cultural factors that may arise with the implementation of knowledge management systems and can use the frameworks proposed in this chapter to guide thinking on potential implementation strategies.

References

Alavi, M., & Leidner, D. (1999). Knowledge management systems: issues, challenges, and benefits. *Communications of the AIS, 1*, article 7. http://cais.isworld.org/

Alavi, M., Kayworth, T., & Leidner, D. (2005–2006). An empirical examination of the influence of organizational culture on knowledge management practices. *Journal of Management Information Systems, 22*(3), 191–224.

Applegate, L. M. (1987). *Lockheed-Georgia company: executive information systems*, Harvard Case (9-187-147). Harvard Business School.

Applegate, L. M., & Osborn, C. S. (1988). *Phillips 66 company: Executive information systems*, Harvard Case (9-189-006). Harvard Business School.

Bacharach, S. B. (1989). Organizational theories: some criteria for evaluation. *Academy of Management Review, 14*(4), 496–515. https://doi.org/10.5465/AMR.1989.4308374

Barley, S. R. (2006). When I write my masterpiece: thoughts on what makes a paper interesting. *Academy of Management Journal., 49*(1), 16–20.

Bartunek, J. M., Rynes, S. L., & Ireland, R. D. (2006). What makes management research interesting, and why does it matter? *Academy of Management Journal, 49*(1), 9–15.

Bergh, D. D. (2003). Thinking strategically about contribution. *Academy of Management Journal., 46*(2), 135–136.

Brown, J. S., & Duguid, P. (1991). Organizational learning and communities-of-practice: Toward a unified view of working, learning, and innovation. *Organization Science, 2*(1), 40–57.

Burack, E. (1991). Changing the company culture – the role of human resource development. *Long Range Planning, 24*(1), 88–95.

Burton-Jones, A., McLean, E. R., & Monod, E. (2015). Theoretical perspectives in IS research: From variance and process to conceptual latitude and conceptual fit. *European Journal of Information Systems, 24*(6), 664–679.

Carlsson, S., Leidner, D. E., & Elam, J. J. (1996). Individual and organizational effectiveness: perspectives on the impact of ESS in multinational organizations. In P. Humphreys et al. (Eds.), *Implementing systems for supporting management decisions.* Chapman and Hall.

Carter, N. M. (1984). *Computerization as a predominate technology: Its influence on the structure of newspaper organizations* (Vol. 27, pp. 247–270). Academy of Management Journal.

Chatman, J. A., & Barsade, S. G. (1995). Personality, organizational culture, and cooperation: Evidence from business simulation. *Administrative Science Quarterly, 40*, 423–443.

Chatman, J., & Jehn, K. (1994). Assessing the relationship between industry characteristics and organizational culture: How different can you be? *Academy of Management Journal, 37*(3), 522–553.

Chipidza, W., & Leidner, D. (2019). A review of the ICT-enabled development literature: towards a power parity theory of ICT4. *Journal of Strategic Information Systems, 28*(2), 145–174.

Cortese, A. (1996). Here comes the intranet. *Business Week, 26*, 76–84.

Corley, K. G., & Gioia, D. A. (2011). Building theory about theory building: What constitutes a theoretical contribution? *Academy of Management Review, 36*(1), 12–32. https://doi.org/10.5465/amr.2009.0486

Daft, R. L., & Lengel, R. H. (1986). Organizational information requirements, media richness and structural design. *Management Science, 32*(5), 554–571.

Davenport, T. H. (1997a). *Knowledge management at Ernst and Young, 1997.* http://knowman.bus.utexas.edu/E&Y.htm

Davenport, T. H. (1997b). *Some principles of knowledge management.* http://knowman.bus.utexas.edu/kmprin.htm

Davis, M. S. (1971). That's interesting! Towards a phenomenology of sociology and a sociology of phenomenology. *Philosophy of the Social Sciences, 1*(2), 309–344.

Dawson, P., & McLaughlin, I. (1986). Computer technology and the redefinition of supervision: A study of the effects of computerization on railway freight supervisors. *Journal of Management Studies, 23*, 116–132.

Delone, W. H., & McLean, E. R. (1992). Information systems success: The quest for the dependent variable. *Information Systems Research, 3*, 60–95.

Denison, D., & Mishra, A. (1995). Toward a theory of organizational culture and effectiveness. *Organization Science, 6*(2), 204–223.

DiMaggio, P. J. (1995). Comments on 'what theory is not'. *Administrative Science Quarterly, 40:3*, 391. https://doi.org/10.2307/2393790

Earley, P. C. (1994). Self or group? Cultural effects of training on self-efficacy and performance. *Administrative Science Quarterly, 39*, 89–117.

Elliott, D. *Executive information systems: Their impact on executive decision making.* Doctoral Dissertation. The University of Texas at Austin, May, 1992.

Feldman, D. (2004). What are we talking about when we talk about theory? *Journal of Management, 30*(5), 565–567. https://doi.org/10.1016/j.jm.2004.05.001

Foster, L. W. & Flynn, D. M. Management information technology: Its effects on organizational form and function. *MIS Quarterly*, December 1984 (pp. 229–236).

Franz, C., Robey, D., & Koeblitz, R. (1986). User response to an online IS: A field experiment. *MIS Quarterly, 10*(1), 29–44.

Friend, D. *Helping corporate executives wade through data to find information.* Datacommunications, September 1986.

George, J., & Leidner, D. (2019). From clicktivism to hacktivism: understanding digital activism. *Information and Organization, 29*(3), 100249.

Grant, R. M. (1996). Prospering in dynamically-competitive environments: organizational capability as knowledge integration. *Organ Sci, 7*(4), 375–387.

Gregor, S. (2006). The nature of theory in information systems. *MIS Quarterly, 30*(3), 611–642.

Gregory, R. W., & Henfridsson, O. (2021). Bridging art and science: phenomenon-driven theorizing. *Journal of the Association for Information Systems, 22*(6), 1509–1523. https://doi.org/10.17705/1jais.00703

Gudykunst, W. B. (1997). Cultural variability in communication. *Communication Research, 24*(4), 327–348.

Gudykunst, W. B., & Ting-Toomey, S. (1988). *Culture and interpersonal communication.* Sage.

Gudykunst, W. B., Matsumoto, Y., Ting-Toomey, S., Nishida, T., Linda, K. S., & Heyman, S. (1996). The influence of cultural individualism-collectivism, self construals, and individual values on communication styles across cultures. *Human Communication Research, 22*, 510–543.

Hall, E. T. (1976). *Beyond culture.* Anchor Books/Doubleday.

Hanssen-Bauer, J., & Snow, C. C. (1996). Responding to hypercompetition: The structure and processes of a regional learning network organization. *Organ Sci, 7*(4), 413–237.

Heinzl, A., & Leidner, D. E. (2012). Information systems and culture. *Business and Information Systems Engineering, 4*(3), 109.

Hemmer, E., Heinzl, A., & Leidner, D. (2014). Foregrounding the "I" in IS Research: A plea for research on computer-mediated human information behaviour. *Working Paper Series in Information Systems* 14.

Hofstede, G. (1980). *Culture's consequences.* Sage.

Hofstede, G. (1991). *Cultures and organizations: Software of the mind.* McGraw-Hill.

Hofstede, G., Neuijen, B., Ohayv, D. D., & Sanders, G. (1990). Measuring organizational cultures: A qualitative and quantitative study cross twenty cases. *Administrative Science Quarterly, 35*, 286–316.

Hogue, J. T. (1987). A framework for the examination of management involvement in decision support systems. *Journal of Management Information Systems, 4*(1).

Holub, A. *What happens when info regarding the quality of a bank's services become visible, July 1988 EIS Conference Report,* Vol. 1, no. 4.

Houdeshel, G., & Watson, H. The MIDS system at lockheed-Georgia. *MIS Quarterly,* March 1987.

Huber, G. P. (1990). A theory of the effects of advanced information technologies on organizational design, intelligence, and decision making. *Academy of Management Review, 15*(1), 47–71.

Huber, G. (1991). Organizational learning: The contributing processes and the literatures. *Organization Science, 2*(1), 88–115.

Huber, G. P., & McDaniel, R. R. (1986). The decision-making paradigm of organizational design. *Management Science, 32*(5), 572–589.

Ives, B., & Olson, M. (1984). User involvement and MIS success: A review of research. *Management Science, 30*(5), 586–603.

Johnson, G. (1992). Managing strategic change–strategy, culture and action. *Long Range Planning, 25*(1), 28–36.

Junnarkar, B., & Brown, C. V. (1997). Re-assessing the enabling role of IT in knowledge management. *Journal of Knowledge Management, 1*(2), 142–148.

Kador, J. (1988). ESSs keep execs in control. *Planner, 11*(2).

Keen, P. G. W., & Morton, M. S. S. (1982). *Decision support systems: An organizational perspective.* Addison-Wesley.

King, W., & Rodriguez, J. (1981). Participative design of strategic DSS. *Management Science, 27*(6), 717–726.

Klatzky, S. R. (1970). Automation, size, and the locus of decision making: The cascade effect. *Journal of Business, 43*, 141–151.

Laudon, K., & Laudon, J. (1997). *Essentials of management information systems* (2nd ed.). Prentice Hall.

Le Blanc, L. A., & K. A. Kozar (1990). An empirical investigation of the relationship between DSS usage and system performance: A case study of a navigation support system. *MIS Quarterly* (pp. 263–277).

Lee, A. S. (2014). Theory is king? But first, what is theory? *Journal of Information Technology, 29*(4), 350–352. https://doi.org/10.1057/jit.2014.23

Leidner, D. E. (1992). *Reasons for EIS failure: An analysis by phase of development.* Working paper, Baylor University.

Leidner, D. E. (1998a). *Understanding information culture: Integrating knowledge management systems into organizations.* INSEAD Working Paper. Flora.INSEAD.edu.

Leidner, D. E. (1998b). *Personal interview.*

Leidner, D. E. (2020). What's in a Contribution?. *Journal of the Association for Information Systems, 21*(1), 2.

Leidner, D. E., & Elam, J. J. (1995). The impact of executive information systems on organizational design, intelligence, and decision making. *Organization Science, 6*(6), 645–665.

Leidner, D., & Jarvenpaa, S. (1995). The use of information technology to improve management education: The theoretical view. *MIS Quarterly, 19*(3), 265–292.

Leidner, D., & Kayworth, T. (2006). A review of culture in information systems research: Towards a theory of IT-culture conflict. *MIS Quarterly, 30*(2), 357–399.

Leidner, D., & Tona, O. (2021a). The CARE theory of dignity amid personal data digitalization. *MIS Quarterly, 45*(1), 343–370.

Leidner, D. E., & Tona, O. (2021b). A thought-gear model of theorizing from literature. *Journal of the Association for Information Systems, 22*(4), 874–892. https://doi.org/10.17705/1jais.00683

LePine, J. A., & King, A. S. (2010). Developing novel theoretical insight from reviews of existing theory and research. *Academy of Management Review., 35*(4), 506–509.

Lyytinen, K., & Hirschheim, R. (1987). Information systems failures – A survey and classification of the empirical literature. *Oxford Surveys in Information Technology, 4*, 257–309.

Markus, L., & Benjamin, R. (1996). Change agentry – The next IS frontier. *MIS Quarterly, 20*(4), 385–408.

Mitchell, P. An EIS is good for you. *July 1988 EIS Conference Report*, Vol. 1, no. 4.

Molloy, S., & Schwenk, C. (1995). The effects of IT on strategic decision making. *Journal of Management Studies, 32*(5), 283–311.

Mowshowitz, A. (1976). *Information processing in human affairs.* Addison-Wesley.

Newman, V. (1997). Redefining knowledge management to deliver competitive advantage. *Journal of Knowledge Management, 1*(2), 123–128.

Nonaka, I. (1994). A dynamic theory of organizational knowledge creation. *Organization Science, 5*(1), 14–37.

Patterson, M., Payn, R., & West, M. (1996). Collective climates: A test of their sociopsychological significance. *Academy of Management Journal, 28*(6), 1675–1691.

Poole, M. S., & van de Ven, A. (1989). Using paradox to build management and organization theories. *Academy of Management Review., 14*(4), 562–678.

Pyburn, P. Linking the MIS plan with corporate strategy. *MIS Quarterly*, June 1983 (pp. 1–14).

Quinn, R. E., & Rohrbaugh, J. (1983). A spatial model of effectiveness criteria: Towards a competing values approach to organizational analysis. *Management Science, 29*(3), 363–377.

Ravishankar, M. N., Pan, S., & Leidner, D. E. (2011). Aligning KMS with organizational strategy: The influence of subculture. *Information Systems Research, 22*(1), 39–59.

Robey, D. (1977). Computers and management structure: Some empirical findings re-examined. *Human Relations, 30*, 963–976.

Rockart, J., & DeLong, D. (1988). *Executive support systems: The emergence of top management computer use.* Dow-Jones-Irwin.

Rooney, P. Imposing order from chaos. *INTRANETS, 2*(8), November 24, 1997, Computerworld Supplement.

Sata, R. (1989). Organizational learning – The key to management innovation. *Sloan Management Review*, Spring, pp. 63–74.

Schein, E. (1996). Culture: The missing concept in organization studies. *Administrative Science Quarterly, 41*, 229–240.

Shepherd, D. A., & Sutcliffe, K. M. (2011). Inductive top-down theorizing: A source of new theories of organization. *Academy of Management Review, 36*(2), 361–380. https://doi.org/10.5465/amr.2009.0157

Simon, H. A. (1977). *The new science of management decision*. Prentice-Hall.

Skyrme, D. J., & Amidon, D. (1997). *Creating the knowledge-based business*. Business Intelligence Limited.

Somogyi, E. K., & Galliers, R. D. (1987). Applied information technology: From data processing to strategic information systems. *Journal of Information Technology, 2*(1), 30–41. Reproduced in Galliers, R. D. & Baker, B. S. H. (Eds.) (1984). op cit., under the title "Information technology in business: from data processing to strategic information systems", pp. 9–27.

Sprague, R. H., & Carlson, E. D. (1982). *Building effective decision support systems*. Prentice Hall.

Stewart, R. (1971). *How computers affect management*. MIT Press.

Sutton, R. I., & Staw, B. M. (1995). What theory is not. *Administrative Science Quarterly, 40*(3), 371–384. https://doi.org/10.2307/2393788

Thyfault, M. E. The intranet rolls in. *InformationWeek*, 564, January 29, 1996, pp. 15, 76–78.

Todd, P., & Benbasat, I. An experimental investigation of the impact of computer-based decision aids on decision making strategies. *Information Systems Research*, June 1991 (pp. 87–115).

Vandenbosch, B., & M. J. Ginzberg (1996–1997) Lotus notes and collaboration: Plus ça change, *Journal of Management Information Systems, 13*(3), 65–82.

Vandenbosch, B., & Higgins, C. (1996). Information acquisition and mental models: An investigation into the relationship between behavior and learning. *Information Systems Research*, 198–214.

Vidal, F., Saintoyant, P. Y., & Meilhaud, J. (1998). *Objectif intranet: Enjeux et applications*. Les Editions d'Organisation.

Weick, K. E. (1989). Theory construction as disciplined imagination. *Academy of Management Review, 14*(4), 516–531.

Whetten, D. A. (1989). What constitutes a theoretical contribution? *The Academy of Management Review, 14*(4), 490–495. https://doi.org/10.2307/258554

Whisler, T. L. (1970). *The impact of computers on organizations*. Praeger Publishers.

Young, A. G., Majchrzak, A., & Kane, G. C. (2021). Reflection on writing a theory paper: How to theorize for the future. *Journal of the Association for Information Systems, 22*(5), 1212–1223.

Yourdan, E., & Constantine, L. L. (1978). *Structured design* (2nd ed.). Yourdan Press.

IT or Not IT? A Female View on Inhibiting and Promoting Factors in Young Women's Decisions for a Career in IT

Birte Malzahn, Jessica Slamka, and Daniela Scheid

Abstract Despite efforts to increase the share of women in IT, women remain largely underrepresented in higher IT education as well as in the IT workplace. Yet, in order to address the shortage of IT professionals and to enlarge diversity in the workplace, increasing the proportion of women who choose a career in IT is both an economic and societal imperative. Understanding career choice as a biographical decision-making process—rather than a one-point-in-time decision—the present work systemizes factors that inhibit young women to choose an IT career along the different phases of the career choice process. Taking these factors into account, approaches to increase girls' motivation for a career in IT are discussed. The findings indicate that a combination of different factors comes into play early in the process already when attitudes and self-concepts develop. A lack of experiences as well as gender attributions of girls' competences and of the IT profession play a decisive role. A concerted effort from childhood to young adulthood is needed to eliminate both gender and IT-related stereotypes and to provide girls and young females with relevant IT experiences, thus increasing their motivation and enabling a career choice solely on the basis of their own abilities and preferences.

B. Malzahn (✉)
Hochschule für Technik und Wirtschaft Berlin, Berlin, Germany
e-mail: Birte.Malzahn@HTW-Berlin.de

J. Slamka
Fakultät für Betriebswirtschaft, Hochschule München – University of Applied Sciences, München, Germany
e-mail: jessica.slamka@hm.edu

D. Scheid
MaibornWolff GmbH, Berlin, Germany
e-mail: daniela.scheid@maibornwolff.de

© The Author(s), under exclusive license to Springer Nature Switzerland AG 2022   109
J. Dibbern et al. (eds.), *Digitalization Across Organizational Levels*, Progress in IS,
https://doi.org/10.1007/978-3-031-06543-9_5

1 Introduction

Competences in the STEM (science, technology, engineering, and mathematics) field are seen as particularly important in order to keep pace with advancing digitalization (Bundesministerium für Bildung und Forschung, 2021). In recent years, the speed at which companies adopt new technologies is increasing, making technical skills a key element of the workplace of the future (World Economic Forum, 2020). In this respect, it can be considered problematic that the shortage of skilled workers in the IT sector in Germany is still very high (Jansen et al., 2020).

In the acquisition of required skills, a "digital gender gap" can be observed. This term describes the fact that women are underrepresented in education in the field of information and communication technology and often show a low level of interest in corresponding professions (Bollag et al., 2021). This lack of interest is problematic from an economic perspective, as it increases the shortage of skilled workers, leaving companies with great problems to fill vacant positions in the IT sector (Jansen et al., 2020). Besides the need to find more qualified IT professionals, there are other reasons why companies seek to increase the proportion of women in IT, such as an improvement in the working climate or the introduction of new ideas and point of views (Weitzel et al., 2017).

It can be deduced that there is a high economic interest in increasing the proportion of women who choose a career in IT. To achieve this goal, it is necessary to take a closer look at the reasons for women (not) choosing an IT career. What factors in which stages of life lead to this decision? And is it possible to influence these factors in the career choice process?

The following work seeks to shed light on these questions. The status quo regarding the digital gender gap in Germany is presented in Sect. 2. In Sect. 3, factors that inhibit girls in the choice of IT degree programs or IT professions are systemized along the career choice process. Taking these factors into account, Sect. 4 discusses effective approaches to increase girls' motivation for a career in IT. Section 5 summarizes the main findings and closes with a conclusion.

2 The Digital Gender Gap in Higher IT Education

Although there are no longer any formal gender-related restrictions on access to occupational fields (Micus-Loos et al., 2016), serious differences between genders in the choice of occupation can still be noted. The educational and labor market can still be differentiated into male and female occupations (Ihsen et al., 2017).

The proportion of women in various STEM subjects at the university level varies considerably (Cheryan et al., 2017). For example, among students in the winter term 2020/2021 in Germany, there are different gender distributions in the following STEM subjects, with a particularly large gap in Computer Science with less than 20% female students (see Fig. 1).

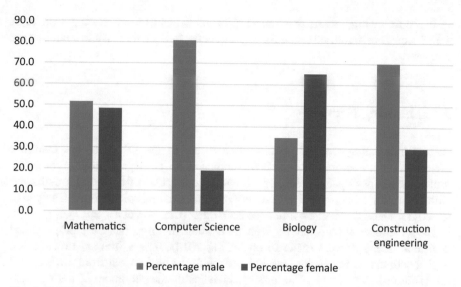

Fig. 1 Students in Germany in selected STEM subjects in winter term 2020/2021; Source: Statistisches Bundesamt (Destatis) (2021); (Own representation)

Female technology distance can be observed particularly in European industrialized nations (Esch, 2011). Boys are much more likely than girls to imagine pursuing a career in the field of information and communication technologies (Microsoft Corporation, 2017). However, the gender ratio for IT subjects in itself must be viewed in a differentiated manner, as the proportion of women in different computer science courses in Germany varies considerably. For example, the proportion of female students in the winter term 2020/2021 in Germany was 19% in engineering informatics/technical informatics, 22% in business informatics, 43% in media informatics, 45% in bioinformatics, and 49% in medical informatics (Statistisches Bundesamt (Destatis), 2021).

There are several initiatives to increase the percentage of women in STEM subjects as well as IT subjects in particular. For example, the German Federal Government is promoting qualifications in STEM subjects with a "MINT-Aktionsplan" from 2019 to 2022 with 55 million euros (Presse- und Informationsamt der Bundesregierung, 2022). The action plan includes the field "Chancen von Mädchen und Frauen in MINT" (Bundesministerium für Bildung und Forschung, 2021). Here, the Federal Ministry of Education and Research supports girls and women in discovering their own STEM abilities and in pursuing their STEM interests. Activities in this regard include the annual Girls Day—"Mädchen Zukunftstag" or the funding program "Erfolg mit MINT—Neue Chancen für Frauen" (Bundesministerium für Bildung und Forschung, 2019). Unfortunately, all initiatives so far do not seem to increase the proportion of women in the IT sector sustainably.

In the following, factors that inhibit girls and women from choosing a career in the IT sector are identified (Sect. 3). Subsequently, in Sect. 4, possible solutions are discussed.

3   Inhibiting Factors

Factors influencing women's choice of a career in the IT sector are manifold (Scheid, 2021). Factors that inhibit the choice of an IT degree program or an IT profession can be on a micro level, e.g., own experiences, self-confidence, skills and attitudes, or on a macro level, e.g. stereotypes and existing role models (Cheryan et al., 2017). These factors also influence each other (Cheryan et al., 2017).

Career choice should not be seen as a point in time, but as a biographical decision-making process (Micus-Loos et al., 2016). It is a lifelong process that begins with childhood aspirations and ends with the withdrawal from professional life (Driesel-Lange, 2011). The process includes the development of a vocational orientation (growth phase, exploration phase) up to the decision for an initial vocational qualification (Micus-Loos et al., 2016).

3.1   Growth Phase

In the growth phase (up to 14 years), the self-concept is formed through identification with reference persons in family and school (Driesel-Lange, 2011). The subject-related self-concept is the assessment of one's own competences and possibilities in the corresponding subject (Haselmeier et al., 2019). The importance of subject-related interest and subject-related self-concept for educational development is undisputed (Haselmeier et al., 2019).

Early in child development, boys are more likely than girls to be exposed to technological activities (Master et al., 2017). Lack of hands-on experience with STEM topics can prevent girls from building interest in this content (Microsoft Corporation, 2017). Parents' role perceptions also have a strong influence on girls' later career choices (Sorger & Willsberger, 2004). If girls are not encouraged by their parents and school to engage with STEM content, this can lead to girls not developing an interest in this content (Microsoft Corporation, 2017).

A student's subject-related self-concept and her/his actual subject-related competences do not have to correspond. Thus, a too low subject-related self-concept can often be observed in female pupils, while male pupils already in primary school show a significantly higher, often exaggerated, self-concept with the same competence—especially in "male" subjects (Haselmeier et al., 2019).

Gender stereotypes are already formed at the age of two to three (Driesel-Lange, 2011). The preferences and aptitudes associated with a gender attribute award or deny certain knowledge and experiences to girls/women, respectively, boys/men.

These attributions are not based on verified facts but are often the result of gender-related stereotyping (Driesel-Lange, 2011).

Technical competences are attributed to men (Friedrich et al., 2018). There is a common social assumption that technology is occupied by male protagonists (Sorger & Willsberger, 2004). People in the IT field are said to be socially incompetent or nerdy (Völkel et al., 2018; Friedrich et al., 2018). To be successful in IT, technical and mathematical skills are seen as most necessary (Bollag et al., 2021). Women are more likely to be attributed competences in social and communication-oriented areas (Friedrich et al., 2018). These skills—on the other hand—tend to be assessed as only complementary to be successful in IT (Bollag et al., 2021). In the media, such as television and magazines, gender-stereotypical portrayals of women and men predominate (Sorger & Willsberger, 2004). Individuals, educational institutions and the labor market also reproduce a stereotypical image of people in the IT sector on a daily basis (Friedrich et al., 2018).

The early and continuing classification of computer science as a "male subject" has an influence on the self-concept of female students in this regard (Haselmeier et al., 2019). Girls or women assess themselves differently from the propagated stereotype, which can influence their interest in computer science (Ehrlinger et al., 2018). As computer science is not a compulsory subject in most German states, most girls do not have the opportunity to correct this image (Haselmeier et al., 2019).

3.2   Exploration Phase

At the age of 13 and 14, adolescents are confronted with real conditions of society and therefore include requirements of professions in their considerations (Driesel-Lange, 2011). The exploration phase extends from adolescence into early adulthood. In this phase, young people try out different roles. By exploring their own occupational interests, skills, and values, they form occupational preferences (Driesel-Lange, 2011).

A female technology distance can be observed from adolescence onward (Esch, 2011). For example, the proportion of girls in the school computer science competition "Informatik Biber" decreases with increasing age from 49% in grade 5/6 to 33% in grade 11–13 (Bundesweite Informatikwettbewerbe, 2020).

Confidence in one's own abilities in the STEM field is significantly different for boys and girls in this phase of life. As early as the fifth grade, male pupils assess their competences in mathematics as higher than female pupils, without this being confirmed by correspondingly better school grades. This difference can be observed up to the twelfth grade (Weinhardt, 2017). In the ICILS 2013 study, noticeable gender-specific differences were also found with regard to the assessment of computer and information-related competences: Girls in grade 8 show higher computer and information-related competences than boys. However, boys in all participating countries have a significantly higher computer-related self-efficacy expectation with regard to advanced skills than girls (Lorenz et al., 2014).

A correspondingly pessimistic assessment of their own abilities can lead to girls developing preferences for other subjects (Weinhardt, 2017) and thus deciding less often on an IT career path later on.

Pupils in general are often afraid of choosing the wrong career path (McDonald's Deutschland LLC, 2019). Information about possible career paths is therefore very important (McDonald's Deutschland LLC, 2019). Among others, people who work in the corresponding profession are considered important (McDonald's Deutschland LLC, 2019). Thus, girls (as well as boys) often orientate themselves on role models when choosing a profession (Sorger & Willsberger, 2004). However, children and young people rarely encounter female role models in STEM professions in their environment (Esch, 2011), thus these professions are perceived as male-dominated. Choosing a male-dominated occupation brings with it for girls and women the consequence of a minority position as well as the risk of discrimination (Micus-Loos et al., 2016) and therefore rises concerns (Sorger & Willsberger, 2004).

Individual interests have a significant influence on the choice of occupation, as a match between one's own individual characteristics and those of the occupation is sought (Micus-Loos et al., 2016). In adolescence, however, stereotypical gender images can have a decisive influence on career choice, regardless of individual interests and abilities (Micus-Loos et al., 2016). Girls and boys can be restricted in their choice of occupation if a gender stereotype does not correspond to their interests (Driesel-Lange, 2011). A perceived incongruity between "real femaleness" and technology affinity can thus result in career choices compliant with stereotypical gender conceptions (Schmid-Thomae, 2012).

3.3 Decision

When it comes to the actual choice of career, additional factors can have an impact: For example, generation-specific values are more pronounced among young women (Scholz, 2016). They place greater value than men on a conscious lifestyle and have a stronger social orientation (Albert et al., 2019). If no or only a weak reference to social topics is recognizable in computer science degree programs, their attractiveness for women may be low.

Women also prefer degree programs with a stronger practical orientation, for example with the integration of practical phases or dual degree programs (Friedrich et al., 2018). A lack of practical relevance in IT degree programs can therefore lead to a low number of women opting for them.

The association of a subject with a male culture may reduce its attractiveness to women (Cheryan et al., 2017). Furthermore, computer science degree programs that integrate little content from degree programs that are more frequently chosen by women—such as medicine or biology—are less attractive to women (Friedrich et al., 2018). This is shown by the different gender ratios in various IT subjects (see Sect. 2).

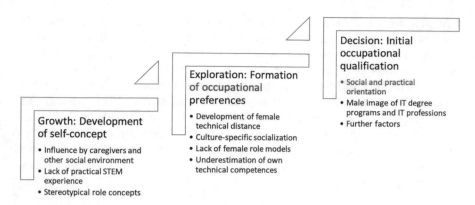

Fig. 2 Summary of inhibiting factors (Own representation)

Regardless of the content, the mere designation of an education program can be an inhibiting factor. For example, Sorger and Willsberger (2004) describe the case of a company that changed a job title from "mathematical-technical assistant" to "IT specialist"; as a result, the proportion of women applying dropped from about 60% to 20%.

Overall, it can be stated that young women shortly before their concrete career choice have a less broad spectrum of aspired occupations than younger girls (Sorger & Willsberger, 2004). The concentration of women on traditionally female professions can thus not be traced back to originally existing interests of girls, but—among others—to social factors (Sorger & Willsberger, 2004). Gender-dependent occupational preferences are thus also an expression of culture-specific socialization (Esch, 2011).

A summary of inhibiting factors presented above is provided in Fig. 2.

4 Promoting Factors and Approaches

Understanding young women's choices for or against a career in IT along different phases in the development of their vocational orientation allows the identification of effective approaches to increase girls' motivation toward IT in consideration of the relevant inhibiting factors in the respective phase.

4.1 Early Experiences and Support

Providing girls with *early experience with IT* contributes to a positive development of their subject-related interest and self-concept in the *growth phase*. Girls with specific IT experience at elementary school level are found to have both a higher interest in programming as well as higher levels of self-efficacy and a stronger self-concept, respectively (Haselmeier et al., 2019; Master et al., 2017). Making IT an integral part of school curricula in early education would thus enable girls to be equally exposed to IT activities in a phase when their interests and self-concept develop. An early integration is essential in order to achieve this effect on self-concept development. Furthermore, as girls' underestimation of their mathematical competences is already prevalent in elementary school (Weinhardt, 2017) and persists for IT competences in secondary school alike (Lorenz et al., 2014), *support from both teachers and caregivers* through *positive feedback* is key to strengthen girls in their perception of these competences, thus promoting their self-efficacy (Weinhardt, 2017).

4.2   Addressing Stereotypes

The need to *address stereotypes* becomes apparent throughout the whole development process in which vocational orientation takes place. Stereotypes are especially problematic as they exist on two different levels that are intertwined in their contribution to the gender gap in IT: *gender stereotypes* regarding girls' competences and *stereotypes about IT as a field* including competences, tasks and people. This leads to a "double gendering" effect where essentially the field of IT is connotated as "male" and where boys—in contrast to girls—are attributed with competences according to the stereotype (Bollag et al., 2021).

As gender stereotypes begin to be formed already at early ages, *awareness and sensibility must be created to avoid* explicit or implicit *gender attributions* of traits and competences in the *growth phase* starting in early childhood education, especially among a child's caregivers and educational personnel. Support by *role models* in their social environment, e.g., by one or both parents working in technical professions, promotes an open and curious attitude toward technology in girls. The self-concept of girls with a higher affinity for IT has been found to differ from traditional concepts of femininity, expressed by an emotional affinity for maleness which however does not put their female gender identity into question (Ripke & Siegeris, 2012).

While positive experiences with IT are especially important in girls' self-concept development, leading to higher technology motivation, such experiences do not change stereotypes about the field of IT, e.g. about programming or robotics (Master et al., 2017). In order to improve the perceived identity compatibility of girls with the field of IT, *stereotypes about the IT profession need to be addressed. Exposure to female role models*, such as successful female IT professionals, can be an effective way to change these stereotypes (Shin et al., 2016).

As in adolescence, stereotypical gender images have an effect on career choice regardless of individual interests and abilities (Micus-Loos et al., 2016), girls' cognition of and identification with female role models in IT becomes even more decisive during the *exploration phase*. The presence of female role models as part of girls' experiences with IT in school programs and extracurricular activities can change their stereotypes about IT, e.g., as *female IT professionals* give first-hand insight into their daily work in presentations or as part of mentoring programs. Encounters with such role models can alleviate girls' concerns of being the only female in a professional IT environment. *Female IT founders* and *female celebrities* promoting digital education can also serve as role models and thereby change the image of IT in the public perception. Prominent examples include public figures such as founder and digital expert Verena Pausder as part of "Digital Education for All" in Germany (https://digitalebildungfueralle.org/) or supermodel Karlie Kloss and her program 'KODE with KLOSSY' (https://www.kodewithklossy.com) which promotes coding as an empowerment for girls. Especially for students with little exposure to real-life female IT role models, featuring role models in digital media can be an effective way to challenge girls' stereotypes about IT (Steinke et al., 2021).

As in the current generation of digital natives adolescents are particularly engaged with social media (Shankleman et al., 2021), achieving continuous encounter with role models in adolescent girls' social environments calls for a *targeted use of social media* in the *exploration phase* (Tijtgat & Franck, 2018). As a first step, such role models or influencers must enter girls' identity bubbles in social media, which become manifested as users identify with online social networks and are inclined to interact with like-minded others and rely on like-minded information (Kaakinen et al., 2018). This could be enabled through deliberate postings of encounters with female role models as these are taking place as part of school programs or extra-curricular activities. Once continuous experiences with IT and encounters with role models are exchanged ongoingly online in a second step, these can ultimately be part of identity bubble formation and reinforcement themselves and can further be strengthened in terms of filter bubbles that are created by algorithmic filtering technology (Kaakinen et al., 2018).

4.3   Targeted Design of IT Experiences

Coming back to *IT experiences*, which have been shown to be a relevant part of girls' self-concept development, the question remains how these experiences should be designed in order to strengthen girls' motivation for IT and to ultimately promote girls' choices for a career in IT. Aspects in the design of these experiences include both the choice of topics and didactics. Moreover, the way an IT experience is designed also needs to be reflected in terms of whether stereotypes (regarding both gender and the field of IT) are counteracted or reproduced.

As the gender gap varies considerably across different STEM fields (as shown in Fig. 1), initiatives aimed at increasing girls' interest in STEM subjects in general fall short of creating a particular interest in IT. In order to develop a particular interest in IT, programs should be designed to *foster IT-specific competences*. Also, it needs to be noted that learning processes differ between different STEM subjects: While natural sciences and mathematics are insight-oriented and technology is design-oriented, IT is both. In IT, digital products and systems are designed by humans, implying they can be studied in terms of artifacts to be designed. Likewise, digital artifacts can be studied as given phenomena in an insight-oriented way. It is important to distinguish between these *"designing" and "exploring" learning processes* and to include both in early IT education (Franke-Wiekhorst et al., 2019).

From a design perspective, *adding creative elements* to activities such as programming has been identified as a way to make experiences with IT more appealing to girls (Aufenanger, 2019; Microsoft Corporation, 2017), thus fostering their motivation for IT (Master et al., 2017). Including "arts" in STEM subjects— "STEAM"—is a central element of the so-called Maker Education where activities of "doing" or "making" are combined with digital functions (such as building a robot that can be controlled digitally). In IT, this leads to a shift of focus for example in programming from a technical to a creative and design-oriented activity (Aufenanger, 2019). That way, IT artifact design closely links IT topics with creative processes, enabling an easier access to IT topics and fostering girls' self-efficacy (Pancratz et al., 2019; Pröbster & Marsden, 2021). *Including social elements* in IT experiences, such as *collaboration and team work* in IT design tasks has further been found to increase girls' motivation for IT (Master et al., 2017; Zimmermann & Sprung, 2008). Working in teams that each contribute to the final IT product enables girls to experience IT development activities as a collaborative process (Pancratz et al., 2019). Both collaboration through digital technologies as well as the ability to creatively use digital tools and technology are seen as key dimensions in digital competence development (Carretero Gomez et al., 2017).

Other approaches suggest to *embed experiences with technology into girls' social contexts* (Pancratz et al., 2019). Shifting the focus of IT activities such as coding from a pure technical one to a context that is more relatable to girls' everyday lives has been found to make these activities more attractive to girls (Aufenanger, 2019). Yet, choosing such context requires caution: Trying to make IT activities explicitly feminine (e.g., designing blinking bracelets or using pink materials) can positively contribute to girls' situational interest in IT; however, at the same time, such approaches contribute to the reinforcement of existing gender stereotypes (Bollag et al., 2021; Master et al., 2017).

Similar challenges need to be addressed on a *didactical level*: Despite professional socialization and education, educators need to carefully reflect in what ways their own image of the IT discipline and their teaching didactics are based on gender constructions (e.g., by highlighting the basics of the discipline as "dry" and "theoretical" or by mystifying IT in a way that it requires a certain intelligence or a positively connotated nerdiness to succeed as a professional in IT) (Bollag et al., 2021). One way to avoid gender constructions is to de-contextualize IT in a sense that IT education focuses on *teaching ways of thinking and problem-solving competences* that are universally applicable and relevant in various contexts (Bollag et al., 2021; Fritz & Luger-Bazinger, 2019). This can be achieved with the concept of "computational thinking" as a general analytic ability to describe problems and develop, represent and evaluate solutions by applying techniques including algorithmic thinking, abstraction, decomposition, generalization or evaluation (Curzon & McOwan, 2018; Wing, 2006).

Designing IT experiences that are appealing to girls by means described above allows to trigger girls' interest in IT topics in the first place. In order to *develop this situational interest into enduring motivation* that keeps girls engaged with IT topics over time, educational programs must be designed accordingly to *enable an ongoing exposure to experiences with IT* (Master et al., 2017). This calls for a change in the educational system in Germany to provide both *early* and *continuous* experiences with IT in the form of compulsory IT classes in both elementary and secondary school. Currently, in Germany, IT education is only part of school curricula in secondary education from seventh grade onward in most federal states. Moreover, IT education is highly heterogeneous across the federal states in Germany, with compulsory IT classes only in one-third of the 16 federal states in secondary education (grades five to ten) (Schwarz et al., 2021).

4.4 Informing the Decision

In the *decision phase* when young females choose their initial vocational qualification, both the image of IT as a profession and the image of IT degree programs play a decisive role. While companies already take part in programs to promote girls in IT such as "Girls' day" to a greater extent (Weitzel et al., 2017), further *employer campaigns* are needed to *promote IT career prospects to young females*, demonstrating the creative, collaborative and interdisciplinary elements of IT jobs.

Furthermore, *IT degree programs can be designed* in a way to make them more appealing to girls. Apart from interdisciplinary programs that combine IT with disciplines that traditionally show higher enrolment shares of female students, such as bioinformatics (Statistisches Bundesamt (Destatis), 2021), IT degree programs can be designed to include elements that are especially attractive to young females during their vocational orientation. This can be achieved by integrating a greater share of modules with a practical orientation, by including elements that foster social competences, e.g., through team projects and a high degree of interaction, or by including social components that emphasize the role of IT as a means to achieve societal purposes (Ripke & Siegeris, 2012). An example effective in this way is the degree program "Informatik und Wirtschaft" (Informatics and Business) at Hochschule für Technik und Wirtschaft Berlin (University of Applied Sciences), which is a mono-educational program for female students. The program further highlights its temporal flexibility and that previous IT knowledge is no prerequisite (https://fiw.htw-berlin.de/studium/).

In order to convey a respective image of IT jobs and IT degree programs to young females, the *choice of job titles* and the *designation of education programs* is a decisive factor (Schmid-Thomae, 2012; Sorger & Willsberger, 2004). These labels should also express content that is appealing to females, however, without reflecting existing gender stereotypes.

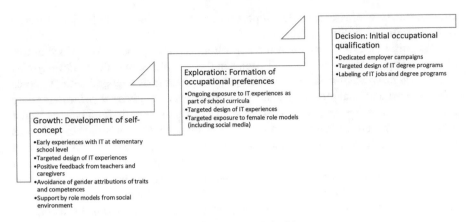

Fig. 3 Summary of promoting factors (Own representation)

Figure 3 shows a summary of the promoting factors discussed above.

5   Conclusion

The present work has pointed out that despite efforts to increase the share of women in STEM subjects and professions, the "digital gender gap" continues to exist in IT education as well as in the IT workplace. In light of the advancing digitization, the general shortage of IT professionals and companies' aims to increase diversity in the workplace, getting more women into IT is both an economic and societal imperative.

The systematization of inhibiting factors shows that a combination of different factors contributes to a decision against a career in IT that come into play in the earlier phases of the career choice process. Gender attributions of girls' competences and of IT as a profession play a decisive role.

Efforts are needed at various levels to break down traditional perceptions and attitudes and to build a more feminine image of IT professions. Initiatives shortly before the actual career choice often come too late, as attitudes and self-concepts have already been formed over a long period of time by this point. Society and the state, as well as early caregivers, must make a concerted effort from childhood to young adulthood to eliminate IT-related stereotypes and to provide girls and young females with relevant IT experiences, thus enabling girls to decide for or against an IT career solely on the basis of their own abilities and preferences.

References

Albert, M., Hurrelmann, K., Quenzel, G., Schneekloth, U., Leven, I., Utzmann, H., & Wolfert, S. (2019). *Jugend 2019 – 18. Shell Jugendstudie: Eine Generation meldet sich zu Wort* (1. Auflage). Beltz.

Aufenanger, S. (2019). MINT schon im Kindergarten!? *Frühe Bildung, 8*(1), 53–55.

Bollag, J., Bühler, C., Clerc, I., Ducommun, M., & Schär, S. (2021). *Auf dem Weg zu einer gendergerechten Informatikdidaktik—Einstellungen und Erfahrungen von Lehrpersonen auf verschiedenen Stufen des schweizerischen Bildungssystems [Abschlussbericht]*. PHBern und Berner Fachhochschule Wirtschaft. Accessed January 28, 2022, from https://arbor.bfh.ch/14453/

Bundesministerium für Bildung und Forschung. (2019). *Mit MINT in die Zukunft! Der MINT-Aktionsplan des BMBF*. Accessed January 28, 2022, from https://www.nationalesmintforum.de/

Bundesministerium für Bildung und Forschung. (2021). *MINT-Aktionsplan*. Accessed January 28, 2022, from https://www.bildung-forschung.digital/digitalezukunft/de/unsere-ueberzeugungen/digitalstrategie-des-bmbf/mint-aktionsplan/mint-aktionsplan_node.html

Bundesweite Informatikwettbewerbe. (2020). *Informatik-Biber 2020 Teilnahmezahlen*. Accessed January 28, 2022, from https://bwinf.de/biber/archiv/archivierte-seiten/2020/zahlen-und-bewertung/

Carretero Gomez, S., Vuorikari, R., & Punie, Y. (2017). *DigComp 2.1: The digital competence framework for citizens with eight proficiency levels and examples of use*. Publications Office of the European Union. Accessed January 28, 2022, from https://publications.jrc.ec.europa.eu/repository/bitstream/JRC106281/web-digcomp2.1pdf_%28online%29.pdf

Cheryan, S., Ziegler, S. A., Montoya, A. K., & Jiang, L. (2017). Why are some STEM fields more gender balanced than others? *Psychological Bulletin, 143*(1), 1–35.

Curzon, P., & McOwan, P. W. (2018). *Computational thinking: Die Welt des algorithmischen Denkens – in Spielen, Zaubertricks und Rätseln*. Springer.

Driesel-Lange, K. (2011). *Berufswahlprozesse von Mädchen und Jungen: Interventions-möglichkeiten zur Förderung geschlechtsunabhängiger Berufswahl*. LIT.

Ehrlinger, J., Plant, E. A., Hartwig, M. K., Vossen, J. J., Columb, C. J., & Brewer, L. E. (2018). Do gender differences in perceived prototypical computer scientists and engineers contribute to gender gaps in computer science and engineering? *Sex Roles, 78*(1–2), 40–51.

Esch, M. (2011). MINT und Chancengleichheit in fiktionalen Fernsehformaten—Einführung und ausgewählte Ergebnisse einer Programmanalyse. In *MINT und Chancengleichheit in fiktionalen Fernsehformaten*. BMBF. Accessed January 28, 2022, from https://publica.fraunhofer.de/dokumente/N-208544.html

Franke-Wiekhorst, A., Günther, C., Brünger, K., Magenheim, J., & Romeike, R. (2019). "Der Informatikkreis": Kinder von drei bis zehn Jahren beim Forschen in Informatik begleiten–ein methodisch-didaktisches Material. *GdSU-Journal, 9*, 95–105.

Friedrich, J.-D., Hachmeister, C.-D., Nickel, S., Peksen, S., Roessler, I., & Ulrich, S. (2018). *Frauen in Informatik: Welchen Einfluss haben inhaltliche Gestaltung, Flexibilisierung und Anwendungsbezug der Studiengänge auf den Frauenanteil? (Arbeitspapier No. 200)*. CHE Centrum für Hochschulentwicklung. Accessed January 28, 2022, from www.che.de/downloads/CHE_AP_200_Frauen_in_Informatik.pdf

Fritz, A., & Luger-Bazinger, C. (2019). *Evaluationsbericht des Programms Go4IT* (pp. 1–20). Österreichisches Zentrum für Begabtenförderung und Begabungsforschung. Accessed January 28, 2022, from https://www.oezbf.at/wp-content/uploads/2019/08/Endbericht_Go4IT.pdf

Haselmeier, K., Humbert, L., Killich, K., & Müller, D. (2019). *Interesse an Informatik und Informatikselbstkonzept zu Beginn der Sekundarstufe I des Gymnasiums*. Accessed January 28, 2022, from http://dl.gi.de/handle/20.500.12116/28969

Ihsen, S., Mellies, S., Jeanrenaud, Y., Wentzel, W., Kubes, T., Reutter, M., & Diegmann, L. (2017). Weiblichen Nachwuchs für MINT-Berufsfelder gewinnen: *Bestandsaufnahme und Optimierungspotenziale*. LIT.

Jansen, A., Flake, R., & Schirner, S. (2020). *Die Fachkräftesituation in IT-Berufen und Potentiale der Zuwanderung* (No. 4/2020; KOFA-Studie). Institut der deutschen Wirtschaft Köln e. V. Accessed January 28, 2022, from https://www.iwkoeln.de/studien/regina-flake-anika-jansen-sebastian-schirner-die-fachkraeftesituation-in-it-berufen-und-potentiale-der-zuwanderung.html

Kaakinen, M., Sirola, A., Savolainen, I., & Oksanen, A. (2018). Shared identity and shared information in social media: Development and validation of the identity bubble reinforcement scale. *Media Psychology, 23*(1), 25–21.

Lorenz, R., Gerick, J., Schulz-Zander, R., & Eickelmann, B. (2014). Computer- und informations-bezogene Kompetenzen von Mädchen und Jungen im internationalen Vergleich. In *ICILS 2013. Computer- und informationsbezogene Kompetenzen von Schülerinnen und Schülern in der 8. Jahrgangsstufe im internationalen Vergleich*. Waxmann.

Master, A., Cheryan, S., Moscatelli, A., & Meltzoff, A. N. (2017). Programming experience promotes higher STEM motivation among first-grade girls. *Journal of Experimental Child Psychology, 160*, 92–106.

McDonald's Deutschland LLC. (2019). *Kinder der Einheit—Same Same but (still) different!* (Die McDonals's Ausbildungsstudie 2019). Accessed January 28, 2022, from https://karriere.mcdonalds.de/docroot/jobboerse-mcd-career-blossom/assets/documents/McD_Ausbildungsstudie_2019.pdf

Microsoft Corporation. (2017). *Why Europe's girls aren't studying STEM* [White Paper]. Accessed January 28, 2022, from http://bit.ly/2qiFT5u

Micus-Loos, C., Plösser, M., Geipel, K., & Schmeck, M. (2016). *Normative Orientierungen in Berufs- und Lebensentwürfen junger Frauen*. Springer VS.

Pancratz, N., Fandrich, A., Chytas, C., Daeglau, M., & Diethelm, I. (2019). Blöcke, Blumen, Mikrocontroller und das Internet of Things. In A. Pasternak (Ed.), *Informatik für alle* (pp. 295–304). Gesellschaft für Informatik.

Presse- und Informationsamt der Bundesregierung. (2022). *Initiativen für MINT-Bildung: So fördert der Bund den MINT-Bereich*. Accessed January 28, 2022, from https://www.bundesregierung.de/breg-de/suche/bundesregierung-foerdert-mint-1929848

Pröbster, M., & Marsden, N. (2021). A matter of identity? Designing personas for the development of makerspaces for girls with migration background considering complex social identities: Eine Frage der Identität? Die Erstellung von Personas für die Entwicklung von Makerspaces für Mädchen mit Migrationshintergrund unter Berücksichtigung komplexer sozialer Identitäten. *Mensch Und Computer, 2021*, 484–489.

Ripke, M., & Siegeris, J. (2012). Informatik—Ein Männerfach?! *Informatik Spektrum, 35*(5), 331–338.

Scheid, D. (2021). *Untersuchung der Motivation von Frauen der Generation Z, einen informatik-nahen Studiengang zu ergreifen [Bachelorarbeit]*. Hochschule für Technik und Wirtschaft Berlin.

Schmid-Thomae, A. (2012). *Berufsfindung und Geschlecht: Mädchen in technisch-handwerklichen Projekten*. Springer.

Scholz, C. (2016). *Generation Z: "Ticken" Mädchen anders?* (Working Paper No. 132). Universität des Saarlandes. Accessed January 28, 2022, from https://1v.com/publizieren/

Schwarz, R., Hellmig, L., & Friedrich, S. (2021). Informatikunterricht in Deutschland – eine Übersicht. *Informatik Spektrum, 44*(2), 95–103.

Shankleman, M., Hammond, L., & Jones, F. W. (2021). Adolescent social media use and well-being: A systematic review and thematic meta-synthesis. *Adolescent Research Review, 6*, 471–492.

Shin, J. E. L., Levy, S. R., & London, B. (2016). Effects of role model exposure on STEM and non-STEM student engagement. *Journal of Applied Social Psychology, 46*, 410–427.

Sorger, C., & Willsberger, B. (2004). *Analyse der IST-Situation zum österreichischen Frauen-Technologie-Projekt (L&R Sozialforschung)*. Lechner, Reiter und Riesenfelder Sozialforschung OEG.

Statistisches Bundesamt (Destatis). (2021). *Studierende an Hochschulen* (Fachserie 11; Reihe 4.1). Accessed January 28, 2022, from https://www.destatis.de/DE/Themen/Gesellschaft-Umwelt/Bildung-Forschung-Kultur/Hochschulen/Publikationen/_publikationen-innen-hochschulen-studierende-endg.html

Steinke, J., Applegate, B., Penny, J. R., & Merlino, S. (2021). Effects of diverse STEM role model videos in promoting adolescents' identification. *International Journal of Science and Mathematics Education, 20*, 255–276.

Tijtgat, P., & Franck, K. (2018). STEMfluence/Amper Slim: Role models on social media encourage STEM-carriers. *Ecsite Annual Conference*, Geneva, 68.

Völkel, S. T., Wilkowska, W., & Ziefle, M. (2018). Gender-specific motivation and expectations toward computer science. *Proceedings of the 4th Conference on Gender & IT - GenderIT '18*, pp. 123–134.

Weinhardt, F. (2017). Ursache für Frauenmangel in MINT-Berufen? Mädchen unterschätzen schon in der fünften Klasse ihre Fähigkeiten in Mathematik. *DIW Wochenbericht, 84*(45), 1009–1028.

Weitzel, T., Laumer, S., Maier, C., Oehlhorn, C., Wirth, J., & Weinert, C. (2017). *Women in IT - Ausgewählte Ergebnisse der Recruiting Trends 2017 und der Bewerbungspraxis 2017* [Research Report]. Accessed 28 Jan 2022, from https://www.uni-bamberg.de/fileadmin/uni/fakultaeten/wiai_lehrstuehle/isdl/4_Women_in_IT_20170210_WEB.pdf

Wing, J. M. (2006). Computational thinking. *Communications of the ACM, 49*(3), 33–35.

World Economic Forum. (2020). *The future of jobs report*. Accessed January 28, 2022, from https://www.weforum.org/reports/the-future-of-jobs-report-2020

Zimmermann, L., & Sprung, G. (2008). Technology is female: How girls can be motivated to learn programming and take up technical studies through adaptations of the curriculum, changes in didactics, and optimized interface design. *Proceedings of ICEE*, 8.

Part IV
Digital Platforms and Ecosystems: Outcomes and Implications

How Access to Resources Affects Complementor Innovation in Platform Ecosystems

Thomas Huber, Thomas Hurni, Oliver Krancher, and Jens Dibbern

Abstract Platform owners must ensure that the ecosystems around their platforms remain as innovative as possible to meet market needs and keep pace with competing platform ecosystems. To this end, platform owners either attract new complementors with innovative complements or foster innovation among existing complementors. This study takes the perspective of complementors to understand the conditions under which access to the platform owner's resources contributes to the complementor's innovativeness. Based on survey data from 179 complementors of different software ecosystems, our findings support the supposition that access to the platform owner's valuable technical and commercial capital drives the complementor's product and process innovativeness. When it comes to access to social capital (e.g., reputation effects, quality signaling), benefits for innovation (limited to production innovation) only accrue under the condition that the platform owner invests in partner-specific information sharing. Our findings contribute to a better understanding of the role of platform design and partnership management practices by the platform owner in shaping complementor innovation.

1 Introduction

In recent years, platform ecosystems have become the dominant organizational arrangement through which innovative software products and services are created (Evans et al., 2008; Iansiti & Levien, 2004). As a consequence, major software

T. Huber
ESSEC Business School, Cergy, France
e-mail: huber@essec.edu

T. Hurni (✉) · J. Dibbern
Universität Bern, Bern, Switzerland
e-mail: thomas.hurni@iwi.unibe.ch; jens.dibbern@iwi.unibe.ch

O. Krancher
IT University Copenhagen, Copenhagen, Denmark
e-mail: olik@itu.dk

companies like Apple, Google, Microsoft, or SAP have become platform owners that offer certain resources and capabilities to third-party developers, including a platform with core functionality and application programming interfaces (APIs), development environments, and channels for app distribution (Eaton et al., 2015; Tiwana, 2013; Wareham et al., 2014). Referred to as complementors (Huber et al., 2017; Hurni et al., 2020, 2022) or spokes (Kude et al., 2012), these partners use these platform resources to provide innovative add-on functionality and services that build on and extend digital platforms (Boudreau, 2012; Eaton et al., 2015). While past research has established that the technological, commercial, and social resources offered by the platform owner will influence the complementor's motivation to partner with a platform owner (Ceccagnoli et al., 2012; Kude et al., 2012; Tiwana, 2015), little is known about the impact that such different types of resources may have on the cocreation of innovation in platform partnerships (Hein et al., 2019). This lack of understanding is an important gap because the promise of generativity requires complementors to join a platform and use the resources offered by the platform owner to create innovation (Evans et al., 2008; Iansiti & Levien, 2004).

Our study addresses this gap by theorizing and testing how the access to different types of resources offered by the platform owner (i.e., technological, commercial, and social) affects two types of innovation: Product innovation and process innovation. Informed by the firm's resource- and knowledge-based views, we hypothesize that the effect of the access to technological, commercial, and social resources on innovation will vary with the degree to which the platform owner engages in information exchange with the complementor. We test our hypotheses using survey data from 179 complementors. Our findings show that access to the platform owner's technological and commercial capital is critical for product and process innovation. By contrast, social capital does not have significant main effects on process and product innovation. However, social capital contributes to product innovation when the platform owner exchanges extensive information with the complementor. Our findings contribute to the literature on platform ecosystems and input-oriented theories of inter-firm partnerships.

The remainder of this chapter is organized as follows. First, we review the theoretical and conceptual background to develop our hypotheses. Then, we describe our method before presenting our results. We conclude by discussing our results, elaborating on theoretical contributions and implications for practice, and addressing the limitations of our study.

2 Theoretical and Conceptual Background

2.1 Platform Ecosystems: Resources as Input, Innovation as Outcome

The input-oriented perspective of platform ecosystems holds that third-party developers partner with a platform owner to access resources and capabilities that they lack, but the platform owner possesses (Kude et al., 2012). In the spirit of this input-oriented perspective, much research on platform ecosystems has pointed to the importance of boundary resources such as a digital platform with core functionality and application programming interfaces (APIs), development environments, knowledge resources, technical support, marketing material, and a channel for app distribution (Eaton et al., 2015; Tiwana, 2013; Wareham et al., 2014). Such boundary resources are created and provided by the platform owner and made accessible only to those complementors that join an ecosystem (Huber et al., 2017; Kude et al., 2012; Sarker et al., 2012; Wareham et al., 2014). Whether or not complementors will join an ecosystem hinges on providing three types of resources, i.e., the platform owner's technological, commercial, and social capital (Kude et al., 2012). Building on Kude et al. (2012), we refer to *technological capital* as the technical resources that the platform owner makes available to complementors, which most importantly includes a modern, extensible platform that integrates with third-party products and services. We refer to *commercial capital* as the resources provided by the platform owner to enable complementors to address better or penetrate different markets. For example, distribution channels like the app store allow complementors to address new customers by giving access to a global audience. Moreover, platform owners sometimes provide standardized marketing tools and materials or provide monetary support for campaigns to help complementors access new sources of revenue (Huber et al., 2017). Finally, we refer to *social capital* as the resources that enable complementors to benefit from the platform owner's reputation. For example, reviewed and curated app stores or certificates issued by the platform owner are often regarded as positive signals for quality and reliability, helping complementors to benefit from the platform owner's reputation.

Across partner dyads, the exploitation of technological, commercial, and social resources will vary for three reasons. First, each platform owner offers a set of resources to their ecosystems to systematically vary across ecosystems. Second, although some resources are available to all complementors within an ecosystem, platform owners may choose to give different complementors different levels of access to resources, e.g., in response to their partner level (Huber et al., 2017; Hurni et al., 2022; Wareham et al., 2014). Third, even if resources are identical, the extent to which complementors access (i.e., make use of) the resources is likely to vary due to the heterogeneity of complementor resources with which they need to be combined and integrated. The resources and capabilities of complementors are often highly idiosyncratic, as expressed by their usually narrow yet deep expertise about specific industry niches, use cases, or technologies (Ceccagnoli et al., 2012; Foerderer et al., 2019; Huber et al., 2017; Kude et al., 2012). Therefore, even if complementors are members of the same ecosystem, they vary in how they access specific resources provided by the platform owner. Therefore, our study focuses on the extent to which individual complementors access specific platform resources rather than on the availability of resources in an ecosystem. This complementor-centric perspective is previously under-researched (McIntyre & Srinivasan, 2017).

The notion of "generativity"—widely seen as the key promise of platform ecosystems (Evans et al., 2008; Iansiti & Levien, 2004)—is closely related to the input-oriented perspective (Kude et al., 2012). The basic idea is that through platform partnerships, third-parties can access complementary resources that they could not have created themselves and that they can then use these resources to create often surprising outside innovation (Boudreau, 2012; Foerderer et al., 2018, 2019; Huber et al., 2017). The literature distinguishes between two types of (outside) innovation: Product and process innovation (Adner & Levinthal, 2001; Tarafdar & Gordon, 2007; Trantopoulos et al., 2017). In our context, product innovation refers to creating a third-party software product or service that is new or has considerably improved characteristics, while a process innovation refers to a new or significantly enhanced software development or delivery method.

2.2 Hypotheses Development

While much research has acknowledged the importance of platform resources in general (Eaton et al., 2015; Ghazawneh & Henfridsson, 2015; Wareham et al., 2014), the specific impact that these resources may have on outcomes other than "motivation to partner" (Kude et al., 2012) is not understood. Most importantly, to the best of our knowledge, no prior study has explicitly investigated the impacts of different resources on different types of innovation. This study develops and tests six hypotheses on the direct and contingent effects of technological, commercial, and social capital on product and process innovation to address this gap. Figure 1 provides an overview of the hypotheses.

2.3 Direct Effects

The technical resources offered by a platform owner to its ecosystem of complementors are designed for innovative reuse and recombination through third-parties (Eaton et al., 2015; Ghazawneh & Henfridsson, 2015; Wareham et al., 2014). These resources are made broadly and easily accessible through online partner portals (Foerderer et al., 2019; Huber et al., 2017) and standardized application programming interfaces (Baldwin & Clark, 2000). Complementors then combine these generic technological resources offered by the platform owner with their resources and capabilities in the process of value cocreation. However, because the resources and capabilities of complementors are often highly specific or

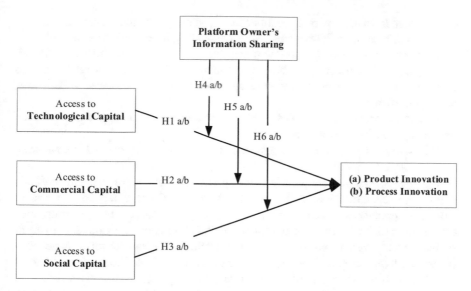

Fig. 1 Hypotheses

even idiosyncratic (Ceccagnoli et al., 2012; Foerderer et al., 2019; Huber et al., 2017; Kude et al., 2012), the mere presence of platform resources per se may not automatically translate into innovation. Instead, the complementor's ability to use and exploit these resources to create innovative products or services will hinge on the extent to which the standardized platform resources complement the complementor (Rochet & Tirole, 2003). For example, a complementor with specific enterprise software expertise is more likely to complement SAP's ERP platform with an innovative niche solution than a complementor with expertise in consumer software.

We also expect the technical resources offered by the platform owner to drive process innovation. Designed for extensibility and often sponsored by leading software companies such as Microsoft, Apple, Google, and SAP, digital platforms are often at the forefront of architectural innovations (Bozan et al., 2020). These architectural innovations spill over to the complementors development processes because using the platform requires embracing the architectural principles embedded in the platform. Therefore we hypothesize:

H1a: Stronger access to the platform owner's technological capital is associated with higher product innovation.

H1b: Stronger access to the platform owner's technological capital is associated with higher process innovation.

By providing commercial capital, platform owners enable complementors to address new and, therefore, a wider variety of markets. The more accessible this valuable commercial capital is to a particular complementor, the more diverse the customer base that the complementors can potentially serve. This will expose complementors to more varied customer needs, helping them innovate their products and services to address these needs. Moreover, having access to a broader and more varied customer base may force complementors into professionalizing their software development and delivery processes. For example, higher levels of reliability and scalability will call for optimized development and delivery processes. Therefore, we hypothesize:

H2a: Stronger access to the platform owner's commercial capital is associated with higher product innovation.

H2a: Stronger access to the platform owner's commercial capital is associated with higher process innovation.

Platform owners are frequently industry and technology leaders and routinely enjoy high reputation levels (Huifang et al., 2019). Complementors can benefit from this reputation in various ways and to varying degrees. For example, they can undergo different levels of platform-specific certifications. Depending on their partner level, they can advertise their partnership with the platform owner to a lower or a higher degree. The more they can access and use the platform owner's social capital, the stronger the quality and reliability signals complementors can send to their customers. Thus, exploiting social capital will give complementors the confidence and latitude to take the risk of experimenting with creating novel product features or improving processes. Therefore, we hypothesize:

H3a: Stronger access to the platform owner's social capital is associated with higher product innovation.

H3b: Stronger access to the platform owner's social capital is associated with higher process innovation.

2.4 The Moderating Role of Platform Owner Information Sharing

Even though platform partnerships tend to be more hands-off or arm's length than other inter-organizational arrangements such as joint ventures or alliances (Tiwana et al., 2010), it is critical that the disparate resources of complementors and platform owners result in a coherent whole to ensure platform owners and complementors co-create value for customers (Huber et al., 2017; Sarker et al., 2012). In other words, integration is needed to ensure the unification and synergistic combination of the complementors' resources and capabilities with the platform owner's technical, commercial, and social capital (Nevo & Wade, 2010). In platform ecosystems, the division of labor is such that complementors carry out and lead this integration effort (Sarker et al., 2012; Wareham et al., 2014). However, platform owners can facilitate this integration task if they frequently provide complementors with useful and valuable information (Sarker et al., 2012; Wareham et al., 2014). Past research suggests that sometimes platform owners are willing to go above and beyond their contractual obligations and provide complementors with exclusive and/or confidential knowledge (Foerderer et al., 2019; Huber et al., 2017; Hurni et al., 2020, 2022). For example, platform owners can give complementors hints on how to better leverage existing APIs and inform them about upcoming platform features and interfaces, changes to their app store rules, and relevant certificates. In this way, complementors can better use the different resources made available by the platform owner. Therefore, we hypothesize:

H4a: The positive relationship between access to technological capital and product innovation is stronger when the platform owner shares more information with the complementor.

H4b: The positive relationship between access to technological capital and process innovation is stronger when the platform owner shares more information with the complementor.

H5a: The positive relationship between access to commercial capital and product innovation is stronger when the platform owner shares more information with the complementor.

H5b: The positive relationship between access to commercial capital and process innovation is stronger when the platform owner shares more information with the complementor.

H6a: The positive relationship between access to social capital and product innovation is stronger when the platform owner shares more information with the complementor.

H6b: The positive relationship between access to social capital and process innovation is stronger when the platform owner shares more information with the complementor.

3   Methods

3.1   Data Collection

We tested our hypotheses through an online survey among complementors in platform ecosystems. Our sampling frame was companies that (1) operated in the software industry (software companies), (2) were part of at least one platform ecosystem, and (3) had activities in Switzerland. We focused on companies from Switzerland to reduce confounding effects, e.g., due to culture or legal norms.

To identify respondents, we relied on a commercial contact database, the contact databases of multiple industry associations in Switzerland, and the contact database of a leading Swiss IT consulting company. We matched these databases and screened each contact to verify that the company existed and operated in the software industry. From initially about 15,000 contacts, 4955 hand-sorted contacts remained in the database. We deployed the survey in May 2015 using a commercial online survey tool (Qualtrics). Invitations for the survey were sent out by email to

Table 1 Distribution of complementors over platform owners

	Microsoft	Oracle	IBM	SAP	Apple	Other
No. of complementors with the most important platform owner	76	14	10	10	10	59

senior members of the companies. Six hundred thirty-two surveys were completed (12.75% response rate). To identify the complementors among these 632 companies, we asked whether they collaborated with a platform owner. For this purpose, we defined our understanding of a software platform: *"Under software partner, we understand legally independent companies which develop own software based on a software platform [e.g., an extension of SAP R/3], or configure an existing platform [e.g., parameterization of SAP ERP in customer projects], and are members of the partner program of the corresponding platform owner."* Of the 632 companies, 196 indicated a relationship with a platform owner. These 196 companies were then asked questions about their relationship with their most important platform owner. We screened the responses of the 196 companies that indicated to be in a relationship with a platform owner using the recommendations by Hair et al. (2006). We dropped 17 responses because they were either unengaged or showed missing values in more than 10% of the survey items or the dependent variables (Hair et al., 2006, p. 36). The data screening resulted in our final sample of 179 complete survey responses.

Table 1 shows the distribution of complementors by the platform owner. By far, most complementors (76) indicated Microsoft as their platform owner, followed by Oracle (14), IBM (10), SAP (10), and Apple (10). As a free-text field in the survey indicated, the complementors that mentioned Microsoft as their most important platform owner contributed to Microsoft Dynamics, SharePoint, Azure, .Net, and Microsoft SQL. The descriptive statistics in Table 4 provide further insights into the composition of our sample.

3.2 Instrument Development and Validation

We measured each construct through a block of questionnaire items. All items were measured on a five-point Likert scale, ranging from "strongly disagree" (1) to "strongly agree" (5). Table 3 shows the items. We used scales from prior literature (see the references in Table 3) to measure the platform owner's information sharing, product innovation, and process innovation. However, we adapted the scales to the context of platform ecosystems. Since we were not aware of survey research measuring technological capital, commercial capital, and social capital, we developed scales for these constructs based on the qualitative data and definitions provided in Kude et al. (2012). Our questionnaire also included several control

Table 2 Control variables

Variable	Measure
Complementor Size	The count of full time employed equivalents in Switzerland (logarithmic transformation)
Export	1 if the complementor sells software or services outside Switzerland
Specific Industry	1 if the complementor addresses the requirements of a particular industry; 0 otherwise
Microsoft	1 if the most important platform owner was Microsoft; 0 otherwise
Multihoming	1 if the complementor complements platforms of more than one platform owner; 0 otherwise
Software Development Company	1 if the primary business purpose of a complementor was software development; 0 otherwise
Partnership Age	The number of years the complementor was in a partnership with the platform owner.
Layer Distance	The distance between the platform owner's and the complementor's layer level. The layer level is coded as 2 for the application software layer, 1 for the middleware layer, and 0 for the systems software layer.

variables to account for factors affecting our independent and dependent variables. The control variables are shown in Table 2.

To validate the questionnaire, we first invited three practitioners working for complementors and four senior IS scholars to review our constructs to assess and ensure content validity. We asked both the scholars and the practitioners to provide feedback and rate the extent to which each item captures each aspect of the construct domain (i.e., construct definition) using five-point Likert scales (Hinkin & Tracey, 1999). We refined our items based on the feedback obtained. We used the information gleaned from this construct review to refine our items. We then performed a pre-test among complementors from Austria and analyzed the scales through exploratory factor analysis. This led to further refinements of the items used for the final survey. Table 3 shows our final survey items.

After collecting the data for the final survey, we used confirmatory factor analysis procedures in SmartPLS to assess validity and reliability. Convergent validity and reliability were supported by Cronbach alpha values above.7, AVE values above.5, and outer loading above.7 for all constructs and items (see Table 3). Discriminant validity was supported by construct correlations below the AVE square roots for all construct pairs (Fornell & Larcker, 1981). Moreover, the differences between construct and cross-loadings were greater than.2 for all items, supporting discriminant validity.

Table 3 Survey items

Construct (in parentheses: Cronbach's alpha, AVE)	Items (in parentheses: Outer loadings)	Source
Technological Capital ($\alpha = 0.83$, AVE $= 0.75$)	Our partnership with \<platform owner\> ... [TC1] ... provides us with knowledge about the future development of its platform (0.83). [TC2] ... helps us to develop marketable software (0.86). [TC3] ... helps us to develop state-of-the-art software (0.91).	Self-developed based on Kude et al. (2012)
Commercial Capital ($\alpha = 0.86$, AVE $= 0.78$)	Our partnership with \<platform owner\> ... [CC1] ... gives us access to its attractive customer base (0.90). [CC2] ... supports us in our public relations network (e.g., marketing campaigns) (0.88). [CC3] ... helps us to increase our sales (0.88).	Self-developed based on Kude et al. (2012)
Social Capital ($\alpha = 0.88$, AVE $= 0.81$)	Our partnership with \<platform owner\> ... [SC1] ... signals to our customers that our products are of high quality (e.g., through certification) (0.89). [SC2] ... signals to our customers that our company is highly reliable (e.g., through a joint market presence) (0.91). [SC3] ... increases our reputation toward customers (0.90).	Self-developed based on Kude et al. (2012)
Platform Owner's Information Sharing ($\alpha = 0.73$, AVE $= 0.65$)	\<Platform owner\> provides us ... [IS1] ... with all information that may be useful to us (0.80). [IS2] ... regularly with information beyond of what is contractually mandated (0.89). [IS3] ... with confidential information (0.71)	Adapted from Heide and John (1992), Heide and Miner (1992), Kaufmann and Dant (1992), Lusch and Brown (1996)
Product Innovation ($\alpha = 0.87$, AVE $= 0.72$)	Our partnership with \<platform owner\> enabled us ... [Prod1] ... to develop radically new products (0.76). [Prod2] ... to give our customers unique advantages with our software \<software\> (0.91). [Prod3] ... to address new customers (0.86). [Prod4] ... to be the market leader in our segment (0.88).	Adapted from Atuahene-Gima (1996)
Process Innovation ($\alpha = 0.87$, AVE $= 0.79$)	Our partnership with \<platform owner\> enabled us ... [Proc1] ... to shorten innovation cycles (0.90). [Proc2] ... to reduce development costs (0.87). [Proc3] ... to continuously improvement our development processes (0.90).	Adapted from Atuahene-Gima (1996)

3.3 Data Analysis

We tested our hypotheses using Ordinary Least Squares Regression. To reduce multicollinearity threats and easy interpretation, we standardized all continuous variables. Following a hierarchical regression approach, we first estimated baseline models with control variables only (model 1a for product innovation and 1b for process innovation). Then we estimated models with control variables and main effects (models 2a/2b) to test the main effects hypothesized in H1a/b, H2a/b, H3a/b. Then we added interaction effects (models 3a/3b) to test our interaction hypotheses H4a/b, H5a/b, and H6a/b. We verified that variance inflation factors were below 3.3, indicating no issues with multicollinearity. We also verified that the residuals followed a normal distribution, suggesting that the assumption of normally distributed error terms was met.

4 Results

Table 4 shows descriptive statistics, Table 5 provides bivariate correlations and Table 6 shows the regression results.

In H1a/b through H3a/b, we hypothesized positive associations between access to different types of capital and product and process innovation. As models 2a/b show, access to technological capital had strong positive relationships with both product innovation (Model 2a, $\beta = 0.46$, $p < 0.001$) and process innovation (Model 2b, $\beta = 0.41$, $p < 0.001$), supporting H1a and H1b. Access to commercial capital was also significantly related with higher product innovation (Model 2a, $\beta = 0.17$, $p < 0.05$) and higher process innovation (Model 2b, $\beta = 0.26$, $p < 0.01$), supporting

Table 4 Descriptive statistics

	Min	Max	Mean	Std. Dev
Product innovation	1	5	3.45	0.92
Process innovation	1	5	3.38	1.00
Complementor size	0.15	400	24.77	56.06
Export	0	1	0.45	0.499
Specific industry	0	1	0.26	0.441
Multihoming	0	1	0.51	0.501
Software development company	0	1	0.88	0.323
Partnership age	0	40	11.68	7.983
Layer distance	0	2	0.76	0.870
Commercial capital	1	5	3.31	1.05
Technical capital	1	5	3.78	0.88
Social capital	1	5	3.67	0.93
Information exchange	1	5	3.00	0.86

Table 5 Bivariate correlations

	(1)	(2)	(3)	(4)	(5)	(6)	(7)	(8)	(9)	(10)	(11)	(12)	(13)	(14)
(1) Product Innovation	1	0.66	-0.17	0	-0.15	0.02	0.02	0.14	0.01	-0.07	0.46	0.61	0.45	0.52
(2) Process Innovation	0.66	1	-0.19	-0.1	-0.12	0	-0.03	0.03	-0.07	-0.01	0.4	0.5	0.31	0.37
(3) Complementor Size	-0.17	-0.19	1	0.09	0.04	0.04	0.08	-0.03	-0.07	-0.15	0.03	-0.04	-0.02	-0.1
(4) Export	0	-0.1	0.09	1	0.1	-0.04	0	0.08	-0.01	0.05	0.04	-0.08	0.09	-0.03
(5) Specific Industry	-0.15	-0.12	0.04	0.1	1	0.06	-0.08	0.06	-0.09	0.09	-0.01	0.01	-0.04	-0.14
(6) Microsoft	0.02	0	0.04	-0.04	0.06	1	0.11	-0.03	-0.08	0.08	-0.03	0.15	0	-0.04
(7) Multihoming	0.02	-0.03	0.08	0	-0.08	0.11	1	-0.01	0.1	-0.05	0.12	0.04	0.01	0.01
(8) Software Development Company	0.14	0.03	-0.03	0.08	0.06	-0.03	-0.01	1	0.01	0.1	0.15	0.14	0.18	0.06
(9) Partnership Age	0.01	-0.07	-0.07	-0.01	-0.09	-0.08	0.1	0.01	1	-0.07	-0.03	-0.05	0.02	-0.01
(10) Layer Distance	-0.07	-0.01	-0.15	0.05	0.09	0.08	-0.05	0.1	-0.07	1	-0.18	0.04	-0.07	-0.22
(11) Commercial Capital	0.46	0.4	0.03	0.04	-0.01	-0.03	0.12	0.15	-0.03	-0.18	1	0.42	0.57	0.43
(12) Technical Capital	0.61	0.5	-0.04	-0.08	0.01	0.15	0.04	0.14	-0.05	0.04	0.42	1	0.58	0.39
(13) Social Capital	0.45	0.31	-0.02	0.09	-0.04	0	0.01	0.18	0.02	-0.07	0.57	0.58	1	0.36
(14) Information Exchange	0.52	0.37	-0.1	-0.03	-0.14	-0.04	0.01	0.06	-0.01	-0.22	0.43	0.39	0.36	1

Table 6 Regression results

	Models 1a/b: Controls only		Models 2a/b: Controls and main effects		Models 3a/b: Controls, main effects, and interaction effects	
	a: Product Innovation	b: Process Innovation	a: Product Innovation	b: Process Innovation	a: Product Innovation	b: Process Innovation
Intercept	0.00(0.31)	−0.52(0.31)	0.14(0.23)	0.68(0.27)	0.12(0.23)	0.71(0.27)
Complementor size	−0.14 * (0.06)	−0.15 * (0.06)	−0.10 * (0.04)	−0.12 * (0.05)	−0.08 * *(0.04)	−0.13 * (0.05)
Export	0.04(0.15)	−0.14(0.15)	0.11(0.11)	−0.08(0.13)	0.13(0.11)	−0.05(0.13)
Specific Industry	−0.33 * *(0.17)	−0.26(0.17)	−0.26 * (0.13)	−0.23(0.14)	−0.25 * (0.12)	−0.24(0.14)
Microsoft	0.09(0.16)	0.02(0.16)	−0.04(0.12)	−0.08(0.13)	−0.04(0.11)	−0.11(0.13)
Multihoming	0.04(0.15)	−0.04(0.15)	−0.03(0.11)	−0.13(0.13)	−0.08(0.11)	−0.15(0.13)
Software Development Company	0.47 * (0.23)	0.13(0.23)	0.13(0.17)	−0.16(0.20)	0.06(0.17)	−0.22(0.20)
Partnership Age	0.00(0.00)	−0.01(0.01)	0.00(0.00)	−0.01(0.01)	0.00(0.00)	−0.01(0.01)
Layer Distance	−0.12(0.09)	−0.05(0.09)	−0.02(0.07)	0.03(0.08)	−0.02(0.07)	0.01(0.08)
Technological Capital			0.46 ****(0.07)	0.41 ****(0.08)	0.48 ****(0.08)	0.44 ****(0.09)
Commercial Capital			0.17 * (0.07)	0.26 *** (0.08)	0.18 * (0.07)	0.28 *** (0.08)
Social Capital			−0.02(0.08)	−0.10(0.09)	0.03(0.08)	−0.12(0.09)
Information Sharing			0.24 ****(0.07)	0.11(0.07)	0.16 * (0.07)	0.09(0.08)
Tech. Cap × Information Sharing					0.04(0.07)	0.08(0.08)
Com. Cap × Information Sharing					−0.05(0.06)	0.10(0.07)
Soc. Cap × Information Sharing					0.19 * (0.08)	−0.04(0.09)

(continued)

Table 6 (continued)

	Models 1a/b: Controls only		Models 2a/b: Controls and main effects		Models 3a/b: Controls, main effects, and interaction effetcs	
	a: Product Innovation	b: Process Innovation	a: Product Innovation	b: Process Innovation	a: Product Innovation	b: Process Innovation
ΔF	1.86 **	0.147	37.47 ****	20.00 ****	4.27 ***	1.41
R^2	0.08	0.07	0.52	0.37	0.55	0.39
Adj. R^2	0.04	0.02	0.48	0.32	0.51	0.33

Standard errors in parentheses

$*p < 0.05$

$*p < 0.1$

$**p < 0.01$

$***p < 0.001$

H2a and H2b. Conversely, access to social capital was not significantly related to product innovation (Model 2a, $\beta = -.02, p > 0.1$) or process innovation (Model 2b, $\beta = -0.10, p > 0.1$). The three types of capital and the platform owner's information sharing increased the explained variance from.08 (product innovation)/0.07 (process innovation) to 0.52/0.37, highlighting the high explanatory power of the four variables.

In H4a/b through H6a/b, we had hypothesized that the platform owner's information sharing strengthens the relationships between different types of capital and product and process innovation. As models 3a/b show, we did not find significant interaction effects for technological and product/process innovation and commercial capital and product/process innovation. However, the model shows that information sharing strengthened the relationship of social capital with product innovation (Model 3a, $\beta = 0.19, p < 0.05$), though not with process innovation (Model 3a, $\beta = 0.04, p > 0.1$). Thus H6a is supported while H4a/b, H5a/b, and H6b are not supported. Figure 2 visualizes the significant interaction between social capital and the platform owner's information sharing on product innovation. As the solid line indicates, social capital had a slightly negative association with product innovation when the platform owner's information sharing was low (i.e., one standard deviation below the mean). Conversely, there was a strong positive association between social capital and product innovation under high information sharing.

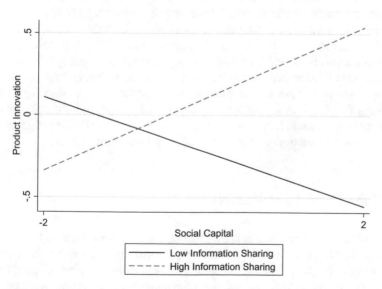

Fig. 2 Interaction of social capital and information sharing

5   Discussion and Implications

The objective of this study was to theorize and test how the complementors' access to different types of resources offered by the platform owner (i.e., technological, commercial, and social) affects two distinct types of innovation: Product innovation and process innovation. Our results on 179 partnerships between complementors and platform owners support our first two hypotheses that complementors are more likely to create product and process innovations when they have strong access to the valuable technical (H1 a/b) and the commercial capital (H2 a/b) of the platform owner. At the same time, we did not find support for our third hypothesis (H3 a/b), that stronger access to valuable social capital also leads to more product and process innovation. However, we found support for our hypothesis (H6a) that the platform owner's information sharing strengthens the relationships between the accessibility to social capital and product innovation. It is also notable that—other than expected—information sharing does not contribute to a stronger positive effect of technical and commercial capital access on complementor innovativeness. This suggests that innovation benefits are more difficult to achieve from access to social capital than technical and commercial capital. Specifically, social capital effects are more oriented toward influencing market reactions than directly affecting product and process innovations. However, if combined with access to exclusive information by the platform owner, complementors can use this information for enhancing products and, at the same time, use the social capital effects to attract customers with new product offerings. This points to the need for platform owners to go the extra mile to exploit their social capital and transfer its positive effects to its complementors through information sharing. Overall, our findings add to a better understanding of the sources of platform innovation. Specifically, they provide new insights into how to drive outside innovation in a platform ecosystem, specifically concerning the development of new or significantly improved software products or services (i.e., product innovations) or concerning new or significantly improved software development or delivery methods (i.e., process innovations).

5.1   Theoretical Contributions

Our results make several important contributions to theory. First, our study contributes to the literature on innovation in platform ecosystems by showing that access to valuable technical and commercial resources can lead to product and process innovation at the side of the complementors. In doing so, our study extends prior literature that has identified three types of resources of the platform owner, namely technical, commercial, and social capital, on the provision of which it depends on whether complementors join an ecosystem (Kude et al., 2012). However, joining a platform ecosystem is not enough to survive in the constant and continuously growing competition between ecosystems. Rather, it requires constant innovation and thus an increase in the attractiveness of the entire ecosystem vis-à-vis the customers. In this respect, platform ecosystems are characterized by their generativity, generally regarded as platform ecosystems' main promise (Evans et al., 2008; Iansiti & Levien, 2004). The idea behind generativity in platform ecosystems is that complementors can create surprising outside innovations by accessing complementary resources they could not have created themselves (Boudreau, 2012; Foerderer et al., 2018, 2019; Huber et al., 2017). In this regard, prior literature distinguishes between two types of (outside) innovation: Product and process innovation (Adner & Levinthal, 2001; Tarafdar & Gordon, 2007; Trantopoulos et al., 2017). Our study finds that the more accessible valuable technical and commercial resources, the more likely complementors create new software products or services or have considerably improved characteristics (i.e., product innovations), or significantly enhance software development or delivery method (i.e., process innovations). In that our study finds positive direct associations between the accessibility of valuable technical and commercial resources and both product and process innovations, it makes an important contribution to prior literature on outside innovation in and the generativity of platform ecosystems (Boudreau, 2010; Boudreau & Lakhani, 2009; Gawer & Cusumano, 2014).

Our study also supports the view that investigating into providing standard platform resources, i.e., boundary resources, pays off for platform owners (Hein et al., 2019). It leverages value-creation potential as a visibly enhanced product and process innovativeness at the complementor side.

Second, however, our study also points at the limitations of investing in generally applicable platform resources in the process of standardization toward achieving scalable infrastructures. Especially to benefit from less tangible platform resources, such as social capital, complementary investments into particular platform partnerships may be needed in the form of information sharing by the platform owner. Specifically, when it comes to product innovations, signaling effects of the platform owner's reputation are of limited use, if not accompanied with dyadic investments that help the complementor gain additional information about how to frame and position its new innovative product so that it appears as a synergistic complement to the platform, i.e., being aligned with the reputation of the platform owner.

5.2 Managerial Implications

Platform ecosystems are facing increasingly fierce competition from other platform ecosystems. To survive in this environment, platform owners must ensure that their platforms and surrounding ecosystems remain competitive. In this context, innovative processes and complements are key success factors. Our study provides three pieces of advice for nurturing such complement and process innovations in platform ecosystems. First, our study underscores the importance of platform owners making technological resources available and easily accessible to their complementors. Platform operators can take advantage of this insight by revisiting their support infrastructures to make their platform-specific technological resources accessible. Second, our study underscores the importance of platform owners making commercial resources available to their complementors. Platform operators can take advantage of this insight by providing their complementors access to commercial resources. Third, our study underscores the importance of platform owners providing social resources to their complementors, but only if they are willing to share vital information. Platform operators can take advantage of this insight by making their partnership managers aware of the beneficial role of information sharing for enhancing product innovation of their complementors, with a special focus on allowing their complementors to benefit from the platform's social capital. This means that partnerships managers need to be aware of the platform's various sources of social capital [see, e.g., Kude et al. (2018), Nahapiet and Ghoshal (1998)] and how these can be brought to fruition in a particular partnership to enhance their partners' product innovations. For example, a platform owner may use its relational links to other complementors to bring together experts from different domains to infuse the innovation process.

5.3   Limitations and Future Research

This study is not without limitations. First, our cross-sectional research design inherently limits the study of causal relationships. Therefore, future studies should rely on longitudinal or experimental methods to capture the dynamic and complex interactions between the different resources. Second, our study included numerous firms from different ecosystems, but all from the same country. Therefore, under some circumstances, the cultural norms of that country may have biased our results. Therefore, future research should test the relationships examined in this study in other cultural or geographic settings. Third, we relied on data from a single source, making our study vulnerable to methodological bias. However, ex-post-tests did not reveal any such biases. Moreover, interaction effects, which are at the heart of our study, cannot be artifacts of common method biases (Siemsen et al., 2010).

References

Adner, R., & Levinthal, D. (2001). Demand heterogeneity and technology evolution: implications for product and process innovation. *Management Science, 47*(5), 611–628. https://doi.org/10.1287/mnsc.47.5.611.10482

Atuahene-Gima, K. (1996). Differential potency of factors affecting innovation performance in manufacturing and services firms in Australia. *Journal of Product Innovation Management, 13*(1), 35–52. https://doi.org/10.1016/0737-6782(95)00090-9

Baldwin, C. Y., & Clark, K. B. (2000). *Design rules: The power of modularity* (Vol. 1). The MIT Press.

Boudreau, K. J. (2010). Open platform strategies and innovation: granting access vs. devolving control. *Management Science, 56*(10), 1849–1872. https://doi.org/10.1287/mnsc.1100.1215

Boudreau, K. J. (2012). Let a thousand flowers bloom? An early look at large numbers of software app developers and patterns of innovation. *Organization Science, 23*(5), 1409–1427. https://doi.org/10.1287/orsc.1110.0678

Boudreau, K. J., & Lakhani, K. R. (2009). How to manage outside innovation. *MIT Sloan Management Review, 50*(4), 69–76.

Bozan, K., Lyytinen, K., & Rose, G. (2020). Software architecture and outsourcing governance: Raising thoroughbreds versus cultivating schools of goldfish. In R. Hirschheim, A. Heinzl, & J. Dibbern (Eds.), *Information systems outsourcing: the era of digital transformation* (pp. 23–41). Springer International Publishing.

Ceccagnoli, M., Forman, C., Huang, P., & Wu, D. J. (2012). Cocreation of value in a platform ecosystem: The case of enterprise software. *MIS Quarterly, 36*(1), 263–290. https://doi.org/10.2307/41410417

Eaton, B., Elaluf-Calderwood, S., Sorensen, C., & Yoo, Y. (2015). distributed tuning of boundary resources: The case of apple's ios service system. *MIS Quarterly, 39*(1), 217–243. https://doi.org/10.25300/misq/2015/39.1.10

Evans, D. S., Hagiu, A., & Schmalensee, R. (2008). *Invisible engines: How software platforms drive innovation and transform industries*. The MIT Press.

Foerderer, J., Kude, T., Mithas, S., & Heinzl, A. (2018). Does platform owner's entry crowd out innovation? Evidence from Google photos. *Information Systems Research, 29*(2), 444–460. https://doi.org/10.1287/isre.2018.0787

Foerderer, J., Kude, T., Schuetz, S. W., & Heinzl, A. (2019). Knowledge boundaries in enterprise software platform development: Antecedents and consequences for platform governance. *Information Systems Journal, 29*(1), 119–144. https://doi.org/10.1111/isj.12186

Fornell, C., & Larcker, D. F. (1981). Structural equation models with unobservable variables and measurement error: algebra and statistics. *Journal of Marketing Research (JMR), 18*(3), 382–388. https://doi.org/10.2307/3150980

Gawer, A., & Cusumano, M. A. (2014). Industry platforms and ecosystem innovation. *Journal of Product Innovation Management, 31*(3), 417–433. https://doi.org/10.1111/jpim.12105

Ghazawneh, A., & Henfridsson, O. (2015). A paradigmatic analysis of digital application marketplaces. *Journal of Information Technology, 30*(3), 198–208. https://doi.org/10.1057/jit.2015.16

Hair, J. F. J., Black, W. C., Babin, B. J., Anderson, R. E., & Tatham, R. L. (2006). *Multivariate data analysis* (Vol. 6). Pearson Prentice Hall Upper.

Heide, J. B., & John, G. (1992). Do norms matter in marketing relationships? *Journal of Marketing, 56*(2), 32–44. https://doi.org/10.2307/1252040

Heide, J. B., & Miner, A. S. (1992). The shadow of the future: effects of anticipated interaction and frequency of contact on buyer-seller cooperation. *The Academy of Management Journal, 35*(2), 265–291. https://doi.org/10.2307/256374

Hein, A., Weking, J., Schreieck, M., Wiesche, M., Böhm, M., & Krcmar, H. (2019). Value co-creation practices in business-to-business platform ecosystems. *Electronic Markets, 29*(3), 503–518. https://doi.org/10.1007/s12525-019-00337-y

Hinkin, T. R., & Tracey, J. B. (1999). An analysis of variance approach to content validation. *Organizational Research Methods, 2*(2), 175–186. https://doi.org/10.1177/109442819922004

Huber, T. L., Kude, T., & Dibbern, J. (2017). Governance practices in platform ecosystems: Navigating tensions between cocreated value and governance costs. *Information Systems Research, 28*(3), 563–584. https://doi.org/10.1287/isre.2017.0701

Huifang, L., Yulin, F., Lim, K. H., & Youwei, W. (2019). Platform-based function repertoire, reputation, and sales performance of e-marketplace sellers. *MIS Quarterly, 43*(1), 207–236. https://doi.org/10.25300/MISQ/2019/14201

Hurni, T., Huber, T. L., Dibbern, J., & Krancher, O. (2020). Complementor dedication in platform ecosystems: Rule adequacy and the moderating role of flexible and benevolent practices. *European Journal of Information Systems, 30*(3), 237–260. https://doi.org/10.1080/0960085X.2020.1779621

Hurni, T., Huber, T. L., & Dibbern, J. (2022). Power dynamics in software platform ecosystems. *Information Systems Journal, 32*(2), 310–343. https://doi.org/10.1111/isj.12356

Iansiti, M., & Levien, R. (2004). *The keystone advantage: What the new dynamics of business ecosystems mean for strategy, innovation, and sustainability.* Harvard Business School Press.

Kaufmann, P. J., & Dant, R. P. (1992). The dimensions of commercial exchange. *Marketing Letters, 3*(2), 171–185. https://doi.org/10.2307/40216254

Kude, T., Dibbern, J., & Heinzl, A. (2012). Why do complementors participate? An analysis of partnership networks in the enterprise software industry. *IEEE Transactions on Engineering Management, 59*(2), 250–265. https://doi.org/10.1109/TEM.2011.2111421

Kude, T., Huber, T., & Dibbern, J. (2018). Successfully governing software ecosystems: competence profiles of partnership managers. *IEEE Software, 36*(3), 39–44.

Lusch, R. F., & Brown, J. R. (1996). Interdependency, contracting, and relational behavior in marketing channels. *Journal of Marketing, 60*(4), 19–38. https://doi.org/10.2307/1251899

McIntyre, D. P., & Srinivasan, A. (2017). Networks, platforms, and strategy: Emerging views and next steps. *Strategic Management Journal, 38*(1), 141–160. https://doi.org/10.1002/smj.2596

Nahapiet, J., & Ghoshal, S. (1998). Social capital, intellectual capital, and the organizational advantage. *Academy of Management Review, 23*(2), 242–266. https://doi.org/10.5465/amr.1998.533225

Nevo, S., & Wade, M. R. (2010). The formation and value of IT-enabled resources: Antecedents and consequences. *MIS Quarterly, 34*(1), 163–183. https://doi.org/10.5555/2017447.2017456

Rochet, J.-C., & Tirole, J. (2003). Platform competition in two-sided markets. *Journal of the European Economic Association, 1*(4), 990–1029. https://doi.org/10.1162/154247603322493212

Sarker, S., Sarker, S., Sahaym, A., & Bjørn-Andersen, N. (2012). Exploring value cocreation in relationships between an ERP vendor and its partners: A revelatory case study. *MIS Quarterly, 36*(1), 317–338. https://doi.org/10.2307/41410419

Siemsen, E., Roth, A., & Oliveira, P. (2010). Common method bias in regression models with linear, quadratic, and interaction effects. *Organizational Research Methods, 13*(3), 456–476. https://doi.org/10.1177/1094428109351241

Tarafdar, M., & Gordon, S. R. (2007). Understanding the influence of information systems competencies on process innovation: A resource-based view. *The Journal of Strategic Information Systems, 16*(4), 353–392. https://doi.org/10.1016/j.jsis.2007.09.001

Tiwana, A. (2013). *Platform ecosystems: Aligning architecture, governance, and strategy.* Morgan Kaufmann Publishers.

Tiwana, A. (2015). Platform desertion by app developers. *Journal of Management Information Systems, 32*(4), 40–77. https://doi.org/10.1080/07421222.2015.1138365

Tiwana, A., Konsynski, B., & Bush, A. A. (2010). Platform evolution: Coevolution of platform architecture, governance, and environmental dynamics. *Information Systems Research, 21*(4), 675–687. https://doi.org/10.1287/isre.1100.0323

Trantopoulos, K., von Krogh, G., Wallin, M. W., & Woerter, M. (2017). External knowledge and information technology: Implications for process innovation performance. *MIS Quarterly, 41*(1), 287–A288. https://doi.org/10.25300/MISQ/2017/41.1.15

Wareham, J., Fox, P. B., & Giner, J. L. G. (2014). Technology ecosystem governance. *Organization Science, 25*(4), 1195–1215. https://doi.org/10.1287/orsc.2014.0895

The Economic and Social Consequences of Digital Platforms: A Systematic and Interdisciplinary Literature Review

Michaela Lindenmayr, Tobias Kircher, Alexander Stolte, and Jens Foerderer

Abstract To monetize digital technologies, many firms use platform-based business models. While such digital platforms can yield tremendous profits, they also pose new challenges, among them privacy, harmful content such as hate speech, cyberbullying, or discrimination, as well as competition and innovation. These challenges have seen an uptick in research interest in the past years yet lack a structured and holistic overview. To resolve, this chapter reports a structured and interdisciplinary literature review. We document open research questions and outline mutual dependencies between the topics under consideration.

1 Introduction

New digital platforms constantly emerge from innovative business ideas and are able to disrupt traditional businesses. They bring together different market actors via technologies that allow interactions which benefit from direct and indirect network effects and create value for individuals (Foerderer et al., 2018; Parker et al., 2016; Shapiro et al., 1998). Platform models allow to carry out transactions more easily through the underlying technology (e.g., Uber, Netflix), on the other hand enhance innovation through collaborative platforms (e.g., Microsoft, SAP), while other platforms combine both functionalities (e.g., Apple, Facebook, Amazon) (Evans & Gawer, 2016).

Although in the first place, platforms offer a convenient place for interaction without restrictions in time and space, at the same time the digital world strengthens the challenges we face in the offline world. Missing regulation (Fisman & Luca, 2016) complemented by freedom of expression and high anonymity (Rauf, 2021) provide room for harmful content and competitive fraud, while platform providers are also faced by the scope of privacy they want to impose on their platforms. Also,

M. Lindenmayr · T. Kircher · A. Stolte · J. Foerderer (✉)
TUM School of Management, Technische Universität München, Heilbronn, Germany
e-mail: michaela.lindenmayr@tum.de; tobias.kircher@tum.de; alexander.stolte@tum.de; jens.foerderer@tum.de

© The Author(s), under exclusive license to Springer Nature Switzerland AG 2022   147
J. Dibbern et al. (eds.), *Digitalization Across Organizational Levels*, Progress in IS,
https://doi.org/10.1007/978-3-031-06543-9_7

recent debates question whether large digital platforms are beneficial for social welfare or whether they misuse their power to set disadvantageous standards in terms of privacy or prevent innovation (Khan, 2016).

While there have been literature reviews on digital platforms, there is no literature review that addresses the societal challenges of digital platforms related to privacy, harmful content such as hate speech, as well as competition and innovation. Literature reviews have been conducted on multi-sided platforms (e.g., Sanchez-Cartas & Leon, 2021; Trabucchi & Buganza, 2022) from a general perspective including investigations on platform design and use (e.g., Asadullah et al., 2018; Faber & de Reuver, 2019; Fischer et al., 2020; Soto Setzke et al., 2019). Tensions on digital platforms have been investigated from the perspective of business models (e.g., Mini & Widjaja, 2019), governance (e.g., Halckenhaeusser et al., 2020a), competition (e.g., Rietveld & Schilling, 2021), and market dominance (e.g., Hermes et al., 2020). Prior reviews on privacy carefully and fruitfully studied the economics of privacy (e.g., Acquisti et al., 2016) and digital platforms (e.g., Bonina et al., 2021; Rochet & Tirole, 2006; Rysman, 2009) but miss the intersection of these two intertwined phenomena. In addition, the literature reviews on hate speech mostly cover automated detection approaches (e.g., Fortuna & Nunes, 2018), while others also address different forms of hate speech (e.g., Chetty & Alathur, 2018). However, a holistic approach to derive societal challenges and find interdependencies between the phenomena that are imposed by digital platforms has not been provided to our knowledge.

To fill this gap, we investigate the following economic and social consequences of digital platforms: (1) privacy, (2) hate speech, cyberbullying, and discrimination, and (3) competition and innovation. To look into these focus areas, we conduct a systematic literature review on these controversial topics to sort the large amounts of literature that have been published. This allows us to find out what has been addressed by previous scholars to connect the topics based on the previous literature. In particular, we want not only to look into these three topics separately, but we want to find the trade-offs that stakeholders face when trying to solve these challenges.

This chapter is organized as follows. Section 2 describes the conceptual background on digital platforms. Section 3 continues by explaining the approach we took for collecting, selecting, and analyzing the literature for the review, and Section 4 provides the results of the separate literature streams we studied. Section 5 combines the main findings from the review and outlines the trade-offs that are faced when dealing with these challenges. Section 6 concludes the paper.

2 Conceptual Background

2.1 Digital Platforms and Network Effects

A digital platform refers to a business model that enables interactions between different market actors and enhances innovation derived from these interactions by using digital technologies and exploiting network effects (Tiwana et al., 2010). Compared to traditional companies that follow a linear value creation by producing goods that are sold to consumers, digital platforms allow interactions of consumers and producers that use the infrastructure of the platform (Parker et al., 2016). The main goal is to bring together different market actors in order to facilitate these interactions with the underlying digital technology that is able to ignore limitations in time and space, while also sophisticated algorithms allow an easier matching of the different market sides (Parker et al., 2016). The nature of digital platforms enhances network effects according to which the value of the platform for new users depends on the number of users that are already on the platform (Parker et al., 2016; Shapiro et al., 1998).

Generally, we observe positive network effects on digital platforms that can either be direct or indirect (Rochet & Tirole, 2003). Whereas for direct network effects, platform users benefit from an increasing number of participants of the same market side, for indirect network effects, the value of the platform increases with a larger number of users of the opposite market side (Katz & Shapiro, 1994). This phenomenon can be derived from an increasing number of possible interactions with an increasing number of platform users, to carry out interactions either with the opposite market side, e.g., for purchasing, or with the same market side, e.g., to connect on social networking platforms. Once a critical mass is attained, reinforcing network effects make a digital platform business develop into a winner-takes-it-all market where only one major player or few platforms will be able to capture most of the market share (Eisenmann et al., 2006; Evans & Schmalensee, 2010). This is enhanced by the missing limitation of growth by physical assets, capital, or geographical proximity (Parker et al., 2016).

While these positive network effects are the predominant dynamic on digital platforms, also negative network effects can appear when platforms are overcrowded and poorly managed (Parker et al., 2016). Among others, negative externalities can occur when private information of users is collected, analyzed, and passed on, when missing measures to prevent from harmful activities such as cyberbullying, or the posting of discriminating or hateful content lead to negative communication, or when platform initiatives result in a competitive environment that puts users at a disadvantage.

2.2 Privacy

Seeking for user adoption and growth during the initial stages of the platform and the winner-takes-it-all race can come at the expense of privacy. We define privacy as individuals' control of the information about themselves and their activities (Westin, 1968). Digital platform firms harness user data for three purposes that translate into the facilitation of valuable interactions, user adoption, and platform growth. First, platform firms use user characteristics and behavioral data in recommendation systems for facilitating valuable interactions for users (Hagiu & Jullien, 2011).

Second, platform firms include user ratings to ensure valuable interactions (Parker & Van Alstyne, 2005). Third, platform firms support the data collection and targeted advertising of complementors (Bhargava et al., 2020; De Corniere, 2016), allowing advertising-financed digital experience goods priced at zero marginal costs under competition (Lambrecht et al., 2014; Schumann et al., 2014; Shampanier et al., 2007). While some individuals might benefit from personalization based on data disclosure, the risks involved in disclosing one's information are data breaches, data misuse and data-based market exclusion from jobs, credit and healthcare, inhibiting individuals and constraining their freedom. If individuals are concerned with respect to their privacy, they protect themselves by using privacy-enhancing technologies (Heurix et al., 2015) and misrepresenting their data (Son & Kim, 2008). In addition to self-protection, governmental privacy legislation and industry self-regulation protect the privacy of individuals (Milberg et al., 2000; Xu et al., 2012).

2.3 Harmful Content

Another form of negative effects on digital platforms can be traced back to harmful content. Related to the growth of the Internet and the increasing amount of online interaction, the communication behavior of individuals changes (Burnap & Williams, 2016) and the volume of online content constantly increases on social platforms (Schmidt & Wiegand, 2017). Interacting in an anonymous way and being unaccountable for the contents that are published and shared, individuals tend to not only exchange ideas, but also to spread harmful content such as hate speech (Neshkovska & Trajkova, 2018). While a clear definition of hate speech is missing, the European Commission (2016, p. 1) describes hate speech as "all conduct publicly inciting to violence or hatred directed against a group of persons or a member of such a group defined by reference to race, colour, religion, descent or national or ethnic origin". As this definition is used for the code of conduct initially signed by Facebook, Microsoft, Twitter, and YouTube, later also by Instagram, Snapchat and Dailymotion, Jeuxvideo.com, TikTok, and LinkedIn, we consider this a relevant definition in our context. Closely related to hate speech are the phenomena of cyberbullying and discrimination. According to Fortuna and Nunes (2018), hate speech can be described as verbal discrimination, and cyberbullying refers to a specific person. However, as all of those concepts relate to some harmful content directed towards platform users online, we treat them equally in our review. In order to meet the challenge of harmful content on digital platforms, providers implement measures to detect (e.g., Lee, 2015; Ransbotham et al., 2016) and anticipate harmful content (e.g., Fisman & Luca, 2016; Klausen et al., 2018). However, with respect to the relevance of online harm for the offline world, also third parties such as companies advertising on social media proceed against these challenges (Pritchard, 2021).

2.4 Competition and Innovation

The third topic considered for our review is competition and innovation. The concept of competition describes a situation in which a given company tries to be more successful than another (Vickers, 1995). Ultimately, this can be narrowed down to two individuals racing against each other with respect to selling or purchasing (Marshall, 1920; Stigler, 1957).

Competition can refer to different dimensions. First, it encompasses all kinds of competition between firms. This includes market trading and auctions but also attempts for attrition. As competitive instruments, firms use prices, advertisement spending, R&D spending approximating innovating effort, and takeover bids. Finally, the measures implemented by the firms have an impact on performance metrics such as profits or market share but more widely also include corporate control and prices that in the end guarantee the survival of the firms (Vickers, 1995). Second, competition can be defined by behavioral terms. The concept of perfect competition refers to a state or a situation (Robinson, 1934) and thus neglects competitive processes. These strong assumptions are often violated. In most markets, information is imperfectly distributed and consequently imperfect competition is realized (Vickers, 1995). Third, describing competition as rivalry does not assume that more competition is always beneficial. This opens up the question of which degree of competition is desirable. Competitive pressure provides an incentive for firms to produce more efficiently, thus reducing costs. This again makes products and services cheaper for consumers. Often products compete in quality and variety and therefore meet heterogeneous preferences of users more accurately (Vives, 1984). In order to win competitive races, which inherit the perspective of a dynamic process, companies need to innovate, which provides advantages for the company as well as society (Aghion et al., 2001; Vickers, 1995).

3 Method

To find and analyze the papers used for the research, we carry out a structured literature review. The procedure is divided into the collection of papers related to the contents based on a structured scope (Sect. 3.1), the selection of the most relevant papers according to pre-defined criteria (Sect. 3.2), and the analysis of those papers (Sect. 3.3).

3.1   Collection of the Literature

To collect relevant papers for review, the journals are selected as well as key words for the search defined to retrieve the papers. First, in order to limit the scope of the literature, we only look into the FT50 journals being the standard basket for journals in their discipline. To get a holistic picture of publications in the field of societal challenges with regard to digital platforms, we might lose some relevant papers by only focusing on the literature related to information systems. Although the phenomenon of digital platforms refers to information systems, its applications are rather broad, ranging from business applications such as marketing or finance, to rather economics-related implementations in policy, while its effects can also be related to psychological constructs.

Second, based on the different topics to be covered in the literature review, different key words are used to entirely capture the contents. To select the papers to be included in this review on the phenomenon privacy on digital platforms, we filter for articles that contain the words *privacy* and *platform$* in the abstract and either *privacy* or *platform$* in the title. This allows us to capture all publications on privacy with respect to platforms while excluding those papers that are irrelevant to our purpose. To limit the results to a manageable number of results, we filter for articles in the categories Technology, Marketing and Advertising, Management and Organizational Behavior, Economics and Business according to the JSTOR database.

For the search on hate, cyberbullying, and discrimination, two separate searches on hate speech or cyberbullying as well as discrimination are carried out. The main purpose of this part is to analyze harmful content in the interaction between users on digital platforms. To define the scope in which this harmful content appears, the word *platform* is used in the string combined with several ways in which this harm can appear. To separate the phenomenon of hate speech and discrimination on platforms, we use two separate search strings. While discrimination can rather be referred to any unfair treatment of people because of protected characteristics such as race, gender, nationality, or religion, the form in which discrimination can be expressed is much wider compared to terms such as hate speech, offensive language, or cyberbullying. These phenomena rather only capture the textual expression of dislike. Consequently, one search query connects *platform* to *discrimination*, while a second query is used to capture also the more narrow papers by combining *platform* with *hate speech*, *offensive language*, or *cyberbullying*. Those three terms are not necessarily synonyms; however, all refer to some level of harm targeted at others online in order to disparage them. Although terms such as *radicalization*, *extremism*, or *profanity* are also related terms, they are intentionally excluded from the query as these terms are very specific and therefore would most probably not add any further value. While the papers that mention the more broader terms will still be retrieved through the search, the very detailed papers are less relevant to get a general understanding of the phenomenon on digital platforms.

To get papers with respect to competition and the effects on innovation, we only review papers that appeared at the intersection of those two topics. This approach translates into four key words to conduct a structured literature review. First, we use the term *platform* to identify all papers that touch in their scope of analysis platforms in a broader sense. To rule out physical platforms, such as credit card and telecommunication networks, we add the term *digital*. This ensures that we find only the literature that analyzes or contributes to modern digital technology and related research questions. In contrast to Rietveld and Schilling (2021), we are interested in the literature combining competition and innovation. Therefore, purely reviewing contributions mentioning *platforms* and *competition* would be insufficient. Consequently, we add *innovation* as our final key word.

3.2 Selection of the Literature

Based on the papers that are retrieved from the key word search in the FT50 journals, we need to reduce and filter the number of matches for the relevant ones. In order to do so, we consider three main aspects:

1. **Title**: Mostly, the title already provides a good understanding of the content of the paper. By skimming the titles, we can remove a broad number of papers from the set of relevant papers.
2. **Abstract**: For those that are kept based on the title, in the next step, we scan the abstracts and assess them in terms of the content of the paper. Based on that, we discard some more papers which are not further be used for the review.
3. **Main Body**: Those papers that are not removed from the set of relevant papers are fully read. Based on the full reading of the text, we remove some further papers if they do not fulfill the purpose of the review.

Although the detailed investigation of the papers depends on the topic, some general criteria help to assess whether a paper should be used for the review or not. First, all papers should study the phenomena in relation to digital platforms instead of only investigating them from a general perspective. Second, the relevant papers need to cover the topic as a central part, not only mentioning it. Particularly, this refers to papers that mention the social implications such as privacy, hate, cyberbullying, and discrimination, as well as competition and innovation only as examples, side aspects, or secondary phenomena that not further investigated.

3.3 Analysis of the Literature

To analyze the literature that was retrieved from the collection and selection strategy, we use a qualitative approach. We apply content analysis in the form of 5-step human-scored schemata (Morris, 1994). First, we identify the unit under analysis, which in our case are the full papers selected for the review. Second, we develop categories for each single topic. To do so, we identify the relevant research streams of each topic by clustering the papers according to the topics they cover. Third, we match the research streams to the papers, where also one paper can be part of several research streams when covering multiple categories. In our case, this does not require several coders; therefore, we do not need the steps for comparing the classifications and aggregating them. For retrieving the contents of each stream, the papers found in the literature review as well as upstream literature cited in those papers are used to be able to understand the contents of the main papers.

4 Results

To outline what has been addressed by scholars in the previous literature, we outline the economic and social consequences of user privacy (Sect. 4.1), hate, cyberbullying, and discrimination (Sect. 4.2), and competition and innovation (Sect. 4.3) with respect to digital platforms.

4.1 Privacy

Privacy-enhancing and privacy-reducing mechanisms can have critical business and societal implications. The main literature streams covered in the previous literature include consequences for platform providers (Sects. 4.1.1–4.1.3), complementors (Sect. 4.1.4), and users (Sect. 4.1.5).

4.1.1 Privacy Regulation on Digital Platforms

Digital platforms' collection of user data and their promotion of developers' collection of user data have evoked privacy concerns by users. Privacy concerns by users are not exclusively triggered but to a great extent driven by platforms. Regulators and users have raised concerns that the data collection on digital platforms includes private information, invades personal privacy, and carries the risk of data misuse (Foerderer & Schuetz, 2022). For example, Google's Android platform has traditionally allowed app developers to collect personal user information such as their location and communication (Kummer & Schulte, 2019; Mayya & Viswanathan, 2021).

Governments have passed numerous privacy laws to protect consumers for whom platforms have become an integral part of their lives. Governmental privacy regulations, e.g., the General Data Protection Regulation (GDPR), impose requirements that platform firms need to enforce, putting pressure on the business model of platform firms. Yet, a platform firm may also exercise its discretionary power and set privacy rules that go beyond what the law requires, in order to compete with privacy for users (Casadesus-Masanell & Hervas-Drane, 2015; Gal-Or et al., 2018), allay users' privacy concerns, and foster user adoption, a phenomenon that has been occurring increasingly in recent years. Among others, Apple introduced the requirement for developers to obtain opt-in consent for tracking and targeted advertising with iOS14 on its mobile platform iOS (Sokol & Zhu, 2021). In a recently published paper, arguments are being made for regarding privacy as a platform governance instrument (Kuan & Lee, 2020).

In regulating privacy on the platform, a platform firm acts as a regulator, reconciling differing interests, a duty resembling the role of a public regulator. Yet, in enforcing privacy guidelines, the platform owner is typically more effective than a public policymaker because of its unique power to enforce privacy. In contrast to a public regulator, a platform firm owns proprietary data and algorithms to monitor quality compliance and a scarce asset that facilitates interactions (Gawer, 2009), resulting in an extraordinary ability and power to enforce privacy guidelines and to curate the platform's value propositions.

In deciding what level of privacy digital platform providers should impose, the interests of platform providers, users, and complementors need to be balanced. Users and complementors are both pivotal parties in platform ecosystems that are characterized as two-sided markets. For attracting users, the platform firm needs to implement certain privacy-related measures but also is dependent on the entry and innovation by complementors supplying "ancillary products that expand the platform's market" (Cusumano & Gawer, 2002, p. 52), a dependency particularly salient for mobile platforms such as Android with uncoordinated complementary innovation (Thomas et al., 2014). Users and complementors typically have opposing preferences as to privacy because it constrains complementors' use of data as input factor to production, for personalization of the user experience, and for monetization through targeted advertising, purposes vital for the capacity and incentive to innovate.

Platform privacy regulations differ in terms of configuration. Privacy policies on digital platforms vary in terms of their intensity and dimension. Previous research on privacy's impact on digital platforms studied the impact of an opt-out regime on publishers' advertising revenue (Johnson et al., 2020), but not of opt-in policies or complete bans on targeted advertising. Regarding the dimension of privacy, prior work focused on information privacy (Sokol & Zhu, 2021) and, except for a study of anonymity on dating platforms (Bapna et al., 2016), neglected other forms of privacy such as disclosure of personal matters, relations, thoughts, portrayal, body, secrets, and ratings.

4.1.2 Economic Consequences of Privacy on Platform Governance Outcomes

User privacy is a platform governance instrument. Among the decisions as part of platform governance are decisions regarding pricing and control (Tiwana, 2013). Decisions as to pricing aim at promoting third-party production and increasing platform profits. Decisions regarding control intend to foster user adoption.

Privacy relates to both pricing and control on the platform. For platform firms, advertising represents an important revenue stream. For example, Google earns revenue on its Android platform with its Admob advertising network that has by far the largest market share. At the same time, offering advertising as an opportunity to price and monetize apps and content to third-party complementors is a strategic means to raise the ability and incentive of third parties to produce apps or content (Bhargava, 2021a; Bhargava et al., 2020). Developers of apps and providers of digital content rely on display advertising for monetization as digital goods are experience goods, which aggravates charging upfront prices, while they are also non-rival and imply zero marginal costs of production and distribution, leading to free digital goods under competition (Shapiro et al., 1998).

Also, research is concerned about the consequences of privacy on platform firms' profits. Theoretical research proposes that platform firms and complementors compete with the level of privacy at the extensive rather than the intensive margin. Regarding the platform firm's decision on privacy as a platform pricing instrument, Gal-Or et al. (2018) make three predictions. First, they propose that users face a trade-off between relevance of advertisements and privacy concerns in terms of data collection for targeted advertising. Second, when users' preferences as to this trade-off are heterogeneous, then platform firms will differentiate themselves with the level of user privacy. Third, when users' privacy concerns globally increase or when competition between platforms intensifies, platform firms will more compete with privacy safeguards, earn less revenue from advertisements, and start to compete on prices. This competition on prices and preceding reduction of privacy differentiation will compound profits (Gal-Or et al., 2018). Therefore, economically, platform firms are predicted to forego profits when they tighten up user privacy on their platforms.

Regarding the control function of privacy within platform governance, user privacy is either a developer guideline by platform firms to ensure quality among complements and to promote user adoption or a user right to foster user adoption. Within the platform governance literature, one stream of research evaluates platform firms' quality-related guidelines intended to control the quality of complementary products, promote valuable interactions for users, and induce user adoption (Claussen et al., 2013; Gawer, 2009; Wareham et al., 2014). This stream of literature examines whether a high quality, limited in quantity portfolio of complements achieved by exclusionary variance-decreasing rules is more effective for user adoption than a large quantity of complements with variable, lacking quality (Wareham et al., 2014). Prior empirical research studied the effect of a soft rule change on Facebook, an intervention that tied the allowed number of notifications sent by apps to users to the quality assessment of the apps and that indeed increased the quality of apps (Claussen et al., 2013). Excluding undesired content and malicious publishers from the iOS platform for safeguarding user adoption, Apple has long been using stringent rules and an application review process (Ghazawneh & Henfridsson, 2013).

Previous research also looked into how privacy as a control instrument impacts user adoption and third-party production. Theoretical arguments would point to a possible positive effect of privacy, which promotes the quality of complements and grants users more control rights of their disclosed information, on user demand. When it comes to the question of how privacy control affects third-party production, there are competing arguments. On the one hand, privacy could impose compliance costs to third parties and reduce their advertising revenues (Campbell et al., 2015). On the other hand, privacy raises the quality and, thereby, demand by users (Hui et al., 2007). In addition, privacy might also promote the supply of complements directly as it requires third parties to adjust their business model towards a higher quality justifying alternative monetization schemes and to beneficially comply with the new regulations (Ghose & Han, 2014; Porter & Van der Linde, 1995). Nascent studies examining the impact of GDPR, a European governmental privacy regulation instead of a platform owner-imposed privacy policy, find a negative impact of GDPR with respect to the number of competing apps on iOS (Wu & Pang, 2021) and on the financing of app startups (Kircher & Foerderer, 2021). When it comes to the impact of privacy as a user right on user behavior, prior research found in the context of Facebook that a privacy policy change that gives users global control over the disclosure of their published content to other users increases content sharing by privacy-sensitive users and decreases content sharing by less privacy-sensitive users (Cavusoglu et al., 2016). Further empirical work related to Facebook exploited a policy change that increased users' privacy control. After this policy change that only affected the perceived control but not the actual targeting of the advertisements, users' likelihood of clicking on an advertisement almost doubled (Tucker, 2014).

4.1.3 Economic Consequences of Privacy on Platforms' Core Value Propositions

From a different angle, user privacy also impacts the overall value creation of digital platforms. While privacy affects platform governance outcomes rather during a later stage of platform evolution, privacy influences the value propositions of platforms already during the launch and growth stages. The value that digital platforms provide to consumers can be summarized as the facilitation of interactions between consumers and producers. More precisely, platforms facilitate valuable interactions by reducing search and verification costs and allowing advertising-financed digital experience goods priced at zero marginal costs. For these value propositions, data is a crucial input factor (Bhargava et al., 2020; Cusumano & Gawer, 2002; Parker & Van Alstyne, 2005).

Regarding the reduction of the search costs function of digital platforms, privacy would potentially compromise the reduction of search costs by disabling the recommendation systems. Platforms such as Amazon and Delivery Hero reduce search costs and make matches between buyers and sellers through three main mechanisms. First, they host large-scale supply and demand markets. Second, they integrate search and filter options. Third, they recommend products based on consumers' characteristics, behavior, and ratings.

With respect to the reduction of verification costs on digital platforms, privacy in the form of private ratings could influence both supply and demand. Platforms such as Android and Netflix reduce verification costs by including ratings of apps and content on the platform. Users rate the apps and content, thereby making it simpler for future interested users to detect the product quality. Recently, platforms got under pressure due to their alleged damage of mental health of their users, a damage that would be caused not solely, but also by ratings. A privacy policy by a platform firm that makes ratings private would benefit the mental health of individuals, but likely makes it more difficult for users to verify the quality of the products on the platform before using them. An increase in the verification costs poses a theoretical problem as to how it affects the suppliers on platforms. On the one hand, providers of digital content, especially those of lower quality, could be encouraged to provide more content. On the other hand, less transparent ratings and verification costs could decrease competition and cut off content providers from valuable feedback for improving their content. In turn, privacy would again detrimentally affect the value of the interactions.

As to the promotion of advertising-financed digital experience goods priced at zero marginal costs, privacy in the form of a restriction of targeted advertising could potentially reduce users' access to free digital goods. Privacy reduces revenues from targeted advertising (Johnson et al., 2020), compounding the advertising-supported business model of app developers and content providers and forcing them to charge prices. This harms the utility of users because their willingness to pay for digital experience goods is limited (Lambrecht et al., 2014).

4.1.4 Economic Consequences of Privacy on Complementors' Business Model

User privacy is expected to harm the business model of complementors. Developers on mobile platforms and content creators rely on monetization through advertising (Hermann, 2021). Though, privacy regulation that demands opt-in consent to or opt-out options of data collection reduces advertising revenues of complementors for opted-out users by about 50% (Johnson et al., 2020). Advertising-dependent complementors arguably lack the ability and incentive to continuously develop apps and content when privacy is tightened up and cuts advertising revenues (Chellappa & Shivendu, 2010).

Previous research on the economic consequences of privacy on the business model of complementors is composed of emerging theoretical and empirical work.

Theoretical work conjectures that complementors compete with the level of privacy at the extensive rather than the intensive margin, developers either charging prices in return for greater levels of user privacy or relying on revenues from targeted advertising. When competition among developers intensifies and there is a price mechanism for privacy, that is when users are willing to pay prices for greater levels of privacy, developers would compete with privacy and, hence, tighten up privacy (Casadesus-Masanell & Hervas-Drane, 2015).

Also, researchers look into the actual consequences of privacy on the performance of third-party complementors. Nascent research with respect to mobile app developers shows that advertising-supported complementors avoid privacy (Kummer & Schulte, 2019; Mayya & Viswanathan, 2021) but only provides suggestions for the consequences of privacy on complementary innovation. Mayya and Viswanathan (2021) found that Android app developers delay their app upgrades to Android 6.0 to defer the changeover from requesting blanket permissions before the download to requesting permissions during runtime. The delay of the upgrade was particularly strong for apps that sought permissions irrelevant to their functionality, indicating that developers need data for a purpose other than functionality, such as monetization. This suggests that the majority of Android developers have no price mechanism for privacy and, thus, need to avoid privacy when privacy is restricted on the platform (Mayya & Viswanathan, 2021). Correlational evidence from Android suggests that developers pursuing privacy-preserving business models are more likely to charge prices for their apps, prices that compensate the lost revenues from targeted advertising but are difficult to enforce in the ad-supported Internet (Kummer & Schulte, 2019). At least for some developers, there seems to be a price mechanism for privacy.

4.1.5 Social, Socio-Economic, and Economic Consequences of Privacy on Users

User privacy impacts users socially, socio-economically, and economically. As regards the social impact of privacy on users, anonymity in dating apps allows users to keep their secret interest in other users undisclosed, but also lowers the likelihood of finding a match (Bapna et al., 2016).

In regard to socio-economic consequences, prior work in the crowdfunding context revealed that privacy-related questions before the transaction reduce funding but increase the average funding amount, compared to privacy setting made after the transaction (Burtch et al., 2015). Keeping one's information in social networks private helps users to ensure that they do not experience any data-based discrimination in hiring (Acquisti & Fong, 2020).

The economic consequences of privacy on users mainly revolve around their ability and willingness to participate in economic transactions. The impact of privacy on user demand still is unexplored and underlies a theoretical tension. On the one hand, privacy could promote usage by reducing privacy concerns (Hui et al., 2007). However, privacy could stifle the supply of digital goods (Campbell et al., 2015). When investigating the effect of privacy on prices of digital goods in the entire market, the essential question is whether there is a price mechanism for the average digital good when privacy is restricted for all goods. For some app developers, there should be a price mechanism. Android developers were found to charge higher prices for greater levels of user privacy (Kummer & Schulte, 2019).

4.2 Hate, Cyberbullying, and Discrimination on Digital Platforms

Besides the challenges that privacy concerns impose on digital platforms, there are further societal implications that refer to the way those platforms are used for disparaging others. Hate speech, cyberbullying, and discrimination are the result of anonymous interaction in the digital age. The main streams in the published literature investigate the reasons for harmful behavior (Sect. 4.2.1), particularly with respect to the role of anonymity (Sect. 4.2.2). Also, researchers show the consequences of online harm (Sect. 4.2.3) and present countermeasures that are applied to reduce harmful content on social platforms (Sect. 4.2.4).

4.2.1 The Presence of Hate and Discrimination on Digital Platforms

Being a place for free speech and unlimited interactions, digital platforms make it easy to spread extreme opinions and harmful content. On the one hand, any form of content can easily be published in an anonymous way, and anyone can join ongoing conversations (Rauf, 2021); on the other hand, low cost for spreading ideas and easy dissemination across online-based networks make contents go viral (Ransbotham et al., 2016).

One main difficulty of dealing with harmful content on digital platforms is closely related to the human right of freedom of expression, which also includes the freedom to express harmful content (Rauf, 2021). Particularly when operating on a global scale and integrating legal backgrounds of several countries, the trade-off between freedom of expression and harmful content becomes increasingly difficult to solve (Cohen-Almagor, 2012).

Moreover, there are further reasons that facilitate the emergence and spread of online harm. This relates to the nature of online platforms, algorithms embedded in platforms, and discriminatory behavior duplicated from the offline world. First, the nature of digital platforms is a reason for harmful content. The Internet does not impose any limitations in time or space to the communication of people, therefore allowing like-minded groups to easily get together, which is enhanced by extremist celebrities spreading their views (Rauf, 2021). Also, the need to disclose personal data to increase the quality of a service (Mejia & Parker, 2021) and to increase trust, such as the uploading of photos, makes users vulnerable to discrimination

(Fisman & Luca, 2016). In addition, certain social relationships and individual characteristics increase the likelihood of participating in online harm. When users experience negative social influence encouraged by the belonging to a group that performs harmful activities, such behavior becomes an accepted norm and users are more likely to participate (Bocij & McFarlane, 2003). Also, an increased time spent on social media makes users more likely to participate in online harm (Lowry et al., 2016).

Aside from social platforms that allow the emergence of harm, algorithms embedded in platforms can be prone to discrimination and harm. Discrimination via artificial intelligence (AI) is able to reinforce imbalances in the offline world (Hermann, 2021). Particularly for the so-called black-box AI, it is increasingly difficult to detect such bias (Hermann, 2021). Although in the first place, algorithms might seem objective and unbiased, a biased training data is replicated by algorithms, therefore making their predictions or analyses prone to discrimination (Leicht-Deobald et al., 2019). This can lead to negative feedback loops when a certain group is overrepresented in the training data (Leicht-Deobald et al., 2019). Also, the inclusion or exclusion of certain features can be a reason for discrimination to arise (Arrieta et al., 2020), as certain relationships might be omitted or highlighted. Besides these technical issues, discriminatory attitudes based on the culture and beliefs of developers integrated in the development process can be translated into algorithms and AI making the algorithm take discriminatory decisions (Leicht-Deobald et al., 2019; Rich & Gureckis, 2019; Seaver, 2017). While discrimination can happen based on beliefs or unintentionally due to algorithmic failure, discrimination can also be a result of the optimized cost-effectiveness, e.g., when advertising directed at young women is more expensive (Lambrecht & Tucker, 2019).

Related to platform discrimination, a third category is the discrimination related to stereotypes that can also be observed in the offline world. Although gender-specific characteristics can be a crucial factor in recruiting as outlined by Cook et al. (2021) who analyzed the gender earnings gap on Uber, according to an experiment on Amazon Mechanical Turk, female applicants are associated with a higher level of attractiveness and trustworthiness and are considered more cooperative, making discrimination a result of gender stereotypes (Chan & Wang, 2018).

4.2.2   Role of Anonymity on Digital Platforms

Considering the particularities of online interactions, one main characteristic is the high degree of anonymity. Such anonymity can be an enabler as well as an inhibitor of online harm, therefore making it increasingly difficult for platform providers to decide on the right level of anonymity.

Anonymity enhances fairness, while at the same time, it becomes increasingly difficult to build personal relationships with strangers in anonymous environments. While anonymity of identities is considered fair to avoid biases, the challenge in building trust and assessing reliability between different parties of an interaction increases due to a high level of anonymity (Etzioni, 2019).

In contrast to enhance fairness, anonymous interactions make individuals more likely to participate in online harm. Cloaking enhanced through digital means allows to interact anonymously on social platforms, which makes harm spread more easily (Ransbotham et al., 2016) as anonymity makes individuals more likely to share thoughts they would not make public if their identity could be traced (Rauf, 2021). In online social networks, individuals believe their identity will not be made public, they cannot be hold accountable for their online actions, their devices are physically not close enough to others that could observe cyberbullying, they cannot be recognized as those in the online world by others, and the system will keep them anonymous (Lowry et al., 2013, 2016; Pinsonneault & Heppel, 1997). Those effects of anonymity that are enhanced by the nature of digital technologies lead to disinhibition and deindividuation that make individuals more likely to engage in harmful activities online although they would hesitate to perform them in the offline world (Lowry et al., 2013, 2016; Suler, 2004). This deindividuation effect results from a lower level of self-awareness when interacting anonymously and therefore a reduced feeling of accountability for harmful actions (Zimbardo, 1969). Also, negative feelings related to situational morality are less likely to appear in an anonymous environment (Lowry et al., 2016).

The high level of anonymity also makes users less identifiable and accountable for their harmful activities on digital platforms. The detection of individuals is way more difficult in the online world, which significantly reduces the likelihood for punishment and societal reluctance (Lowry et al., 2016). Also, anonymity fosters the power of the bullies by allowing to create content that involves several profiles based on fake people, anonymous messages, etc. (Lowry et al., 2016). According to Lee (2015), laws need to accept tracing for societal benefit, however, ensuring that privacy of individuals is only restricted if there is substantial suspicion for harmful behavior.

4.2.3 Consequences of Discrimination and Hate on Platforms

Discrimination and harmful content have three main implications: unfair treatment, mental health problems, and value loss with respect to the platform.

In terms of digital technologies, algorithmic bias can lead to discrimination of certain groups resulting in unfair treatment or access restrictions (Ransbotham et al., 2016). While on the one hand, algorithms applied in company processes allow to take data-driven decisions that are more rational and objective, they are also applied to a wider extent to evaluate and interpret machines, which induces employees to not question and blindly trust results (Leicht-Deobald et al., 2019). This becomes increasingly concerning if it leads to reinforcing effects (Lambrecht & Tucker, 2019).

Users who are directly or indirectly affected by harmful content on digital platforms face psychological problems. Almost half of the Americans who reported to be targeted by online hate suffer from physical and mental problems, also in terms of depression and anxiety, sleeping problems, or fears in the offline world

(Forbus, 2021). Besides direct effects, also second-order effects can appear such as the silencing of targets of harassment, but also a general decrease in the willingness to interact online (Ransbotham et al., 2016). Also third parties on platforms often do not remain unaffected, and unconscious differences in processing information or mental health can appear (Ransbotham et al., 2016).

Besides the problems that arise for individuals, also businesses face negative implications of harmful content. People are more likely to leave a platform where they feel harassed, which makes advertising on such platforms less effective (Forbus, 2021). Also, advertisement that is placed next to harmful content that appears on platforms is not adequately considered by consumers or in worst case fosters distrust (Pritchard, 2021).

4.2.4 Mechanisms to Reduce Harmful Online Content

Platforms are concerned with the removal and anticipation of harmful content, but their measures are often insufficient. When considering the increase of harm on social platforms, the failure of corporations and law in restricting such content can be observed (Rauf, 2021). Besides platform-initiated measures to reduce online harm, external pressure from platform users can be an effective measure.

First, companies can introduce own mechanisms on the platform to fight against harmful contents on their platform by closely monitoring user-generated content with technology or human moderators, while also implementing the option to report such content in order to enhance platform users to become active supporters of a clean platform. Detection of harmful content becomes increasingly difficult and requires precise content monitoring. As hate is case-specific, it becomes increasingly difficult to detect it via machine learning, which requires a substantial training data set (Rauf, 2021). This forces social platforms to have alternative means of detecting harmful content, e.g., with a highly skilled workforce observing deviations on the platform (Rauf, 2021). According to Lee (2015), outgoing content should be monitored and controlled more closely by still ensuring an adequate level of user privacy, e.g., by implementing digital software agents that follow rule-based content monitoring. Besides the detection of harmful content on platforms, most platform providers also rely on users to report abuse happening on the platform. Wong et al. (2021) analyzed what encourages bystanders to use reporting functions. As a result of the immense content that is published on digital platforms and the limited intelligence of automated systems (Harris, 2017), platform owners require the help of these bystanders in order to combat hate and cyberbullying (Wong et al., 2021). In general, an increased perceived responsibility, confidence in system anonymity, perceived self-efficacy, perceived outcome effectiveness, and perceived reporting climate have a positive impact on using the available reporting functions (Wong et al., 2021).

Besides reactive measures to remove harmful content on digital platforms, anticipatory actions are most effective in preventing from negative consequences. Even if hateful content gets removed, it might have already spread widely (Rauf,

2021) based on the velocity in which the online world evolves. This makes it crucial to prevent from harmful user behavior even before it can appear on the platform. Platform providers can implement certain measures that enhance safe interactions on digital platforms by making use of technical content restrictions, but also by sensitizing users. Dhillon and Smith (2019) define the protection of online interactions, the establishment of security procedures and technical security, strong value systems, and the definition of intermediaries that ensure the minimization of cyberstalking as fundamental objectives to prevent from cyberstalking. Users should be familiarized with dangers online and should be provided means to carry out safe interactions, while security measures such as authentication or monitoring, as well as intermediaries, are also crucial (Dhillon & Smith, 2019). In addition, strong value systems need to be taught to children so that they will not participate in misbehavior (Dhillon & Smith, 2019). Besides, profiling of a user could help to identify users as harmful even before they post-related content (Klausen et al., 2018) by assessing the likelihood for creating harm. As there is the danger that extremist users suspended from a social network are likely to create a new account, it also needs to be ensured that user profiles similar to suspended profiles are detected as such (Klausen et al., 2018). To further reduce harmful content and discrimination on digital platforms, it can be effective to determine thoughtful rules for the exclusion or inclusion of personal data, or timing the displaying of personal data accordingly. Fisman and Luca (2016) conducted experiments on how discrimination can be reduced, e.g., by showing personal information only at a later point in the booking process or showing anti-discrimination rules more prominently. However, Mejia and Parker (2021) showed in an experiment on a ridesharing platform that even if identity-revealing characteristics are only shown after the booking has been completed, discrimination in terms of race and LGBT support can be observed in cancellation rates. In terms of discrimination based on algorithms, monitoring of potentially discriminating algorithms is required (Fisman & Luca, 2016). Fu et al. (2021) propose a debiasing method that makes input variables independent from sensitive attributes to ensure that the algorithmic output does not contain bias by only slightly reducing the accuracy the algorithm can achieve, while also human questioning of results is required (Leicht-Deobald et al., 2019). As a particularity of the opportunities that social platforms provide, an effective measure in enhancing trust and lowering the risk for discrimination based on unrelated characteristics are reviews. Cui et al. (2020) detected in an experiment that discrimination against African–Americans can significantly be reduced if there are reviews. Especially on sharing platforms such as Airbnb or eBay, rating systems are a popular mechanism to enhance trust (Whelan, 2019). While this increases trust for future transactions, it also helps platform providers in identifying users that do not perform according to guidelines (Etzioni, 2019). However, anonymity on social networks makes review systems a popular place for fraud through fake reviews or offer new potential for hate (Scott & Orlikowski, 2014).

Finally, also users can further enhance the removal of harm on digital platforms, either actively by using reporting functions, but also by exerting pressure on platform providers. Not only platform providers and policymakers have a responsibility in ensuring safe online interactions, also users take an important role in supporting this goal. People in the digital age have a double responsibility to enhance safe online interaction: On the one hand, they should not initiate harm, on the other hand, they should react to harm caused by others (Pundak et al., 2021). Being used for advertising, platforms also need to constitute a safe place for companies (Pritchard, 2021). This lead to initiatives in 2020 such as the #StopHateForProfit boycott to stop advertising on Facebook as a pressure to address the problem of hate as well as the #EngageResponsibly initiative that wants to connect platforms with consumers and brands to target the problem of social media harassment and hate by creating awareness in the consumer environment (Forbus, 2021). In order to ensure that algorithms do not result in mistreatment, highly qualified third parties should intervene in ensuring fairness. On digital labor crowdsourcing platforms, such as Amazon Mechanical Turk, Fieseler et al. (2019) propose to include a third party that ensures fairness, regulates complaints, and prevents from unfair treatment. With AI becoming increasingly complex, it is also required to hold a company accountable for their algorithms, being aware of the underlying technology and the features used for prediction (Hermann, 2021).

4.3   Competition and Innovation

To outline the topic of competition and innovation on digital platforms, the main literature streams cover the mutual rivalry between platforms, ecosystems, and contributors (Sect. 4.3.1). Underlying economic forces determine who rivals against whom (Sect. 4.3.2). Platform interventions and ecosystem contributors often aim at deterring further competition or incentives to innovate (Sect. 4.3.3).

4.3.1   Mutual Rivalry Between Platforms, Ecosystems, and Contributors

Competition can occur among businesses, but also among ecosystems and contributors. First, the breadth of competition of platforms includes the core product or technology and features a value co-creating ecosystem. This circumstance leads to platforms competing against other platforms (Liu et al., 2011; Marx et al., 2014; Niculescu et al., 2018). Second, ecosystems can compete against each other, while individual ecosystem participants compete against each other regarding attention and range (Bauer et al., 2016; Cennamo et al., 2018; Foerderer, 2020). Third, competition can appear among complementors. Complementors can use multi-homing strategies to maximize their range, which negatively impacts the contribution's quality and hurts the platform (Cennamo et al., 2018).

Beyond that, ecosystems contribute positively to the size of a platform's network effects. This contribution creates additional value, whose distribution can be a subject of competition between the platform and ecosystem complementors (Casadesus-Masanell & Yoffie, 2007; Ghose & Han, 2014). As a result, the ecosystem can create potential competitors that use the ecosystem's strength to endanger the incumbent platform's market position (Karhu et al., 2018). The incumbent platform will likely intervene in the ecosystem to maintain control.

Platforms compete against each other in various dimensions, the most important one being innovation, that can take place at two different levels. First, the platform can provide innovation by itself. Second, the platform acts as a host for innovative activity performed by the contributors and participants of the ecosystem (Foerderer, 2020; Jung et al., 2019). Within the ecosystem, innovations are often developed by novel combinations of the existing features from the platform and the corresponding ecosystem (Ganco et al., 2020). These two distinct places for innovation have different implications. An innovative platform attempting to replace an incumbent platform has to overcome a high market entry barrier, as the innovation itself is not sufficient for gaining a large market share. Furthermore, the platform must accumulate large network effects (Murthy & Madhok, 2021; Sheremata, 2004) and overcome stickiness and inertia of customers (Kumar et al., 2021). Many digital platforms could reach a critical mass and platformize conventional markets (Eisenmann et al., 2006; Evans & Schmalensee, 2010). For instance, Airbnb represents one of the major changes in tourism. Its superior matching can be seen as the innovation itself (Guttentag, 2019). Similarly, Uber entered the ride-hailing market and could improve the allocative efficiency of a market (Cramer & Krueger, 2016). Another example is the market entry of Craigslist, which significantly affected newspapers (Seamans & Zhu, 2014). In all of the three cases, traditional markets could less effectively match supply and demand than the platform entrant.

To enhance innovation, platforms can implement different measures that promote such actions (Evans & Gawer, 2016). Using the example of Apple, the platforms foster innovative complements for its app store, while also organizing the cooperation between ecosystem members to create positive knowledge spillovers (Foerderer, 2020).

4.3.2 Ecosystem Contributors

To enhance a vibrant ecosystem, the platform can leverage its ecosystem to increase the attractiveness. The platform systematically builds strategic partnerships and supports the supply of complements from the ecosystem. The complexity and volume of such complements have a positive effect on the platform performance (Gnyawali et al., 2010). This effect can be reduced by multi-homing strategies from complementors, which weaken the network effects if content is not provided exclusively on one platform (Cennamo et al., 2018). Overall, the platform has to navigate between openness supporting innovative and fast-growing ecosystems, while this enables hostile attacks against the market position of the incumbent platform.

The provision of resources in order to secure a thriving ecosystem creates a trade-off between control and openness of the platform. Its openness is subject to a variety of governing decisions. Giving up control by increasing the openness is beneficial, as this increases the degrees of freedom for ecosystem members developing their own complements. As a result, the development rate of complements can rise (Boudreau, 2010; Ghose & Han, 2014). Complementors and even potential new platforms can use these resources to maximize network effects of the incumbent platform. However, this strategy is only rational at intermediate levels of network effects to establish a monopoly (Niculescu et al., 2018). This kind of support can utilize boundary resources, which can represent an API, an app store, or open-source agreements. On the one hand, these resources are relevant for an ecosystem to emerge and grow. On the other hand, they provide access for complementors to the network and enable hostile forking attempts. The complementor can potentially outgrow the incumbent platform and might take over the installed user base (Karhu et al., 2018). Such a hostile takeover becomes more realistic with a growing shared base of users between the platform and ecosystem participants (Eisenmann et al., 2011).

Platform innovations also affect the ecosystem (Foerderer et al., 2014), as new technology requires a transition of the ecosystem. If this innovation becomes disruptive in its character, grown ties between the platform and its ecosystem members can be irreversibly damaged. This has two important implications for an incumbent platform. First, it opens up the opportunity for a new incumbent to enter the market. Second, the long-run growth potential is reduced, as the ecosystem loses additional value for users (Ozalp et al., 2018).

4.3.3 Platform Interventions

If a platform fears losing control over its ecosystem and thus an important feature of its own attractiveness, interventions to regain control can become necessary.

Changing the access of intellectual property for participants from the ecosystem can be one potential solution. Similarly, the usage of intellectual property can be restricted, by making key components proprietary again. This limits the capabilities of potential challengers. Exercising the market power by adjusting standards and norms can be a second feasible way to maintain control over an ecosystem. Whenever a platform has the ability to set standards, potential innovators have to ensure compatibility of their innovation, otherwise losing access to the network of the platform (Sheremata, 2004). Maintaining a certain standard becomes easier with a base of firms supporting the platform's decision and can be one decisive factor in setting the standard in a competitive market (Wang & Xie, 2011). However, protection of a standard can be alleviated by the use of digital conversion technologies, which restores compatibility between platforms (Liu et al., 2011). Google used its market power, or more specifically ownership of the Play Store, to successfully set the standard for photography apps by entering the sphere of complementors with the app Google Photos. As a result, this spurred innovation as complementing app developers substantially increased their development effort (Foerderer et al., 2018).

In a similar manner, even a potential entry threat can have significant effects. In an environment with network effects, the present incumbents react with an increase in innovative effort (Pan et al., 2019). The least favored option can be a controlled loss of control if no other strategy is available. Intellectual property, which is highly protected due to patents, can be disclosed intentionally. This creates an incentive for competitors to imitate rather than innovate. Such a strategy establishes a technological leadership and might relieve competitive pressure (Pacheco-de Almeida & Zemsky, 2012).

5 Mutual Dependencies in Research

After having outlined the three different topics of privacy, hate, cyberbullying, and discrimination, as well as competition and innovation separately, this section aims at bridging the different topics and finding dependencies. To do so, we develop a framework that looks into the relationship between the concepts.

We find positive as well as negative relationships as outlined in Fig. 1. While applying mechanisms to enhance privacy and positivity can lead to a competitive advantage, high competition makes it often necessary for companies to put less effort in solving these challenges to be able to compete with rivals. Also, privacy-enhancing mechanisms can reduce harmful content by exposing less vulnerable details to potential attackers, while high privacy also makes it increasingly difficult to detect harm.

5.1 Privacy Decisions to Reduce Harm

Privacy reduction as well as privacy enhancement can both be promising in reducing harmful content on digital platforms. While the previous literature has commonly looked into mechanisms to reduce harm on online platforms, particularly privacy measures can be a mechanism to control harm. Platform owners find themselves in a trade-off of balancing privacy on their platform where high privacy provides less vulnerability of potential targets of harm, while low privacy makes the identification of those that attack others easier.

On the one hand, privacy reduction can be a promising measure to make online places more transparent and less prone to online harm. Although privacy is highly valued in times of digital platforms, a restriction of this privacy could help when it comes to malicious activity or certain webpages mainly used to perform such activity (Rauf, 2021). It was observed by previous scholars that anonymity is a major factor for harmful content, which can be reduced by lowering privacy restrictions imposed on digital platforms. By being able to trace contents back to users and

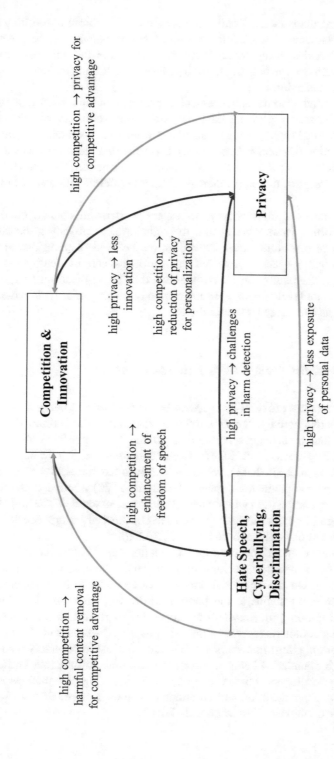

Fig. 1 Mutual dependencies between concepts

publicly revealing the personal identity of users, toxic disinhibition resulting from anonymity on platforms that leads to rude and hateful contents can be prevented (Suler, 2004). Besides, using more data that is available through less privacy-enhancing mechanisms can help in improving algorithms and make them less prone to discriminatory behavior.

On the other hand, also the enhancement of privacy can reduce harm on digital platforms. Disclosure of personal data provides some room for discrimination (Mejia & Parker, 2021) by exposing personal characteristics that make one vulnerable to discrimination (Fisman & Luca, 2016). Ensuring that identity disclosure that potentially leads to unfair treatment, such as skin colour, gender, race, or ethnicity, is covered by privacy restrictions to increase fairness in online processes can lower discrimination.

Facing this trade-off of privacy with respect to harmful content on digital platforms, platform owners need to find the right level of privacy to be able to face the challenge of online harm. Depending on the kind of harm that appears on the platform with respect to protected characteristics, certain identity-revealing properties can be excluded to lower the likelihood of being discriminated; on the other hand, a certain level of data revealing can be promising in order to reduce the danger of harm as a result of its traceability.

5.2   Privacy in the Competitive Environment

The reviewed literature provides a consensus about competition being a force that increases innovative activity. It was confirmed that more competition is strictly beneficial and that a thriving ecosystem is crucial for a platform to maintain attractiveness (Gnyawali et al., 2010). Complementors can try to replace the platform (Eisenmann et al., 2011), while the platform has the ability to intervene and even enter the complementor's sphere (Foerderer, 2020) where complementors find themselves in competition with owners (Halckenhaeusser et al., 2020b). At the same time, integrating external parties requires to take crucial governance decisions about the collaboration (Halckenhaeusser et al., 2020a).

Innovation and competition have a mutual relationship: While innovative activities improve the competitive position of platforms, increased competition also fosters innovation. On the one hand, incentives can enhance complementors in developing further extensions to the platform; however, such award-giving also results in multi-homing, the serving of competitive platforms at the same time, while also further complementors are attracted by awards (Foerderer et al., 2021). To enhance innovation, platform owners are required to invest in boundary resources, with knowledge boundaries being a substantial resource to integrate knowledge across different developers (Foerderer et al., 2019). Entering new markets results in increased customer attention and an attention spillover effect that encourages complementors to innovate (Foerderer et al., 2018).

Considering the importance of innovation on digital platform to attain a competitive edge, also the relevance of privacy with respect to innovation needs to be considered. On the one hand, privacy-enhancing mechanisms can reduce the possibilities for complementors to use user data, therefore making the platform less attractive. The lower participation of third parties on a platform reduces external innovation and makes the platform highly dependent of own ideas. Also, many platforms rely on user data to offer functionalities for free in exchange of user data that is used for targeted advertising. When applying privacy-enhancing strategies that prevent from using private data for targeted advertising, this likely reduces the revenues for platform firms (Bhargava, 2021b). On the other hand, also self-developed extensions of the platform can possibly be less effective if they are built on less user data that allows to detect user preferences.

Facing high competition, privacy enhancement as well as privacy reduction can be a possible solution to remain competitive. High competition requires that content is more targeted toward users, ensuring that they are satisfied with the contents presented on the platform. To ensure that such a personalization of the content and therefore user satisfaction can be achieved, it is necessary to use personal data. On the other hand, users that highly value privacy might be more likely to join a platform that takes care of private information to a larger extent, therefore making privacy-enhancing mechanisms a tool to attain a competitive advantage.

Depending on the sort and the main purposes of a platform, owners need to decide on the level of privacy also with respect to the competition they are confronted with. Taking innovation threats and a lack of personalization into account, privacy might rather negatively impact the business, while depending on the user group, privacy enhancement can be a successful tool to create an effective contrast to competitive firms.

5.3   Discrimination, Hate, and Cyberbullying in the Competitive Environment

Besides privacy-enhancing mechanisms on digital platform, also the level of positivity and therefore the attempts to remove harmful content present a challenge with respect to competition.

Considering that digital platforms enhance freedom of expression, implementing mechanisms that reduce such freedom, e.g., through automated filters, can have a negative impact on platform growth. On the one hand, people might leave the platform as they do not feel like being able to freely express their opinions; on the other hand, others might leave the platform if they feel like the information they can retrieve from the platform is filtered and therefore does not show the overall public opinion. This also refers to ranking feeds that are often applied on digital platform and are criticized for enhancing harmful content, particularly on Facebook (Oremus, 2021). Such automated algorithms are a main enabler of the growth of platforms by showing the most popular content, considerably reducing the growth by using alternative means of showing content to users. Particularly if automated filters are not able to effectively distinguish between harmful and non-harmful content, this challenge aggravates.

In contrast to the slowdown of growth as a result of increased measures for reducing harm, this can, equally to privacy enhancement, also be a mechanism to achieve a competitive advantage. There are individuals and businesses that preferably join platforms that support positive values and stand up for online positivity on platforms. While some companies actively force platform providers to implement strategies for removing harmful content (Forbus, 2021), in general focusing on such measures can help to reach this part of the society that does not feel comfortable using alternative platforms on which hate and cyberbullying commonly appear.

As a result, companies need to evaluate what strategies they want to follow and which values they want to represent, by considering the advantages of strictly removing hateful—and possibly non-hateful—content from their platform or enhancing freedom of expression.

6 Conclusion

In this chapter, we carried out a literature review of three literature streams on digital platforms that result in conflicts of interest. We investigated privacy, hate speech, cyberbullying and discrimination, as well as competition and innovation and identified trade-offs between those phenomena that are to be solved by platform providers and external stakeholders. We find that privacy should be closely evaluated with respect to its impact on harmful content, while also the relationship between privacy and innovation and competition requires mature concepts to find the right strategy. Finally, harmful content removal should be evaluated in terms of its potential to reach a competitive advantage or suffering from decreased growth.

References

Acquisti, A., & Fong, C. (2020). An experiment in hiring discrimination via online social networks. *Management Science, 66*(3), 1005–1024.

Acquisti, A., Taylor, C., & Wagman, L. (2016). The economics of privacy. *Journal of Economic Literature, 54*(2), 442–92.

Aghion, P., Harris, C., Howitt, P., & Vickers, J. (2001). Competition, imitation and growth with step-by-step innovation. *The Review of Economic Studies, 68*(3), 467–492.

Arrieta, A. B., Díaz-Rodríguez, N., Del Ser, J., Bennetot, A., Tabik, S., Barbado, A., García, S., Gil-López, S., Molina, D., Benjamins, R., et al. (2020). Explainable artificial intelligence (XAI): Concepts, taxonomies, opportunities and challenges toward responsible AI. *Information Fusion, 58*, 82–115.

Asadullah, A., Faik, I., & Kankanhalli, A. (2018). Digital platforms: A review and future directions. In *Proceedings of the 22nd Pacific Asia Conference on Information Systems (PACIS 2018)*.

Bapna, R., Ramaprasad, J., Shmueli, G., & Umyarov, A. (2016). One-way mirrors in online dating: A randomized field experiment. *Management Science, 62*(11), 3100–3122.

Bauer, J., Franke, N., & Tuertscher, P. (2016). Intellectual property norms in online communities: How user-organized intellectual property regulation supports innovation. *Information Systems Research, 27*(4), 724–750.

Bhargava, H. K. (2021a). Bundling for flexibility and variety: An economic model for multiproducer value aggregation. *Management Science, 67*(4), 2365–2380.

Bhargava, H. K. (2021b). The creator economy: Managing ecosystem supply, revenue-sharing, and platform design. *Management Science*. https://doi.org/10.1287/mnsc.2021.4126

Bhargava, H. K., Rubel, O., Altman, E. J., Arora, R., Boehnke, J., Daniels, K., Derdenger, T., Kirschner, B., LaFramboise, D., Loupos, P., et al. (2020). Platform data strategy. *Marketing Letters, 31*(4), 323–334.

Bocij, P., & McFarlane, L. (2003). Cyberstalking: The technology of hate. *The Police Journal: Theory, Practice and Principles, 76*(3), 204–221.

Bonina, C., Koskinen, K., Eaton, B., & Gawer, A. (2021). Digital platforms for development: Foundations and research agenda. *Information Systems Journal, 31*(6), 869–902.

Boudreau, K. (2010). Open platform strategies and innovation: Granting access vs. devolving control. *Management Science, 56*(10), 1849–1872.

Burnap, P., & Williams, M. L. (2016). Us and them: Identifying cyber hate on Twitter across multiple protected characteristics. *EPJ Data Science, 5*(11).

Burtch, G., Ghose, A., & Wattal, S. (2015). The hidden cost of accommodating crowdfunder privacy preferences: A randomized field experiment. *Management Science, 61*(5), 949–962.

Campbell, J., Goldfarb, A., & Tucker, C. (2015). Privacy regulation and market structure. *Journal of Economics & Management Strategy, 24*(1), 47–73.

Casadesus-Masanell, R., & Hervas-Drane, A. (2015). Competing with privacy. *Management Science, 61*(1), 229–246.

Casadesus-Masanell, R., & Yoffie, D. B. (2007). Wintel: Cooperation and conflict. *Management Science, 53*(4), 584–598.

Cavusoglu, H., Phan, T. Q., Cavusoglu, H., & Airoldi, E. M. (2016). Assessing the impact of granular privacy controls on content sharing and disclosure on Facebook. *Information Systems Research, 27*(4), 848–879.

Cennamo, C., Ozalp, H., & Kretschmer, T. (2018). Platform architecture and quality trade-offs of multihoming complements. *Information Systems Research, 29*(2), 461–478.

Chan, J., & Wang, J. (2018). Hiring preferences in online labor markets: Evidence of a female hiring bias. *Management Science, 64*(7), 2973–2994.

Chellappa, R. K., & Shivendu, S. (2010). Mechanism design for "free" but "no free disposal" services: The economics of personalization under privacy concerns. *Management Science, 56*(10), 1766–1780.

Chetty, N., & Alathur, S. (2018). Hate speech review in the context of online social networks. *Aggression and Violent Behavior, 40*, 108–118.

Claussen, J., Kretschmer, T., & Mayrhofer, P. (2013). The effects of rewarding user engagement: The case of Facebook apps. *Information Systems Research, 24*(1), 186–200.

Cohen-Almagor, R. (2012). Freedom of expression, Internet responsibility, and business ethics: The Yahoo! saga and its implications. *Journal of Business Ethics, 106*(3), 353–365.

Cook, C., Diamond, R., Hall, J. V., List, J. A., & Oyer, P. (2021). The gender earnings gap in the gig economy: Evidence from over a million rideshare drivers. *The Review of Economic Studies, 88*(5), 2210–2238.

Cramer, J., & Krueger, A. B. (2016). Disruptive change in the taxi business: The case of Uber. *American Economic Review, 106*(5), 177–182.

Cui, R., Li, J., & Zhang, D. J. (2020). Reducing discrimination with reviews in the sharing economy: Evidence from field experiments on Airbnb. *Management Science, 66*(3), 1071–1094.

Cusumano, M. A., & Gawer, A. (2002). The elements of platform leadership. *MIT Sloan Management Review, 43*(3), 51–58.

De Corniere, A. (2016). Search advertising. *American Economic Journal: Microeconomics, 8*(3), 156–188.

Dhillon, G., & Smith, K. J. (2019). Defining objectives for preventing cyberstalking. *Journal of Business Ethics, 157*(1), 137–158.

Eisenmann, T., Parker, G., & van Alstyne, M. (2011). Platform envelopment. *Strategic Management Journal, 32*(12), 1270–1285.

Eisenmann, T., Parker, G., & Van Alstyne, M. W. (2006). Strategies for two-sided markets. *Harvard Business Review, 84*(10), 92–101.

Etzioni, A. (2019). Cyber trust. *Journal of Business Ethics, 156*(1), 1–13.

European Commission. (2016). Code of conduct of countering illegal hate speech online. https://ec.europa.eu/info/policies/justice-and-fundamental-rights/combatting-discrimination/racism-and-xenophobia/eu-code-conduct-countering-illegal-hate-speech-online_en. Accessed 27 December 2021.

Evans, D. S., & Schmalensee, R. (2010). Failure to launch: Critical mass in platform businesses. *Review of Network Economics, 9*(4).

Evans, P. C., & Gawer, A. (2016). *The rise of the platform enterprise: A global survey.* New York: The Center for Global Enterprise.

Faber, R., & de Reuver, M. (2019). Consumer studies on digital platform adoption and continuance: A structured literature review. In *Proceedings of the 27th European Conference on Information Systems (ECIS 2019).*

Fieseler, C., Bucher, E., & Hoffmann, C. P. (2019). Unfairness by design? The perceived fairness of digital labor on crowdworking platforms. *Journal of Business Ethics, 156*(4), 987–1005.

Fischer, S., Lohrenz, L., Lattemann, C., & Robra-Bissantz, S. (2020). Critical design factors for digital service platforms - A literature review. In *Proceedings of the 28th European Conference on Information Systems (ECIS 2020).*

Fisman, R., & Luca, M. (2016). Fixing discrimination in online marketplaces. *Harvard Business Review, 94*(12), 88–95.

Foerderer, J. (2020). Interfirm exchange and innovation in platform ecosystems: Evidence from Apple's Worldwide Developers Conference. *Management Science, 66*(10), 4772–4787.

Foerderer, J., Kude, T., Mithas, S., & Heinzl, A. (2018). Does platform owner's entry crowd out innovation? Evidence from Google photos. *Information Systems Research, 29*(2), 444–460.

Foerderer, J., Kude, T., Schuetz, S., & Heinzl, A. (2014). Control versus generativity: A complex adaptive systems perspective on platforms. In *Proceedings of the 35th International Conference on Information Systems (ICIS 2014).*

Foerderer, J., Kude, T., Schuetz, S. W., & Heinzl, A. (2019). Knowledge boundaries in enterprise software platform development: Antecedents and consequences for platform governance. *Information Systems Journal, 29*(1), 119–144.

Foerderer, J., Lueker, N., & Heinzl, A. (2021). And the winner is...? The desirable and undesirable effects of platform awards. *Information Systems Research, 32*(4), 1155–1172.

Foerderer, J., & Schuetz, S. (2022). Data breach announcements and stock market reactions: A matter of timing? *Management Science.* https://doi.org/10.1287/mnsc.2021.4264.

Forbus, P. (2021). Commentary: The case for a healthier social customer journey. *Journal of Marketing, 85*(1), 93–97.

Fortuna, P., & Nunes, S. (2018). A survey on automatic detection of hate speech in text. *ACM Computing Surveys, 51*(4).

Fu, R., Huang, Y., & Singh, P. V. (2021). Crowds, lending, machine, and bias. *Information Systems Research, 32*(1), 72–92.

Gal-Or, E., Gal-Or, R., & Penmetsa, N. (2018). The role of user privacy concerns in shaping competition among platforms. *Information Systems Research, 29*(3), 698–722.

Ganco, M., Kapoor, R., & Lee, G. K. (2020). From rugged landscapes to rugged ecosystems: Structure of interdependencies and firms' innovative search. *Academy of Management Review, 45*(3), 646–674.

Gawer, A. (Ed.). (2009). *Platforms, markets and innovation*. Edward Elgar E-Book Archive. Cheltenham, UK; Northampton, MA: Edward Elgar Publishing

Ghazawneh, A., & Henfridsson, O. (2013). Balancing platform control and external contribution in third-party development: The boundary resources model. *Information Systems Journal, 23*(2), 173–192.

Ghose, A., & Han, S. P. (2014). Estimating demand for mobile applications in the new economy. *Management Science, 60*(6), 1470–1488.

Gnyawali, D. R., Fan, W., & Penner, J. (2010). Competitive actions and dynamics in the digital age: An empirical investigation of social networking firms. *Information Systems Research, 21*(3), 594–613.

Guttentag, D. (2019). Progress on Airbnb: A literature review. *Journal of Hospitality and Tourism Technology, 10*(4), 814–844.

Hagiu, A., & Jullien, B. (2011). Why do intermediaries divert search? *The RAND Journal of Economics, 42*(2), 337–362.

Halckenhaeusser, A., Foerderer, J., & Heinzl, A. (2020a). Platform Governance Mechanisms: An Integrated Literature Review and Research Directions. In *Proceedings of the 28th European Conference on Information Systems (ECIS 2020)*.

Halckenhaeusser, A., Foerderer, J., & Heinzl, A. (2020b). Wolf in a sheep's clothing: When do complementors face competition with platform owners? In *Proceedings of the 40th International Conference on Information Systems (ICIS 2020)*.

Harris, R. (2017). *Detecting cyber bullying: But can it be stopped?* https://www.wvtf.org/post/detecting-cyber-bullying-can-it-be-stopped#stream/0. Accessed 09 August 2021.

Hermann, E. (2021). Leveraging artificial intelligence in marketing for social good—An ethical perspective. *Journal of Business Ethics*. https://doi.org/10.1007/s10551-021-04843-y

Hermes, S., Pfab, S., Hein, A., Weking, J., Böhm, M., & Krcmar, H. (2020). Digital platforms and market dominance: Insights from a systematic literature review and avenues for future research. In *Proceedings of the 24th Pacific Asia Conference on Information Systems (PACIS 2020)*.

Heurix, J., Zimmermann, P., Neubauer, T., & Fenz, S. (2015). A taxonomy for privacy enhancing technologies. *Computers & Security, 53*, 1–17.

Hui, K.-L., Teo, H. H., & Lee, S.-Y. T. (2007). The value of privacy assurance: An exploratory field experiment. *MIS Quarterly*, 31(1), 19–33.

Johnson, G. A., Shriver, S. K., & Du, S. (2020). Consumer privacy choice in online advertising: Who opts out and at what cost to industry? *Marketing Science, 39*(1), 33–51.

Jung, D., Kim, B. C., Park, M., & Straub, D. W. (2019). Innovation and policy support for two-sided market platforms: Can government policy makers and executives optimize both societal value and profits? *Information Systems Research, 30*(3), 1037–1050.

Karhu, K., Gustafsson, R., & Lyytinen, K. (2018). Exploiting and defending open digital platforms with boundary resources: Android's five platform forks. *Information Systems Research, 29*(2), 479–497.

Katz, M. L., & Shapiro, C. (1994). Systems competition and network effects. *Journal of Economic Perspectives, 8*(2), 93–115.

Khan, L. M. (2016). Amazon's antitrust paradox. *The Yale Law Journal, 126*(3), 710–805.

Kircher, T., & Foerderer, J. (2021). Does EU-consumer privacy harm financing of US-app-startups? Within-US evidence of cross-EU-effects. In *Proceedings of the 42nd International Conference on Information Systems (ICIS 2014)*.

Klausen, J., Marks, C. E., & Zaman, T. (2018). Finding extremists in online social networks. *Operations Research, 66*(4), 957–976.

Kuan, J., & Lee, G. (2020). Governance strategy for digital platforms: Differentiation through information privacy. *Strategic Management Review, 48*(1), 147–184.

Kumar, V., Nim, N., & Agarwal, A. (2021). Platform-based mobile payments adoption in emerging and developed countries: Role of country-level heterogeneity and network effects. *Journal of International Business Studies, 52*(8), 1529–1558.

Kummer, M., & Schulte, P. (2019). When private information settles the bill: Money and privacy in Google's market for smartphone applications. *Management Science, 65*(8), 3470–3494.

Lambrecht, A., Goldfarb, A., Bonatti, A., Ghose, A., Goldstein, D. G., Lewis, R., Rao, A., Sahni, N., & Yao, S. (2014). How do firms make money selling digital goods online? *Marketing Letters, 25*(3), 331–341.

Lambrecht, A., & Tucker, C. (2019). Algorithmic bias? An empirical study of apparent gender-based discrimination in the display of STEM career ads. *Management Science, 65*(7), 2966–2981.

Lee, J. K. (2015). Research framework for AIS grand vision of the bright ICT initiative. *MIS Quarterly, 39*(2), iii–xii.

Leicht-Deobald, U., Busch, T., Schank, C., Weibel, A., Schafheitle, S., Wildhaber, I., & Kasper, G. (2019). The challenges of algorithm-based HR decision-making for personal integrity. *Journal of Business Ethics, 160*(2), 377–392.

Liu, C. Z., Gal-Or, E., Kemerer, C. F., & Smith, M. D. (2011). Compatibility and proprietary standards: The impact of conversion technologies in IT markets with network effects. *Information Systems Research, 22*(1), 188–207.

Lowry, P. B., Moody, G. D., Galletta, D. F., & Vance, A. (2013). The drivers in the use of online whistle-blowing reporting systems. *Journal of Management Information Systems, 30*(1), 153–190.

Lowry, P. B., Zhang, J., Wang, C., & Siponen, M. (2016). Why do adults engage in cyberbullying on social media? An integration of online disinhibition and deindividuation effects with the social structure and social learning model. *Information Systems Research, 27*(4), 962–986.

Marshall, A. (1920). *Principles of economics* (8th ed.). London: Macmillan.

Marx, M., Gans, J. S., & Hsu, D. H. (2014). Dynamic commercialization strategies for disruptive technologies: Evidence from the speech recognition industry. *Management Science, 60*(12), 3103–3123.

Mayya, R., & Viswanathan, S. (2021). Delaying informed consent: An empirical investigation of mobile apps' upgrade decisions. *Available at SSRN*.

Mejia, J., & Parker, C. (2021). When transparency fails: Bias and financial incentives in ridesharing platforms. *Management Science, 67*(1), 166–184.

Milberg, S. J., Smith, H. J., & Burke, S. J. (2000). Information privacy: Corporate management and national regulation. *Organization Science, 11*(1), 35–57.

Mini, T., & Widjaja, T. (2019). Tensions in digital platform business models: A literature review. In *Proceedings of the 40th International Conference on Information Systems (ICIS 2019)*.

Morris, R. (1994). Computerized content analysis in management research: A demonstration of advantages & limitations. *Journal of Management, 20*(4), 903–931.

Murthy, R. K., & Madhok, A. (2021). Overcoming the early–stage conundrum of digital platform ecosystem emergence: A problem–solving perspective. *Journal of Management Studies, 58*(7), 1899–1932.

Neshkovska, S., & Trajkova, Z. (2018). The essentials of hate speech. *Teacher, 14*(1), 71–80.

Niculescu, M. F., Wu, D. J., & Xu, L. (2018). Strategic intellectual property sharing: Competition on an open technology platform under network effects. *Information Systems Research, 29*(2), 498–519.

Oremus, W. (2021). *Facebook under fire: Why Facebook won't let you control your own news feed*. https://www.washingtonpost.com/technology/2021/11/13/facebook-news-feed-algorithm-how-to-turn-it-off/. Accessed 15 December 2021.

Ozalp, H., Cennamo, C., & Gawer, A. (2018). Disruption in platform–based ecosystems. *Journal of Management Studies, 55*(7), 1203–1241.

Pacheco-de Almeida, G., & Zemsky, P. B. (2012). Some like it free: Innovators' strategic use of disclosure to slow down competition. *Strategic Management Journal, 33*(7), 773–793.

Pan, Y., Huang, P., & Gopal, A. (2019). Storm clouds on the horizon? New entry threats and R&D investments in the U.S. IT industry. *Information Systems Research, 30*(2), 540–562.

Parker, G. G., & Van Alstyne, M. W. (2005). Two-sided network effects: A theory of information product design. *Management Science, 51*(10), 1494–1504.

Parker, G. G., Van Alstyne, M. W., & Choudary, S. P. (2016). *Platform revolution: How networked markets are transforming the economy and how to make them work for you.* New York: Norton & Company.

Pinsonneault, A., & Heppel, N. (1997). Anonymity in group support systems research: A new conceptualization, measure, and contingency framework. *Journal of Management Information Systems, 14*(3), 89–108.

Porter, M. E., & Van der Linde, C. (1995). Toward a new conception of the environment-competitiveness relationship. *Journal of Economic Perspectives, 9*(4), 97–118.

Pritchard, M. (2021). Commentary: "Half my digital advertising is wasted...". *Journal of Marketing, 85*(1), 26–29.

Pundak, C., Steinhart, Y., & Goldenberg, J. (2021). Nonmaleficence in shaming: The ethical dilemma underlying participation in online public shaming. *Journal of Consumer Psychology, 31*(3), 478–500.

Ransbotham, S., Fichman, R. G., Gopal, R., & Gupta, A. (2016). Special section introduction—Ubiquitous IT and digital vulnerabilities. *Information Systems Research, 27*(4), 834–847.

Rauf, A. A. (2021). New moralities for new media? Assessing the role of social media in acts of terror and providing points of deliberation for business ethics. *Journal of Business Ethics, 170*(2), 229–251.

Rich, A. S., & Gureckis, T. M. (2019). Lessons for artificial intelligence from the study of natural stupidity. *Nature Machine Intelligence, 1*(4), 174–180.

Rietveld, J., & Schilling, M. A. (2021). Platform competition: A systematic and interdisciplinary review of the literature. *Journal of Management, 47*(6), 1528–1563.

Robinson, J. (1934). What is perfect competition? *The Quarterly Journal of Economics, 49*(1), 104–120.

Rochet, J.-C., & Tirole, J. (2003). Platform competition in two-sided markets. *Journal of the European Economic Association, 1*(4), 990–1029.

Rochet, J.-C., & Tirole, J. (2006). Two-sided markets: A progress report. *The RAND Journal of Economics, 37*(3), 645–667.

Rysman, M. (2009). The economics of two-sided markets. *Journal of Economic Perspectives, 23*(3), 125–143.

Sanchez-Cartas, J. M., & Leon, G. (2021). Multisided platforms and markets: A survey of the theoretical literature. *Journal of Economic Surveys, 35*(2), 452–487.

Schmidt, A., & Wiegand, M. (2017). A survey on hate speech detection using natural language processing. In *Proceedings of the 5th International Workshop on Natural Language Processing for Social Media (SocialNLP 2017)*.

Schumann, J. H., von Wangenheim, F., & Groene, N. (2014). Targeted online advertising: Using reciprocity appeals to increase acceptance among users of free web services. *Journal of Marketing, 78*(1), 59–75.

Scott, S. V., & Orlikowski, W. J. (2014). Entanglements in practice: Performing anonymity through social media. *MIS Quarterly, 38*(3), 873–894.

Seamans, R., & Zhu, F. (2014). Responses to entry in multi-sided markets: The impact of Craigslist on local newspapers. *Management Science, 60*(2), 476–493.

Seaver, N. (2017). Algorithms as culture: Some tactics for the ethnography of algorithmic systems. *Big Data & Society, 4*(2).

Shampanier, K., Mazar, N., & Ariely, D. (2007). Zero as a special price: The true value of free products. *Marketing Science, 26*(6), 742–757.

Shapiro, C., Varian, H. R., Carl, S., et al. (1998). *Information rules: A strategic guide to the network economy*. Boston: Harvard Business Press.

Sheremata, W. A. (2004). Competing through innovation in network markets: Strategies for challengers. *Academy of Management Review, 29*(3), 359–377.

Sokol, D. D., & Zhu, F. (2021). Harming competition and consumers under the guise of protecting privacy: An analysis of Apple's iOS 14 Policy Updates. *Available at SSRN*.

Son, J.-Y., & Kim, S. S. (2008). Internet users' information privacy-protective responses: A taxonomy and a nomological model. *MIS Quarterly, 32*(3), 503–529.

Soto Setzke, D., Böhm, M., & Krcmar, H. (2019). Platform openness: A systematic literature review and avenues for future research. In *Proceedings of the 14th International Conference on Business Informatics (WI 2019)*.

Stigler, G. J. (1957). Perfect competition, historically contemplated. *Journal of Political Economy, 1957*(65), 1–17.

Suler, J. (2004). The online disinhibition effect. *Cyberpsychology & Behavior, 7*(3), 321–326.

Thomas, L. D., Autio, E., & Gann, D. M. (2014). Architectural leverage: Putting platforms in context. *Academy of Management Perspectives, 28*(2), 198–219.

Tiwana, A. (2013). *Platform ecosystems: Aligning architecture, governance, and strategy*. Burlington: Morgan Kaufmann.

Tiwana, A., Konsynski, B., & Bush, A. A. (2010). Research commentary—Platform evolution: Coevolution of platform architecture, governance, and environmental dynamics. *Information Systems Research, 21*(4), 675–687.

Trabucchi, D., & Buganza, T. (2022). Landlords with no lands: A systematic literature review on hybrid multi-sided platforms and platform thinking. *European Journal of Innovation Management, 25*, 64–96.

Tucker, C. E. (2014). Social networks, personalized advertising, and privacy controls. *Journal of Marketing Research, 51*(5), 546–562.

Vickers, J. (1995). Concepts of competition. *Oxford Economic Papers, 1995*, 1–23.

Vives, X. (1984). Duopoly information equilibrium: Cournot and Bertrand. *Journal of Economic Theory, 34*(1), 71–94.

Wang, Q., & Xie, J. (2011). Will consumers be willing to pay more when your competitors adopt your technology? The impacts of the supporting-firm base in markets with network effects. *Journal of Marketing, 75*(5), 1–17.

Wareham, J., Fox, P. B., & Cano Giner, J. L. (2014). Technology ecosystem governance. *Organization Science, 25*(4), 1195–1215.

Westin, A. F. (1968). Privacy and freedom. *Washington and Lee Law Review, 25*(1).

Whelan, G. (2019). Trust in surveillance: A reply to Etzioni. *Journal of Business Ethics, 156*(1), 15–19.

Wong, R. Y. M., Cheung, C. M., Xiao, B., & Thatcher, J. B. (2021). Standing up or standing by: Understanding bystanders' proactive reporting responses to social media harassment. *Information Systems Research, 32*(2), 561–581.

Wu, X., & Pang, M.-S. (2021). How data privacy regulations affect competition: Empirical evidence from mobile application market. In *Proceedings of the 42nd International Conference on Information Systems (ICIS 2014)*.

Xu, H., Teo, H.-H., Tan, B. C., & Agarwal, R. (2012). Research note—Effects of individual self-protection, industry self-regulation, and government regulation on privacy concerns: A study of location-based services. *Information Systems Research, 23*(4), 1342–1363.

Zimbardo, P. G. (1969). The human choice: Individuation, reason, and order versus deindividuation, impulse, and chaos. In W. J. Arnold & D. Levine (Eds.), *Nebraska Symposium on Motivation* (pp. 237–307). Lincoln: University of Nebraska Press.

Part V
Emerging Technologies: Affordances and Opportunities

The Affordances of Blockchain Platforms: Why Service Providers Use Blockchains

Kai Spohrer and Marten Risius

Abstract Contemporary blockchain platforms differ in their technological features and are under active development as open-source projects. Nonetheless, they have the potential to fuel substantial socio-economic changes. The scale of such changes, however, requires not only blockchain platforms but also organizations that develop and provide services on top of these platforms. Yet, little is known as to why service providers use specific blockchain platforms to offer their services or how they deal with the developmental state of blockchain platforms. This study, therefore, strives to identify the general affordances of blockchain platforms for service providers and aims to understand how service providers respond to different affordances on distinct platforms. Based on Affordance Theory and grounded in the analysis of 19 cases of blockchain service providers on the three most prominent blockchain platforms, we identify five types of salient affordances (i.e., validity affordances, analytical affordances, automation affordances, decentralization affordances, generative affordances). We explain how they result from specific features of blockchain platforms and from properties of the provided service. We lastly show that service providers' use of a blockchain platform depends not only on the salient affordances of the platform but also on the values that are enacted by the open-source community behind it.

Financial support for Marten Risius from the Algorand Foundation through the Algorand Centre of Excellence (ACE) on Sustainability Informatics for the Pacific is gratefully acknowledged.

K. Spohrer (✉)
Frankfurt School of Finance & Management, Frankfurt am Main, Germany
e-mail: k.spohrer@fs.de

M. Risius
The University of Queensland, Brisbane, Australia

1   Introduction

Blockchain technology is considered to be disruptive for various areas of economy both by research and practice (Tapscott & Tapscott, 2016). In particular, blockchain-based services are assumed to have the potential to overcome the need for intermediary services in financial fields such as securities issuance, insurance, trading, and settlement (Harvey, 2016; Nofer et al., 2017), in accounting (Dai & Vasarhelyi, 2017), supply-chain management (Zhao et al., 2016), enterprise resource planning (Tapscott & Tapscott, 2017), copyright management (Savelyev, 2017), and healthcare (Yue et al., 2016). Consequently, it is important to understand how this emergent technology unfolds its value and how to use it effectively.

Given the great expectations, there is a proliferation of services that are being developed on blockchain platforms. As such, blockchain startups amassed 2.6 billion U.S. dollars in worldwide venture-capital funding in the first quarter of 2021, more than in the whole year of 2020 (Statista, 2021). There are blockchain services as diverse as storage services (e.g., Filecoin), predictions markets (e.g., Gnosis), and digital advertising platforms (e.g., BAT). However, despite the fast progress and the ample expectations regarding the socio-economic impact, a comprehensive understanding regarding the effective use of blockchains for such services is missing (Risius & Spohrer, 2017). While blockchain technology is generally appealing due to its promises of disintermediation, immutability, redundancy, and increased transparency (Savelyev, 2017), contemporary blockchain platforms differ in their technological features, for example regarding permissioning, modularity, power of scripting languages, and the provision of a native cryptocurrency (Du et al., 2019; Ostern et al., 2020; Shin & Hwang, 2020). Moreover, all major blockchain platforms are under active development as open-source projects and are therefore subject to continuous change. This makes it hard for complementary service providers to select and use the blockchain platform that is most beneficial for them.

Thus, it is necessary to create an understanding of how the diverse features of blockchain platforms influence their value for service providers and what determines how service providers can use blockchain platforms for their services over time. The latter is particularly challenging with platforms being under active development. First approaches toward guiding the decision process have broadly distinguished four types of applications dependent on the degree of innovativeness and coordination (Iansiti & Lakhani, 2017). Such conceptualizations, however, model the blockchain application market but offer little guidance for the individual service provider. Valuable case studies have provided detailed insights for service providers but have focused on specific use cases and domains (e.g., Hyvärinen et al., 2017; Savelyev, 2017; Ying et al., 2018; Zhao et al., 2016). Consequently, there is no comprehensive understanding of the general possibilities and constraints that blockchain platforms entail for service providers.

Against this backdrop, we follow the suggestion of Volkoff & Strong (2017) to take an Affordance Theory perspective for looking differently at the phenomenon of blockchain platforms and service providers. Specifically, we aim to answer the research questions:

1. What are the general affordances of blockchain platforms for service providers?
2. How do service providers respond to the different affordances of distinct blockchain platforms under development?

Based on Affordance Theory (Markus & Silver, 2008), we develop empirically grounded answers to these questions. To do so, we analyze 19 different cases of professional service providers on three major blockchain platforms (Bitcoin, Ethereum, Hyperledger Fabric).

The remainder of this paper is structured as follows. We first describe the conceptual background of blockchain technology and technical features of blockchain platforms. We introduce and draw on Affordance Theory to frame our research. Subsequently, we describe the research design and results of our empirically grounded investigation before discussing the study's implications for theory and practice.

2 Conceptual Background

Analyzing the affordances of blockchain platforms for service providers, we base our investigation on foundational literature on blockchain technology and on affordance theory. The following sections provide an overview of the literature streams on blockchain technology and functional affordances. We then present a preliminary framework of service providers' use of specific blockchain platforms.

2.1 Blockchain Technology

Blockchain is a decentralized peer-to-peer distributed ledger that enables cryptographically secured transactions between participants. Blockchain technology has certain foundational technological features, which may differ in their characteristics between specific blockchains (e.g., Bitcoin, Ethereum, Hyperledger Fabric). Blockchains are commonly considered to be a distributed ledger. This means that each participant has access to the entire database as well as its complete history (Iansiti & Lakhani, 2017). This shared database of all transactions that occur on the blockchain is continuously synchronized between all participants (Ølnes et al., 2017), enabling immediate peer-to-peer transmissions (Iansiti & Lakhani, 2017). Thereby, a distributed ledger offers great transparency (Giancaspro, 2017) and irreversibility of records (Iansiti & Lakhani, 2017), which assures data as well as transaction integrity (Ølnes et al., 2017).

While blockchains are commonly considered to be some form of distributed ledger, not all blockchains contain native digital currencies in their core protocol. Prominent examples for blockchains with native coins are Bitcoin and Ethereum, whereas Hyperledger does not have a built-in currency. These currencies are designed as a medium of cryptographically secured exchange between participants. Mining these currencies serves as an incentive for participants to invest their computing power and, thereby, maintain the blockchain network to enable transactions (Ying et al., 2018). Other blockchains like Hyperledger do not require computationally intensive mining, as they apply, for example, a Practical Byzantine Fault Tolerance (PBFT) consensus mechanism, which relies on a primary trusted validating node that multicasts the transaction request to all other validating peers to reach consensus and ultimately execute transactions (Castro & Liskov, 1999). Due to the required intensive network communication, this algorithm is applicable to platforms with a limited number of participating nodes to achieve a comparatively large number of transactions (Vukolić, 2015). Thereby, this approach lowers the mining costs but requires hosting a dedicated server infrastructure. Enabling organizations to create their own cryptocurrency on a blockchain has been found to offer the potential of significantly improving operational efficiency, while also requiring trust between participants to adopt these currencies as a valuable token of exchange (Ying et al., 2018).

The question of whether a blockchain offers its own cryptocurrency is related to the decision of permissioning regarding who participates to what extent in a blockchain environment. The permissioning detail describes restrictions in becoming a miner as a "transaction processor who submits data and is eligible to create blocks of data" (Walsh et al., 2016). On permissioned blockchains, such as Hyperledger, only predefined users can validate data, while permissionless blockchains (e.g., Bitcoin, Ethereum) have no such restrictions (Bakos et al., 2021). It is important to acknowledge that the permission requirement refers to participation in the consensus decision and does not necessarily exclude users from accessing and reading the blockchain (Gramoli, 2017). Ethereum, moreover, enables permissioning on higher development layers (i.e., the application layer). Consortia of large corporations, for example, have adapted the open-source protocol to operate their own permissioned, private instance of Ethereum.

Furthermore, blockchains also differ regarding their modularity in terms of whether the stored and exchanged assets remain on the blockchain or can be externally distributed off-chain. While transactions might be stored in a blockchain, the underlying data about the exchanged entity might be stored in an off-chain database (Ølnes et al., 2017). One of the key questions in digital rights management is whether or not to store copyrighted content on- or off-chain (Savelyev, 2017). For example, Blockstream offered "Lightning" early on as an off-chain payment solution to avoid Bitcoin protocol-related transaction delays (Back et al., 2014). On Ethereum, for example., on-chain tokens can be linked to off-chain assets (Hyvärinen et al., 2017; Ying et al., 2018) in order to secure the real-world value of the exchange (Glaser, 2017). While Hyperledger does not have a native currency to perform transactions, it has a modular architecture offering plug-in implementations of functions (Cachin, 2016).

Due to their digital nature, transactions between nodes on blockchains are tied to computational logics that can be automatically triggered (Iansiti & Lakhani, 2017). However, various blockchains differ regarding their scripting power in terms of the support for building decentralized Apps (DApps) through smart contracts, which can interact with each other. The Turing complete Ethereum Virtual Machine (EVM), for example, is one of Ethereum's major advantages and allows complex programs written in a high-level programming language (Solidity) to be compiled and run on the blockchain. To support complementors, Ethereum provides full programming language documentations as well as a browser-based compiler, a specialized web IDE (Ethereum Studio), and a Solidity plug-in for Microsoft's Visual Studio (Ethereum, 2018). Bitcoin, for example, is comparatively limited as it uses a non-Turing complete language that does not support smart contracts with complex loops but rather simple if-then functions (Antonopoulos, 2014). "Chaincode" smart contracts on Hyperledger are based on Google's GoLang (IBM, 2018).

In sum, while blockchain platforms share certain technical features (i.e., distributed ledger functionality), technological details differ substantially between blockchains (i.e., native cryptocurrency, detailed permissioning, modularity, scripting power). The various features have been argued to determine the appropriateness of different blockchains for blockchain applications and service providers (Iansiti & Lakhani, 2017). Currently, however, we lack a comprehensive and systematic understanding of how the fragmented technological details contribute to the actual usefulness of applications. This might lead to a duplication of development and research efforts, and calls have been made for more standardization (Ølnes et al., 2017). Extant research has mostly focused on isolated use cases with technical details of the particular blockchain (e.g., Hyvärinen et al., 2017; Ying et al., 2018), while neglecting potentially better-suited blockchain environments (e.g., permissioned blockchain) due to a lack of understanding of how features of blockchain platforms influence their affordances. Furthermore, many case studies have focused on specific technical features relevant only to their context. Finance, for example, tends to focus on the log immutability to secure transactions (Underwood, 2016), supply-chain management emphasizes the distributed ledger to identify product provenance (Zhao et al., 2016), HR services providers put an emphasis on privacy (Ying et al., 2018), and digital rights management considers the transparency for proper revenue distribution (Savelyev, 2017). Thus, it is necessary to move beyond the isolated use cases and purely technical analyses toward building an understanding of the general, underlying affordances of blockchain platforms for service providers (Risius & Spohrer, 2017).

2.2   Understanding Blockchain Platform Use Through Affordance Theory

The question of how technology is selected and used by individuals, groups, and organizations constitutes a perennial topic in IS research that has been significantly advanced by Affordance Theory (Volkoff & Strong, 2017). In particular, Affordance Theory provides a theoretical fundament to overcome the dichotomous view of social constructivism versus technological determinism in the use and application of technology (Robey et al., 2013). It holds that both the material elements of a technology as well as the context of an actor causally influence which potentials for goal-directed action the technology offers to the actor (Markus & Silver, 2008; Volkoff & Strong, 2013). These potentials for action are called affordances and relate the immediate, concrete outcomes that an actor wants to achieve to the underlying features of a technology (Strong et al., 2014). They constitute the necessary but not sufficient conditions for the appropriation and use of a technology.

Affordance Theory has recently been applied in areas as diverse as collective engagement in social media (Vaast et al., 2017), organizational change to green IT (Seidel et al., 2014), and effective use of electronic health records (Burton-Jones & Volkoff, 2017), as well as in the blockchain context regarding financial markets (Du et al., 2019; Ostern et al., 2020) and trust building heuristics (Shin & Hwang, 2020). But its usefulness is at a peak "when we start utilizing it as a lens for changing how we look at [. . .] IS topics rather than simply examining the theory itself" (Volkoff & Strong, 2017, p. 234). In line with this idea, we leverage Affordance Theory to provide a new perspective on the often claimed but rarely specified value of blockchain technology.

As emphasized by Risius and Spohrer (2017), evidence on the value provided by blockchain technology is primarily anecdotal and has largely been confined to very specific use cases. Even valuable and rigorous examinations of single blockchain service providers have recently opened more questions than they have answered (Beck et al., 2018; Rossi et al., 2019). Our investigation of service providers on blockchains, therefore, takes one step back and examines the value that these companies see in blockchain technology for achieving their goals and how they come to use a specific blockchain technology. Based on Affordance Theory, we can remain sensitive to the context of the blockchain technology and single companies but nonetheless achieve a more general understanding of blockchain affordances for service providers. Facilitating such mid-range theories is a particular strength of Affordance Theory (Volkoff & Strong, 2013), and prior work has recently called for more research that applies this lens to understand how technology is effectively used in context (Burton-Jones & Volkoff, 2017).

An affordances perspective on service providers' use of blockchain platforms suggests that the companies evaluate the features of a given blockchain platform in the light of their own needs in providing a service. Examining which immediate, concrete goals they can or cannot achieve with the features of a blockchain platform, they conclude what the platform affords to them. Service providers may then use a

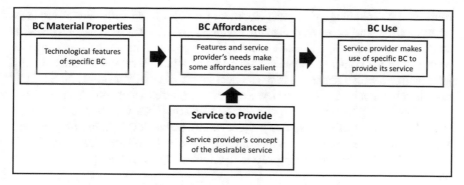

Fig. 1 Conceptual framework of service provider's use of a blockchain platform

specific platform to make use of its salient affordances. However, as blockchain platforms are still under active development in open-source communities, service providers may not necessarily use a platform based solely on its affordances. Instead, they may also take the open-source communities and their inherent dynamics into account. The present study seeks to understand the affordances for service providers that result from blockchain platform features and how these service providers come to use a blockchain. Figure 1 depicts this as a conceptual model.

Although we acknowledge that a collection of blockchain affordances will necessarily be non-exhaustive due to their relational nature (Markus & Silver, 2008), a focus on recurring affordances allows research on the value of blockchain technology to move away from the idiosyncrasies of single-use cases which are predominant in prior work (Risius & Spohrer, 2017). Affordance Theory enables us to look for commonalities and demi-regularities while still remaining technologically specific about blockchain platforms (Volkoff & Strong, 2013; Zachariadis et al., 2013). This elevates the analysis of the impact of blockchain technology to a level of a mid-range theory as opposed to current literature which primarily focuses on single-use cases or isolated features, their design, or their consequences (Risius & Spohrer, 2017).

The specific context of blockchain platforms moreover enriches the literature on Affordance Theory. Specifically, blockchain platforms are currently emerging technologies and several open-source blockchain platform projects compete for attracting the most powerful ecosystem. In doing so, the technological features of each blockchain platform are under constant development. The dynamics of different technological developments may therefore influence how service providers use the blockchain platforms, an aspect that has scarcely been looked at in affordance literature. Prior work on affordances has, in fact, mostly looked at established systems and their use (e.g., Burton-Jones & Volkoff, 2017; Strong et al., 2014) but only rarely examined systems that are under active development. As a mentionable exception, Leonardi (2011) found that users tend to change their routines if a technology under development provides them with new affordances whereas they tend to rework custom-developed technology if it is perceived as constraining. In contrast to such custom development settings, however, service providers in the context of blockchain platforms aim to leverage the benefits of a joint platform with other actors in the respective ecosystem (Mini et al., 2021). They may therefore not be free to rework the underlying platform technology on their own without deviating from their aim of a shared platform (Overhage & Widjaja, 2022). How the dynamics of open-source projects under active development play into the appropriation of technology is a new theoretical area for affordance research. We tap into this field by examining service providers that use emerging blockchain platforms.

3   Research Design

To understand the affordances of blockchain platforms for service providers and to explore how service providers react to the distinct affordances of diverse platforms, we chose a multiple case study approach (Yin, 2009). We selected engagements of 19 professional service providers in three different blockchain platforms: Bitcoin, Ethereum, and Hyperledger Fabric. These platforms are arguably the most widely used blockchain platforms currently in the market. All of them are under active development and manage their source code as part of separate open-source projects. While instances of all three blockchains can be set up as new and isolated networks, Bitcoin and Ethereum additionally provide publicly accessible instances of their blockchains. The three platforms differ strongly in their features, and professional service providers make use of this by relying on a single or even multiple platforms for their services. Table 1 contrasts the features of the three blockchain platforms. Examining the ends toward which service providers use the features of different blockchain platforms allows us to draw inferences on the general affordances of blockchain technology for service providers. Taking a closer look at the distinct open-source communities that develop each blockchain allows us to understand the role they play in service providers' use of blockchains.

3.1   Data Collection

Interviews and documents were our primary data sources. We approached professional service providers that were featured in trade press for the blockchain services they already provided on at least one of the three blockchain platforms. That is, we aimed to capture data from companies that were already experienced in and actively using blockchain technology for their services as opposed to companies that only had vague ideas about potential use cases. As the vast majority of these blockchain service providers were small enterprises and start-ups, we interviewed

Table 1 Features of contemporary blockchain platforms

Feature	Bitcoin	Ethereum	Hyperledger Fabric
Native crypto currency	Yes	Yes	No
Cryptographically secured distributed ledger	Focused; transaction ledger primarily focused on ownership of native currency	Broad; transaction ledger for transactions of native currency and generic tokens	Broad; transaction ledger for transactions of generic tokens
Detailed permissioning	Low; data visible to all participants; all participants incentivized to validate transactions	Medium; all participants can validate transactions; network access configurable	High; only predefined nodes validate transactions; data visibility adaptable
Powerful scripting	Low; limited scripting possibilities	High; various Turing complete programming languages	High; Turing complete programming language
Modularity	Low; consensus, mining, and currency tightly entangled	Medium; virtual machine provides some abstraction; consensus mechanism to be changed but still tight entanglement	High; core elements like consensus mechanisms can be exchanged easily

key informants that gave us insight into both the decisions underlying technical choices and details of how they leveraged specific blockchain features as well as the business elements specific to their context and service. The semi-structured interviews lasted between 35 and 90 min, were conducted in English or the national language of the interviewees, recorded and transcribed (resulting in 363 pages of transcript). Interviewees were asked questions about the companies' services, their use of underlying platforms, the perceived importance of single features, and their experiences with the respective open-source communities. To extend the results from the interviews and to create a clearer mapping of blockchain features and affordances, we gathered documents about these companies and their services, partly from publicly accessible sources and partly from the interviewees. Specifically, we collected whitepapers about the services, documentation from code-sharing platforms such as GitHub, and press articles on the services provided and their relation to underlying blockchain platforms. Table 2 provides an overview of the data we collected from service providers.

To deepen our understanding of the open-source projects behind each blockchain in our sample and to triangulate the views of service providers, we collected publicly available documents on the projects' missions, values, and governance approaches. We moreover interviewed one to two informants per project that could provide key insights due to their roles in the respective open-source communities. As such, we interviewed a leading member in developing smart contract languages of the Ethereum Foundation, one executive board member and one member of the

Table 2 Interview data collected by case

Service provider	Platform	Service	Interviewee(s)	Pages
S1	HF	250+ employees; founded in 2001; provides blockchain consultancy services and custom-developed blockchain solutions	Blockchain Lead	20
S2	ETH	14 employees; founded in 2014; provides decentralized prediction market platform	2: COO & Team Lead	20
S3	ETH	8 employees; founded in 2015; provides decentralized platform for insurance and reinsurance markets	Founder	14
S4	BTC& ETH	40+ employees; founded in 2014; provides platform for issuing and exchanging local crypto-currencies for B2C transactions	CEO	15
S5	ETH	15 employees; founded in 2016; provides on-demand issuance and administration of financial instruments automating document structuring, marketing, distribution, execution, clearing, settlement	Founder	19
S6	ETH	40+ employees; entered blockchain market in 2013; blockchain consultancy services and has developed about 30 proofs of concepts	Blockchain Consultant	16
S7	HF	2 founder startup; since 2016; provides services focused on financial derivatives clearing solutions	Co-Founder	15
S8	ETH	21 employees; founded in 2016; provides a platform for decentralized insurance	Founder	24
S9	BTC	27 employees; founded in 2014; provides notary services and proof of existence	Senior Developer	33
S10	ETH	28 employees; founded in 2015; provides a prediction market platform	Co-Founder	24
S11	HF	100+ employees in cooperative project of 2 multinationals; since 2016; developing a platform for global logistics processes	VP Blockchain	11
S12	ETH & HF	3 people dedicated to blockchain consultancy services, proofs of concept	2: Principal & Senior Consultant	31
S13	HF	10+ employees; founded in 2012; facilitate distributed systems recording state data and tamper-proof event logs in a complete audit trail	CTO	10
S14	BTC & ETH	5 employees; inc. 2015; notary service to certify and ensure existence, integrity, and attribution of data	CEO	13
S15	BTC & ETH	30+ employees; provides services to validate workflow execution in operations, e.g., in fleet management	CEO	16
S16	ETH	open-source project; since 2016; provides a decentralized market infrastructure to create generic p2p commercial transactions	Project Lead	29

(continued)

Table 2 (continued)

Service provider	Platform	Service	Interviewee(s)	Pages
S17	HF	10+ employees; founded in 2013; creates recycling platform for collecting and reselling recyclable waste	Co-Founder	18
S18	BTC & ETH	5 employees; since 2014; customer identification service for finance with integrated solutions with hardware vendors	CEO	22
S19	ETH	30+ employees; since 2015; provides blockchain consulting services and custom development	Co-Founder	13

HF Hyperledger fabric, *ETH* Ethereum, *BTC* Bitcoin

Technical Steering Committee of Hyperledger, as well as a senior Bitcoin developer who has contributed significantly to the development of the Bitcoin core technology that is currently in use. These interviews lasted 70 min on average and resulted in 21–29 pages of transcript per interview. Together with documents describing rules and processes in each community, the interviews helped us to better understand the dynamics inherent to each of the blockchain platform projects.

3.2 Data Analysis

Our data analysis followed an iterative approach of moving back and forth between analyzing data and building tentative theory using open, axial, and selective coding (Corbin & Strauss, 1990). Knowledge and literature on blockchain systems and Affordance Theory allowed us to define a set of concepts a-priori that we sought during data collection and expected to find relevant during data analysis. These concepts thereby served as a sensitizing device to inform data collection and theorizing (Charmaz, 2006). We started our analysis by openly coding these concepts. To do so, we attached labels to them in transcripts and documents. For example, we examined where service providers made use of specific features of blockchain platforms by evaluating technical descriptions of their services on websites and further documents, attaching the labels of blockchain features to them (cf. Table 1). We additionally made sure to gather and analyze responses from interviewees that assessed how important they judged each feature for a blockchain platform and how they used the particular feature for their own services. This led us to open codes for tentative functional affordances of blockchain platforms to specific service providers such as speeding up claim settlement (insurance) and rewarding individual collectors (recyclables). Following suggestions for research into the effective use of technology (Burton-Jones & Volkoff, 2017), we remained open for other ideas and emerging concepts that allowed for inductive theory building. For example, community values and service provider values emerged from open coding as relevant concepts. Although these concepts emerged from our data analysis, we

Table 3 Core concepts after data analysis

Core concept	Definition	Sources and illustrative codes
Salient affordance	The potentials for action provided by blockchain platforms that service providers perceive as most important in achieving their immediate, concrete service goals [based on Strong et al. (2014)]	"This is the core of blockchain technology for us" "That is what a blockchain really is about"
Community value of • immutability • innovativeness	A community's expressed or unexpressed promise to [based on Huber et al. (2017), Tiwana et al. (2010)]: • Ensure the immutability of their blockchain and its historic records • Swiftly incorporate innovative ideas for the better of the technical quality of the platform	• Interviews with leading members of all three blockchain platform communities • Websites, wikis, blogs
Focus and extended engagement	A service provider intensifies its use of a specific blockchain platform	Contribution of code to the open-source platform project Actively influencing community discussions Engagement at community developer conferences
Decoupling and diversification	A service provider reduces its use of a specific blockchain platform	Creating a middleware layer Striving to "become agnostic to underlying blockchain"

could relate them to prior work on platforms which suggests that values and their enactment play a crucial role in how companies engage in providing services based on platforms (Huber et al., 2017; Tiwana et al., 2010). By iterating the concepts between the authors, consulting literature, discussing the concepts with colleagues and research assistants, and refining them over time, we achieved a higher level of robustness for the main concepts (Yin, 2009). Table 3 displays these main concepts.

Axial coding helped us explore patterns of commonalities and differences in the relationships between the main concepts. Drawing on memos, case write-ups, and data displays, we engaged in pattern matching (Miles & Huberman, 1994; Yin, 2009) to identify regularities in how material properties of blockchain technology were used by service providers to achieve immediate, concrete outcomes and how they responded to the affordances of distinct blockchain platforms. For example, this led us to the insight that companies with similar service offerings mostly perceived the same salient affordances of blockchain technology but did not necessarily rely on the same platforms to make use of them.

We lastly identified the theoretical mechanisms underlying service providers' use of specific blockchain platforms and how the dynamics of open-source communities, in which the platforms were rooted, played into it through selective coding (Charmaz, 2006; Corbin & Strauss, 1990). Following Burton-Jones and

Volkoff's (2017) recommendation, we not only looked at the lower level affordances that were reported quite frequently but also examined the aggregate, higher-level affordances of blockchain platforms that aided service providers in achieving their more abstract organizational goals. In sum, this approach enabled us to identify the salient affordances of blockchain systems for service providers and to understand how service providers responded to the affordances of distinct blockchain platforms.

4 Results

In the following, we first present the salient affordances that we recurrently found in the case studies. These affordances pertain to five higher-level categories of affordances that facilitate the achievement of organizational goals of service providers. We elaborate on the enabling relationship between material properties of blockchain platforms and these higher-level affordances. By examining how these higher-level affordances influence each other, we moreover show why specific blockchain platforms fit more than others with the organizational goals of specific service providers. Lastly, we show how the actual use of a blockchain platform by a service provider depends not only on the salient affordances of this platform for the service provider but also on the values that are enacted in the open-source community behind it.

4.1 Functional Affordances of Blockchain Platforms

Our analyses elicited several recurring, salient affordances that service providers perceived as central to their services. These affordances were the result of service providers' perspectives on the features of specific blockchain platforms and could be aggregated into five groups. Not all groups were equally important to all service providers. After introducing the affordances, we address this fact in more detail. Table 4 depicts the salient categories of affordances.

The most fundamental affordances of blockchain platforms are validity affordances. As such, service providers in our sample emphasized that a major novelty of blockchain platforms, compared to traditional information systems, is their ability to achieve consensus between an undefined large number of actors regarding a global state and history of transactions that cannot be altered. For example, the public Bitcoin blockchain contains a history of all payment transactions of Bitcoins that have been made since the launch of this platform in 2009. The near certainty that this commonly agreed-on transaction history is immutable and cannot be altered ex-post by any malicious attacker constitutes the very basis of blockchain systems. It also enables blockchain users to ensure the validity of each new transaction by comparing it to prior history. For example, a user must only be able to spend a token if the token is actually in her possession according to the transaction history. As a last validity affordance, blockchain platforms afforded storing data in a durable way to several service providers in our sample. As such, service provider S14 anchors cryptographic representations of documents on the Bitcoin blockchain to prove their existence from a given point in time on. Certified by S14 and verifiable by all participants on the respective blockchain, S14 customers can then prove that their documents, for example, identification documents necessary for financial transactions, are authentic and can be used in business transactions without the need to re-evaluate the originals each time.

Although validity affordances may emerge from any public or private distributed ledger, they are particularly salient in the presence of a native cryptocurrency in public blockchains with many participants. More specifically, intrinsic crypto-currencies allow public blockchains to provide the incentives for large numbers of validators who keep the blockchain immutable, accept only valid transactions, and make sure it does not cease to exist. The extensiveness of the network and the inherent diversity of validators thereby fosters the salience of validity affordances. Provider S14 put this as follows:

> In my opinion, blockchains need to have a native token [. . .] because that's what guarantees that the incentives of the participants are aligned. [. . .] There is a consensus algorithm, and this consensus algorithm, it's related to economic incentives. And for those economic incentives to work, you need a token! So I don't believe in token-less blockchains.— Provider S14

Analytical affordances constitute a second category of affordances salient with many service providers. As such, tracking the ownership of assets, digital or physical, is an analytical affordance that directly results from putting validity affordances into action. For example, the provider S11 established a private blockchain based on Hyperledger Fabric to provide services for international trade and logistics. As such, S11 tracks the ownership of internationally shipped and traded goods to facilitate the necessary exchange of documents, e.g., for customs processing. At the same time, S11 data records can be audited because they are stored as an immutable transaction history in the distributed ledger. This is perceived as particularly important in a regulated environment like international trade and logistics.

Table 4 Categories of salient affordances

Validity affordances	Analytical affordances	Automation affordances	Decentralization affordances	Generative affordances
Retaining an immutable transaction history Ensuring validity of each transaction Storing durable data	Tracking ownership Auditing transaction history Selectively disclosing information	Reliably executing processes Speeding up complex transactions Efficiently scaling the service	Dividing and aggregating tasks and decisions Rewarding distributed actors based on rules	Quickly creating new services Changing underlying optimization criteria

> We decided to go into blockchain. [. . .] And we went into it knowing that our customers are enterprises. [. . .] And this means a number of different things. It means that they're scalable, it means they're secure, it means they are auditable, it means things are reliable.— Provider S11

Only detailed permissioning possibilities, moreover, allow clearly differentiating between internal and external auditors and provide the means to selectively disclose information from the transaction history. Like for S11, this is important for provider S7 who operates in the regulated financial industry providing transaction clearing services. The possibility to analyze historical data transactions in a detailed way differentiated by roles is a central reason for S7 to rely on permissioned blockchain technology like Hyperledger Fabric.

> In short, we don't wanna go to jail. The longer story is, we're dealing with a very regulated business. Ahm, we're not talking about moving a few hundred dollars payments around the globe. What we're talking about is, moving billion dollar risks between hedge funds.— Provider S7

We moreover find that automation affordances are salient in blockchain platforms for many service providers if the platforms entail powerful scripting features and permissioning possibilities. Scripting features allow service providers to define clear rules for reliably executing processes and workflows. Such reliable, rule-based execution then actually enables service providers to speed up complex transactions. For example, service providers like S3, S5, and S7 address the time-consuming hand-over phases in the financial industry. As such, S3 defines the workflow and process steps that are necessary in handling claim processing between insurance and re-insurance organizations. They perceive that blockchain platforms primarily enable them to securely execute predefined steps in an interorganizational process while all participants have the same perspective on the state of the process and the data that leads to decisions. Detailed permissioning enables some of these service providers to rely on more efficient transaction validation schemes than public blockchains. At the same time, they strictly limit the access to their private blockchain because this reduces the danger of attacks and data leakage. Detailed permissioning is therefore seen as a crucial necessity to efficiently scale their services in terms of transaction speed.

Generative affordances were primarily found salient by service providers on blockchain platforms that provide them with powerful scripting features to quickly create new services. As such, the consultancy company S6 develops custom-made blockchain solutions for its clients, often starting with a sole proof of concept. Consequently, they emphasize that blockchain platforms must primarily provide them with flexibility regarding scripting and permissioning so that they can develop strongly varying applications with ease:

> But the quality of the technology is around how many options you have to deliver one function. If you look at Ethereum, you can use a lot of different apps on top of Ethereum already. That does not exist in Hyperledger, yet.—Provider S6

Nonetheless, the same company acknowledges that architectural modularity may provide it with more possibilities to change underlying optimization criteria of a blockchain and thereby react more swiftly to changing requirements of their customers. For example, their customers may decide to shift their focus from security to higher transaction speed over time. Provider S6 perceives that modularity, for example in terms of exchangeable consensus mechanisms like in Hyperledger Fabric, can provide a central value to their service offering. Primarily, however, they perceive that the central affordance of specific blockchains to their service is the ability to easily generate varying solutions for their customers.

Lastly, decentralization affordances refer to affordances that facilitate the meaningful integration of large numbers of actors in services. Blockchain platforms on which automation affordances are already being leveraged afford service providers functions for dividing tasks and decisions and for rewarding distributed actors based on rules. Platforms that include a native currency facilitate rewarding through the intrinsic value of the currency, which can be leveraged to motivate consumers to participate in distributed tasks. The effective division and re-aggregation of tasks and decisions is seen as crucially dependent on the effective execution of rule-based processes and the validity of transactions in the immutable history. Decentralization affordances thereby depend strongly on both the successful execution of automation affordances and validity affordances. For example, service provider S8 engages consumers in peer-to-peer insurances through its platform based on Ethereum. Using smart contracts, users can bet on the occurrence of a specific event if at least one user wants to insure against this event. Depending on the occurrence of the event, the stakes go to the insuree or to the betting insurer including a fee. Providers S10 and S2 use similar wager mechanism to crowdsource predictions of real-world events. Provider S17 also perceives decentralization affordances as most crucial to its service as they allow S17 to contract recyclables collectors in developmental countries, purchase recyclable waste from them, and reward them accordingly via smart contracts. However, S17 is very aware that their use of decentralization affordances would be damned to failure if underlying automation affordances were not successfully executed:

> Step one of our decision making was unlimited scalability, which is why we were starting on essentially the largest enterprise system we could. You know, even when [. . .] we hit a billion users [. . .] we're already on the platform for that.—Provider S17

In sum, we identified five categories of functional affordances in our case studies. Single service providers differed in the affordances that they perceived as salient, and several salient affordances required the successful actualization of other affordances before they became salient. Next, we present the results of a dual examination of the technical features of blockchain platforms that enable these affordances and the organizational goals of service providers which puts these results into a coherent picture. It shows that blockchain affordances not only build on each other but vary depending on the group of service providers and can even detrimentally affect each other.

4.2   A Network of Salient Blockchain Affordances

Figure 2 depicts a network view of salient blockchain platform affordances for service providers. Following Burton-Jones & Volkoff et al. (2017), this view takes into account that affordances do not exist independent of actors who can make use of them and that higher-level affordances may require the successful actualization of lower-level affordances. In line with the above analysis, the figure depicts that analytical affordances and automation affordances are only enabled by successfully executed validity affordances. That is, without the successful retention of an immutable transaction history of valid transactions and without the durable storage of data on a distributed ledger, neither analytical nor automation affordances become salient for service providers. Similarly, decentralization affordances only become salient if complex processes can effectively be automated through the underlying blockchain platform. Only if the platform provides enough scripting and permissioning capabilities to efficiently automate complex transactions, it becomes feasible for service providers to engage large numbers of actors in decentralized tasks and decisions, because only then can they automate the management of dividing and aggregating tasks and decisions.

Interestingly, however, enabling higher-level affordances is not the only effect that the actualization of affordances has in this network. Specifically, service providers who primarily rely on salient lower-level affordances feel that the use of higher-level affordances can constrain basic affordances of a blockchain platform. As such, abundant use of automation affordances and generative affordances are seen very critical by service providers who focus on lower-level validity affordances. Their reasoning is that more complexity in the transactions that need to be validated increases the chance for errors, successful hacker attacks, and for diminishing the most fundamental validity affordances of blockchain platforms. As such, for service provider S9, validity affordances are salient in its service of ensuring the authenticity and correctness of documents for its customers. Consequently, provider S9 sees powerful scripting capabilities merely as a feature that would not benefit them much but could lead to problems if others use it extensively. This is in line with the reasoning of a Bitcoin core developer:

> Eventually, an easy-to-use language can give you the illusion that (developing Dapps) is easier than it actually is. And this practically motivates people who do not really have the know-how to engage with it. And this can lead, as in the DAO case, to costly mistakes.— Bitcoin platform developer

Lastly, Fig. 2 also highlights that service providers with similar core service offerings base their use of blockchain platforms on the same salient affordances. Four categories of service providers emerged from our data analysis. Table 5 depicts these categories. Authenticity services, which mostly engage in proving the existence and authenticity of data and documents (e.g., notaries and know-your-customer service providers), make primarily use of validity affordances. Blockchain consultancies, which develop software solutions for their customers, primarily make use of generative affordances. Efficiency services of various kinds target

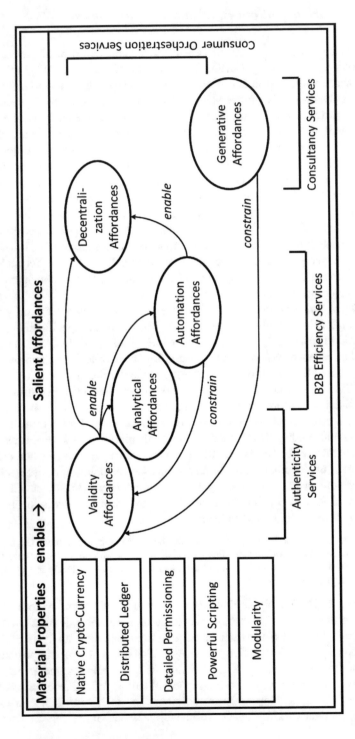

Fig. 2 Blockchain features as necessary antecedents of salient affordances for service providers

Table 5 Categories of service providers and their salient affordances

Category	Authenticity services	Consumer orchestration services	Efficiency services	Consultancy services
Core service area	Proving authenticity and existence of data and documents; notary services	New forms of orchestrating consumer actions and interactions	Increasing efficiency in extant processes (esp. interorganizational)	Consultancy and custom software development for customers
Service providers (chosen platforms)	S9 (BTC)	S2 (ETH)	S5 (ETH)	S1 (ETH, HF)
	S14 (BTC, ETH)	S8 (ETH)	S7 (HF)	S6 (ETH)
	S18 (BTC, ETH)	S10 (ETH)	S3 (ETH)	S12 (ETH, HF)
		S17 (HF)	S11 (HF)	S19 (ETH)
		S16 (ETH)	S13 (HF)	
		S4 (BTC, ETH)	S15 (BTC, ETH)	
Salient affordances	Validity affordances	Decentralization and generative affordances	Automation and analytical affordances	Generative affordances

inefficient hand-overs and time-consuming process steps in different industries. They particularly focus on interorganizational transactions that often suffer from inefficiencies but are typically subject to regulation and, therefore, require effective auditability. For efficiency services, the primary salient affordances are analytical and automation affordances. Lastly, consumer orchestration services aim to create value by connecting and interconnecting large numbers of consumers and engaging them in business activities that were previously hard to orchestrate. Examples include prediction markets, peer-to-peer insurances, and e-commerce platforms for sharing and exchanging goods in regionally bounded economies. Accordingly, consumer orchestration services rely primarily on decentralization affordances and generative affordances.

In sum, Fig. 2 shows how the salient affordances of blockchain platforms for service providers emerge from two necessary preconditions: the material properties of the platform and the core service area of the service to provide. Where specific platform characteristics come together with the matching core service area, service providers tend to make use of the respective affordances. Contrary to conventional expectation, however, actualizing affordances does not necessarily lead to further affordances but can also be detrimental and constraining to lower level affordances. Thus, our results so far answer the question of what the affordances of blockchain platforms for service providers are and explain where they come from. Given that blockchain platforms are under active development and constantly evolve, we now turn to the question of how service providers respond to the emergent affordances of distinct blockchain platforms.

4.3 Using Emergent Blockchain Platforms: The Role of Community Values

Extant blockchain platforms differ in those material properties that result in salient affordances for service providers (cf., Table 1). Consequently, service providers that have to decide which platform they want to join typically examine each platform's affordances and select the one they perceive to fit best.

However, all major blockchain platforms are under ongoing development in open-source communities. Consequently, there are ongoing changes in all platforms that have the potential to create new affordances for service providers or remove extant ones. Affordances may even emerge for a service provider from other platforms than the one it is currently providing its services on. This begs the question of how service providers respond to these emergent affordances and how they adapt their use patterns of blockchain platforms in order to make the most effective use of the technology under development.

We analyzed all cases in our sample for how the service providers reacted to new features and resulting affordances within and outside their respective blockchain platforms. Although not all service providers did follow what was happening in other blockchain open-source projects, there were cases of several providers that allowed us to draw meaningful conclusions. We could study reactions to emergent features in other platforms because several service providers were already active before the platforms Hyperledger Fabric or even Ethereum became available. Abstracting from the single cases in our sample, we identified two patterns of how service providers adapt their use of blockchain platforms over time. Figure 3 depicts these patterns. For reasons of brevity, we illustrate each pattern with the case of one service provider.

4.3.1 Illustrating Blockchain Use Pattern 1: Decoupling and Diversification

In technical domains as specific as blockchain platforms, there is generally some exchange of ideas and opinions across different communities. In projects under ongoing development, there are consequently situations when open-source communities discuss and argue about the directions in which to go and whether comparable strategies in related other communities constitute viable alternatives.

We find that service providers tend to decouple from their focal blockchain platform if the values that the community enacts at such times of discussion and argument do not match the service provider's values. In these cases, service providers act to become less dependent on their focal blockchain platform and its open-source community. For example, service providers introduce middleware layers between their service and the underlying platform, create versions of their service running on another blockchain platform, or leave the focal platform altogether. That is, service providers decouple from their original blockchain platform and diversify to other platforms.

The major value conflicts that we observed and that caused such adaptations in blockchain platform use related all to values of immutability and innovativeness. Where the former constitutes an expressed or unexpressed promise of the community to ensure the immutability of their blockchain and historic records, the latter constitutes a promise to swiftly incorporate innovative ideas for the better of the platform's technical quality. Where the values of a service provider regarding immutability and innovativeness collide with differently enacted values of its community, the service provider reacts by decoupling or diversifying.

For example, service provider S18 had been working exclusively on the Bitcoin blockchain to provide its authentication service when performance scalability became a highly discussed topic in the community. Scalability could be addressed in different ways that were also proposed and implemented in other blockchain platform communities. However, the Bitcoin core community engaged in months of discussions and arguments. And even then, they could not agree on a change in protocol that would provide scalability but would have marginal consequences for the immutability of the blockchain. A Bitcoin core developer put it as follows:

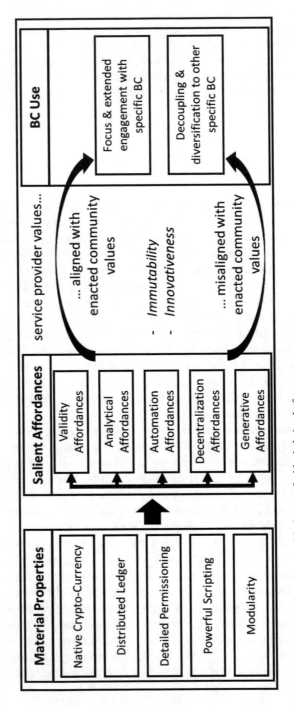

Fig. 3 Refined model of service provider's use of a blockchain platform

> At the moment we have this giant chaos with [name of the proposed code change], which is actually backward compatible. However, some people realized that they can use their leverage to some degree to block this. So, even backward compatible changes are relatively difficult to get through.—Bitcoin core developer

For service provider S18, this constituted an undesirable over-emphasis on immutability at the expense of investments in innovativeness. In reaction, S18 developed a connector for its service to the Ethereum blockchain platform because they attributed more of the desirable community value of innovativeness to Ethereum's open-source community. From this point on, S18 provided its service on both Bitcoin and Ethereum platforms.

> Ethereum is very interesting for us, because they are moving faster, experimenting more and they are finding their hybrid solution that will allow to increase throughput. And bitcoin is kind of stuck in the world of more conservative approaches, slow solution. And we need both! We need a community that moves faster and breaks things faster. And then we need a community that is more conservative.—Provider S18

Although the new scalability feature of Ethereum did not directly benefit S18 or provide them with any new affordances, S18 decoupled from Bitcoin and built a connection to the community behind Ethereum. They did so to make sure they do not miss out on new affordances of innovative blockchain platforms because they perceived an underappreciation of innovativeness in the Bitcoin community.

4.3.2 Illustrating Blockchain Use Pattern 2: Focus and Extended Engagement

By contrast, when community decisions and actions reinforced the perspective of service providers on the values of immutability and innovativeness, then the service providers were more often found to intensify their focus on their original blockchain platform. As such, service providers engaged more in the community, communicated more intensively with open-source developers, or started contributing to the source code of the core platform.

For example, service provider S8 observed the discussions and arguments when the Ethereum community was facing the disastrous hacker attack on the crowdfunding platform DAO and had to decide whether and how to react on it. In favor of working against the hackers, S8 supported the community decision to violate the value of immutability by changing the transaction history of the public Ethereum blockchain back to the state before the attack. The Ethereum community did interfere with the transaction history and changed it, thereby neutralizing the hackers' attack. This community decision reinforced S8's value of working in a highly dynamic environment where innovation and technical quality sometimes needed to overrule other values.

> [. . .] and we also lost a lot of money because of it [the DAO hack and the ensuing rollback]. But hey, we all know this is a high risk system. [. . .] I would sometimes wish for more tolerance [on behalf of the critics] and a confession that we all are experimenting a lot and that we are all allowed to make mistakes.—Provider S8

After the decision, S8 engaged more actively in the Ethereum community. They started to attend workshops and summits and openly presented their decentralized insurance service at international conferences so that other service providers could learn from their approach. At the end of our data collection period, S8 pointed out that "more bureaucratic" or "slow and rudimentary" blockchain platform communities (referring to Hyperledger and Bitcoin) would definitely not constitute viable alternatives for developing their service.

In sum, we find that such situations - when the open-source communities behind blockchain platforms need to act in favor or against values of immutability and innovativeness - constitute the events when service providers decide on their further engagement on a specific platform. If the values enacted in community decisions conform to those of the service providers, then they tend to focus more on the specific platform and extend their engagement in its community. If the values enacted in community decisions conflict with those of the service providers, then they tend to decouple their services from the focal platform and diversify to other blockchain platforms.

5 Discussion

This study explored the affordances of blockchain platforms to service providers. Drawing on Affordance Theory and a grounded theory investigation, we found that blockchain platforms provide validity affordances, analytical affordances, automation affordances, decentralization affordances, and generative affordances to service providers. We outlined the complex interrelationships of blockchain platform features, properties of the service, and resulting affordances. Lastly, we showed that service providers' engagement on a blockchain platform depends not only on the salient affordances of the platform but also on the values that are enacted in the open-source community behind it. These findings have several implications for theory and practice.

5.1 Implications for Theory on Blockchain Platforms and Affordances

First, this study adds to the growing body of research on blockchain systems by outlining and explaining the provenance of functional affordances of blockchain platforms for service providers. Prior research has emphasized the flexible nature of blockchain technology (Risius & Spohrer, 2017). It showcased that blockchain technology provides value in very different ways, depending on the specifics of use cases in finance (Underwood, 2016), supply chain management (Zhao et al., 2016), human resources management (Ying et al., 2018), or digital rights management

(Savelyev, 2017). What was missing so far is an understanding of the more general affordances of blockchain platforms. This study elaborated on five different categories of affordances (validity affordances, analytical affordances, automation affordances, decentralization affordances, generative affordances) and how they depend on features of blockchain platforms and characteristics of services. It thereby presents a more comprehensive, theory-driven understanding of the usefulness of blockchain platforms.

Second, by providing an affordances perspective on blockchain platforms, we also contribute to the discussion of how blockchain technology can facilitate decentralization in our economy (Beck et al., 2018). Specifically, our affordances lens provides insight into the necessary but non-sufficient requirements for decentralization (Volkoff & Strong, 2017). As such, our findings suggest that decentralization affordances cannot be actualized without the proper actualization of validity and automation affordances. At the same time, abundant actualization of automation affordances can result in constraints to validity affordances. These adverse effects need to be considered when aiming to devise systems with decentralization affordances. Our findings, therefore, constitute a promising starting point for future research on decentralization in blockchain systems.

Third, our study helps understand why service providers rely on specific blockchain platforms rather than others. As such, service providers generally select those blockchain platforms that provide the best fitting salient affordances for their service. However, our study highlights that the ongoing use of blockchain platforms by service providers also depends on the open-source communities behind these platforms. If the communities enact values that conflict with those of the service providers, then the service providers tend to decouple from the respective platform. Although this resonates with prior work on platform ecosystems, where the alignment of values between platform providers and complementors strongly influences their joint performance (Huber et al., 2017), the idea has previously not received attention in the context of blockchain research. In our study, this relationship emerged from inductive data analysis. Future research may, however, draw more explicitly on prior work on platform ecosystems. For example, it may capture phenomena that have been theoretically addressed in platform ecosystems but remain little understood in blockchain research. Thereby, we advance insights beyond the mere conceptualization of potential blockchain application developments (Iansiti & Lakhani, 2017) into a case-specific understanding of platform selection by blockchain-based service providers.

Fourth, this study is one of the first to follow the call by Burton-Jones and Volkoff (2017) to use networks of affordances for understanding the effective use of innovative technology in context. We showed that blockchain platform affordances unfold as networks and can not only be enabling but also mutually constraining. Our study may consequently serve as evidence that the proposed perspective of networks of affordances provides fruitful insights.

Lastly, prior research on functional affordances has often emphasized that higher-level affordances depend on the actualization of lower-level ones (e.g., Burton-Jones & Volkoff, 2017; Strong et al., 2014). We find similar patterns of emergence.

In addition, however, we find that the actualization of higher-level affordances (e.g., automation affordances) can not only enable but also constrain the execution of lower-level affordances (e.g., validity affordances). This suggests that adverse emergent effects, such as the one observed, may have hitherto been overlooked and need to be examined in future research.

5.2 Practical Implications

This study provides a general understanding of the generic affordances of blockchain platforms. Service providers may use the different categories of affordances and the knowledge of how they relate to platform features to evaluate how well a specific blockchain platform suits their needs. Our work moreover suggests that open-source communities should take good care which values they enact in their decisions. Extreme decisions have the potential to drive valuable complementary service providers away, particularly when the decisions weigh the immutability of a blockchain against its innovativeness.

6 Conclusion

This study set out to understand the affordances of blockchain platforms for service providers. Based on Affordance Theory, we conducted a grounded theory investigation of 19 service providers on three platforms. We found that blockchain platforms provide five different types of affordances for service providers. We showed that complex interrelationships exist between blockchain platform features, properties of the service domain, and resulting affordances. Lastly, we showed that service providers' use of a blockchain platform depends not only on the salient affordances of the platform but also on the values that are enacted by the open-source community behind it.

References

Antonopoulos, A. M. (2014). *Mastering Bitcoin: Unlocking digital cryptocurrencies*. O'Reilly Media.

Back, A., Corallo, M., Dashjr, L., Friedenbach, M., Maxwell, G., & Miller, A., Wuille, P. (2014). *Enabling blockchain innovations with pegged sidechains*. Retrieved March 31, 2018, from http://www.blockstream.com/sidechains.pdf

Bakos, Y., Halaburda, H., and Mueller-Bloch, C. 2021. "When Permissioned Blockchains Deliver More Decentralization Than Permissionless," *Communications of the ACM, 64*(2), 20–22. https://doi.org/10.1145/3442371

Beck, R., Müller-Bloch, C., & King, J. L. (2018). *Governance in the blockchain economy: A framework and research agenda*. Journal of the Association for Information Systems. https://doi.org/10.17705/1jais.00518

Burton-Jones, A., & Volkoff, O. (2017). How can we develop contextualized theories of effective use? A demonstration in the context of community-care electronic health records. *Information Systems Research*. https://doi.org/10.1287/isre.2017.0702

Cachin, C. (2016). *Architecture of the hyperledger blockchain fabric*. IBM.

Castro, M., & Liskov, B. (1999). Practical Byzantine fault tolerance. Paper presented at the *OSDI*.

Charmaz, K. (2006). *Constructing grounded theory: A practical guide through qualitative research*. Sage.

Corbin, J., & Strauss, A. (1990). Grounded theory research: Procedures, canons, and evaluative criteria. *Qualitative Sociology, 13*(1), 3–21.

Dai, J., & Vasarhelyi, M. A. (2017). Toward blockchain-based accounting and assurance. *Journal of Information Systems, 31*(3), 5–21.

Du, W. D., Pan, S. L., Leidner, D. E., & Ying, W. (2019). Affordances, experimentation and actualization of fintech: A blockchain implementation study. *The Journal of Strategic Information Systems, 28*(1), 50–65.

Ethereum. (2018). *Solidity*. Retrieved March 30, 2018, from https://solidity.readthedocs.io/en/develop/

Giancaspro, M. (2017). Is a 'smart contract' really a smart idea? Insights from a legal perspective. *Computer Law and Security Review, 33*(6), 825–835.

Glaser, F. (2017). Pervasive decentralisation of digital infrastructures: A framework for blockchain enabled system and use case analysis. Paper presented at the *50th Hawaii International Conference on System Sciences (HICSS 2017)*, Waikoloa, Hawaii.

Gramoli, V. (2017). *From blockchain consensus back to Byzantine consensus*. Future Generation Computer Systems.

Harvey, C. R. H. (2016). *Cryptofinance*. SSRN.

Huber, T., Kude, T., & Dibbern, J. (2017). Governance practices in platform ecosystems: Navigating tensions between co-created value and governance costs. *Information Systems Research, 28*(3), 563–584.

Hyvärinen, H., Risius, M., & Friis, G. (2017). A blockchain-based approach towards overcoming financial fraud in public sector services. *Business and Information Systems Engineering, 59*(6), 441–456.

Iansiti, M., & Lakhani, K. R. (2017). The truth about blockchain. *Harvard Business Review, 1*.

IBM. (2018, January 11). *Developing blockchain smart contracts*. Retrieved March 30, 2018, from https://console.bluemix.net/docs/services/IoT/blockchain/dev_blockchain.html

Leonardi, P. (2011). When flexible routines meet flexible technologies: Affordance, constraint, and the imbrication of human and material agencies. *MIS Quarterly, 35*(1), 147–167.

Markus, M. L., & Silver, M. S. (2008). A foundation for the study of IT effects: A new look at DeSanctis and Poole's concepts of structural features and spirit. *Journal of the Association for Information Systems, 9*(10), 609–632.

Miles, M. B., & Huberman, M. A. (1994). *Qualitative data analysis: An expanded sourcebook*. Sage.

Mini, T., Ellinger, E. W., Gregory, R. W., & Widjaja, T. (2021). "An Exploration of Governing via IT in Decentralized Autonomous Organizations," in Proceedings of the 42nd International Conference on Information Systems, Austin

Nofer, M., Gomber, P., Hinz, O., & Schiereck, D. (2017). Blockchain. *Business and Information Systems Engineering*, 1–5.

Ølnes, S., Ubacht, J., & Janssen, M. (2017). *Blockchain in government: Benefits and implications of distributed ledger technology for information sharing*. Elsevier.

Ostern, N., Rosemann, M., & Moormann, J. (2020). Determining the idiosyncrasy of blockchain: An affordances perspective. In *Proceedings of the 41st International Conference on Information Systems (ICIS): Making Digital Inclusive: Blending the Local and the Global*. Association for Information Systems.

Overhage, S., & Widjaja, T. 2022. "A Taxonomy of Forks in the Context of Decentralized Autonomous Organizations," in Proceedings of the European Conference on Information System (ECIS 2022), Paper 1410, Timisoara, June 18. https://aisel.aisnet.org/ecis2022_rp/77

Risius, M., & Spohrer, K. (2017). A blockchain research framework: What we (don't) know, where we go from here, and how we will get there. *Business and Information Systems Engineering, 59*(6), 385–409.

Robey, D., Anderson, C., & Raymond, B. (2013). "Information Technology, Materiality, and Organizational Change: A Professional Odyssey," *Journal of the Association for Information Systems, 14*(7), 379–398.

Rossi, M., Müller-Bloch, C., Thatcher, J. B., & Beck, R. (2019). "Blockchain Research in Information Systems: Current Trends and an Inclusive Future Research Agenda," *Journal of the Association for Information Systems, 20*(9), 247–265.

Savelyev, A. (2017). Copyright in the blockchain era: Promises and challenges. *Computer Law and Security Review*.

Seidel, S., Recker, J., & vom Brocke, J. (2014). "Sensemaking and Sustainable Practicing: Functional Affordances of Information Systems in Green Transformations," *MIS Quarterly, 37*(4), pp. 1275–1299.

Shin, D., & Hwang, Y. (2020). *The effects of security and traceability of blockchain on digital affordance*. Online information review.

Statista. (2021). Accessed 13-12-2021, from https://www.statista.com/statistics/621207/worldwide-blockchain-startup-financing-history/

Strong, D. M., Volkoff, O., Johnson, S. A., Pelletier, L. R., Tulu, B., Bar-On, I., Trudel, J., & Garber, L. (2014). A theory of organization-EHR affordance actualization. *Journal of the Association for Information Systems, 15*(2), 53–85.

Tapscott, D., & Tapscott, A. (2016). *Blockchain revolution: How the technology behind bitcoin is changing money, business, and the world*. Penguin.

Tapscott, D., & Tapscott, A. (2017). How blockchain will change organizations. *MIT Sloan Management Review, 58*(2), 10.

Tiwana, A., Konsynski, B., & Bush, A. A. (2010). Platform evolution: Coevolution of platform architecture, governance, and environmental dynamics. *Information Systems Research, 21*(4), 675–687.

Underwood, S. (2016). Blockchain beyond bitcoin. *Communications of the ACM, 59*(11), 15–17.

Vaast, E., Safadi, H., Lapointe, L., & Negoita, B. (2017). Social media affordances for connective action: An examination of microblogging use during the gulf of Mexico oil spill. *MIS Quarterly, 41*(4), 1179–1206.

Volkoff, O., & Strong, D. M. (2013). Critical realism and affordances: Theorizing IT-associated organizational change processes. *MIS Quarterly, 37*(3), 819–834.

Volkoff, O. & Strong, D. M. (2017). Affordance theory and how to use it in IS research, in Galliers, R. D. & Stein, M.-K. (Eds.) The Routledge companion to management information systems, Routledge Handbooks Online, 232–243. https://doi.org/10.4324/9781315619361.ch16

Vukolić, M. (2015). The quest for scalable blockchain fabric: Proof-of-work vs. BFT replication. Paper presented at the *International Workshop on Open Problems in Network Security*.

Walsh, C., O'Reilly, P., Gleasure, R., Feller, J., Li, S., & Cristoforo, J. (2016). New kid on the block: a strategic archetypes approach to understanding the Blockchain. Paper presented at the *37th International Conference on Information Systems (ICIS)*, Dublin.

Yin, R. K. (2009). *Case study research* (5th ed.). Sage.

Ying, W., Jia, S., & Du, W. (2018). Digital enablement of blockchain: Evidence from HNA group. *International Journal of Information Management, 39*, 1–4.

Yue, X., Wang, H., Jin, D., Li, M., & Jiang, W. (2016). Healthcare data gateways: Found healthcare intelligence on blockchain with novel privacy risk control. *Journal of Medical Systems, 40*(10), 218.

Zachariadis, M., Scott, S., & Barrett, M. (2013). Methodological implications of critical realism for mixed-methods research. *MIS Quarterly, 37*(3), 855–879.

Zhao, J. L., Fan, S., & Yan, J. (2016). *Overview of business innovations and research opportunities in blockchain and introduction to the special issue*. Springer.

Process Mining for Carbon Accounting: An Analysis of Requirements and Potentials

Lars Brehm, Jessica Slamka, and Andreas Nickmann

Abstract Organizations are considered as key contributors to environmental deterioration caused by resource consumption, waste, and carbon emissions. In an aim to reduce their carbon footprints, organizations are increasingly starting to account for their environmental impact and are seeking new ways to improve their operations. Previous research indicates that only through changing their processes, companies can become more sustainable. This, however, requires a sound understanding of how unsustainable processes are and to what extent a change can facilitate more sustainable ways to operate. For this purpose, this paper examines how process mining can support carbon accounting in terms of decision support for carbon reduction. Based on a review of related literature and interviews with process mining experts, requirements and potentials of process mining to support carbon accounting are identified. The findings indicate that with process mining, it becomes possible to create the much-needed process transparency by incorporating carbon data into the process model. This allows to measure the carbon footprint per process step and along the execution of processes. Thereby, practitioners are not only able to evaluate the carbon performance on granular process levels but in fact are empowered to establish carbon reduction measures without neglecting the process design and process workflow.

1 Introduction

The accounting for and disclosure of carbon-related information in the context of carbon accounting is increasingly becoming an economically relevant topic for corporate management (Burritt et al., 2011, p. 91; Schaltegger & Csutora, 2012, p. 6ff). Carbon tax regulations and emissions trading influence the costs of fossil-based energy usage within supply chains, production, and logistics, resulting in

L. Brehm (✉) · J. Slamka · A. Nickmann
Am Stadtpark 20, Munich, Germany
e-mail: lars.brehm@hm.edu; jessica.slamka@hm.edu; andreas.nickmann@hm.edu

© The Author(s), under exclusive license to Springer Nature Switzerland AG 2022
J. Dibbern et al. (eds.), *Digitalization Across Organizational Levels*, Progress in IS,
https://doi.org/10.1007/978-3-031-06543-9_9

higher product prices (Schaltegger & Csutora, 2012, p. 13). Through regulations and changing consumer behavior, politics and society are increasingly forcing companies to reduce their carbon footprint, which requires the implementation of effective methods, tools, and technologies to support this endeavor (Schaltegger & Csutora, 2012, p. 3).

The ever-increasing growth of public interest in climate change issues acts as a catalyst for the large increase in carbon auditing (Tang, 2019, p. 388). However, although carbon accounting and respective reduction initiatives have gained significant attention over the last decades, companies are still not able to realize the full potential of existing corporate carbon accounting methods (Burritt et al., 2011, p. 92). Current carbon accounting methods and tools have been found to lack standardization (Schaltegger et al., 2015, p. 19; Schaltegger & Csutora, 2012, p. 7), decision support (Zvezdov & Schaltegger, 2015, p. 40f; Schaltegger & Csutora, 2012, p. 13) as well as capabilities to identify reduction potentials (Schaltegger & Csutora, 2012, p. 13). Moreover, existing literature mostly focuses on carbon disclosure rather than achieving actual carbon reductions (He et al., 2021, p. 29). In order to identify effective levers for carbon reduction, the focus should be shifted towards the implementation of performance measurement and actual reduction of carbon emissions (Qian & Schaltegger, 2017, p. 377).

Organizations primarily contribute to environmental degradation through their business processes (Seidel et al., 2012, p. 3ff). Consequently, the need arises to develop methods that create transparency about the carbon impact of past and current business operations on a process level. This would allow an identification of reduction potentials and an assessment of environmental implications and effectiveness in order to derive measures that ultimately reduce a firm's carbon footprint (Qian et al., 2018, p. 1616; Brander & Ascui, 2015, p. 116f; Schaltegger & Csutora, 2012, p. 7). For this purpose, there is a need to further research new carbon accounting practices that consider state-of-the-art technologies and more innovative methods to measure and effectively find ways to reduce CO_2 emissions for improved carbon performance (He et al., 2021, p. 27).

The application of process-centered techniques and dedicated consideration of environmental consequences on a business process level is framed under the notion of Green Business Process Management (BPM) (Seidel et al., 2012, p. 6f). While the BPM domain has elevated to the status of becoming an important management discipline (vom Brocke & Rosemann, 2015, p. 1ff), Green BPM is expanding this view of process-related concepts with a strong focus on sustainable development (Seidel et al., 2012, p. 6ff). By being able to document and measure the environmental impact of a business process, practitioners are empowered to make informed decisions about processes and the improvement of these processes towards environmental and traditional business objectives (Recker et al., 2012, p. 107).

Process mining as a state-of-the-art technology has recently received attention as an enabler of Green BPM. Process mining can be described as a technology that enables the discovery, monitoring, and improvement of real processes (i.e., not assumed processes) by extracting knowledge from event logs readily available in information systems (van der Aalst, 2016, p. 31). Analyses in process mining can be enhanced by enriching the data with external attributes such as information related to time which allows to calculate the throughput time between two occurring events (van Eck et al., 2015, p. 6). In practice, recent efforts by process mining experts from Celonis and Ernst & Young have been made to develop a solution design that considers carbon emission data and thus facilitates the measurement and evaluation of carbon emissions on process levels along the value chain (Ueda, 2021).

In contrast to the versatile optimization potential of process mining, to date, academic research that investigates process mining adoption as a potential method to support carbon reduction is scarce. The general capability of Green BPM to consider carbon management has been pointed out in a few previous studies, with process mining enhancing the process view by creating a true "as-is" process model (Ghose et al., 2010; Lübbecke et al., 2015; Ortmeier et al., 2021) and enabling effective decision-making through business process simulation (Lübbecke et al., 2015) in first (fictional) use cases. Yet, the actual requirements of how to implement process mining to support carbon management as well as the potentials of process mining to measure and improve carbon performance on process levels remain unclear.

Given the capabilities of process mining to measure process performance considering economic factors, the question arises how process mining can support carbon accounting in terms of decision support for carbon reduction. Accordingly, this paper addresses the following research question: How can process mining support carbon accounting in the recognition, measurement, and reduction of carbon emissions?

The objective is to identify necessary requirements for implementing process mining for carbon accounting and to create an understanding of the specific potentials of process mining to identify and realize carbon saving potentials on the process management level.

With this objective, we contribute to the overall "Green IS" resp. "Green BY IT" initiatives (Calero & Piattini, 2015, p. 15f), and to be more specific, we combine the Green IS Practices of environmental management systems and process re-engineering as defined by Loeser et al. (2017, p. 515).

The remainder of this paper is organized as follows: The remainder of this paper is organized as follows: Sect. 2 provides the conceptual foundation by introducing the concepts of carbon accounting and process mining in light of the current state of research. The research design for the empirical study including interviews with experts experienced in the implementation of process mining for carbon reduction described in Sect. 3. Section 4 presents the findings of the empirical study in terms of requirements and potentials of process mining to support carbon accounting. Section 5 proceeds with a discussion of the study's theoretical and practical contribution, followed by limitations and avenues for future research. The paper concludes in Sect. 6 with a short summary and an outlook.

2 Conceptional Foundation: Process Mining for Carbon Accounting

The concepts of carbon accounting and process mining are introduced in this section based on current literature. For this purpose, Sect. 2.1 outlines goals of and current approaches in carbon accounting, while basic process mining techniques are presented in Sect. 2.2. Section 2.3 gives insight into existing literature on the potentials of process mining in terms of sustainable development and carbon reduction.

2.1 Carbon Accounting

To measure environmental impacts including carbon emissions, carbon accounting emerged as a discipline over the last decades with growing attention from the business sector.

2.1.1 Corporate Carbon Footprint

In order to combat global warming and mitigate the effects of climate change, the United Nations reached two major international binding agreements that resulted in the adoption of the Kyoto Protocol in 1997 (United Nations, 2005, p. 2ff) and the subsequent Paris Agreement in 2015 (United Nations, 2016, p. 1ff). The objective of these agreements aims at undertaking joint actions on reducing greenhouse gas (GHG) emissions on domestic levels. As a consequence, governments around the world started to introduce emission trading schemes, carbon taxes, and disclosure regulations which invoke organizations to report on their carbon performance and expose their corporate carbon footprint (Qian et al., 2018, p. 1608; Schaltegger et al., 2015, p. 2). This creates the need for organizations to start gaining a sound understanding and knowledge of their corporate carbon footprint, as they would otherwise not be able to develop and pursue any effective carbon mitigation strategies (Matthews et al., 2008, p. 5839). Thus, measuring the corporate carbon footprint has become a topic of interest to many business organizations in order to calculate their carbon emissions and derive measures to mitigate their environmental impact (Seidel et al., 2012, p. 95).

In scientific literature, various definitions of the term carbon footprint have been proposed. Although there are slight differences in the scope of each definition, the term carbon footprint is generally understood as the quantified assessment of CO_2 emissions caused directly and indirectly by a certain activity, product, or population (Damert et al., 2020, p. 59; Wright et al., 2011, p. 64). Carbon footprints represent measures of climate change impact and provide indication of contributions to global GHG emissions entering the atmosphere (Schaltegger & Csutora, 2012,

p. 9). On a corporate level, these indicators for carbon intensity can be allocated on different scales ranging from internal operations (e.g., production, logistics) to product value chains (e.g., in upstream and downstream activities) up to sector and even nation-wide carbon accounts (Wright et al., 2011, p. 66f). Measuring the carbon footprint in form of CO_2 emissions and equivalents becomes crucial when it comes to identifying alternative, less carbon-intensive ways of production, sourcing, and product design (Schaltegger & Csutora, 2012, p. 7).

A common way to measure carbon footprints is the assessment of CO_2 equivalents in tons (tCO_2e), including the accounts for global warming effects of various other GHGs (Wright et al., 2011, p. 63). Since different GHGs can have different effects on the earth's warming, the introduction of the global warming potential allows for better comparison by simplifying a specific measure of how much energy the emissions of one ton of other GHGs will absorb over a given period of time, relative to the emissions of one ton of CO_2 (EPA, 2016). The efficient and effective collection and processing of such carbon-related information allow for improved carbon management performance (Burritt et al., 2011, p. 92f). In fact, there is scientific evidence indicating that good carbon performance is generally positively related to superior financial performance (Busch & Lewandowski, 2018, p. 755). As a consequence, the effective management and processing of carbon-related information to reduce the corporate carbon footprint and improve a firm's carbon performance has become a managerial economic imperative. To that end, the development of appropriate measures for effective carbon management is a specific challenge for carbon accounting (Schaltegger & Csutora, 2012, p. 9).

2.1.2 Corporate Carbon Accounting

With the increasing demand of corporate carbon disclosure and the carbon impact on business organizations, growing efforts have been made in designing and implementing new methods and tools to improve the measurement and management of corporate carbon performance (Qian et al., 2018, p. 1608ff; Burritt et al., 2011, p. 80ff; Schaltegger & Csutora, 2012, p. 1ff). Carbon accounting emerged as a business practice to measure, calculate, monitor, audit, and report greenhouse gas emissions on various levels (Schaltegger & Csutora, 2012, p. 4f; Csutora & Harangozo, 2017, p. 13f). Besides the geographical levels, Schaltegger and Csutora (2012, p. 4) separate also between three institutional levels. For our analysis, we focus on the corporate level as marked in Fig. 1 within the red box.

The term carbon accounting is widely used by scientists and often discussed in the context of integrating different aspects of climate into accounting (Stechemesser & Günther, 2012, p. 17). Despite the heterogeneity in the conceptualization of carbon accounting, there is a general consensus when defining the term (He et al., 2021, p. 28). Stechemesser and Günther (2012, p. 35) present the first systematic literature review on carbon accounting on different levels and define carbon accounting as "the recognition, the non-monetary and monetary evaluation and the monitoring of greenhouse gas emissions on all levels of the value chain

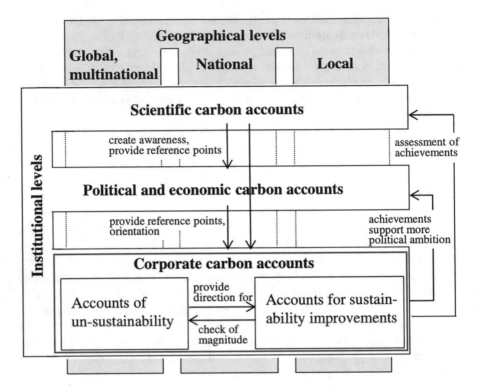

Fig. 1 Different levels of carbon accounts [source: Schaltegger and Csutora (2012, p. 4)]

and the recognition, evaluation, and monitoring of the effects of these emissions on the carbon cycle of ecosystems." Similarly, Tang (2017, p. 10) refers to "a system that uses accounting methods and procedures to collect, record, and analyze climate change–related information [. . .] to inform the decision-making processes of internal managers and external stakeholders."

Several efforts have been made to review the development of carbon accounting literature (He et al., 2021, p. 9ff; Saraswati, 2020, p. 17ff; Csutora & Harangozo, 2017, p. 3ff; Schaltegger & Csutora, 2012, p. 1ff; Stechemesser & Günther, 2012, p. 17ff; Ascui, 2014, p. 3ff; Ascui & Lovell, 2011, p. 978ff). Current research on carbon accounting has particularly focused on the conceptualization of carbon accounting (Tang, 2017, p. 33f; Ortas et al., 2015, p. 77ff), different types and levels of carbon accounts (Schaltegger & Csutora, 2012, p. 4ff; Csutora & Harangozo, 2017, p. 3ff; Ascui & Lovell, 2011, p. 982ff), and carbon accounting practices, methods, and functions (Burritt et al., 2011, p. 80ff; Gibassier, 2015, p. 129ff; Csutora & Harangozo, 2017, p. 8ff; Schaltegger & Csutora, 2012, p. 7ff). Kasbun et al. (2019, p. 1918ff) provide a conceptual framework to improve carbon performance, emphasizing the importance of a close fit between corporate carbon strategy and carbon accounting. A recent study by Ong et al. (2021, p. 16f) found that the implementation of carbon accounting positively influenced the firm's carbon performance. Moreover, Busch and Lewandowski (2018, p. 755) identified a positive correlation of a firm's carbon performance and financial performance.

Despite these advantages and the ever-increasing need for mandatory disclosure of carbon levels for business organizations, current literature on carbon accounting practices and methods remains largely under-researched (Zvezdov & Schaltegger, 2015, p. 27f; Hartmann et al., 2013, p. 558f) with only a few empirical studies on internal carbon accounting approaches (Gibassier & Schaltegger, 2015, p. 340ff; Burritt et al., 2011, p. 80ff). The need for further research is suggested with a strong focus on increases in awareness, the identification of reduction potentials, decision support, and the effective implementation of reduction measures (Schaltegger & Csutora, 2012, p. 13f; Gibassier & Schaltegger, 2015, p. 361f; Zvezdov & Schaltegger, 2015, p. 27f; He et al., 2021, p. 29).

2.1.3   Carbon Accounting Standards and Approaches

Various standards exist that provide guidelines for corporate carbon accounting. Besides the Intergovernmental Panel on Climate Change (IPCC) Guidelines for National Greenhouse Gas Inventories (IPCC, 2006) and the International Institute for Standardization (ISO) who published their carbon accounting standard ISO 14067 (ISO, 2018), the Greenhouse Gas Protocol is currently the dominant and most widely used standard (Schaltegger & Csutora, 2012, p. 13). Developed by the World Business Council for Sustainable Development and the World Resources Institute (WBCSD and WRI, 2015), the GHG Protocol provides guidelines to organizations to distinguish and categorize their corporate carbon emissions into three distinct scopes:

- *Scope 1 refers to direct GHG emissions* from resources that are owned or controlled by the company (e.g., emissions from combustion in owned or controlled boilers, vehicles, process equipment, etc.).
- *Scope 2 refers to indirect GHG emissions* from the generation of purchased electricity, steam, heat, and cooling that is brought into the organizational boundary and consumed by the company.
- *Scope 3 refers to other indirect GHG emissions* as a consequence of a firm's activities occurring from sources not owned or controlled by the company (e.g., transportation and production of purchased materials and use of sold products and services).

Thus, when assessing business-related carbon emissions, there are three fundamental approaches to be considered (Csutora & Harangozo, 2017, p. 8f).

First, the *top-down approach* considers an input-output analysis (Leontief, 1936, p. 105ff) by applying OECD or Eurostat statistics to develop a rough estimate of the environmental impacts a company caused by purchasing intermediate products for its production processes supports. This crude benchmarking of a company's performance against the industrial sector average establishes a rough estimate of the environmental impacts a company caused by purchasing intermediate products for its production processes (Schaltegger & Csutora, 2012, p. 13). Although Mozner (2015, p. 143) suggests that this approach is particularly appropriate to account for emissions along supply chains (i.e., Scope 3), it yet encompasses limitations in setting system boundaries for detailed process or product assessment (Ozawa-Meida et al., 2013, p. 187).

Second, the *bottom-up approach*, which is also proposed within the GHG Protocol (WBCSD and WRI, 2004, p. 59), focuses on GHG emissions of a certain product or organization by analyzing individual process activities in which emissions occur (Csutora & Harangozo, 2017, p. 8). While this approach delivers more accurate emission results on process and product levels (Csutora & Harangozo, 2017, p. 8), the complexity of products including several thousand processes may become difficult to assess, which results in a constraint in terms of time and budget leading to data gaps as the corresponding process or product is being disregarded (Müller & Schebek, 2013, p. 504).

The third and often recommended approach is the *hybrid approach* (Ozawa-Meida et al., 2013, p. 187; Schaltegger & Csutora, 2012, p. 8) which allows to overcome the trade-offs between accuracy and low costs of data (Schaltegger & Csutora, 2012, p. 8). This approach entails the detail and accuracy of bottom-up primary and secondary process data in lower order stages (i.e., Scope 1 and Scope 2), while indirect, higher order stages from purchased goods and services can be covered through input-output estimations (i.e., Scope 3) (Ozawa-Meida et al., 2013, p. 187). In fact, scope 3 emissions are often cited 'optional' with little guidance given as to the cut-off procedure for external upstream process emissions (Wright et al., 2011, p. 66), although estimates suggest that scope 3 emissions could account for 75% of total GHG emissions of a company (Huang et al., 2009, p. 8509).

Nevertheless, it must be noted that these approaches and standards are rather voluntary codes of practice and thus, constitute mere guidelines to support organizations in estimating their carbon footprint (Damert et al., 2020, p. 62). This creates uncertainties on how to set system boundaries and avoid double counting (Wiedmann & Minx, 2008, p. 5; Csutora & Harangozo, 2017, p. 14). Thus, similar companies might achieve different carbon performance results due to different scopes and system boundaries set for the calculation and evaluation of the carbon performance (Damert et al., 2020, p. 65). Hence, researchers and practitioners are challenged to propose and test new and more standardized carbon accounting approaches that provide the ability to integrate carbon information into routine business process operations for better-informed decision-making towards sustainable development (Zvezdov & Schaltegger, 2015, p. 41) and improved corporate carbon performance (Burritt et al., 2011, p. 93).

2.2 Process Mining

Process mining emerged as a research discipline that bridges the gap between data science and process science by combining traditional model-based process analysis and data-centric analysis techniques (van der Aalst, 2016, p. 17). Van der Aalst (2011, p. 337) views process mining as "the missing link between data mining and traditional model-driven BPM" (van der Aalst, 2011, p. 337). Business Process Management (BPM) is a discipline that combines various approaches for the design, execution, control, measurement, and optimization of business processes (van der Aalst, 2016, p. 16). By being able to document and measure the environmental impact of a business process, practitioners are empowered to make informed decisions about processes and the improvement of these processes towards environmental and traditional business objectives (Recker et al., 2012, p. 107).

From an academic perspective, the establishment of the IEEE Task Force on process mining and the creation of the Process Mining Manifesto in 2012 have laid the foundation upon which extant research and the evolution of log-based process analysis have been unfolded (van der Aalst et al., 2012). Likewise, the current market for process mining solutions is growing rapidly. In 2018, Gartner evaluated the process mining market at $110 million and predicted the market to triple in the upcoming years. In fact, the market size reached the $320 million mark already at the end of 2019 (Gartner, 2020, p. 14). Furthermore, Celonis—the current market leader in process mining which was founded in 2011—recently received a $1 billion dollar funding round which values the company at $11.1 billion, ranking it the highest-valued tech startup in New York City and Germany (Konrad, 2021, p. 2f).

Fundamentally, process mining revolves around the idea of deriving process models from log data stored as digital traces within today's information systems (van der Aalst, 2016, p. 31). In the context of designing processes and process models, people often tend to think in the form of an idealized and simplified process flow (commonly referred to as "To-Be" process), while the reality appears to be more complex with multiple process variants (known as "As-Is" process) that may deviate significantly from the idealized version (Reinkemeyer, 2020a, p. 4).

The objective of process mining is to extract knowledge from logged events stored in the information systems and provide the full picture of the process to then visualize the actual and often times very complex process flows (Reinkemeyer, 2020a, p. 6). This process-related information that is sequentially being recorded and stored within information systems in form of data can be referred to as event logs, which consist of different features describing the context of the events recorded (Peters & Nauroth, 2019, p. 15).

In summary, an event log is therefore a collection of events that denotes the execution of business processes whereby each event corresponds to a specific activity or process step that took place at a certain moment in time and can be assigned to a unique case. An event log is typically illustrated by a table whereby each line corresponds to an event, an activity, and a timestamp. The minimum required features of an event log include the case ID (i.e., unique identifier) and an activity (i.e., a description of the executed process step) (Reinkemeyer, 2020a, p. 3f; van der Aalst, 2016, p. 35). In this context, Reinkemeyer (2020a, p. 3) argues that the timestamp (i.e., a record of the time of occurrence of an activity) is likewise an essential requirement to specify the precise time of every action taken. However,

Table 1 Types of process mining (source: adopted from van der Aalst et al. (2012, p. 175f))

Type	Characterization
Discovery	This technique takes an event log and (re)produces a process model based on example executions in the event logs without using any a-priori information.
Conformance checking	Here, an existing process model is compared with an event log of the same process. Conformance checking is applied to validate if the as-is process, as recorded in the log, conforms to the to-be process model and vice versa. By scanning the event log using a model specifying these requirements, it is possible to show whether a rule is followed or not and thus detect and measure unwanted deviations.
Enhancement	This technique allows to extend or improve an existing process model using information about the actual process recorded in some event log. In contrast to conformance checking, enhancement aims at changing or extending the a-priori model to derive a new, optimized model. With the help of timestamps in the event logs, it would be possible to portray bottlenecks, service levels, throughput times, and frequencies in the process model.

it must be noted that any additional attributes such as the timestamp or associated resources and costs can become useful, especially when analyzing performance-related properties such as the time in between two activities or resource-related process performance (van der Aalst, 2016, p. 128f).

To "mine" a process, these digital traces need to be identified, extracted, and visualized to generate a process model that reproduces the observed process flows, thus providing transparency regarding the sequence of activities as they have actually taken place (Reinkemeyer, 2020a, p. 4).

In general, there are three distinct types of process mining techniques: *discovery*, *conformance checking* and *enhancement* (van der Aalst, 2016, p. 33f; van der Aalst et al., 2012, p. 175f). These types can be characterized as shown in Table 1.

Each process mining type employs different input and output forms for a different purpose, as described by van der Aalst et al. (2012, p. 175). As shown in Fig. 2, techniques for (a) *discovery* require the event log as an input to produce a process model as an output which oftentimes is visualized in form of a Business Process Model and Notation (BPMN) model or Petri net. To highlight differences and commonalities between model and log, (b) *conformance checking* uses both an event log and a model as inputs to achieve diagnostic information as an output. Techniques for (c) model *enhancement* also require an event log and a process model as inputs, which generates an improved or extended model as an output (van der Aalst et al., 2012, p. 175).

2.3   Process Mining and Carbon Accounting

Despite the capabilities of process mining to create end-to-end transparency starting on a very granular process level and scaling up to an organization-wide picture

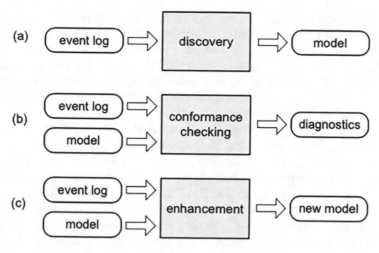

Fig. 2 Process mining types in terms of input and output [source: van der Aalst et al. (2012, p. 175)]

on how businesses actually run their entire operations, current scientific literature barely investigated the potential of process mining in terms of sustainable development and carbon reduction. While the main objectives of improving business processes are often related to economic imperatives of cost, quality and time, there is scarce research that focused on process mining adoption to reduce the corporate carbon footprint and support a firm's sustainable development. In the following, insights from existing studies in this field of research are summarized.

Lübbecke et al. (2015) conducted a study where process mining was implemented as a simulation technique to identify and measure the energy consumption and the carbon footprint of business processes. This was done by implementing a smart sensor that recorded the energy consumption of the activities executed within an IT-based process. Doing so, the authors were not only able to map the energy consumption of each process activity but also simulate different process scenarios and apply measures to reduce the energy consumption by a total margin of 29.98% of that given process (Lübbecke et al., 2015, p. 874). Their study demonstrated the simulation capabilities of process mining and identified that business process simulation through process mining can support the analysis of path complexities for various business process models. To that end, process mining can serve as preparation for effective decision-making in an ecological context (Lübbecke et al., 2015, p. 867). However, the authors expressed the need for a more automated data import and efficient mapping of energy-related data to the process models as well as the need for an automatic generation of simulation models to speed up actual process optimization (Lübbecke et al., 2015, p. 874).

Moreover, Liao et al. (2014, p. 995ff) developed a general framework for semantic process mining which essentially provides a guideline on how to enrich system event logs with external domain knowledge. In their study, the authors applied their proposed semantic framework to exemplify a potential carbon footprint analysis whereby carbon footprint ontologies are used as a basis to assist the semantic annotation. The domain semantics behind those carbon-related labels in event logs then form the carbon footprint perspective. However, the paper is limited to the fact that it merely describes how their semantic framework could potentially be applied in theory and thus represents a mere analogy that is lacking practicality due to the lack of real-world parameters.

A fictional case study conducted by Ghose et al. (2010, p. 103ff) confirms the notion of associating carbon footprints with process designs through Green BPM. By assigning contextual assumptions of process emissions ontology to the process activities, the authors found that it is possible to derive the overall carbon footprint of that given process with the help of BPM. Thereby, process mining enhances the process view by creating the true "as-is" process model and any unwanted process executions that deviate from the originally planned process. As such, it becomes possible to better evaluate and measure the activities that contribute to the carbon footprint the most (Ghose et al., 2010, p. 115). While the fictional case study clearly demonstrates the capabilities of Green BPM to consider carbon management using a hybrid approach (i.e., top-down and bottom-up), the integration of process mining in their paper remains unclear as to how it must be technically implemented to support carbon management.

A more recent paper by Ortmeier et al. (2021, p. 163ff) examined how process mining can be applied for Life Cycle Assessment (LCA) in vehicle manufacturing. The authors demonstrated that the application of process mining addresses several barriers of LCA in manufacturing and therefore facilitated the implementation of LCA in companies. The study examined the selection process of an algorithm and inductive miner best suitable for LCA and demonstrates how process mining can visualize the process model and animate the process flow. This allows to evaluate the control flow and perform hotspot analyses and in order to identify changing bottlenecks. To perform a systematic analysis of the environmental impacts of products throughout the entire life cycle, the authors highlighted the importance to enrich the event logs with information about the physical flows in terms of energy and raw material data (Ortmeier et al., 2021, p. 168). However, their study is limited to the fact that the input and output flows of the machines and production data acquisition of the processes was not performed, and thus the authors were simply not able to implement the processing of energy and material flow data into their process mining interface.

From a practical standpoint, initial efforts have been made by Celonis, the leading vendor in the global process mining market (Everest Group, 2021, p. 10), and Ernst & Young, a large auditing and financial advisory organization. Both organizations in cooperation developed first applications that enable practitioners to calculate carbon emissions based on real-time data mapped to process activities throughout the value chain of a manufacturing company (Ueda, 2021). This way, raw materials, manufacturing activities, transport, and other related business activities can be assigned with their respective carbon footprint, thus providing a complete picture of actual emissions induced by every single business activity and process step

(Reinkemeyer, 2020b, p. 1ff). Within their developed dashboards, users can perform drill-down analyses for various areas from upstream to downstream, including material supplier, production process, carbon performance per plant. This not only allows to simulate alternative production volume or logistics methods by creating various scenarios with different outputs in terms of cost and throughput time but also considering the carbon impact along the entire value chain (Ueda, 2021). While this indeed appears to be a promising use case for process mining and carbon management, no information is published about the actual procedure and requirements on how to adopt process mining to develop such applications for carbon measurement.

3   Research Design

Since the phenomenon of study—how process mining can support carbon accounting in the recognition, measurement, and reduction of carbon emissions—is still emerging and not well researched to date, a qualitative research approach is considered suitable (Recker, 2013, p. 88). For this study, we collected empirical data via interviews with experts. Expert interviews can be used as a means to collect practical knowledge and experiences (Helfferich, 2014, p. 570) when the development of special knowledge is necessary (Gläser and Laudel 2010, p. 12). The following sections outline the data collection procedure (Sect. 3.1) as well as the data analysis (Sect. 3.2).

3.1   Data Collection

Data collection with expert interviews requires the definition of a certain target group (Helfferich, 2014, p. 560). In line with our research focus how process mining can support carbon accounting, decisive selection criteria for interview partners were framed as shown in Table 2.

A prior screening procedure of qualified interview candidates is crucial as it allows to identify the appropriate experts relevant for the investigation of the study focus (Yin, 2018, p. 105f). In a two-phased approach, relevant data was collected

Table 2 Selection criteria for interview candidates (source: own illustration)

Selection criteria	
Industry:	Sector independent
Professional experience with process mining:	2+ years
Process mining and CO_2 emissions affiliation:	Professional experience with process mining as a means to reduce carbon emissions is required

about the entire candidate pool using a database. In the first phase, a total of 27 eligible candidates were being identified of which three candidates were contacted directly from the authors' professional network within the process mining field. The remaining 24 candidates were identified using LinkedIn, a professional networking platform that allows users to publicly disclose their resumes and to connect with other professionals. The screening was done using the LinkedIn search function to filter for candidates considering the combination of three keywords: *process mining*, *sustainability,* and *carbon*. In the second phase, the total number of interviewees was reduced to only include those with relevant practical experience in the application of process mining as a means to reduce carbon emissions as specified in our selection criteria. This resulted in a total number of eight expert interviews. Given the exploratory phenomenology of this study topic, the sampling size is adequate to reach saturation, meaning that additional cases will not spark equally new findings (Creswell & Creswell, 2018, p. 186). Table 3 provides an overview of the interview partners. In terms of the required focus topic affiliation towards process mining and carbon emission, all identified interview partners provided a substantial expertise in process mining and carbon emissions.

For the purpose of our study, a semi-structured interview design with open-ended questions was considered appropriate. This choice was based on the following considerations. Semi-structured interviews allow to assess the participants' opinions while at the same time also eliciting narratives about their personal experiences (Nohl, 2017, p. 17f). The semi-structured characteristic gives the participants the freedom to express their diverse views and allows the researcher to react to and follow up on emerging ideas (Nohl, 2017, p. 18). Ultimately, the results obtained through semi-structured interviews can be compared with each other since all participants are required to express their views about the same general themes (Nohl, 2017, p. 17). The interview guideline was designed to include open-ended questions that allowed the interviewees to answer freely and in their preferred form, as opposed to closed-ended questions (Creswell, 2012 p. 386f).

The first part of the interview guideline (section A) was mainly about understanding the interview partner's background and expertise. The second part (section B) was to discuss the term process mining in order to establish a common understanding of the topic and to validate the process mining expertise of the interviewee. The third part (section C) drew on the interview partner's experiences with the adoption of process mining to identify carbon reduction potentials, i.e., how the interview partner has used process mining in the past as means to optimize processes whereby carbon reduction potentials were identified and realized. The questions that were raised addressed aspects including the process steps, application areas, requirements, and challenges that occurred. The fourth part (section D) intended to identify the interviewee's assessment as to what extent process mining qualifies as method to support carbon accounting. Ultimately, the fifth and last part (section E) gathered the personal opinion of the interviewed expert regarding the relevance of process mining in the future in general but also particularly with emphasis for the role of corporate sustainability of future companies.

Table 3 Overview of interview partners (source: own illustration)

Interview partner	Industry	Process mining affiliation	CO_2 affiliation
Interview Partner #1	Consulting	Client consultation	Development of carbon emission dashboards
Interview Partner #2	Manufacturing (formerly consulting)	Client consultation	Development of carbon emission dashboards
Interview Partner #3	Enterprise Software	Process mining vendor incl. Implementation	Process mining implementation with carbon footprint focus
Interview Partner #4	Consulting	Client consultation	Process mining projects with carbon performance evaluation focus
Interview Partner #5	Consulting	Client consultation	Process mining projects with carbon performance evaluation focus
Interview Partner #6	Enterprise Software	Process mining vendor incl. Implementation	Process mining projects with sustainability benchmarking focus
Interview Partner #7	Enterprise Software	Process mining vendor incl. Implementation	Process mining projects with sustainability benchmarking focus
Interview Partner #8	Consulting	Client consultation	Process mining implementation with carbon footprint focus

The interviews were conducted online using Microsoft Teams in July and August 2021. They were recorded in order to be analyzed within the data analysis phase. Each interview covers a length between 30 and 45 min.

3.2 Data Analysis

After the data has been collected, the information was examined in seven consecutive steps by applying an adapted scheme by Creswell and Creswell (2018, p. 193ff). The first step was to organize and prepare the data by transcribing the interviews. Each interview was transcribed and analyzed by using the qualitative data analysis software MAXQDA. The second step considers reading through and reflecting on the interview data to gain an overall impression and understanding of the collected data. The third step was to define a coding scheme to segment the sentences or paragraphs from the transcribed interviews into categories and labelling those categories with a descriptive term and color. Transcribing and coding the interviews with MAXQDA enhances the analysis process significantly as it allows to quickly locate all passages or text segments assigned to the same code and determine whether the interviewees are responding to a code idea in similar or different ways (Creswell & Creswell, 2018, p. 193). The developed coding scheme is strongly based on the structure of the interview guideline. The fourth step included assigning the coding scheme to the in-text paragraphs to categorize and label certain text passages. To affirm the reliability of the research, the exact same coding scheme was applied in all interviews. This procedure allowed results to be collected in a standardized and systematic manner. The fifth step was to sort the empirical data by the terms and then to consolidate the findings for each code from the different interviews in the sixth step. In the final step, the different interviews were compared, and the compiled results are presented in the following section.

4 Results

In line with our research objective, this section outlines the results of our empirical study in terms of requirements (Sect. 4.1) and potentials (Sect. 4.2) of process mining to support carbon accounting. A summary of findings is provided in Sect. 4.3.

4.1 Requirements

In the following, we present the findings regarding requirements necessary for applying process mining for carbon accounting. Here we separate between requirements for (1) retrieving and integrating carbon-related data and (2) necessary technical and process know-how.

4.1.1 Retrieving and Integrating Carbon-Related Data

In terms of recognizing new information about carbon emissions, all interviewed experts conclude that process mining as a technology itself is not capable to detect the carbon footprint of process activities. This is because process mining simply does not produce new data but solely relies on the data considered in the underlying data model and is thus dependent on the quality and type of data being loaded into the model.

> Recognition does not work at all. So, process mining itself does not know [. . .] what the carbon footprint of each activity is. You have to train process mining accordingly. (Interview Partner 4)

> When it comes to recognizing the carbon footprint, I have a hard time seeing a use case for process mining. Maybe for lack of my creativity, but I rather don't see that. Of course, you can take that to some extent as a basis for calculation, I say, to derive [CO_2] with different standardized input factors. But that's always based on assumptions. It would not be capturing actual as-is values. (Interview Partner 5)

Most concerns raised were related to data availability.

> So, the data is certainly 80, 90% of the main challenges. (Interview Partner 5)

With regard to carbon data, it is particularly given that sustainability-related data such as tons of carbon dioxide being emitted needs to be incorporated into the event log, i.e., the event logs need to be enriched by CO_2 emission factors. In contrast to the already available process traces being logged as a result of the execution of business processes, CO_2 information is often not available due to the fact that emission data is not being recorded or stored explicitly in the existing IT systems. Some experts argue that the reason for this are legacy systems prevalent in many organizations which do not consider the processing or storing of such information, given that these systems date back to a time when sustainability simply was not yet in the interest of business organizations as it is today. This general lack of carbon data is outlined by interview partner 6:

> The biggest problem is usually that the data is not available at the customer's end. We don't talk about the complete carbon emission data, which is mostly not available in any way, but even just good information about the start and end destination of a transport, the weight, the size, and all those things, so relatively basic information, is already not available. And we have this problem also in many other cases and in many other areas, where we wanted to measure carbon emissions and simply failed because of the lack of available data which made it more difficult. [...] In fact, CO_2 emissions are never measured directly. [...] This means, for this you need another API with which you can calculate the [CO_2] values accordingly. That was something we had to source separately. (Interview Partner 6)

When thinking of data acquisition and what data is being collected, the experts distinguish between two types of data that are required for process mining. At first, data in form of event logs build the fundamental basis for the mining of a process. In line with the prevalent literature, this includes the case ID, activity, and timestamp, which from here on will be further referred to as primary data. The following statement by interview partner 5 exemplifies this data acquisition process:

> We first specified the activities that we wanted to analyze. So, from the business point of view, what are the relevant business activities—unloading pallets, transporting pallets, loading pallets in our case—that we want to analyze. And then we defined the process flow that we wanted to look at. We talked to IT experts to identify the corresponding system events that reflect these activities that the business wants to look at in the underlying IT system, to find out in which tables they are located, whether they have a time and date stamp and a unique identifier that we need. And in which fields they are located. So, we defined our catalog of requirements for the IT data extracts. In this prototype, we worked with a one-time data extract, i.e., we used this list of requirements to extract certain data from the IT systems, which we anonymized to avoid any personal data, and then in this case, load the data into the process mining application. And in this application, we then took the data, transformed it into the process mining event log format, created a data model,

and then based on that, defined KPIs together with the customer that we wanted to analyze. And then we modeled these KPIs and presented them in a dashboard. (Interview Partner 5)

Secondly, the interviewed experts described how additional data in various other forms can be included in the data model and mapped with the event logs. This secondary data also known as attributes can provide further information about the specific process activities. As such, these attributes enrich the event logs with supplementary information and thus add additional dimensions to the analysis. This is where carbon emission-related data can be integrated into the data model as additional attributes to provide an advanced perspective that can measure carbon emissions along the process flow. Interview partner 5 illustrates this based on a process mining solution implemented for a transit process in retail:

> CO_2 emissions would be an additional attribute that we have to take into account in this process. For instance, we have also done that with the weight and size of these pallets, adding them as further attributes. This is possible on case level, meaning on the individual cases that we are looking at, which in this process represent a pallet. Weight and size. And then we have accumulated these different levels of those attributes. Now we know, for example, the processed volume per day, per employee, inbound volume, intra-processed volume, outbound volume. Those are sort of aggregated attributes for the volume, which we have analyzed in various dimensions. [. . .] And from my point of view, exactly the same would work for CO_2 emissions. So, if we know for each piece that we process, what is the standard emission that such a pallet brings with it, which process step, perhaps also has which emission output, then you can aggregate that just as well. And for different process variants with each other. [. . .] But yes, it would be an attribute that we would have to pull in from another external source to source to then aggregate it, and also to understand which activities are the main drivers of CO_2 emissions. Which variants of a process are perhaps CO_2 optimized. And so that can then be a control parameter to design the processes in such a way that this metric is represented according to one's own demands and goals. (Interview Partner 5)

When adopting process mining as means to reduce carbon emissions, the experts agree that this carbon-related information must be provided or made available before being integrated into the data model. To that end, enriching the analysis with additional carbon-related information is technically feasible.

However, collecting carbon information can lead to additional effort and requires specific approaches for the acquisition, such as the use of an Application Programming Interface (API), as explained in the following by interview partner 6:

> Yes, the CO_2 emissions are rarely recorded directly. That means that we had to retrieve them separately. At least now with the shipment emissions, we used some API, in which we then know the existing data points from the shipping process. So, for example, the start and end location. And based on that, the [API] then fed back to us the amount of carbon emissions. And that's another kind of effort that we had to do to make sure that we have these data points. [. . .] So, the bottom line is that we built a second table where we inserted this data. (Interview Partner 6)

An API constitutes a set of software functions by which the software application can make requests to other software services, libraries, or operating systems (Li & Jain, 2009, p. 41). In the light of process mining, interview partner 6 describes the API as a gateway that can be programmed into the process mining application and allows to retrieve meta data related to sustainability from external libraries of service providers. For example, such data encompasses emission values about the distance between a vendor and a warehouse in kilometers and thus can determine how much carbon emissions are released by comparing vendors with different means of transport, as confirmed in the following statement by interview partner 1:

> [. . .] we wanted to map the entire value chain, not just a part of it. That means we start with the purchasing function and see what are the triggers for CO_2. And we took the P2P process and added CO_2 emissions as an additional factor. So, we continue to look at how often a process is being executed and how long it takes related to the cost component. But in addition, we also look at to what extent CO_2 is emitted. And for this we then take the P2P process and enhance it. We do the same with the distribution process at the end. And in between we have production, where we then look at where CO_2 occurs in production. And then we bring it all together, so we have a dashboard where you can see all the sub-areas on one page. You can see the total emissions for all areas, but also per individual subarea. (Interview Partner 1)

Figure 3 shows an example how the data model for the process data needs to be enhanced in order to include the required carbon accounting data.

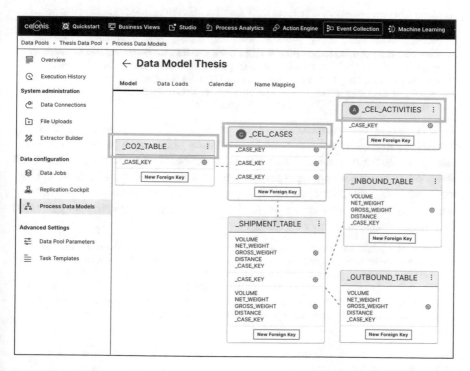

Fig. 3 Example data model in Celonis (source: own illustration derived from the Celonis's academic environment)

4.1.2 Technical and Process Know-How

Another challenge as described by the experts was the transformation and contextualization of the data. This requires the need for domain expertise both from a technical perspective when implementing carbon data into the data model and process expertise to quickly identify and validate improvement potential towards sustainable development. Interview partner 2 described the importance of being able to effectively use SQL joins that allow to combine data from different tables within the process mining tool. The quality of mapping the tables with each other (i.e. combining primary data with secondary data) to create the underlying data model is crucial for the quality and reliability of the derived insights. This is due to the fact that the process mining dashboards are built upon the data model and thus form the output of any analysis.

In the following, interview partner 3 emphasizes that process mining as a technology does not portray the limiting factor but so does the interpretation of the generated insights as only an optimization or a change in the process can ensure less CO_2 emissions are being produced:

> I would not see process mining as the limitation. [...] The technology already provides us a lot. I think the most important challenge we are facing [...] is the interpretation of these results, namely where is CO_2 produced, where can I reduce CO_2. And then the next step, what do I have to do to reduce [CO_2]? Can I automate the process so that this this activity stops producing CO_2? Can I predict this transport from A to B and not let it happen at all, and yet can my other processes continue as usual? So downstream from the realization that I have a transparency where something is created, the difficulties lie in the optimization and the ultimate reduction of CO_2. (Interview Partner 3).

This notion is confirmed by Seidel et al. (2012, p. 7), who indicate that technology itself does not reduce carbon emissions, but only a change in processes can drive sustainable development. In light of becoming more sustainable, all interviewed experts emphasized that process mining does not create sustainability itself, but rather creates the required transparency necessary to make better decisions while considering the carbon impact in direct contrast to process efficiency and cost factors. As interview partner 7 explains:

> I mean if you have the data and the right methodology then it's fine with the technical side. Because you then solved that challenge. Process Mining itself is fine as well if you have your data and your approach. Like it's complete. But the thing is that process mining is only as valuable as the decisions and actions you take based on it. Insight by itself is kind of useless. So that's why you have to be able to use it to identify the improvement actions as to how to translate it into business value. (Interview Partner 7)

4.2 Potentials

Once carbon data is retrieved and integrated, process mining solutions are able to support carbon accounting in the identification of carbon saving potentials. The findings from the expert interviews show how process mining enables (1) transparency of CO_2 emissions and (2) an identification of levers to reduce CO_2 on an operational process level based on (3) a multidimensional analysis that links operational efficiency and sustainability. These potentials are outlined in the following.

4.2.1 Create Transparency About As-Is

With process mining, it is possible to aggregate the CO_2 information within the data model and calculate the carbon performance per activity and process step. This enables adding an additional dimension to the analysis that now measures and tracks the carbon performance along the process flow and for each specific process activity similarly to measuring other factors such as cost, quality, and time. This creates transparency for a given process, as illustrated for a logistics process by interview partner 6:

> We have now started to look at specific carbon emissions, i.e., in the logistics process, because these are relatively similar across several industries. [. . .] This includes looking at what shipments are there. How heavy were the products? How many trucks were driven? How much CO_2 was emitted, based on weight, route or even based on the means of transport used? Was it shipped by sea, air or road transport? We looked at all these things and determined the carbon emissions accordingly. (Interview Partner 6)

Once several adjacent business functions are included in the analysis, transparency about CO_2 emissions can be created along the value chain.

> And process mining helps you to kind of connect things together across the organization. Also, multiple processes which help with building that transparency. (Interview Partner 7)

> Our goal is to create a complete visibility of the CO_2 emissions along the entire value chain. By that, we really want to know what the CO_2 footprint of the end product is in the end. Of course, you have to consider that many different processes are involved in such a value chain. (Interview Partner 6)

These capabilities of process mining enable carbon accountants to get a complete view that contextualizes carbon information with process-related events and enhances the reliability in their considered analysis, as outlined by interview partner 7:

> It [process mining] could help for auditing, so companies that want to do carbon accounting. Let's say they have more reliability in their data set because with process mining you don't really make choices on what to exclude and what to include as much. It is a more complete view on how a company is running. So, when they try to tell you our products are sustainable because of the way we process them. You can verify this more easily. (Interview Partner 7)

4.2.2 Identify Levers to Reduce CO_2 on an Operational Process Level

Any improvement in carbon performance requires actions that need to be undertaken to transform and change the process towards a more sustainable execution with less carbon emissions being produced. Process mining can hereby provide the missing link between top-down defined objectives related to sustainability and bottom-up change initiatives on process levels that consider domain expertise to drive the convergence of both approaches without neglecting the substantial execution of process operations and value creation.

> You can really generate actions from that to manage the issues that are not completely farfetched from the actual business processes. And a simple change in the right place within the processes might then have a measurable impact. So again, this classic principle, I want to achieve a [sustainable] objective, but I don't know how. And then I start to define numerous measures, top-down. However, with process mining you can exactly steer your processes to achieve this objective, because you have the control over your real and organic processes and not somehow try to intervene without knowing [. . .] the impact [change] would have on your business operations. (Interview Partner 8)

In fact, the experts particularize that process mining certainly helps to better understand the execution of processes and thus creates visibility as to how (un)sustainable the processes are. This fundamental process understanding then provides the basis to identify any activities with significant carbon impact upon which measures can be derived to either reduce executions that run through these activities or fundamentally redesign the process towards a more sustainable execution with less carbon emissions being produced. Interview partner 6 points out how process mining allows this identification of measures on an operational process level:

> The thing is that many companies today still have a strong top-down approach, i.e., they calculate carbon emissions based on their general energy consumption. But in order to really reduce them in the long term, they have to incorporate it into their operational processes. So you really have to measure from the bottom up how individual day-to-day decisions influence the carbon footprint. You can't just achieve this through large strategic initiatives, you also have to reduce your energy consumption, for example by deciding that we are now bundling 2 shipments together. And that has to happen at this operational process level, and process mining is exactly the right fit. (Interview Partner 6)

4.2.3 Link Operational Efficiency and Sustainability (Multidimensional Analysis)

When adopting process mining as a means to reduce carbon emissions, the procedural phases and undertaken steps are no different from other use cases because the formulated objectives often times remain the same, where sustainability is just added as another dimension to the process analysis. Interview partner 4 outlines this approach for freight management and shipment planning:

> In fact, we set it up like any other project. That means we defined KPIs, we connected the process, [. . .] and then we added certain dimensions to the process graph in order to examine the process. The dimensions were primarily lead time, cost rates and the like. And then we optimized the freight management and shipment planning to ensure that one has hardly any delay and can deliver just-in-time. Then we expanded the view and actually included CO_2 values provided by the customer directly [. . .] and integrated them accordingly as approximate values in the dashboard and were then able to evaluate from a sustainability perspective. Does sustainability now compete against my efficiency? Or does

it possibly converge? And how does it compare to my customer satisfaction? (Interview Partner 4)

That way, process mining considers various dimensions that cover different business areas and therefore does not only focus on one single aspect such as carbon emissions in an isolated way but rather several different areas that are examined synergistically.

> [...] because you're not just trying to reduce CO_2 in a one-dimensional way. [...] The CO_2 [reduction], I would say, is simply just another additional result. It's a complementary one. And you have many of these complementarities when you look at the processes in the whole context. [...] And the interesting thing is, you can make all [potentials] visible. Because you know how much CO_2 is attached to each ton of kerosene, you can make that visible. Then you can also show a Euro symbol on the same report and say that's how much we've saved in purchasing to that end. And that's the beauty of it, this multidimensional view of the process as well as the decision steering in that process. (Interview Partner 8)

To that end, process mining qualifies as a technology to measure the process performance in terms of economic factors while at the same time considering ecological factors such as the carbon impact. Any process transformation can be evaluated with regard to operational efficiency and sustainability. Thereby, it is possible to evaluate processes in terms of their economic performance vs. their ecologic performance. This is of particular interest for businesses as a greater carbon impact increasingly correlates with rising financial burdens that occur as a result of increasing carbon taxes, emissions trading schemes, domestic as well as international regulations such as the Paris Agreement (Schaltegger & Csutora, 2012, p. 9; Schaltegger et al., 2015, p. 2).

> I think it [process mining] is actually one of the best tools to support [carbon accounting]. Simply because [...] you can also see the connection between raw materials and end products. And you still have the possibility to make your decisions not on the sole basis of carbon emissions but also on monetary factors. Hence, you can also combine these carbon emissions with, for example, the margins per product, in order to not only make decisions as a silo function [...] but really make a decision based on monetary as well as emission values. And that is one of the strengths of process mining. (Interview Partner 2)

In the consideration of ecologic and economic performance, divergence of operational and strategic objectives can become an area of conflict. This might require a trade-off between sustainability and strategic goals, as illustrated by interview partner 5:

> What can also be the case, of course, is that there are conflicting goals. So, for example if there is this presumption that a pallet should ideally flow through the distribution center in less than 24 hours. And if I now see that a CO_2-optimized process variant might not achieve this objective, then there might be conflicts with other goals. And this is not a question that cannot be answered technically, but is really strategic. Is there either an activity that allows me to achieve both? Or do I have to weigh between two different corporate objectives. (Interview Partner 5)

This underpins the importance of ensuring a close fit between the process mining initiative and the overall operational and strategic objectives of the organization to ensure that sustainability targets can be combined with the traditional managerial imperatives of cost, quality, and time. Any discrepancy between the operational goals and the strategic goals would simply lead to the fact that the insights gained with the help of process mining would remain worthless as a result of inaction.

4.3   Summary of Findings

Our findings show that process mining has the capabilities to support carbon accounting in terms of identifying and realizing carbon saving potentials without neglecting process design, workflow, and execution. The interviewed experts agree that process mining as a technology does not reduce carbon emissions per se but rather provides the much-needed transparency that ultimately establishes the foundation for practitioners to make better-informed decisions towards more sustainable execution of business processes with less carbon impact.

Extending Schaltegger's and Csutora's (2012, p. 4) framework of carbon accounting on the corporate level, Fig. 4 illustrates our study results by showing how process mining contributes to accounts of un-sustainability and accounts for sustainability improvements. With process mining, transparency about CO_2 emissions can be created on process levels and for entire value chains, thereby detecting areas of un-sustainability. Moreover, process mining enables the identification of activities with significant carbon impact and ultimately the proposal of measures for more sustainable process execution. Through process mining, sustainability improvements and operational efficiency improvements can be identified in a complementary manner, thereby linking ecological and economic performance. As outlined above, the application of process mining for carbon accounting requires the integration of carbon-related data through APIs or a manual

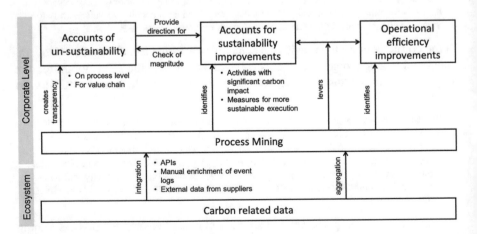

Fig. 4 Summary of findings (source: own illustration)

enrichment of event logs and also an aggregation of CO_2 information within the data model.

5 Discussion

Based on the empirical findings, this section discusses our paper's contribution to theory and practice (Sect. 5.1) and outlines limitations (Sect. 5.2) as well as avenues for future research (Sect. 5.3).

5.1 Contribution to Theory and Practice

Taking deficiencies of current carbon accounting approaches and the capabilities of process mining as an enabler for Green BPM into account, this study was motivated by the need to get a clearer understanding of requirements and potentials of process mining to support carbon accounting in terms of decision support for carbon reduction. Our study offers a number of both theoretical and practical contributions which are outlined in the following.

5.1.1 Process Mining to Support Carbon Accounting in Recognizing the Carbon Footprint

Matthews et al. (2008, p. 5839) note that "without a full knowledge of their footprints, firms will be unable to pursue the most cost-effective carbon mitigation strategies." Therefore, before measuring and evaluating the carbon performance, it is necessary to be able to recognize and capture the amount of carbon emissions that are produced as result of the execution of business processes. Current practices in corporate carbon accounting focus more on disclosure rather than achieving actual carbon reductions (He et al., 2021, p. 29). In fact, Schaltegger and Csutora (2012, p. 7) argue that current practices of carbon accounting have hardly explored ways to consider the design of processes, measures, and indicators to document greenhouse gas emissions in order to identify and allocate carbon within processes, products or activities.

Our study identified the limitations of process mining in terms of recognizing and capturing new carbon information. In fact, the empirical findings indicate that with process mining, it is technically not possible to recognize new physical carbon emission values. However, the findings also highlight that despite the lack of recognizing new carbon values, process mining can support the processing of carbon data in a way that the event logs are being aggregated and form new data perspectives.

Van Eck et al. (2015, p. 5) describe that the aggregation of events and enriching of logs with additional attributes leads to process enhancement, i.e., an extension of the process model with additional performance-related information. This was also emphasized in the empirical findings, which revealed that the loading of carbon data into process mining creates new dimensions that enhance the analysis, such as the consideration of carbon information on aggregated levels. With these aggregated views, it becomes possible to filter on different case notions considering specifications for the carbon impact on various levels, for instance, carbon emissions per purchase order, per shipped pallet, per country, division, unit, city, or many other aggregated levels within a specific time period. This creates unlimited possibilities to calculate the carbon intensity of process activities for different scenarios.

Thus, our empirical findings highlight that although process mining does not recognize and capture new physical carbon emission values, the contextualization of carbon information with other process-related factors creates new data perspectives (e.g., accumulated carbon impact per pallet), which allow to generate new and enhanced insights that without process mining would require significant effort to retrieve. While the fact remains that process mining does not recognize and collect new carbon emission values like a thermometer would measure temperature values, it certainly provides a platform where CO_2 data can be enriched manually through calculation or externally incorporated through APIs.

5.1.2 Process Mining to Support Carbon Accounting in Measuring the Carbon Footprint

Schaltegger and Csutora (2012, p. 8) emphasized the need to measure carbon emissions prior to identifying and establishing carbon reduction plans. When measuring the carbon impact on process levels, our empirical findings reveal that with process mining, it becomes possible to create the necessary transparency about the as-is process to better understand and quantify the carbon intensity of the process activities. This is particularly important since the value of process models is limited if too little attention is paid to the alignment of model and reality, and simulation experiments are then conducted using a model that assumes a mere idealized version of the real process (van der Aalst, 2016, p. 30). Schaltegger and Csutora (2012, p. 8) emphasize the importance to initially create awareness about the (un)sustainability of processes as it is crucial to clarify the sources and drivers for the carbon output to evaluate the carbon performance. This notion was equally supported by the empirical findings as the experts demonstrate that once the event logs are enriched with secondary data in form of CO_2 values, process mining is able to aggregate the data along the process execution and allows to measure the accumulated carbon footprint to create a full picture of the end-to-end carbon impact of a process. The empirical findings further indicate that these capabilities of process mining to measure the carbon footprint entails numerous benefits that emerge.

For one, the aggregation of carbon data with the event logs allows for a contextualization of carbon information with process performance-related factors.

This facilitates enhanced in-depth analyses by adding an ecologic dimension to what was a predominantly a rather economic performance analysis. Thus, the empirical findings show that it becomes possible to measure carbon performance against economic process performance factors. Thereby CO_2 emissions can be put into logical context with factors of cost, quality, and time. This creates new ways to substantially identify measures that can potentially improve the operational carbon performance in both environmental and economic terms.

Moreover, according to Schaltegger and Csutora (2012, p. 6), prevalent carbon management accounting systems are currently missing this ability which is seen as fundamental when supporting decision makers in creating real improvements without neglecting business realities and goals. To that end, process mining would contribute to filling this gap as it evaluates the process-related carbon performance without neglecting how the process is being executed and 'lived' throughout the organization. In fact, process mining would thereby also preserve the value creation of adjacent workflow paths along the value chain.

In addition, process mining creates aggregated views that can be accessed by different stakeholders in the organization. On the one hand, the empirical findings demonstrate that the process performance and the resulting carbon output can be measured and evaluated by operational employees such as process experts. This enables a bottom-up definition of operational targets that meet realistic sustainability standards considering the process design. On the other hand, top management can view process mining dashboards that provide this granular process perspective considering the defined operational targets but allow to put these benchmarks into a more holistic context for other processes, functions, departments and thus, the entire operating model. Process mining could thereby act as an enabler to identify any mismatch between strategy and operations and support the development towards a close fit of both.

In addition to process ownership, responsibility and accountability can be assigned to process stakeholders with regard to sustainability. This would empower greater carbon management control as the stakeholders are held accountable for any sustainable improvements and to evaluate whether the measures taken by the responsible actors are effective and the sustainability goals are achieved (Schaltegger & Csutora, 2012, p. 8). Ultimately, process mining can be carried out across all organizational levels, making it a supportive tool for carbon accountants to increase data reliability for a more fact-based and unbiased interpretation and evaluation of a firm's carbon performance.

To conclude, the empirical findings reveal that process mining enables measuring and evaluating the carbon footprint from a process perspective. This enables practitioners and carbon accountants to compare the execution of an alternative process path through the simulation of different outcomes in terms of cost, quality, time, and carbon impact. Therefore, it becomes possible to measure the process performance while also considering ecologic factors without neglecting critical process performance indicators. The empirical findings demonstrate that process mining adoption facilitates the suggested hybrid approach by Schaltegger and Csutora (2012, p. 6) whereby (1) carbon emissions of processes can be measured,

(2) operational goals in the light of carbon levels can be defined bottom-up and (3) sustainability targets can be established top-down based on the operational goals considering the design and execution of processes.

5.1.3 Process Mining to Support Carbon Accounting in Reducing the Carbon Footprint

To become environmentally sustainable, organizations must implement environmentally sustainable processes (Seidel et al., 2012, p. 7). Seidel et al. (2012) argue that this can only be achieved through continuous change of business processes with dedicated consideration paid to the environmental consequences of these business processes. To that end, the empirical findings reveal that the process mining adoption generally supports decision makers in terms of understanding, documenting, modeling, analyzing, simulating, and executing business processes to better manage and improve the process performance with regard to costs, quality and time. Our findings show that enriching the event logs with carbon data helps to enhance the analysis of the mined process by adding an ecologic dimension that allows evaluation of the carbon impact for different levels of the processes.

Schaltegger and Csutora (2012, p. 7) emphasize the need for carbon accounting to develop functions that allow to take into account of un-sustainability of past and current operations and to identify reduction potentials and the evaluation of reduction measures. Our empirical findings indicate that process mining enables practitioners to not only create this transparency to measure the carbon performance of current process executions, but also identify carbon saving potentials through the simulation of alternative process execution workflows. This makes it possible to recognize less carbon-intensive process paths that continue to be in line with the operational targets and ensure reducing the carbon impact without ignoring throughput times or cost-intensive process activities. To a certain extent, it also becomes possible to predict how the development and change of processes would impact future carbon output. However, little is known about why and how often companies do or should collect carbon information and how this information is or should be used to facilitate implementation of actual improvements (Schaltegger & Csutora, 2012, p. 7). This notion equally applies to process mining as Grisold et al. (2020, p. 12) found that implementation of the technology does not automatically lead to continuous and ongoing use, which requires additional strategies to define how process mining can contribute to the mid- and long-term success of the organization.

To conclude, it becomes evident that process mining adoption can support carbon accounting in terms of reducing the carbon footprint of an organization. To that end, Reinkemeyer (2020a, p. 15) underpins the importance of clearly defining and communicating the purpose of adopting process mining to successfully achieve these economic and ecological benefits accordingly. Thus, it becomes crucial to set boundaries and define the scope related to carbon reduction in order to be able to measure the effects of process change towards becoming a sustainable organization.

Table 4 Summary of process mining levels of support for carbon accounting

Process mining to support carbon accounting	Support level and practical implications
Recognize CO_2 emissions	• Processing of carbon values through APIs or manual enriching of event logs • Aggregates carbon information with event logs • Puts carbon data into context with process data • Creates new data perspectives for carbon accountants to measure and evaluate carbon impact of processes
Measure CO_2 emissions	• Enables carbon accountants to measure carbon impact per process activity along the process execution • Increases carbon awareness on process levels • Contextualizes carbon data considering ecologic and economic performance • Signals carbon accountants if processes deviate in terms of carbon performance • Constitutes a hybrid approach to define realistic operational targets on process levels (bottom-up) and ensure alignment of with strategic carbon targets defined by leadership and management (top-down)
Reduce CO_2 emissions	• Empowers carbon accountants to compare carbon performance vs. process performance without neglecting process design, workflow, and execution • Simulates different scenarios of process flows to juxtapose carbon output with economic factors related to cost, time and quality • Supports carbon accountants in the identification of high CO_2 activities and thus CO_2 reduction potentials

Table 4 provides a summary of the support level that the findings indicate process mining adoption provides for carbon accounting.

5.2 Limitations

In the following, we discuss the limitations of this study.

Carbon accounting has a dedicated focus on evaluating and reducing the carbon impact of an entire organization due to various internal and external drivers. In contrast, process mining as a technology can only help to assess and compare ecologic and economic information on a very granular process level. Therefore, process mining does not necessarily take into consideration the broader ecological effects an entire organization has on its environment. Process mining, as the name implies, starts with a clear focus on one single process. This requires rolling out the technology to other processes throughout the organization to benefit from the network effects of process mining. However, it must be taken into consideration that this requires significant effort both operationally and financially. In combination with the current lack of carbon data availability (which might change in the near future), the costs currently overweigh the benefits.

In addition, the results did not clarify how to consider manual activities for the process mining analysis. Commonly, manual activities are not being recorded by source systems and thus do not provide digital traces to be used for process mining. However, manual activities which take place, for example, in construction can be very carbon-intensive. Thus, such process activities would not be considered in the analysis, which results in an incomplete picture of the mined process. The portrayed results would therefore distort the carbon analysis and thus negatively affect the interpretation and decision-making towards sustainable development accordingly.

Data was gathered using the methodology of qualitative expert interviews. These interviews were constrained in time and scope. In general, the expert interview method only provides an exemplary look into an organization. Different people in the same company (or maybe even same department) might have different technical set-ups, opinions, or insights. Therefore, findings from individual expert interviews must not be generalized as a whole. The quality of findings generated from expert interviews depends by definition on the expertise of the interviewee. The main focus area of the interview partners lies in process mining, not necessarily to the same extent in carbon accounting. The responses from the interview partners might additionally reflect a strong and (un)intentional bias. This bias is particularly more probable among process mining vendors and consulting firms who regularly promote the technology and therefore report only the most impressive results of their use cases.

Interview candidates were chosen regardless of company size, industry, and use cases. Different industries face different challenges when thinking of sustainability and carbon mitigation. Also, the size of the organization plays a role since larger organizations generally tend to produce more carbon emissions than smaller and medium-sized enterprises just by the way they operate at scale. In addition, the maturity of the process mining affiliation can also portray a relevant factor. Thus, the results of how process mining can support in reducing carbon emissions may differ in terms of industry, company size, and experience the company has made with process mining.

5.3   Future Research

The following paragraphs indicate areas for future research to follow up on the findings of this study.

As carbon reduction potentials vary across industries (e.g., with greater potentials in process-heavy industries such as the chemicals, construction, and manufacturing sector as compared to other, less carbon-intensive industries like the financial sector), future research could focus on one industry and analyze the impact of process mining on the carbon reduction within that one specific industry to ensure comparability of the outcomes and quantify the carbon saving potentials of companies in that specific industry.

Likewise, carbon outputs of small and medium-sized enterprises might differ from the carbon output of large organizations as larger companies tend to produce more carbon emissions as a result of operating at larger scale. Thus, another subject for future research is to determine whether the company size plays an important role in identifying carbon reduction potentials through process mining adoption.

Furthermore, it would also be interesting to examine companies that have already implemented and rolled out various process mining initiatives as they appear to have greater expertise in utilizing process mining and thus require less effort both, financially and operationally in enhancing their current process mining initiatives to also address sustainability issues related to carbon emissions.

For a more practical approach to critically assess how process mining can support carbon accounting, it can clearly be helpful to conduct action design research for developing process mining dashboards that consider carbon data in the data model and testing of the applicability of these dashboards with iterative feedback loops together with carbon accountants. This would allow to determine the relevance of the results and whether these insights would support carbon accountants in fulfilling their duties.

6 Conclusion

The purpose of this paper was to examine how process mining can support carbon accounting in reducing carbon emissions. Based on a literature review in the fields of carbon accounting and process mining and eight expert interviews with process mining experts across different industries, requirements and potentials of process mining to support carbon accounting in terms of decision support for carbon reduction were identified. The findings reveal that process mining can support carbon accounting in three different ways. First, process mining creates the end-to-end visibility of the carbon impact on process levels. Second, process mining enables carbon accountants to simulate different process execution scenarios in order to evaluate different carbon outputs and thus, identify alternative and less carbon-intensive ways to operate the processes. Third, through the aggregated views, process mining facilitates the monetary and non-monetary evaluation by allowing to compare ecologic factors (i.e., CO_2 emissions) with process performance indicators (e.g., throughput time, costs, quality, etc.) without neglecting the actual process execution. Primary data in form of event logs and secondary data in form of carbon emission values for the process are needed, whereby the latter can either be manually collected or retrieved through external data libraries and integrated using an API. In summary, the research reveals that process mining can be seen as an auxiliary tool to support carbon accounting as it creates new and enhanced ways to measure and evaluate the carbon footprint on process levels that enable the identification of carbon reduction potentials. Process mining enables practitioners a closer alignment between operational targets and sustainability targets formulated by top management while considering process design, execution, and value generation along the value chain. Future research should focus on carbon reduction in different industries and company sizes to identify different utilization potentials of process mining. Further guidance is also needed to calculate the business impact of reducing carbon emissions through process mining adoption, given that practitioners currently lack this ability. Ultimately, more practical approaches are suggested considering the development and testing of process mining applications together with carbon accountants and process experts to confirm the suitability and effectiveness of process mining adoption to reduce carbon emissions.

References

Ascui, F. (2014). A review of carbon accounting in the social and environmental accounting literature: what can it contribute to the debate? *Social and Environmental Accountability Journal, 34*. https://doi.org/10.1080/0969160X.2013.870487

Ascui, F., & Lovell, H. (2011). As frames collide: Making sense of carbon accounting. *Accounting, Auditing and Accountability Journal, 24*(8), 978–999. https://doi.org/10.1108/09513571111184724

Brander, M., & Ascui, F. (2015). The attributional-consequential distinction and its applicability to corporate carbon accounting. In S. Schaltegger, D. Zvezdov, I. Alvarez Etxeberria, M. Csutora, & E. Günther (Eds.), *Corporate carbon and climate accounting* (pp. 99–120). Springer International Publishing. https://doi.org/10.1007/978-3-319-27718-9_5

Burritt, R. L., Schaltegger, S., & Zvezdov, D. (2011). Carbon management accounting: explaining practice in leading German companies: Carbon management accounting. *Australian Accounting Review, 21*(1), 80–98. https://doi.org/10.1111/j.1835-2561.2010.00121.x

Busch, T., & Lewandowski, S. (2018). Corporate carbon and financial performance: A meta-analysis: Corporate carbon and financial performance. *Journal of Industrial Ecology, 22*(4), 745–759. https://doi.org/10.1111/jiec.12591

Calero, C., & Piattini, M. (2015). Introduction to green in software engineering. In C. Calero & M. Piattini (Eds.), *Green in software engineering* (pp. 3–27). Springer International Publishing. https://doi.org/10.1007/978-3-319-08581-4_1

Creswell, J. W. (2012). *Educational research: Pearson new international edition PDF eBook: Planning, conducting, and evaluating quantitative and qualitative research* (4th ed.) Pearson.

Creswell, J. W., & Creswell, J. D. (2018). *Research design: Qualitative, quantitative, and mixed methods approaches* (5th ed.). Sage.

Csutora, M., & Harangozo, G. (2017). Twenty years of carbon accounting and auditing – A review and outlook. *Society and Economy, 39*, 459–480. https://doi.org/10.1556/204.2017.39.4.1

Damert, M., Morris, J., & Guenther, E. (2020). Carbon footprints of organizations and products. In W. Leal Filho, A. M. Azul, L. Brandli, P. G. Özuyar, & T. Wall (Eds.), *Responsible consumption and production* (pp. 59–72). Springer International Publishing. https://doi.org/10.1007/978-3-319-95726-5_12

EPA. (United States Environmental Protection Agency). (2016, January 12). *Understanding global warming potentials [Overviews and factsheets]*. US EPA. https://www.epa.gov/ghgemissions/understanding-global-warming-potentials

Everest Group. (o. J.). *Process mining—Technology vendor landscape with products PEAK matrix assessment 2021*. Abgerufen 29. August 2021, von https://www.everestgrp.com/published-research/peak-matrix/

Gartner. (2020). Market guide for process mining. . https://www.gartner.com/en/documents/3991229/market-guide-for-process-mining

Ghose, A., Hoesch-Klohe, K., Hinsche, L., & Lê, L.-S. (2010). Green business process management: A research agenda. *Australasian Journal of Information Systems, 16*(2) (2009), 16. doi:https://doi.org/10.3127/ajis.v16i2.597.

Gibassier, D. (2015). Implementing an EMA innovation: The case of carbon accounting. In S. Schaltegger, D. Zvezdov, I. Alvarez Etxeberria, M. Csutora, & E. Günther (Eds.), *Corporate carbon and climate accounting* (pp. 121–142). Springer International Publishing. https://doi.org/10.1007/978-3-319-27718-9_6

Gibassier, D., & Schaltegger, S. (2015). Carbon management accounting and reporting in practice: A case study on converging emergent approaches. *Sustainability Accounting, Management and Policy Journal, 6*(3), 340–365. https://doi.org/10.1108/SAMPJ-02-2015-0014

Gläser, J., & Laudel, G. (2010). *Experteninterviews und qualitative Inhaltsanalyse als Instrumente rekonstruierender Untersuchungen* (4th ed.) VS Verl. für Sozialwiss.

Hartmann, F., Perego, P., & Young, A. (2013). Carbon accounting: Challenges for research in management control and performance measurement: Carbon accounting. *Abacus, 49*(4), 539–563. https://doi.org/10.1111/abac.12018

He, R., Luo, L., Shamsuddin, A., & Tang, Q. (2021). Corporate carbon accounting: A literature review of carbon accounting research from the Kyoto Protocol to the Paris Agreement. *Accounting and Finance*, acfi.12789. doi:https://doi.org/10.1111/acfi.12789.

Helfferich, C. (2014). Leitfaden- und Experteninterviews. In N. Baur & J. Blasius (Eds.), *Handbuch Methoden der empirischen Sozialforschung* (pp. 559–574). Springer Fachmedien Wiesbaden. https://doi.org/10.1007/978-3-531-18939-0_39

Huang, Y. A., Weber, C. L., & Matthews, H. S. (2009). Categorization of Scope 3 emissions for streamlined enterprise carbon footprinting. *Environmental Science and Technology, 43*(22), 8509–8515. https://doi.org/10.1021/es901643a

IPCC, I. P. on C. C. (2006). *2006 IPCC Guidelines for National Greenhouse Gas Inventories*. https://www.ipcc-nggip.iges.or.jp/public/2006gl/

ISO, I. for S. (2018). *DIN EN ISO 14067 Greenhouse gases—Carbon footprint of products—Requirements and guidelines for quantification*. https://www.din.de/en/getting-involved/standards-committees/nagus/publications/wdc-beuth:din21:289443505

Kasbun, N. F., Ong, T. S., Muhamad, H., & Said, R. M. (2019). Conceptual framework to improve carbon performance via carbon strategies and carbon accounting. *Journal of Environmental Management and Tourism, X*, Winter, 1918–1923. doi:https://doi.org/10.14505/jemt.v10.8(40).21.

Konrad, A. (2021). *Celonis raises $1 billion at $11 billion valuation, making it New York's – and Germany's – most valuable startup*. Forbes https://www.forbes.com/sites/alexkonrad/2021/06/02/celonis-process-mining-raises-at-11-billion-valuation/

Leontief, W. W. (1936). Quantitative input and output relations in the economic systems of the United States. *The Review of Economics and Statistics, 18*(3), 105. https://doi.org/10.2307/1927837

Li, S. Z., & Jain, A. (Eds.). (2009). Application programming interface (API). In *Encyclopedia of biometrics* (S. 41–41). Springer US. doi:https://doi.org/10.1007/978-0-387-73003-5_858.

Liao, Y. X., Rocha Loures, E., Portela Santos, E. A., & Canciglieri, O. (2014). The proposition of a framework for semantic process mining. *Advanced Materials Research, 1051*, 995–999. https://doi.org/10.4028/www.scientific.net/AMR.1051.995

Loeser, F., Recker, J., vom Brocke, J., Molla, A., & Zarnekow, R. (2017). How IT executives create organizational benefits by translating environmental strategies into Green IS initiatives:

Organizational benefits of Green IS strategies and practices. *Information Systems Journal,* *27*(4), 503–553. https://doi.org/10.1111/isj.12136

Lübbecke, P., Reiter, M., Fettke, P., & Loos, P. (2015). Simulation-based decision support for the reduction of the energy consumption of complex business processes. *2015 48th Hawaii International Conference on System Sciences* (pp. 866–875). doi:https://doi.org/10.1109/HICSS.2015.109.

Matthews, H. S., Hendrickson, C. T., & Weber, C. L. (2008). The importance of carbon footprint estimation boundaries. *Environmental Science and Technology, 42*(16), 5839–5842. https://doi.org/10.1021/es703112w

Mozner, Z. (2015). Carbon accounting in long supply chain industries. In S. Schaltegger, D. Zvezdov, I. Alvarez Etxeberria, M. Csutora, & E. Günther (Eds.), *Corporate carbon and climate accounting* (pp. 143–162). Springer International Publishing. https://doi.org/10.1007/978-3-319-27718-9_7

Müller, B., & Schebek, L. (2013). Input-output-based life cycle inventory: Development and validation of a database for the German building sector. *Journal of Industrial Ecology, 17*(4), 504–516. https://doi.org/10.1111/jiec.12018

Nohl, A.-M. (2017). *Interview und Dokumentarische Methode: Anleitungen für die Forschungspraxis.* Springer Fachmedien Wiesbaden. https://doi.org/10.1007/978-3-658-16080-7

Ong, T., Kasbun, N., Teh, B., Muhammad, H., & Javeed, S. (2021). Carbon accounting system: The bridge between carbon governance and carbon performance in Malaysian companies. *Ecosystem Health and Sustainability, 1927851.* https://doi.org/10.1080/20964129.2021.1927851

Ortas, E., Gallego-Álvarez, I., Álvarez, I., & Moneva, J. M. (2015). Carbon accounting: A review of the existing models, principles and practical applications. In S. Schaltegger, D. Zvezdov, I. Alvarez Etxeberria, M. Csutora, & E. Günther (Eds.), *Corporate carbon and climate accounting* (pp. 77–98). Springer International Publishing. https://doi.org/10.1007/978-3-319-27718-9_4

Ortmeier, C., Henningsen, N., Langer, A., Reiswich, A., Karl, A., & Herrmann, C. (2021). Framework for the integration of process mining into life cycle assessment. *Procedia CIRP, 98,* 163–168. https://doi.org/10.1016/j.procir.2021.01.024

Ozawa-Meida, L., Brockway, P., Letten, K., Davies, J., & Fleming, P. (2013). Measuring carbon performance in a UK University through a consumption-based carbon footprint: De Montfort University case study. *Journal of Cleaner Production, 56,* 185–198. https://doi.org/10.1016/j.jclepro.2011.09.028

Peters, R., & Nauroth, M. (2019). *Process-Mining: Geschäftsprozesse: smart, schnell und einfach.* Springer Fachmedien Wiesbaden. https://doi.org/10.1007/978-3-658-24170-4

Qian, W., & Schaltegger, S. (2017). Revisiting carbon disclosure and performance: Legitimacy and management views. *The British Accounting Review, 49*(4), 365–379. https://doi.org/10.1016/j.bar.2017.05.005

Qian, W., Hörisch, J., & Schaltegger, S. (2018). Environmental management accounting and its effects on carbon management and disclosure quality. *Journal of Cleaner Production, 174,* 1608–1619. https://doi.org/10.1016/j.jclepro.2017.11.092

Recker, J. (2013). *Scientific research in information systems.* Springer. https://doi.org/10.1007/978-3-642-30048-6

Recker, J., Rosemann, M., Hjalmarsson, A., & Lind, M. (2012). Modeling and analyzing the carbon footprint of business processes. In J. vom Brocke, S. Seidel, & J. Recker (Eds.), *Green business process management: Towards the sustainable enterprise* (pp. 93–109). Springer. https://doi.org/10.1007/978-3-642-27488-6_6

Reinkemeyer, L. (2020a). *Process mining in action: Principles.* Springer International Publishing. https://doi.org/10.1007/978-3-030-40172-6

Reinkemeyer, L. (2020b). *How process mining can turn sustainability targets into action.* https://www.linkedin.com/pulse/how-process-mining-can-turn-sustainability-targets-lars-reinkemeyer.

Saraswati, E. (2020). Carbon accounting, disclosure and measurement: A systematic literature review. *The International Journal of Accounting and Business Society, 28*, 17–44. https://doi.org/10.21776/ub.ijabs.2020.28.2.2

Schaltegger, S., & Csutora, M. (2012). Carbon accounting for sustainability and management. Status quo and challenges. *Journal of Cleaner Production, 36*, 1–16. https://doi.org/10.1016/j.jclepro.2012.06.024

Schaltegger, S., Zvezdov, D., Günther, E., Csutora, M., & Alvarez, I. (2015). Corporate carbon and climate change accounting: Application, developments and issues. In S. Schaltegger, D. Zvezdov, I. Alvarez Etxeberria, M. Csutora, & E. Günther (Eds.), *Corporate carbon and climate accounting* (pp. 1–25). Springer International Publishing. https://doi.org/10.1007/978-3-319-27718-9_1

Seidel, S., Recker, J., & vom Brocke, J. (2012). Green business process management. In J. vom Brocke, S. Seidel, & J. Recker (Eds.), *Green business process management: Towards the sustainable enterprise* (pp. 3–13). Springer. https://doi.org/10.1007/978-3-642-27488-6_1

Stechemesser, K., & Günther, E. (2012). Carbon accounting: A systematic literature review. *Journal of Cleaner Production, 36*, 17–38. https://doi.org/10.1016/j.jclepro.2012.02.021

Tang, Q. (2017). Framework for and the Role of Carbon Accounting in Corporate Carbon Management Systems: A Holistic Approach. SSRN Electronic Journal. DOI: 10.2139/ssrn.2903366.

Tang, Q. (2019). Institutional influence, transition management and the demand for carbon auditing: The Chinese experience. *Australian Accounting Review, 29*(2), 376–394. https://doi.org/10.1111/auar.12224

Ueda, S. (2021). *Process mining will move CO2 reduction goal management one step forward*. Celonis. https://www.celonis.com/blog/process-mining-will-move-co2-reduction-goal-management-one-step-forward/

United Nations, (2005). Kyoto Protocol. Available at: https://unfccc.int/resource/docs/convkp/kpeng.pdf (Accessed: 18 May 2021).

United Nations (2016). Paris Agreement. Available at: https://unfccc.int/sites/default/files/english_paris_agreement.pdf (Accessed: 18 May 2021).

van der Aalst, W. M. P. (2011). *Process mining: Discovery, conformance and enhancement of business processes*. Springer. https://doi.org/10.1007/978-3-642-19345-3

van der Aalst, W. (2016). *Process mining: Data science in action* (2. Aufl.). Springer. doi:https://doi.org/10.1007/978-3-662-49851-4.

van der Aalst, W., Adriansyah, A., de Medeiros, A. K. A., Arcieri, F., Baier, T., Blickle, T., Bose, J. C., van den Brand, P., Brandtjen, R., Buijs, J., Burattin, A., Carmona, J., Castellanos, M., Claes, J., Cook, J., Costantini, N., Curbera, F., Damiani, E., de Leoni, M., et al. (2012). Process mining manifesto. In F. Daniel, K. Barkaoui, & S. Dustdar (Eds.), *Business process management workshops* (pp. 169–194). Springer. https://doi.org/10.1007/978-3-642-28108-2_19

van Eck, M. L., Lu, X., Leemans, S. J. J., & van der Aalst, W. M. P. (2015). PM2: A process mining project methodology. In J. Zdravkovic, M. Kirikova, & P. Johannesson (Eds.), *Advanced information systems engineering* (Bd. 9097, pp. 297–313). Springer International Publishing. doi:https://doi.org/10.1007/978-3-319-19069-3_19.

vom Brocke, J., & Rosemann, M. (2015). *Handbook on business process management 1: Introduction, methods, and information systems*. Springer. https://doi.org/10.1007/978-3-642-45100-3

WBCSD and WRI. (2004). *GHG protocol*. World Business Council for Sustainable Development and World Resource Institute. https://ghgprotocol.org/standards.

WBCSD and WRI. (2015). *The greenhouse gas protocol – A corporate accounting and reporting standard*. (p 116). World Business Council for Sustainable Development and World Resources Institute. https://ghgprotocol.org/sites/default/files/standards/ghg-protocol-revised.pdf

Wiedmann, T., & Minx, J. (2008). A definition of carbon footprint. *CC Pertsova, Ecological Economics Research Trends, 2*, 55–65.

Wright, L. A., Kemp, S., & Williams, I. (2011). 'Carbon footprinting': Towards a universally accepted definition. *Carbon Management, 2*(1), 61–72. https://doi.org/10.4155/cmt.10.39

Yin, R. K. (2018). *Case study research and applications: Design and methods (Hochschule München)*. Sage.

Zvezdov, D., & Schaltegger, S. (2015). Decision support through carbon management accounting – A framework-based literature review. In S. Schaltegger, D. Zvezdov, I. Alvarez Etxeberria, M. Csutora, & E. Günther (Eds.), *Corporate carbon and climate accounting* (pp. 27–44). Springer International Publishing. https://doi.org/10.1007/978-3-319-27718-9_2

Part VI
Recommendation Networks and Industry Structure: Sales and Market Analysis

The Impact of Product Recommendation Networks on Sales: The Moderating Influence of Product Age

Nils Herm-Stapelberg and Franz Rothlauf

Abstract In many online stores, recommender systems create a product recommendation network by placing links to recommended products on a product page. The importance of a product in such a product recommendation network can be measured by its PageRank centrality. Previous research found that the PageRank of books in a product recommendation network is a predictor for its expected sales. However, it is unclear whether this relationship is affected by the age of a book. Consequently, this chapter studies the influence of book age on the relationship between PageRank of a book and expected sales (SalesRank). We use various multivariate regressions to analyze how the relationship between PageRank centrality and SalesRank is moderated by product age. We collected data from a large online bookstore over a period of 35 days and find that the PageRank of a book is a significant predictor of expected sales if only books younger than 170 days are considered. When including also books in the regression models older than 170 days, we find no significant influence of PageRank on expected sales. Thus, book age moderates the influence of PageRank on SalesRank. We do not only find a direct influence of book age on expected sales but also confirm a significant quadratic moderating effect of book age. As a result, if online stores want to increase the demand of a specific product, recommendations should also take the age of a book into account as for very new as well as old books a high centrality of a book in a product network does not lead to higher sales.

1 Introduction

The rise of online e-commerce shops has increased the amount of available products per shop by many magnitudes compared to classic retail stores. This has also created the need for tools capable of filtering the massive amount of information, helping

N. Herm-Stapelberg · F. Rothlauf (✉)
Johannes Gutenberg-University Mainz, Mainz, Germany
e-mail: hermstapelberg@uni-mainz.de; rothlauf@uni-mainz.de

© The Author(s), under exclusive license to Springer Nature Switzerland AG 2022
J. Dibbern et al. (eds.), *Digitalization Across Organizational Levels*, Progress in IS,
https://doi.org/10.1007/978-3-031-06543-9_10

customers find the right products and make purchase decisions. Recommender systems (RS) fulfill these tasks by suggesting relevant items to users, based, e.g., on their previous behavior (such as purchases, clickstreams, etc.). Currently, a variety of different RS have been deployed on e-commerce platforms (e.g., Amazon), video-on-demand, and television platforms (e.g., Netflix), or e-learning platforms (e.g., Coursera) (Klašnja-Milićević et al., 2015; Park et al., 2012; Véras et al., 2015) as well as other domains such as medical decision-making (Jussupow et al., 2018, 2021; Paulussen et al., 2006) or flight planning (Grosche et al., 2001).

Assessing the quality and impact of recommender systems is not trivial. Evaluating RS can lead to different results depending on a number of factors, including the domain in which it is used, the purpose of the platform, or the type of user. Early research focused mainly on "accuracy" measures such as mean absolute error (MAE) or root mean squared error (RSME) measuring the deviation between the system's predicted product ratings and actual product ratings given by the users (Herlocker et al., 2004). Examples for classification accuracy measures are precision (percentage of useful recommendations compared to all given recommendations) and recall (percentage of useful recommendations compared to all possible useful recommendations) (Cremonesi et al., 2010; Herlocker et al., 2004; Shani & Gunawardana, 2011). RS evaluation was later extended by measures such as diversity (how different are recommended products to each other) or novelty (are recommendations new to a user and previously unknown) (Bobadilla et al., 2011; Kotkov et al., 2016). Although RS were also evaluated from a user-based perspective by measuring user satisfaction, trust, or surprise (Ge et al., 2010; Knijnenburg et al., 2012; McNee et al., 2006; Wang & Benbasat, 2005), many e-commerce providers are primarily interested in its economic impact. Proper measures are, e.g., overall sales, the distribution of sales over all products, or cross-sales (Fleder & Hosanagar, 2009; Goolsbee & Chevalier, 2010; Lin et al., 2017; Oestreicher-Singer & Sundararajan, 2012a).

In most online stores, RS generate hyperlinks (i.e., recommendations) pointing from a product website currently visited by a user to other available products. These hyperlinks form a *product recommendation network*, where nodes denote products and hyperlinks are directed connections between these nodes. The importance of a node in a product recommendation network can be described by centrality measures, such as *PageRank*. PageRank centrality has been used in multiple studies to better understand how individual sales and the distribution of product sales are affected by RS (Hu et al., 2012; Leem & Chun, 2014; Lin et al., 2017; Oestreicher-Singer & Sundararajan, 2012a). For example, Hu et al. (2012) gathered the PageRank as well as the SalesRank of newly released books on amazon.com and found that PageRank centrality can serve as a predictor for product demand. For their study, they focused on new books with a maximum age of 45 days.

Since Hu et al. (2012) used only recently released books, it is unclear whether the found effect also holds for older books or might be moderated by the age of a book. Thus, this chapter studies the influence of PageRank and product age on individual product sales. We study different multivariate regression models predicting a product's SalesRank in the next period. The models use only subsets of the books based on the maximum allowed book age. Thus, PageRank centrality and book age are used as predictors, and several product characteristics as well as product dummies are added to the model to control for observed and unobserved heterogeneity among the products. We present models that demonstrate a moderating influence of the product age on the relationship between network centrality (PageRank) and sales (SalesRank).

This chapter contributes to the understanding of the impact of recommender systems in online e-commerce shops. For books, we find that the influence of the position of a product (book) in the product recommendation network on expected sales is moderated by the age of the book.

2 Related Work

In the last years, the impact of recommender systems on sales and sales diversity has received increasing attention. For e-commerce websites, Pathak et al. (2010) find that RS increase overall sales and allow sellers to optimize prices. However, Hinz and Eckert (2010) suggest that RS mainly foster substitution effects and do not increase overall sales volume. Rather, the overall sales volume increases through the optimization of search engines that return a list of products based on user-provided search keywords. A study by Fleder and Hosanagar (2009) finds that the increase in sales may only be due to a "rich get richer" effect as RS often tend to recommend top-selling products.

Taking into account this mixed evidence, Oestreicher-Singer and Sundararajan (2012a,b) adopted a network-centered approach and used product networks to explain the influence of RS on sales diversity for books. For the example amazon.com, they find that RS flatten the distribution of sales over all products so that niche products benefit more from RS than top sellers. Additionally, Oestreicher-Singer et al. (2013) find that individual product sales cannot be viewed separately when assessing the performance of a product. When products are part of a product network, every product receives additional attention (and thus, sales) from all other products that link to it. Similarly, every product also provides additional sales for other (e.g., complementary) products through the network. Lin et al. (2017) extended this approach by distinguishing between ingoing and outgoing connections of a product and by adding network diversity (i.e., diversity of the direct neighbors of a product) and stability (i.e., frequency of updates of recommendations). They find that the diversity of network nodes that point toward a particular product (incoming links) increases product's demand, whereas the stability of the outgoing network decreases demand.

Leem and Chun (2014) used a variety of network centrality measures in a multivariate linear regression to examine the correlation between network position and demand (using the transformation of SalesRank to demand introduced by Goolsbee and Chevalier (2003)). All predictors show a significant influence. However, they did not test whether this effect is also valid for products of different ages (e.g., newly released vs. year-old books). Furthermore, they did not use any product characteristics such as book age, price, or rating. Furthermore, they used data from the co-purchase network of amazon.com that features only one specific point of time although the SalesRank of a product is based on past sales.

Hu et al. (2012) gathered the SalesRank and PageRank of newly released books on amazon.com. They found that PageRank positively predicts demand (thus negatively predicts SalesRank). They consider only newly released books (max. 45 days), leaving it unclear whether the effect is also valid for older books.

Dhar et al. (2010) used historic data and explained future sales of amazon.com books by constructing an autoregressive model, including the network neighbors of each product. They found that the prediction of future SalesRanks improved from a baseline autoregressive model, when past SalesRanks of direct neighbors are considered.

None of these studies explicitly looks at the effect of the age of products on its demand or whether the relationship between a product's network position and sales is moderated by its age. Oestreicher-Singer and Sundararajan (2012a) included a binary "recency" variable to account for newly released books but did not look at changes in other predictors based on the age. Hu et al. (2012) implicitly considered the age of products by only looking at newly released books on Amazon. This chapter extends this approach by building different multivariate regression models for books of different maximum ages.

3 Data and Data Collection

We collected data from individual product websites of a large online bookstore. The bookstore features over 100,000 books and many categories such as "Fantasy," "Cooking," "Crime Novel," and "Tour Guide." We implemented a depth-first web crawler, which started randomly from a top 10,000 product page of each of these categories. After recording the necessary information on the visited book, the web crawler used one of the shown recommendation hyperlinks to travel to the next product. If the next book has already been visited and documented, or if it was not part of the category currently being crawled, the program backtracked to the last successfully recorded book and chose another recommendation. This process continues until 10,000 iterations were reached. This procedure was repeated once a day over a time frame of 35 days. Table 1 lists the recorded information for each book.

Table 2 lists the summary statistics of the crawled data for the different categories. Due to crawler errors, server restarts, or unavailability of the website, some days are missing for certain categories. Since the crawler randomly started in every category once per day, not every book was crawled on every day. On average, each book was recorded approx. 10 times in total. The average rating (AvgRating) overall is fairly high. It has been shown before that user reviews tend to be biased toward positive (or higher) ratings (Chevalier & Mayzlin, 2006). The

Table 1 Recorded book information

BOOK_TITLE	Book title
CATEGORY	Book category, i.e., one of the following: "Fantasy," "Cooking," "Crime Novel," "Tour Guide"
DATE	Date of information gathering
ISBN	Unique identification number of book
SALES_RANK	Associated sales rank of book
PUB_DATE	Publication date
PRICE	Price (in €)
RATING	Rounded average rating $\in \{1, 2, 3, 4, 5\}$
#RATINGS	Total number of ratings that were given to the book
REC1-REC34	Title of shown recommendations. Seven recommendations are shown directly beneath the product description. More recommendations can be viewed by manually clicking on a button, revealing the next 7 recommendations available. The maximum number of recommendations is 34; however, often few recommendations are shown.

Table 2 Summary statistics

Category	#Books	AvgPrice	AvgRating	Avg#Ratings	TotalObs
Fantasy	3052	12.82	4.60	25.55	34,142
Cooking	3287	16.90	4.70	7.86	25,613
Crime	3921	10.98	4.38	23.32	55,303
Tour Guide	3135	15.14	4.50	3.08	26,766

Table 3 Sales rank (SR)

Category	MinSR	MaxSR	AvgSR	MedianSR	StdDevSR
Fantasy	2	90,743	27,441	20,534	24,179
Cooking	6	91,230	34,313	28,501	25,632
Crime Novel	1	91,389	30,146	23,366	25,094
Tour Guide	46	91,453	35,031	28974	24,649

average number of ratings (Avg#Ratings) is considerably higher for Fantasy Novels and Crime Novels (which might be due to popularity and the fact that these books are geared toward entertainment) and low for Cooking Books and Tour Guides. The number of crawled books (#Books) and the average price (AvgPrice) are fairly similar with Crime Novels being the biggest (3921 recorded books) and cheapest (10.98€ AvgPrice) group.

Table 3 gives an overview of the SalesRank distribution in the dataset. The dataset covered a broad range of products, from top sellers to niche products (from a high SalesRank (MinSR) of 1 to a low SalesRank (MaxSR) of 91,453). The average sales rank (AvgSR) was around 30,000 in every category. The standard deviation (StdDevSR) was similar across categories. The different categories represent very diverse types of books since Fantasy and Crime Novels are entertainment books, whereas Cook Books and Tour Guides are utility books.

4 Method and Results

4.1 PageRank Centrality

The importance of a node in a product network can be measured by its PageRank centrality. Although developed for assessing the importance of websites (Brin & Page, 1998), PageRank can be used for a variety of different tasks. The PageRank PR_i of product i is defined as

$$PR_i = \frac{(1 - \alpha)}{n} + \alpha \sum_j \frac{PR_j}{OutDegree_j},$$

where $\alpha \in [0, 1]$ is the damping factor, n is the number of products, PR_j is the PageRank of a product j that has a directed edge (i.e., a hyperlink) pointing toward product i, and $OutDegree_j$ counts the number of outgoing edges of product j. This model describes the behavior of a web surfer, who randomly chooses one of the available recommendations on a product website or jumps to a random product node in the network (with probability $1 - \alpha$). Consequently, the resulting PageRank of a node is the probability that a random surfer is visiting this node (Brinkmeier, 2006). A higher PageRank is expected to lead to more sales (as more users will see the product and buy it) and a lower (i.e., better) SalesRank (Hu et al., 2012; Leem & Chun, 2014; Oestreicher-Singer & Sundararajan, 2012b).

For the crawled books, we calculated the PageRank separately for each of the crawled networks (four categories) and for each day. Table 4 gives an overview of the average PageRank of a book per day and per category. The minimum (MinPR), average (AvgPR), median (MedianPR), and standard deviation (StdDevPR) of the PageRank are similar across categories. Interestingly, the maximum PageRank (MaxPR) of books in the category Fantasy is around 10 times higher in comparison to the maximum PageRank of books in the categories Cooking, Crime Novels, and Tour Guides.

Table 4 PageRank

CATEGORY	MaxPR	MinPR	AvgPR	MedianPR	StdDevPR
Fantasy	0.053967	0.000087	0.000394	0.000232	0.000783
Cooking	0.005762	0.000043	0.000373	0.000247	0.000429
Crime Novels	0.008773	0.000043	0.000294	0.000161	0.000506
Tour Guides	0.004602	0.000051	0.000434	0.000308	0.000416

4.2 Linear Model

To predict the SalesRank of a product, we use multivariate regression models. Since the SalesRank is based on previous sales and we do not know how often it is updated, we use the SalesRank of a book in the next time period as dependent variable. As independent variables, we use PageRank centrality (as a measure of the importance of a node in the product network) and a product's age. Furthermore, we use several control variables such as price and rating of each book. Since attributes such as the inherent quality of a book or its overall popularity influence a product's SalesRank, however most of these attributes are not observed or observable in the crawled data, and we added product dummies to the models accounting for the unobserved heterogeneity among the recorded products. The resulting model is

$$
\begin{aligned}
SR_{i,t+1} = \quad & \beta_0 \\
& + \beta_1 * PAGERANK_{i,t} \\
& + \beta_2 * PRICE_{i,t} \\
& + \beta_3 * BOOK\_AGE_{i,t} \\
& + \beta_4 * RATING_{i,t} \\
& + \beta_5 * NUMBER\_OF\_RATINGS_{i,t} \\
& + \sum_{i \in I} \beta_i * PD_{i,t} \\
& + \epsilon_{i,t},
\end{aligned}
$$

where $SR_{i,t+1}$ is the SalesRank of product i at time $t+1$ and $PAGERANK_{i,t}$ is the PageRank of product i at time t. $\sum_{i \in I} \beta_i * PD_{i,t}$ denotes the product dummies (with I as the set of all products).

Table 5 gives an overview of the used predictor variables. We excluded all observations with missing data (e.g., the SalesRank of the next period) from the model. For each book, we use the global SalesRank (and not the SalesRank within the category) since it better represents the overall demand for a specific book. Additionally, using the SalesRank per category would imply that the best-selling

Table 5 Predictor variables

	Max	Min	Avg	Median	StdDev
PageRank	0.06328	0.00004	0.00038	0.00021	0.00063
Price	300	0.49	13.52	10.95	7.45
BookAge	13022	0	1191	791	1230
Rating	5	1	4.49	5	0.58
NumberOfRatings	409	0	22.33	12	29.9

Table 6 Linear model with product dummies

		Predicted variable: $SALES\_RANK_{t+1}$
PAGERANK		−148,744
		(95,560)
		[−83]
PRICE		101
		(248)
		[655]
BOOK_AGE		54***
		(6)
		[65,610]
RATING		3209**
		(799)
		[1875]
NUMBER_OF_ RATINGS		−7
		(34)
		[−214]
Constant		−66,059***
		(6841)
Observations		51,767
R^2		0.696
Adjusted R^2		0.671
Residual std. error		14,140 (df = 51764)
F-statistic		27,6***
		(df = 4298; 51764)

Note: $^*p < 0.1$; $^{**}p < 0.05$; $^{***}p < 0.01$

Crime Novel (global SalesRank 1) book has as much sales as the best-selling Tour Guide (global SalesRank 46), which is most likely not adequate.

4.3   Quality of Linear Models

Table 6 shows the output of this model (we omitted product dummies for better visualization). The robust standard errors are in brackets; standardized coefficients (i.e., the absolute change in SalesRank that is associated with one standard deviation change in the predictor) are shown in square brackets. The coefficients of PageRank, price, and number of ratings are insignificant. This is counter-intuitive since one would expect that the importance of a node or at least the price of a product should have an impact on the associated SalesRank. The adjusted R-squared value of the model is $Adj.R^2 \approx 0.67$. This model including all books (new books as well as old books) shows no support for an influence of PageRank on SalesRank. This result is in contrast to the findings of Hu et al. (2012) who found a significant predictive power of PageRank on sales. However, as stated before, Hu et al. (2012) ignored book age and used only new books with a maximum age of 45 days.

Consequently, we extend our analysis and calculate 35 different regression models using only subsets of the crawled books depending on the maximum age of the books. Starting with a model that contains only freshly published books (max book age < 20 days), we gradually increased the maximum age of the books included in the model by 10 days up to 360 days. This allows us to assess whether the prediction power of the regression model changes if we include also older books in the model. For all models, we use the same variables (PageRank, price, book age, rating, and the number of ratings) except for the dummies since the number of included books increases if we increase the maximum allowed age of the books.

Figure 1 plots the significance (p-value) of the independent variables (PageRank, price, book age, rating, #ratings) over the maximum age of the books considered for the regression model. High p-values indicate that the variable has no impact on SalesRank. The horizontal dashed black line shows a significance cutoff of 5%. We also added two vertical black lines to split the models into three groups (max book age < 65 days; 65 days $<$ max book age < 175 days; 175 days $<$ max book age) that emerge when comparing the different models. For the models considering only new books (max book age < 65 days), most of the predictor variables are insignificant. The p-values are not robust but show a high variation with respect to maximum book age. This might be also due to the low number of observations for newly released books (e.g., there are only 119 books with a maximum book age of less than 20). In contrast, in all regression models considering books that are not older than half a year (65 days $<$ max book age < 175 days), all predictor variables (except average rating) are highly significant ($p < 0.01$). When considering even older books (175 days $<$ max book age), the predictors PageRank, the number of ratings, and also price become insignificant again, until only book age remains a significant predictor of the SalesRank in the following period.

Motivated by the finding that the maximum age of the books considered for the regression model influences the impact of PageRank on SalesRank, we present more details for three models representing the three different groups of models. Consequently, Table 7 compares three models where the maximum age of the books considered for the model was either set to 60 days (denoted as model M60), 110 days (denoted as model M110), or 180 days (denoted as model M180). For M60 (we considered only books with a maximum age of 60 days), only price and rating are significant predictors; the other variables are not significant. This could be due to a number of reasons. First, when considering only books published in the last 60 days, there are only 941 observations (books) available across all categories. Second, for newly released books, the influence of RS might be limited. Since recommendations are often based on sales, ratings, and/or views of a book, newly released books are not often recommended but are rather found by users through, e.g., advertisement or cross-channel references. For M60, the $Adj.R^2 = 0.873$ and the F-statistic of 57.541 is significant ($p < 0.01$).

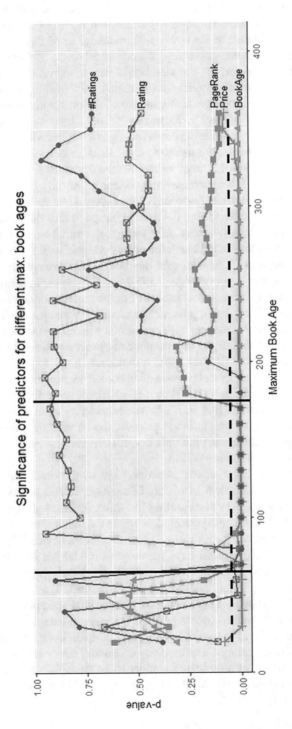

Fig. 1 Significance of predictor variables over the maximum book age

Table 7 Three linear models with maximum book age of either 60 days, 110 days, or 180 days

max. book age	Predicted variable: $SALES\_RANK_{t+1}$		
	60 days	110 days	180 days
	(M60)	(M110)	(M180)
PAGERANK	−1,385,115	−3,462,360***	−97,574
	(964,092)	(889,809)	(55,032)
	[−364]	[−1119]	[−78]
PRICE	−4,643***	2179***	−967***
	(21,047)	(399)	(180)
	[−23,364]	[11,603]	[−5471]
BOOK_AGE	31	194***	173***
	(72)	(31)	(17)
	[482]	[5539]	[8203]
RATING	945**	−181	−120
	(340)	(963)	(876)
	[549]	[−108]	[−72]
NUMBER_OF_	4	−150***	−101***
RATINGS	(56)	(28)	(26)
	[99]	[−4178]	[−3089]
Constant	56,054***	−22,344***	11,566**
	(313,799)	(5882)	(4472)
Maximum book age	60	110	180
Product dummies	Yes	Yes	Yes
Observations	941	2321	3959
R^2	0.888	0.843	0.812
Adjusted R^2	0.873	0.825	0.793
Residual std. error	5172	7626	8580
F-statistic	57.541***	48.217***	43.599***
	(df = 114; 826)	(df = 232; 2088)	(df = 356; 3602)

Note: $^{*}p < 0.1$; $^{**}p < 0.05$; $^{***}p < 0.01$

For the model M110 where we consider books with an age up to 110 days, every predictor variable (except average rating) is highly significant ($p < 0.01$). As expected, the coefficient of PageRank is negative, indicating that a more central position in the recommendation network is associated with a lower sales rank (and thus more sales). This finding also supports previous research (Hu et al., 2012). The coefficients of price and book age are positive, indicating that higher price and higher age lead to higher SalesRank. Since the number of ratings can be used as a proxy for the popularity of a book, we expected to find a negative coefficient, which indicates that a more popular book is sold more frequently than a less popular book. The F-statistic of 48.217 is again significant and the $Adj.R^2 = 0.825$, both indicating a good model fit.

For the model M180 with books up to 180 days old, we observe insignificant coefficients for PageRank, average rating, and the number of ratings. Thus, we cannot support the hypothesis that a more central position in a recommendation network leads to lower sales rank (and therefore a higher sales volume). The $Adj.R^2$ decreases to 0.764, and the F-statistic of 41.544 is lower than the M60 and M110 models.

The results indicate a possible moderating effect of product's age on the influence of PageRank centrality on SalesRank since the prediction changes depending on the age of books considered for the model.

4.4   Moderating Effects

Motivated by these findings, we study two models describing an interaction effect between PageRank centrality and book age. As before, we limit the maximum book age to 360 days, resulting in approx. 10,000 observations. Considering only books that are published in the last year gives us a more unbiased model, as considering all books available in the online book store would lead to a strong bias toward old books.

The first model (denoted as linear moderation model, LMM) assumes a linear moderating effect of book age:

$$
\begin{aligned}
SR_{i,t+1} = \quad & \beta_0 \\
& + \beta_1 * PAGERANK_{i,t} \\
& + \beta_2 * BOOK\_AGE_{i,t} \\
& + \beta_3 * PAGERANK_{i,t} * BOOK\_AGE_{i,t} \\
& + \beta_4 * PRICE_{i,t} \\
& + \beta_5 * RATING_{i,t} \\
& + \beta_6 * NUMBER\_OF\_RATINGS_{i,t} \\
& + \sum_{i \in I} \beta_i * PD_{i,t} \\
& + \epsilon_{i,t}.
\end{aligned}
$$

Table 8 shows the resulting coefficients, robust standard errors (in brackets), and the standardized coefficients (in square brackets). The model with linear moderation (LMM) shows support for a moderating effect of product's age on the relationship between PageRank and SalesRank ($p < 0.01$). However, the direct influence of PageRank on SalesRank is still insignificant. Even though the effect of PageRank on SalesRank gets stronger with increasing book age (i.e., more negative), the effect

Table 8 Two models with moderating effects of book age on PageRank

	Dependent variable: $SALES\_RANK_{t+1}$	
	(LMM)	(QMM)
PAGERANK	−18,776	−1,572,505***
	(133,928)	(346,713)
	[−15]	[−1242]
BOOK_AGE	953,446***	981,043***
	(220,410)	(244,612)
	[5492]	[17,017]
BOOK_AGE^2		−311,962**
		(136,354)
		[−11,059]
PRICE	−325**	−340**
	(150)	(157)
	[−2202]	[−2307]
RATING	−671	−834
	(763)	(769)
	[−407]	[−506]
NUMBER_OF_RATINGS	−3	−40
	(25)	(32)
	[−91]	[−1352]
PAGERANK * BOOK_AGE	−218,257,142***	3,565,890
	(59,319,726)	(39,421,507)
	[−1100]	[4728]
PAGERANK * BOOK_AGE^2		−226,347,475***
		(50,505,576)
		[−4846]
Constant	25,556***	29,548***
	(4196)	(4301)
Observations	9831	9831
Log likelihood	−105,333	−105,320
Akaike Inf. Crit.	212,106	212,083

Note: *$p < 0.1$; **$p < 0.05$; ***$p < 0.01$

is countered by the strongly positive direct effect of product's age on SalesRank (a standardized coefficient of −1100 compared to 5492).

Consequently, we study a second model (denoted as quadratic moderation model, QMM) assuming a linear as well as a quadratic moderating effect of book age on the relationship between PageRank and SalesRank.

$$SR_{i,t+1} = \beta_0$$
$$+ \beta_1 * PAGERANK_{i,t}$$

$$+ \beta_2 * BOOK_AGE_{i,t}$$

$$+ \beta_3 * BOOK_AGE_{i,t}^2$$

$$+ \beta_4 * PAGERANK_{i,t} * BOOK_AGE_{i,t}$$

$$+ \beta_5 * PAGERANK_{i,t} * BOOK_AGE_{i,t}^2$$

$$+ \beta_6 * PRICE_{i,t}$$

$$+ \beta_7 * RATING_{i,t}$$

$$+ \beta_8 * NUMBER_OF_RATINGS_{i,t}$$

$$+ \sum_{i \in I} \beta_i * PD_{i,t}$$

$$+ \epsilon_{i,t}.$$

Table 8 shows the results for this quadratic model (QMM). We find support for a moderating effect of product age on the relationship between PageRank and SalesRank. The squared effect is significant (and negative). The direct influence of PageRank on SalesRank is significant ($p < 0.01$) and negative, which fits the hypothesis that a more central product in the network is associated with a higher sales volume. The quality of the two models (linear versus quadratic moderation) is similar (Log Likelihood $-105,333$ vs. $-105,320$ and AIC $212,106$ vs. $212,083$).

These results support the findings from the linear models presented in Sect. 4.3. We know from previous work that the position of a product can be used to predict its sales (Lin et al., 2017; Oestreicher-Singer & Sundararajan, 2012a,b; Oestreicher-Singer et al., 2013). We extended these studies that it is not enough to only use the PageRank of a product as a linear predictor of its sales, but that the age of a product has to be taken into account as predictor as well as moderator of this relationship.

5 Robustness Checks

To assess the quality and suitability of the presented models, we performed several robustness checks and additional analysis. For all models, an outlier analysis based on the standardized residuals shows that there are only a few observations with a residual over 3.29, less than 1% of residuals over 2.58, and less than 5% over 1.96. Thus, there are only a few outliers in the data. Cook's distance, which measures the influence of individual cases on the models, is never greater than 1. Thus, no cases, including the outliers, have an undue influence on any of the models. A Breusch–Pagan test on the occurrence of heteroscedasticity is significant, indicating that the base assumption of homoscedasticity is violated. Thus, every model uses heteroscedasticity robust standard errors when calculating the significance of

Table 9 Two linear models without product dummies

	Predicted variable: $SALES\_RANK_{t+1}$	
	(PR)	(NPR)
PAGERANK	−4,829,115***	
	(609,524)	
	[−3080]	
PRICE	207***	117***
	(20)	(17)
	[1299]	[736]
BOOK_AGE	2.7***	2.8***
	(0.08)	(0.08)
	[3302]	[3399]
RATING	−2984***	−3210***
	(182)	(182)
	[−1734]	[−1865]
NUMBER_OF_ RATINGS	−137***	−167***
	(4.8)	(3.1)
	[−4275]	[−5192]
Constant	39,310***	39,988***
	(835)	(841)
	[26,623]	[26,495]
Max. book age	Unrestricted	Unrestricted
Product dummies	No	No
Network position	Yes	No
Observations	56,068	56,068
R^2	0.088	0.070
Adjusted R^2	0.088	0.069
Residual std. error	23,545 (df = 56062)	23,784 (df = 56063)
F-statistic	1083.707*** (df = 5; 56062)	1047.175*** (df = 4; 56063)

Note: $^{*}p < 0.1$; $^{**}p < 0.05$; $^{***}p < 0.01$

predictors. In addition, we assume independence of the residuals as the Durbin–Watson test is between 1 and 3.

Since the product dummies may account for larger parts of the explained variance and the influence of including PageRank centrality on the quality of the models is of interest, we tested additional linear models to assess the validity of this approach. Table 9 shows the results of two linear models without product dummies. The first model (denoted as PR) includes PageRank; the second model (denoted as NPR) does not include PageRank. In both models, there are no restrictions on the maximum book age (we considered all available books).

Both models show highly significant coefficients for every included predictor (PageRank, price, book age, rating, and the number of ratings, $p < 0.01$). The coefficient of PageRank is negative, which is in line with the models with product dummies, indicating that a more central position in the product network is associated with higher sales volume. The book age and price have positive coefficients, which indicates that higher priced books and older books tend to sell less. The average rating and the number of ratings describe the popularity and quality of a book, and, as expected, a higher average rating and more ratings lead to higher sales volume.

If we include the centrality of a product (model PR), R^2 increases from 0.070 to 0.088. The $Adj.R^2$ increases from 0.069 to 0.088. The residual standard error decreases from approx. 23,784 to 23,545. This supports the claim that the position of a product in its product network has an influence on its associated sales rank. When PageRank centrality is included, the other coefficients change in strength, but not in direction. These results support the findings of Leem and Chun (2014).

6   Conclusions, Limitations, and Future Research

Previous research (Hu et al., 2012) found that the PageRank of newly published books (published in the last 45 days) in a product network is a predictor for the expected sales. This chapter studies the influence of book age on this relationship and finds that the PageRank of a book is a significant predictor of expected sales if only books younger than 170 days are considered. When including also books older than 170 days, we find no significant influence of PageRank on expected sales. Consequently, we studied whether book age moderates the influence of PageRank on SalesRank. Building several multivariate regression models, we not only find a direct influence of book age on expected sales but also confirm a significant quadratic moderating effect of book age on the relationship between PageRank and SalesRank.

As a result, recommender systems should take into account the age of a book when making recommendations to the user. For very new as well as old books, a high centrality of a book in a product network does not lead to higher sales. Thus, recommender should focus on newer books where a high PageRank leads to higher expected sales. Of course, there are some limitations to this research:

1. Book sales, just like any other product sales, can be influenced by, e.g., promotions, advertisements, and similar time-restricted effects. These might also include non-observable cross-channel effects such as the publication of a new movie or tv advertisements.
2. In the case of newly released books (up to 70 days of age), we found no significant influence of PageRank on its associated SalesRank. This might be due to the restricted number of observations for these books (e.g., we found only 119 books younger than 20 days). To get more robust results for very young books, we recommend repeating this study either over a longer time period or with a higher coverage of the product network, thus capturing more new or recently released books.

3. We do not know how often the observed SalesRank of a product is updated. Therefore, the used SalesRank possibly only approximates the actual sales at a certain point of time.

4. In the used models, we only accounted for observable features (such as price and rating) and used product dummies for fixed but unobserved characteristics. We ignored information on the customer such as preferences, experience, or intent of visit, although Xiao and Benbasat (2007) found that such information could have an influence on recommender system use and user decision, which in turn could influence the product network and the centrality of a product.

5. Finally, we assumed that the recommendations shown to our web crawler were similar in structure to recommendations shown to a human visitor of the book store. Especially, we assume that possible collaborative filtering models used in the studied book store did not bias the observed product network. Thus, we recommend repeating this study and constructing the product network with links actually shown to human users (and not with links observed by a web crawler). This procedure would eliminate possible biases due to the construction of the product network using a web crawler.

Based on these limitations, there are different possible future research directions. First, it would be interesting to better understand how the product recommendation network depends on the type of used recommender system. This information is especially useful to online shop providers since it would allow them to better understand how the introduction of a recommender system (and its design) could influence sales. Second, the effect of the product recommendation network on sales could be different depending on the recommender used. Working together with a shop provider, the results might be more precise since exact sales and more in-depth product characteristics could be added to the model. A typical user of the platform could also be analyzed as it is possible that users who are simply browsing could be more strongly influenced by a product recommendation network than the users who are specifically searching for a product. Finally, it might also be interesting to look at more complex models to further explain why the influence of the network position gets lower with increasing book age.

Acknowledgment The authors would like to thank Nicolas Hasemann for help with the data acquisition.

References

Bobadilla, J., Hernando, A., Ortega, F., & Bernal, J. (2011). A framework for collaborative filtering recommender systems. *Expert Systems with Applications, 38*(12), 14609–14623. https://doi.org/10.1016/j.eswa.2011.05.021

Brin, S., & Page, L. (1998). The anatomy of a large scale hypertextual Web search engine. *Computer Networks and ISDN Systems, 30*, 107–117. https://doi.org/10.1.1.109.4049

Brinkmeier, M. (2006). PageRank revisited. *ACM Transactions on Internet Technology, 6*(3), 282–301. https://doi.org/10.1145/1151087.1151090

Chevalier, J. A., & Mayzlin, D. (2006). The effect of word of mouth on sales: Online book reviews. *Journal of Marketing Research, 43*(3), 345–354. https://doi.org/10.1509/jmkr.43.3.345

Cremonesi, P., Koren, Y., & Turrin, R. (2010). Performance of recommender algorithms on top-n recommendation tasks. In *Proceedings of the Fourth ACM Conference on Recommender Systems - RecSys '10* (pp. 39–46). https://doi.org/10.1145/1864708.1864721, http://portal.acm.org/citation.cfm?doid=1864708.1864721

Dhar, V., Oestreicher-Singer, G., Sundararajan, A., & Umyarov, A. (2010). *The Gestalt in Graphs: Prediction Using Economic Networks* (pp. 1–26). NYU Working Paper No CEDER-09-06

Fleder, D., & Hosanagar, K. (2009). Blockbuster culture's next rise or fall: The impact of recommender systems on sales diversity. *Management Science, 55*(5), 697–712. https://doi.org/10.1287/mnsc.1080.0974

Ge, M., Delgado-Battenfeld, C., & Jannach, D. (2010). Beyond accuracy: Evaluating recommender systems by coverage and serendipity. In *Proceedings of the Fourth ACM Conference on Recommender Systems RecSys'10* (pp. 257–260). https://doi.org/10.1145/1864708.1864761, http://dl.acm.org/citation.cfm?id=1864761

Goolsbee, A., & Chevalier, J. A. (2003). Measuring prices and price competition online: Amazon.com and BarnesandNoble.com. *Quantitative Marketing and Economics, 1*(2), 203–222. https://doi.org/10.2139/ssrn.319701

Grosche, T., Heinzl, A., & Rothlauf, F. (2001). A conceptual approach for simultaneous flight schedule construction with genetic algorithms. In E. J. W. Boers, J. Gottlieb, P. L. Lanzi, R. E. Smith, S. Cagnoni, E. Hart, G. R. Raidl, & H. Tijink (Eds.), *Applications of Evolutionary Computing, EvoWorkshops 2001: EvoCOP, EvoFlight, EvoIASP, EvoLearn, and EvoSTIM, Como, Italy, April 18–20, 2001, Proceedings.* Lecture Notes in Computer Science (Vol. 2037, pp. 257–267). Springer. https://doi.org/10.1007/3-540-45365-2_27

Herlocker, J. L., Konstan, J. A., Terveen, L. G., & Riedl, J. T. (2004). Evaluating collaborative filtering recommender systems. *ACM Transactions on Information Systems, 22*(1), 5–53. https://doi.org/10.1145/963770.963772

Hinz, O., & Eckert, J. (2010). The Impact of search and recommendation systems on sales in electronic commerce. *Business & Information Systems Engineering, 2*(2), 67–77. https://doi.org/10.1007/s12599-010-0092-x

Hu, N., Tian, G., Liu, L., Liang, B., & Gao, Y. (2012). Do links matter? An investigation of the impact of consumer feedback, recommendation networks, and price bundling on sales. *IEEE Transactions on Engineering Management, 59*(2), 189–200. https://doi.org/10.1109/TEM.2010.2064318

Jussupow, E., Spohrer, K., Dibbern, J., & Heinzl, A. (2018). AI changes who we are - Doesn't it? Intelligent decision support and physicians' professional identity. In P. M. Bednar, U. Frank, & K. Kautz (Eds.), *26th European Conference on Information Systems: Beyond Digitization - Facets of Socio-Technical Change, ECIS 2018, Portsmouth, UK, June 23–28, 2018* (p. 53). https://aisel.aisnet.org/ecis2018_rip/53

Jussupow, E., Spohrer, K., Heinzl, A., & Gawlitza, J. (2021). Augmenting medical diagnosis decisions? An investigation into physicians' decision-making process with artificial intelligence. *Information Systems Research, 32*(3), 713–735. https://doi.org/10.1287/isre.2020.0980

Klašnja-Milićević, A., Ivanović, M., & Nanopoulos, A. (2015). Recommender systems in e-learning environments: A survey of the state-of-the-art and possible extensions. *Artificial Intelligence Review, 44*(4), 571–604. https://doi.org/10.1007/s10462-015-9440-z

Knijnenburg, B. P., Willemsen, M. C., Gantner, Z., Soncu, H., & Newell, C. (2012). Explaining the user experience of recommender systems. *User Modelling and User-Adapted Interaction, 22*(4–5), 441–504. https://doi.org/10.1007/s11257-011-9118-4

Kotkov, D., Wang, S., & Veijalainen, J. (2016). A survey of serendipity in recommender systems. *Knowledge-Based Systems, 111*, 180–192. https://doi.org/10.1016/j.knosys.2016.08.014

Leem, B., & Chun, H. (2014). An impact of online recommendation network on demand. *Expert Systems with Applications, 41*(4), 1723–1729. https://doi.org/10.1016/j.eswa.2013.08.071

Lin, Z., Goh, K. Y., & Heng, C. S. (2017). The demand effects of product recommendation networks: An empirical analysis of network diversity and stability. *MIS Quarterly, 41*(2), 397–426. https://doi.org/130.233.243.235

McNee, S. M., Riedl, J., & Konstan, J. A. (2006). Being accurate is not enough: How accuracy metrics have hurt recommender systems. In *CHI'06 Extended Abstracts on Human Factors in Computing Systems* (pp. 1097–1101). https://doi.org/10.1145/1125451.1125659

Oestreicher-Singer, G., & Sundararajan, A. (2012a). Recommendation networks and the long tail of electronic commerce. *MIS Quarterly, 36*(1), 65–84. https://doi.org/10.2139/ssrn.1324064

Oestreicher-Singer, G., & Sundararajan, A. (2012b). The visible hand? Demand effects of recommendation networks in electronic markets. *Management Science, 58*(11), 1963–1981. https://doi.org/10.1287/mnsc.1120.1536

Oestreicher-Singer, G., Libai, B., Sivan, L., Carmi, E., & Yassin, O. (2013). The network value of products. *Journal of Marketing, 77*(3), 1–14. https://doi.org/10.1509/jm.11.0400

Park, D. H., Kim, H. K., Choi, I. Y., & Kim, J. K. (2012). A literature review and classification of recommender systems research. *Expert Systems with Applications, 39*(11), 10059–10072. https://doi.org/10.1016/j.eswa.2012.02.038

Pathak, B., Garfinkel, R., Gopal, R. D., Venkatesan, R., & Yin, F. (2010). Empirical analysis of the impact of recommender systems on sales. *Journal of Management Information Systems, 27*(2), 159–188. https://doi.org/10.2753/MIS0742-1222270205

Paulussen, T. O., Zöller, A., Rothlauf, F., Heinzl, A., Braubach, L., Pokahr, A., & Lamersdorf, W. (2006). Agent-based patient scheduling in hospitals. In S. Kirn, O. Herzog, P. C. Lockemann, & O. Spaniol (Eds.), *Multiagent Engineering, Theory and Applications in Enterprises* (pp. 255–275). Springer. https://doi.org/10.1007/3-540-32062-8_14

Shani, G., & Gunawardana, A. (2011). Evaluating recommendation systems. In F. Ricci, L. Rokach, B. Shapira, & P. Kantor (Eds.), *Recommender systems handbook* (pp. 257–298).

Véras, D., Prota, T., Bispo, A., Prudêncio, R., & Ferraz, C. (2015). A literature review of recommender systems in the television domain. *Expert Systems with Applications, 42*(22), 9046–9076. https://doi.org/10.1016/j.eswa.2015.06.052

Wang, W., & Benbasat, I. (2005). Trust in and adoption of online recommendation agents. *Journal of the Association for Information Systems 6*(3), 72–101. https://doi.org/10.1016/j.jsis.2007.12.002

Xiao, B., Benbasat, I. (2007). E-commerce product recommendation agents: Use, characteristics, and impact. *MIS Quarterly 31*(1), 137–209.

Airline Market Concentration in Europe

Tobias Grosche

Abstract Despite the constant growth in air passengers in Europe until 2019, many airlines had to file for insolvency and left the market. This often raised concerns by competition authorities regarding market concentration by the remaining air service providers. But at the same time, these remaining market participants still complain about protectionism and non-consolidated market structures. Against this backdrop, the aim of this paper is to assess the level of competition in airline service provision in Europe by measuring market concentration for city pairs within and to/from Europe. Market concentration on a city pair is measured using the Herfindahl-Hirschman Index (HHI) based on quality-weighted nonstop and connecting flights, and results for individual city pairs are aggregated based on their weight according to a gravity model. This allows to measure the level of competition on a city, country, or region level or any combination thereof. Results show that despite a reduction in the number of airlines operating in Europe, overall market concentration has been reduced but still is higher than concentration levels in the US market or the worldwide average.

1 Introduction

Before being hit by the Corona pandemic, the aviation industry was on a constant growth path. The number of air passengers climbed from around 2 billion passengers in 2004 to more than 4.5 billion in 2019 (IATA, 2021). Thus, an average annual growth of around 5.6% could be observed worldwide despite events like the financial crisis in 2008 or increasing environmental concerns. And although the Corona pandemic represents the biggest crisis in commercial aviation history since World War 2, the industry is expected to fully recover and to return to growth patterns as in the past.

T. Grosche (✉)
Worms University of Applied Sciences, Worms, Germany
e-mail: grosche@hs-worms.de

However, as aviation markets are at different states of maturity, passenger numbers and growth rates vary around the world. Increased economic activities, higher social incomes, and steps of liberalization in emerging markets especially in South East Asia and India result in higher growth rates compared to more mature markets like Europe or North America (IATA, 2021). Here, competition for market shares is stronger, as can be observed not only by the further expansion of low-cost carriers (LCC) activities but also from airline bankruptcies and the trend of consolidation. As example, in Europe in 2019 alone well-known carriers like Germania, FlyBMI, WOW Air, Thomas Cook, Aigle Azur, and Adria Airways have ceased operations.

In this context, the aim of this paper is to provide an overview about the pre-pandemic state of market concentration of airline services in Europe and its development over the last 10 years. Furthermore, a comparison with the competition level in the USA is made as this region represents an aviation market of roughly the same size and a similar political/competitive framework. While competition in airline markets is often measured based on the number of (nonstop) flights only, this study provides a more realistic assessment by considering the service quality of nonstop and connecting flights between city pairs.

This paper is structured as follows. The most relevant literature and the contribution of this research are presented in Sect. 2. Section 3 describes the scope of the analysis and the methodology used to determine competition levels. Results are presented and discussed in Sect. 4 followed by a conclusion in Sect. 5.

2   Literature Review and Contribution

Airline competition is examined in many studies. If in focus, it serves as explanatory factor for impacts on pricing or service quality (see for example, Obermeyer et al., 2013; Greenfield, 2014; Shen, 2017; Avogadro et al., 2021; Lewis, 2021; Gil & Kim, 2021). Other studies analyze the drivers of competition and the impact of policy decisions like deregulation or taxation (see, for example, Ustaömer et al., 2015; Wang et al., 2016; Ivaldi & Toru-Delibaşı, 2018; Oliveira & Oliveira, 2018; Bilotkach & Hüschelrath, 2019). Especially the rise and expansion of LCC and high-speed rail (HSR) have received much attention in this context (see Alderighi et al., 2012; Detzen et al., 2012; Acar & Karabulak, 2015; Bubalo & Gaggero, 2015; Su et al., 2019; Zhang et al., 2019; Cai et al., 2021).

However, the focus of these studies is usually on specific markets or limited set of routes only, reducing their scope. Furthermore, only nonstop or direct flights between airport pairs are considered when measuring the level of competition. But a passenger usually can choose between nonstop and connection flights and between different departure and arrival airports of the same city (Lijesen & Behrens, 2017). Therefore, a more realistic definition of the relevant market in aviation should include all travel options between any given origin and destination pair (O&D) (Lijesen, 2004; Maertens, 2018).

Focusing on European airline travel, the study of Dobruszkes (2009) represents an example for a wider investigation of competition levels. The author shows that liberalization in Europe has not only increased the level of competition but also led to new (but monopoly) routes. However, competition is measured by the offer of nonstop flights only, omitting indirect flight connections. Direct and indirect flight alternatives are considered by Brueckner et al. (2013). Focusing on domestic O&Ds in the USA, the authors investigate the effect of increased competition by low-cost carriers and legacy carriers on average price levels.

A comprehensive analysis on the competitive landscape in Europe can be found in Lieshout et al. (2016). The authors include direct and indirect flight connections between any two airports in Europe and to the 40 most important destination airports outside of Europe and model competition between different departure airports for municipalities that lie within the relevant catchment areas of the competing airports. Market shares of the available travel alternatives are estimated based on their attractiveness using a Multinomial Logit (MNL) model with frequencies, access cost, and time cost estimates as input variables. The input variables and the MNL model were calibrated using booking and fare data. Aggregating results of different markets, the authors provide an overview about the spatial distribution of competition levels in Europe for 2012. They show that competition in general has increased but still is unevenly distributed with the UK and parts of Spain and Italy being the highest.

Maertens (2018) develops a new metric to measure competition and applies it to the European air transport market. Using industry data from 2015 of estimated total passenger traffic numbers, including its split on the airlines' different travel alternatives, the competitive position of an airline is assessed on the network level. The analysis shows that within Europe, low-cost carriers have the best competitive position, followed by the large network airlines.

Grosche and Klophaus (2020) are measuring market concentrations on O&Ds between German cities and other German, European and worldwide destinations before and after the bankruptcy of the then second-largest German carrier Air Berlin. The competition on any O&D is measured between nonstop and connecting flights and HSR services. Market shares are estimated with a Quality-of-Service (QSI) model using travel time, number of stops, time-of-day, and frequencies as input variables. Similar to Lieshout et al. (2016), results of individual O&Ds are aggregated to provide a more general competition assessment. Findings show that the German air transport market became more concentrated after the exit of Air Berlin with the Lufthansa Group becoming even more dominant.

In this paper, the approach of Grosche and Klophaus (2020) is used to assess the level of competition. Compared to Lieshout et al. (2016), Maertens (2018), and Grosche and Klophaus (2020), the scope of analysis is expanded by calculating competition levels between any given departure city and any destination worldwide and combining them on any aggregation level. This allows to compare the European market with any other market, in this case with the USA and the world. Results are provided for the years 2009 to 2019, including the most recent "regular" year of aviation before being hit by the Corona pandemic.

3 Methodology

3.1 Scope

Airlines are competing with each other if a potential passenger can choose between the flight services of these airlines to travel from a given origin to a destination. The choice of service between an origin city to a destination city is not only between the type of flight (nonstop flight or connecting flights with stopover(s)) but also between different departure and arrival airports at the origin or destination. For example, when traveling between Rome and London, a nonstop flight between the airports Rome-Fiumicino and London-Stansted competes with a connecting flight between airports Rome-Ciampino and London-Gatwick. This study follows this rationale by constructing all relevant airline travel alternatives (or itineraries) between airport pairs and by assessing the level of competition on the level of the corresponding city pairs.

The airline industry was hit hard by the Corona pandemic since early 2020. Although signs of recovery can be observed after 2 years, current traffic figures and forecasts still represent the exceptional development of the industry and must be treated with care. The year 2019 represents the most recent "regular" year of aviation regarding demand and competition levels. Therefore, this analysis is based on a typical week of that year (8th calendar week).

The European Common Aviation Area (ECAA) was created by the EU member states and other European countries in 2006. Its purpose is to create a single market with mutual market access, equal conditions of competition, etc. (EU, 2006). Although not being a formal member of the ECAA, Switzerland acts according to its rules and regulations based on bilateral agreements. Therefore, the analysis of the European air market in this study is based on the ECAA countries, their subdivisions, and Switzerland. Table 1 lists the countries and entities that are referred to as "Europe" in the following.

3.2 Competition Assessment

Competition takes place on the individual O&D level. To provide information about the competitive level for a city or region or pairs of it, it is necessary to aggregate the information of their constituting markets. The level of competition on a single market depends on the number of air service providers and their market shares, respectively. Airline market shares are the cumulated market shares of all itineraries of that airline in the market, and the market share of a single travel alternative depends on its attractiveness for the travelers.

To summarize, the following tasks have to be accomplished:

1. Construction of the set of relevant travel alternatives
2. Market share calculation for each travel alternative
3. Determination of the level of competition for each market
4. Aggregation of individual markets' competition levels

Table 1 European countries/entities

Albania (AL)	France (FR)	Jersey (JE)	Republic of Kosovo (XK)
Austria (AT)	Germany (DE)	Latvia (LV)	Romania (RO)
Belgium (BE)	Gibraltar (GI)	Lithuania (LT)	Serbia (RS)
Bosnia/Herzegovina (BA)	Greece (GR)	Luxembourg (LU)	Slovakia (SK)
Bulgaria (BG)	Greenland (GL)	Macedonia (MK)	Slovenia (SI)
Croatia (HR)	Guernsey (GG)	Malta (MT)	Spain (ES)
Cyprus (CY)	Hungary (HU)	Montenegro (ME)	Svalbard Jan Mayen (SJ)
Czech Republic (CZ)	Iceland (IS)	Netherlands (NL)	Sweden (SE)
Denmark (DK)	Republic of Ireland (IE)	Norway (NO)	Switzerland (CH)
Estonia (EE)	Isle of Man (IM)	Poland (PL)	United Kingdom (GB)
Finland (FI)	Italy (IT)	Portugal (PT)	Åland Islands (AX)

A procedure involving these tasks is presented in previous work (Grosche & Klophaus, 2020). Compared to other approaches dependency on (typically unavailable) data for parameter calibration or direct use is minimized. As a consequence, it allows for a broad range of applications and is therefore also used in the analysis presented here. A brief overview about its steps is provided in the following.

3.2.1   Construction of the Set of Relevant Travel Alternatives

The set of travel alternatives on any O&D consists of nonstop flights and connecting flights. While information about nonstop flights is directly available from schedule data provider OAG, connecting flights have to be created from nonstop flights in a process commonly referred to as "connection building" (CB). Two flights constitute a feasible flight connection if the arrival airport of the first flight is the same as the departure airport of the second flight and there is enough time between the two flights to allow passengers to connect and baggage to be processed. This minimum connection time (MCT) is usually provided by the airport and airline and may take various factors into account (like terminal/gate information, origin/destination country, flight numbers, etc.). Although there is no limit on a maximum connection time or the geographical detour of a flight connection to make it feasible, the increase in total travel time limits the competitiveness of a flight connection. Many different connection building algorithms were used for different purposes that use different rules and parameters to create a set of feasible but at the same time competitive flight connections (see, for example, Burghouwt & Redondi, 2013 or Redondi et al., 2021).

This study uses the CB algorithm developed by Seredyński et al. (2014) that introduces connection lag as additional parameter to reflect the impact of connecting time and geographical detour on the total travel time for any given itinerary. The parameters are distance-dependent and were calibrated with booking data to maximize the number of feasible connections that were chosen by passengers while at the same time limiting the number of connections that were not selected.

3.2.2 Market Share Calculation for Each Travel Alternative

The likelihood of a given travel alternative to be booked and therefore its market share depends on its relative attractiveness to (potential) passengers. The attraction of a flight offer usually is the combination of price and service quality. However, because reliable price information is typically not available for research, service quality is regularly used in market share estimation. Different approaches exist to estimate market shares with different types of estimation models and influencing factors (see, for example, Redondi et al., 2021; Coldren & Koppelman, 2005; Garrow, 2010; Lurkin et al., 2018). Quality-of-Service Index (QSI) models are commonly applied in the airline industry to forecast market shares of travel itineraries (Halpern & Graham, 2015).

In this study, a QSI-model with four service attributes (total travel time, number of stopovers, time of day, frequency) is used. These service attributes are normalized to range between 0 and 1 (with 1 representing the best alternative on the given O&D) and added up to an overall attractiveness value q_i for any given itinerary i. The market share s_i of an itinerary i then is calculated as its share of the total quality of all J itineraries of the given O&D:

$$s_i = \frac{q_i}{\sum_{j=1}^{J} q_j}$$

3.2.3 Determination of the Level of Competition for Each Market

The level of competition is calculated as the Herfindahl–Hirschman Index (HHI). The HHI is a common measure to access market concentration in the airline industry (Alderighi et al., 2012; Lieshout et al., 2016; Oliveira & Oliveira, 2018). The HHI value for any given market is calculated by summing up the squared market shares of the competitors in that market, it ranges between 0 and 1 (or 10,000 when market shares are expressed as percentage points). A value of 1 indicates no competition or a monopoly of a single provider, while values close to 0 indicate a highly fragmented market with many competitors.

An airline's market share s_a on any given O&D is calculated as the sum of market shares s_i of the itineraries that the airline a is offering (the longer flight of a connection of two operating airlines determines its assignment to one airline):

$$s_a = \sum_{i=1}^{I} s_i$$

Many airlines are part of airline groups (for example, International Airlines Group (IAG), Lufthansa Group, etc.) or cooperating in alliances (for example, Star Alliance, OneWorld, SkyTeam) reducing competition intensity in many markets. The levels of cooperation within the many different airline groups and alliances are diverse and are constantly changing, making it too difficult for this wide-ranging study to be taken into account in its details. However, based on the assumption that airlines are avoiding competition within the same airline alliance, market shares are calculated on the alliance level for their member airlines.

The HHI value for any given O&D then is calculated as

$$\text{HHI} = \sum_{a=1}^{A} (s_a)^2$$

with A being the total number of airlines/alliances offering flights on the given O&D.

3.2.4 Aggregation of Individual Markets' Competition Levels

The levels of competition for or between cities, countries, or regions depend on the competition of their constituting O&Ds. Therefore, it is necessary to aggregate the individual HHI values of those O&Ds and weight them according to the O&Ds importance or size. Passenger demand figures are generally not available on the O&D level. Therefore, the size of any O&D is estimated using the gravity model of Lieshout et al. (2016) that was calibrated with booking data:

$$p_{\text{od}} = 2.539 \times 10^{-4} \times \frac{c_o^{0.791} \times c_d^{0.791}}{g_{\text{od}}^{1.037}}$$

Here, p_{od} represents the number of passengers traveling between origin o and desination d, c_o is the total seat capacity of all flights departing at o, c_d for arriving flights at d, and g_{od} being the great circle distance between o and d.

4 Results and Discussion

The methodology presented in Sect. 3 allows to assess the level of competition as capacity weighted average HHI value for any given relation. HHI values range between 0 and 1 with higher values indicating high market concentration. Using the approach presented in this paper, an HHI value of 0.616 is calculated for all O&Ds within Europe and a value of 0.617 for all city pairs to and from Europe. Thus, these HHI values impose a more than less concentrated airline market in Europe. This assessment is supported by the fact that the European Commission (EC) considers markets with HHI values larger than 0.2 as highly concentrated markets (European

Commission, 2004), the US Department of Justice (DoJ) for HHI values above 0.25 (US Department of Justice, 2010). However, these thresholds might be too low for application to the airline industry as many markets are served by a limited number of airlines only. Short-haul markets usually have a very low demand for airline travel as they are competing with other modes of transport. Therefore, operation by more than one air carrier is economically often not feasible. In addition, connection flights are too unattractive to play role for competition on these short routes. Long-haul markets, on the other hand, often connect markets or countries where bilateral air transport agreements are still in place, limiting the number of airlines allowed to provide air service between them (Maertens, 2018).

Besides setting thresholds to categorize a market as highly concentrated, the EC and the DoJ are also monitoring market concentration levels by changes in HHI values. An HHI increase of 0.01–0.02 is taken as an indication of increasing market power by the EC (2004), 0.015 by the DoJ, respectively (US Department of Justice, 2010). Table 2 provides HHI values for the years 2009–2019 and their changes for all O&Ds within Europe and to/from Europe. Furthermore, the total number of airlines/alliances operating the O&Ds are provided.

Market concentration decreased between 2009 and 2019 in general, indicating an increasing level of competition. In years where market concentration increased the changes in HHI were well below the aforementioned threshold. No real difference exists when comparing competition levels between city pairs within Europe and to/from Europe. Thus, in general these results do not give cause for concerns regarding decreasing levels of competition on the European level. The decrease in market concentration within Europe is even more remarkable as the number of operating airlines has decreased by more than 25% in the same time. The increase of competition despite a fewer number of market participants can be partly explained by consolidation (Dunn, 2020) but mainly by the expansion of low-cost carrier (LCC) traffic in Europe and their shift to more primary airports facing competition

Table 2 HHI and number of airlines in Europe 2009–2019

| Year | Within Europe | | | To/From Europe | | |
	HHI	HHI change	Airlines	HHI	HHI change	Airlines
2009	0.645		178	0.634		285
2010	0.645	0.000	193	0.637	0.002	285
2011	0.654	0.009	177	0.630	−0.006	272
2012	0.656	0.003	165	0.638	0.008	281
2013	0.663	0.007	151	0.645	0.008	268
2014	0.652	−0.012	154	0.635	−0.011	267
2015	0.628	−0.024	154	0.626	−0.009	264
2016	0.625	−0.003	143	0.628	0.002	273
2017	0.620	−0.005	145	0.619	−0.008	273
2018	0.628	0.008	142	0.621	0.002	280
2019	0.616	−0.012	132	0.617	−0.004	281

with existing carriers. While the big European LCC Ryanair, Easyjet, WizzAir, Norwegian Express, and Vueling were offering services on around 4200 city pairs in 2009, this number has grown to almost 11,000 in 2019. LCC also expanded into markets to and from the periphery of Europe. There, the number of city pairs with LCC grew by 2000. However, as these markets are reflecting only a limited share of all markets to and from Europe, the drop in HHI is not as strong as within Europe.

In order to assess the levels of competition at the country level, Table 3 presents HHI values for domestic, European, and worldwide O&Ds per country. For a better presentation, only values for the years 2009 and 2019 are shown, and the table is limited and sorted according to the 16 most relevant countries for European air travel, covering 90% of the total passenger (Pax) volume in Europe in 2019 (Eurostat, 2022). Empty entries indicate no air travel for the specific entity (for example, there is no domestic airline market in the Netherlands).

In general, market concentration is higher on domestic markets than on international markets. Domestic O&Ds in Europe are usually short-haul, thus, the explanatory remarks from before can be applied here, too. This is especially true for (smaller) countries with a lower number of domestic O&Ds. However, concentration levels fell in Sweden by 0.321 between 2009 and 2019 as the LCC Norwegian Air Shuttle and its Swedish subsidiary expanded its service in its domestic market. A large portion of the increase of concentration in the largest market Great Britain can be explained by the acquisition of BMI by British Airways from Lufthansa in 2012 and the subsequent closure of its regional subsidiaries. In total, the number of domestic air markets fell by about 20% between 2009 and 2019. However, for international markets within and to and from Europe Great Britain has the lowest market concentration. The city of London has the biggest catchment area for airline travel in Europe and attracts many different airlines that, furthermore, can offer service from four different airports (Heathrow, Gatwick, Stansted, and City). Spain as second-largest aviation market also shows a low market concentration in Europe but a relatively high one for traffic outside of Europe. While the low concentration in Europe resembles the typical development by the LCC expansion, the high concentration on markets outside of Europe results from Spain's links to South America and not having many different options for traffic routes between these two regions. From the largest markets, Germany has the highest market concentration levels for domestic and European routes. This can be explained by the strong presence of Lufthansa and its group airlines but also the high share of high-speed rail services reducing room for economically feasible competition by air. The already relatively high concentration levels and the replacement by LCC services have led to only a limited further increase after Air Berlin left the market in 2017 (Grosche & Klophaus, 2020). Increase in market concentration for domestic Italian markets can be explained by the restructuring and subsequent reduction of the domestic offer of the Italian carrier Meridiana (later Air Italy) and the expansion of high-speed rail.

As mentioned, HHI values for the aviation industry tend to be higher than for other industries. In order to put the results obtained for the European aviation market in perspective, a similar analysis for the US market is used as benchmark. Both markets are not only comparable in terms of traffic volumes and geographical size

Table 3 HHI per European country 2009 vs. 2019

Country	Pax (mill.)	HHI domestic			HHI Europe			HHI worldwide		
		2009	2019	Change	2009	2019	Change	2009	2019	Change
GB	277.4	0.620	0.774	0.155	0.491	0.460	−0.031	0.546	0.531	−0.015
ES	228.3	0.533	0.568	0.035	0.566	0.479	−0.087	0.669	0.636	−0.034
DE	226.8	0.834	0.843	0.009	0.669	0.644	−0.025	0.628	0.613	−0.015
FR	168.7	0.902	0.809	−0.093	0.653	0.563	−0.090	0.592	0.574	−0.018
IT	160.7	0.638	0.793	0.155	0.651	0.584	−0.066	0.642	0.628	−0.014
NL	81.2				0.627	0.586	−0.041	0.581	0.593	0.012
CH	57.2	0.990	1.000	0.010	0.737	0.697	−0.040	0.608	0.569	−0.038
GR	56.1	0.672	0.827	0.155	0.619	0.745	0.126	0.710	0.758	0.048
PT	55.0	0.967	0.827	−0.140	0.613	0.537	−0.076	0.750	0.680	−0.070
PL	46.9	1.000	0.962	−0.038	0.775	0.754	−0.020	0.795	0.724	−0.071
NO	40.3	0.693	0.621	−0.072	0.642	0.597	−0.046	0.659	0.645	−0.013
IE	37.9	0.939	1.000	0.061	0.525	0.502	−0.023	0.527	0.545	0.018
SE	37.6	0.904	0.583	−0.321	0.663	0.626	−0.037	0.659	0.616	−0.044
AT	35.6	0.937	1.000	0.063	0.747	0.743	−0.004	0.723	0.658	−0.066
BE	35.4				0.643	0.678	0.036	0.561	0.533	−0.029
DK	34.8	0.854	0.86	0.006	0.683	0.617	−0.067	0.654	0.602	−0.051

Table 4 HHI and number of airlines in USA 2009–2019

Year	Within USA			To/From USA		
	HHI	HHI change	Airlines	HHI	HHI change	Airlines
2009	0.558		74	0.614		199
2010	0.554	−0.004	68	0.619	0.005	198
2011	0.552	−0.002	65	0.615	−0.004	201
2012	0.547	−0.005	70	0.617	0.003	212
2013	0.544	−0.003	59	0.622	0.004	188
2014	0.547	0.002	63	0.619	−0.003	191
2015	0.523	−0.023	79	0.602	−0.016	189
2016	0.515	−0.009	64	0.598	−0.004	197
2017	0.504	−0.011	59	0.594	−0.004	207
2018	0.500	−0.003	57	0.595	0.000	210
2019	0.511	0.011	54	0.595	0.000	212

Table 5 Traffic numbers EUR vs. USA

Region	Nonstop itineraries	Connecting itineraries	O&Ds	Itineraries per O&D
Europe	109,920	750,967	30,748	28.0
USA	158,189	3,434,326	54,793	65.6

(Whittome, 2017) but also with regard to a liberal market environment. Table 4 corresponds to Table 2 but refers to the US market instead of Europe.

While the general tendency to lower market concentration over time can be observed for US markets, too, and also be explained by the expansion of LCC services (especially from ultra-low-cost airlines like Spirit Airlines and Allegiant Air), clear differences in the level of market concentration are apparent. Market concentration is much lower for city pairs within the USA than in Europe. But on the other hand, significantly less airlines are operating in the USA than in Europe. O&Ds in the USA are longer than in Europe, and a high share of traffic is between distant cities between the West and East coast. In general, the longer the distance, the higher the attractivity of airline traffic (compared to ground traffic that is of less relevance in the USA anyways) and the less important the quality drawbacks of connecting flight services. Thus, connecting flights play a bigger role in the USA than in Europe, and the number of (competing) itineraries on any given O&D is higher on average (see Table 5).

The lower number of airlines in the USA result from a phase of consolidation in the US airline industry. Over the last 20 years and often as a result of economic struggles, large airlines were formed through merges and acquisitions of smaller regional and national airlines (Airlines for America, 2022). As a result, the US market is dominated by the "big four" airlines: American Airlines, Delta Air Lines, United Airlines, and Southwest Airlines. They have a combined market share of more than 75% of the available seat kilometers (ASK) on domestic flights in 2019 (the biggest four European airlines have less than 50%, it needs 12 airlines to get to 75%). But as a result of mergers and acquisitions of various former (regional) airlines, the major airlines are operating in all parts of the country, effectively competing with each other on all relevant O&Ds. Thus, market shares on a given O&Ds are more evenly distributed among the major US airlines resulting in lower HHI values. In contrast, the European aviation industry is still influenced by the legacy of national flag carriers, support or protective actions by national governments, and limited slot availability at the major airports. Although the total number of airlines is higher in Europe and despite the rise of transnational LCC, individual airlines still dominate their "home markets" and competing airlines are having relatively low shares (Burghouwt & de Wit, 2015). As a result of this uneven distribution of competition, the average market concentration (HHI) is higher despite the higher number of airlines (Obermeyer et al., 2013). And at the same time, each airline has to compete against many different airlines on diverse markets, overall reducing efficiencies and limiting economies of scale. For example, in 2017, the average load factor for US domestic flights was 84.5% (Bureau of Transportation Statistics, 2021), while it was 80.3% in Europe (EASA, 2019). And in total profit margins in the USA were higher by almost 10 percentage points than in Europe (IATA, 2020), although this is not solely due to the structure of the competition.

The methodology presented in Sect. 3 is not limited to specific or bounded regions. Applying the methodology to all airline services worldwide, the overall average market concentration level can be calculated on a global scale. Table 6 gives an overview about the worldwide traffic and the HHI values for international and domestic markets for the years 2009 and 2019. Here, traffic within the ECAA-states (see Sect. 3.1) is counted towards the domestic sector. Furthermore, values are provided for worldwide traffic but with the two markets Europe and USA removed from the calculation.

Market concentration decreased on international flights between 2009 and 2019, probably reflecting the overall global trend to more liberal bilateral aviation agreements between countries. A similar but weaker development can be observed for domestic travel. It actually increases if Europe and the USA are removed from the calculation. These two regions represent the two markets with the highest passenger numbers and a decreasing trend in market concentration. Without them, their impact on the global values is removed and other markets gain more relative importance. For example, China represents a regulated market and became the third-largest aviation market in 2019 behind the USA and Europe after showing

Table 6 Worldwide market concentration levels

Scope	Year	Itineraries	O&Ds	HHI domestic	HHI international
Incl. Europe/USA	2009	8,100,000	238,650	0.599	0.630
	2019	9,720,000	326,320	0.585	0.608
Excl. Europe/USA	2009	1,040,000	63,840	0.566	0.628
	2019	2,280,000	117,080	0.614	0.608

Fig. 1 HHI values worldwide

Fig. 2 HHI values in Europe

an average growth rate of 11% per year between 2009 and 2019 (The World Bank, 2022).

Finally, Fig. 1 and Fig. 2 provide an overview about the market concentration levels on a global (Fig. 1) and European scale (Fig. 2). The color intensity represents the level of HHI for all (domestic and international) markets to and from a country.

5   Conclusion

A correct definition of the relevant market is key in competition analysis. From a potential passenger's perspective, on any given city pair airlines are competing with their nonstop and connecting flight offer, often also including different departure and arrival airports. Thus, the relevant market has to be created by the many different flight alternatives that the passenger can choose from. This study follows this market definition and applies a corresponding methodology for market concentration measurement to all markets in and to/from Europe. Thus, it extends existing research by a wider geographical and temporal scope including a comparison of competition levels with the USA and also worldwide.

Results show that the level of market concentration in Europe has been declining throughout the last years. This can mainly be attributed to the rise of transnational LCC operating in Europe. However, despite being a liberalized market, the overall market concentration in Europe is still higher than the world's average and especially the liberal US market. As the number of airlines operating in Europe is significantly higher than in the USA, higher market concentration can be explained by the diverse geographical distribution of the airlines' services in Europe. This conclusion is supported by the different domestic market concentration levels at the different European countries. But as the US market and the trend in Europe show, consolidation is not necessarily at the expense of competition on the market level.

While the industry is expecting (and partially also calling for) more consolidation (Maul et al., 2018; Canelas & Ramos, 2016), often governmental support initiatives for individual airlines or too strict conditions of regulators prevent further airline retirements or merges and acquisitions (Robinson, 2020). As this analysis shows, the smaller the markets, the higher the concentration levels, and if policy makers act with small markets in mind, consolidation on the European level is delayed. Small markets can result not only from national/geographical boundaries (like individual countries in Europe) but also from a to narrow definition of the relevant market (Maertens, 2018). As this and other studies have shown, connecting flights play an important role, especially for longer city pairs where aviation has a time advantage over other modes of transport. But in return, this also means that other modes of transportation have to be taken into account when analyzing competition on shorter distances. Therefore, future research about the competitive landscape in Europe with its shorter city pairs and well-developed (high speed) rail network has to include both modes of transportation, air and rail, into the definition of the relevant market to be able to support sound decision-making by regulating authorities.

References

Acar, A., & Karabulak, S. (2015). Competition between full service network carriers and low cost carriers in Turkish airline market. *Procedia - Social and Behavioral Sciences, 207*, 642–651.

Airlines for America. (2022, 02 10). *U.S. Airline mergers and acquisitions*. Retrieved from https://www.airlines.org/dataset/u-s-airline-mergers-and-acquisitions/.

Alderighi, M., Cento, A., Nijkamp, P., & Rietveld, P. (2012). Competition in the European aviation market: The entry of low-cost airlines. *Journal of Transport Geography, 24*, 223–233.

Avogadro, N., Malighetti, P., Redondi, R., & Salanti, A. (2021). A tale of airline competition: When full-service carriers undercut low-cost carriers fares. *Journal of Air Transport Management, 92*, 102027.

Bilotkach, V., & Hüschelrath, K. (2019). Balancing competition and cooperation: Evidence from transatlantic airline markets. *Transportation Research Part A: Policy and Practice, 120*, 1–16.

Brueckner, J. K., Lee, D., & Singer, E. S. (2013). Airline competition and domestic US airfares: A comprehensive reappraisal. *Economics of Transportation, 2*(1), 1–17.

Bubalo, B., & Gaggero, A. A. (2015). Low-cost carrier competition and airline service quality in Europe. *Transport Policy, 43*, 23–31.

Bureau of Transportation Statistics. (2021). *T-100 Segment data*. US Department of Transportation. Retrieved from https://www.transtats.bts.gov/Data_Elements.aspx?Data=1

Burghouwt, G., & de Wit, J. (2015). In the wake of liberalization: Long-term developments in the EU air transport market. *Transport Policy, 43*, 104–113.

Burghouwt, G., & Redondi, R. (2013). Connectivity in air transport networks an assessment of models and applications. *Journal of Transport Economics and Policy, 47*, 35–53.

Cai, D.-L., Xiao, Y.-B., & Jiang, C. (2021). Competition between high-speed rail and airlines: Considering both passenger and cargo. *Transport Policy, 110*, 379–393.

Canelas, H., & Ramos, P. (2016). *Consolidation in Europe's Airline Industry*. The Boston Consulting Group. https://image-src.bcg.com/Images/BCG-Collaboration-and-Consolidation-in-the-European-Airline-Industry-Aug-2016_tcm38-144749.pdf:

Coldren, G. M., & Koppelman, F. S. (2005). Modeling the competition among air-travel itinerary shares: GEV model development. *Transportation Research Part A: Policy and Practice, 39*, 345–365.

Detzen, D., Jain, K. P., Likitapiwat, T., & Rubin, R. M. (2012). The impact of low cost airline entry on competition, network expansion, and stock valuations. *Journal of Air Transport Management, 18*, 59–63.

Dobruszkes, F. (2009). Does liberalisation of air transport imply increasing competition? Lessons from the European case. *Transport Policy, 16*(1), 29–39.

Dunn, G. (2020, 03 31). *How consolidation has changed the shape of the European airline sector*. Retrieved from FlightGlobal: https://www.flightglobal.com/strategy/how-consolidation-has-changed-the-shape-of-the-european-airline-sector/136649.article.

EASA. (2019). *European aviation environmental report 2019*. European Union Aviation Safety Association. Retrieved from https://www.easa.europa.eu/eaer/system/files/usr_uploaded/219473_EASA_EAER_2019_WEB_HI-RES_190311.pdf

EU. (2006, 10 16). *Decision of the council and of the representatives of the member states of the european union meeting within the council*. Retrieved 01 24, 2022, from https://eur-lex.europa.eu/legal-content/EN/TXT/?uri=uriserv:OJ.L_.2006.285.01.0001.01.ENG

European Commission. (2004, 02 05). *Guidelines on the assessment of horizontal mergers under the Council Regulation on the control of concentrations between undertakings*. Retrieved from https://eur-lex.europa.eu/legal-content/EN/TXT/?uri=celex:52004XC0205(02)

Eurostat. (2022, 01 17). *Air passenger transport by reporting country*. Retrieved from https://ec.europa.eu/eurostat/databrowser/view/AVIA_PAOC__custom_285652/default/table?lang=en.

Garrow, L. A. (2010). *Discrete choice modelling and air travel demand*. Routledge.

Gil, R., & Kim, M. (2021). Does competition increase quality? Evidence from the US airline industry. *International Journal of Industrial Organization, 77*, 102742.

Greenfield, D. (2014). Competition and service quality: New evidence from the airline industry. *Economics of Transportation, 3*, 80–89.

Grosche, T., & Klophaus, R. (2020). Market concentration in German air transport before and after the Air Berlin bankruptcy. *Transport Policy, 94*, 78–88.

Halpern, N., & Graham, A. (2015). Airport route development: A survey of current practice. *Tourism Management, 46*, 213–221.

IATA. (2020). *Industry statistics fact sheet november 2020.* Montreal. Retrieved from https:// www.iata.org/en/iata-repository/publications/economic-reports/airline-industry-economic-performance%2D%2D-november-2020%2D%2D-data-tables/

IATA. (2021, October 5). *Number of scheduled passengers boarded by the global airline industry from 2004 to 2022 (in millions) [Graph].* Retrieved January 21, 2022, from Statista: https:// www.statista.com/statistics/564717/airline-industry-passenger-traffic-globally/

Ivaldi, M., & Toru-Delibaşı, T. (2018). Competitive impact of the air ticket levy on the European airline market. *Transport Policy, 70*, 46–52.

Lewis, M. S. (2021). Identifying airline price discrimination and the effect of competition. *International Journal of Industrial Organization, 78*, 102761.

Lieshout, R., Malighetti, P., Redondi, R., & Burghouwt, G. (2016). The competitive landscape of air trnsport in Europe. *Journal of Transport Geography, 50*, 68–82.

Lijesen, M. G. (2004). Adjusting the Herfindahl index for close substitutes: an application to pricing in civil aviation. *Transportation Research Part E: Logistics and Transportation Review, 40*, 123–134.

Lijesen, M., & Behrens, C. (2017). The spatial scope of airline competition. *Transportation Research Part E: Logistics and Transportation Review, 99*, 1–13.

Lurkin, V., Garrow, L. A., Higgins, M. J., Newman, J. P., & Schyns, M. (2018). Modeling competition among airline itineraries. *Transportation Research A, 113*, 157–172.

Maertens, S. (2018). A metric to assess the competitive position of airlines and airline groups in the intra-European air transport market. *Research in Transportation Economics, 72*, 65–73.

Maul, B., Spear, B., & Usman, K. (2018). *When consolidation makes sense.*https:// www.oliverwyman.com/content/dam/oliver-wyman/v2/publications/2018/september/Velocity-2018/when-consolidation-makes-sense-Velocity.pdf: Oliver Wyman.

Obermeyer, A., Evangelinos, C., & Püschel, R. (2013). Price dispersion and competition in European airline markets. *Journal of Air Transport Management, 26*, 31–34.

Oliveira, M. V., & Oliveira, A. V. (2018). What drives effective competition in the airline industry? An empirical model of city-pair market concentration. *Transport Policy, 63*, 165–175.

Redondi, R., Birolini, S., Morlotti, C., & Paleari, S. (2021). Connectivity measures and passengers' behavior: Comparing conventional connectivity models to predict itinerary market shares. *Journal of Air Transport Management, 90*, 101958.

Robinson, J. (2020, 01 08). Airlines*: The evolving approach to market definition.* Retrieved from Watson, Farely & Williams: https://www.wfw.com/articles/eu-merger-control-and-airlines-the-evolving-approach-to-market-definition/.

Seredyński, A., Rothlauf, F., & Grosche, T. (2014). An airline connection builder using maximum connection lag with greedy parameter selection. *Journal of Air Transport Management, 36*, 120–128.

Shen, Y. (2017). Market competition and market price: Evidence from United/Continental airline merger. *Economics of Transportation, 10*, 1–7.

Su, M., Luan, W., & Sun, T. (2019). Effect of high-speed rail competition on airlines' intertemporal price strategies. *Journal of Air Transport Management, 80*, 101694.

The World Bank. (2022, 02 04). *Air transport, passengers carried.* Retrieved from https://data.worldbank.org/indicator/IS.AIR.PSGR?end=2019&most_recent_value_desc=true&start=1970

US Department of Justice. (2010, 08 19). *Horizontal Merger Guidlines*, Federal Trade Commission. Retrieved from https://www.justice.gov/atr/horizontal-merger-guidelines-08192010

Ustaömer, T. C., Durmaz, V., & Lei, Z. (2015). The effect of joint ventures on airline competition: The case of American Airlines, British Airways and Iberia Joint Business. *Procedia - Social and Behavioral Sciences, 210*, 430–439.

Wang, J., Bonilla, D., & Banister, D. (2016). Air deregulation in China and its impact on airline competition 1994–2012. *Journal of Transport Geography, 50*, 12–23.

Whittome, M. (2017). *Different views on Performance - Benchmarking EU / US.* FABEC. Retrieved from https://www.fabec.eu/images/user-pics/pdf-downloads/Topic_Benchmarking_US_Europe.pdf

Zhang, R., Johnson, D., Zhao, W., & Nash, C. (2019). Competition of airline and high-speed rail in terms of price and frequency: Empirical study from China. *Transport Policy, 78*, 8–18.

Printed in the United States
by Baker & Taylor Publisher Services